SIMON WINCHESTER

The author was born in London in 1944 and became a journalist in 1967, a year after leaving Oxford with a degree in geology. He has been a staff correspondent in Ireland, America and India, and has reported from almost every country in the world. He is currently Pacific Region Correspondent for the *Sunday Times*, based in Hong Kong.

When not travelling, Simon Winchester lives in Oxford with his wife and three children.

'A splendid idea . . . an idea which only a journalist of the highest personal resource, and one with a legendary ability to tap to the full the resources of his mighty newspaper, could have carried through, and very well it is done'

The Guardian

'Fascinating . . . important observations'

Times Literary Supplement

'A most original and enjoyable book'

Books and Bookmen

'A travel book of rare quality . . . Mr Winchester is a first-class investigative journalist who knows how to ask awkward questions and how to give pungent answers to them'

Country Life

'He has brought a sensitivity and openness to the people who inhabit the islands . . . (It is) inaccurate to describe OUTPOSTS as a travel book for it is very much more – a powerful and compelling book'

Glasgow Herald

'A readable account mixing historical résumé with descriptions . . . and Mr Winchester argues cunningly'

Literary Review

Simon Winchester

OUTPOSTS

First published in Great Britain in 1985 by Hodder and Stoughton Ltd

Sceptre edition 1986
Second impression 1987

Sceptre is an imprint of Hodder and Stoughton Paperbacks, a division of Hodder and Stoughton Ltd

British Library C.I.P.

Winchester, Simon
  Outposts.
  1. Great Britain –
  Colonies – Description
  and travel
  I. Title
  910'.09171241   DA11

  ISBN 0-340-40271-7

Printed and bound in Great Britain for Hodder and Stoughton Paperbacks, a division of Hodder and Stoughton Ltd., Mill Road, Dunton Green, Sevenoaks, Kent (Editorial Office: 47 Bedford Square, London, WC1 3DP) by Richard Clay Ltd., Bungay, Suffolk. Photoset by Rowland Phototypesetting Ltd., Bury St Edmunds, Suffolk.

For my Father and Mother

CONTENTS

The British Empire - Ye[s]

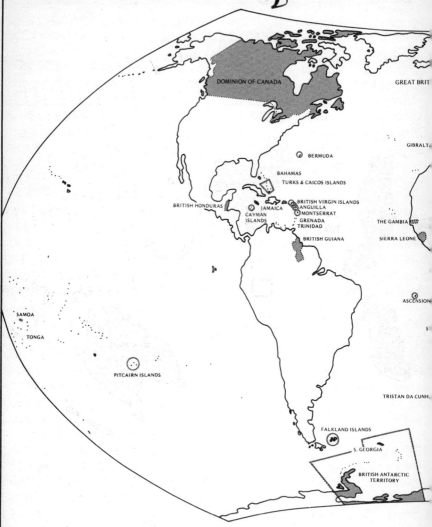

DOMINION OF CANADA

GREAT BRIT[AIN]

GIBRALT[AR]

BERMUDA

BAHAMAS
TURKS & CAICOS ISLANDS

BRITISH HONDURAS

JAMAICA

CAYMAN
ISLANDS

BRITISH VIRGIN ISLANDS
ANGUILLA
MONTSERRAT
GRENADA
TRINIDAD

THE GAMBIA

SIERRA LEONE

BRITISH GUIANA

ASCENSION

S[T]

SAMOA

TONGA

PITCAIRN ISLANDS

TRISTAN DA CUNH[A]

FALKLAND ISLANDS

S. GEORGIA

BRITISH ANTARCTIC
TERRITORY

day & Today

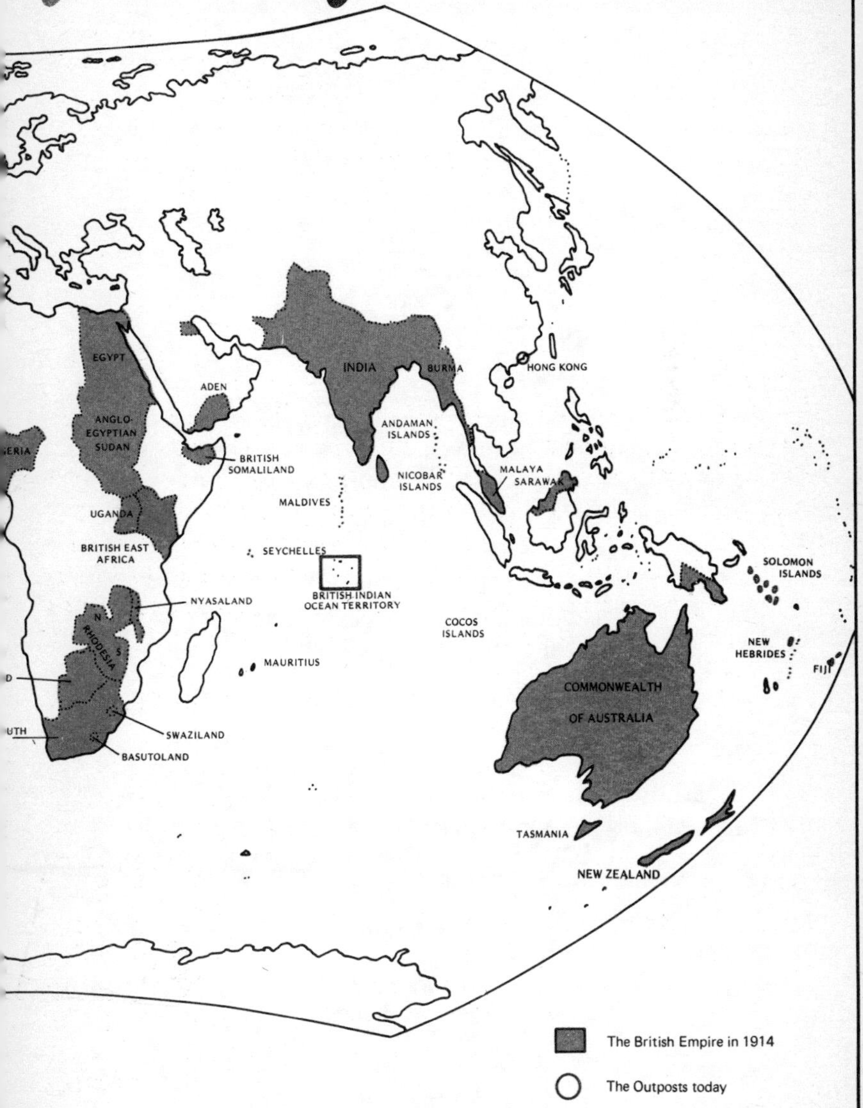

EGYPT

ADEN

INDIA

BURMA

HONG KONG

ANGLO-
EGYPTIAN
SUDAN

ERIA

BRITISH
SOMALILAND

ANDAMAN
ISLANDS

UGANDA

NICOBAR
ISLANDS

MALAYA
SARAWAK

MALDIVES

BRITISH EAST
AFRICA

SEYCHELLES

SOLOMON
ISLANDS

NYASALAND

BRITISH INDIAN
OCEAN TERRITORY

COCOS
ISLANDS

N

NEW
HEBRIDES

FIJI

D

S

MAURITIUS

COMMONWEALTH

OF AUSTRALIA

UTH

SWAZILAND

BASUTOLAND

TASMANIA

NEW ZEALAND

The British Empire in 1914

The Outposts today

ILLUSTRATIONS

St. Helenian family[1]
Ascension[2]
British Antarctic Territory[3]
Hong Kong[4]
Pitcáirn[5]
Admiral Sir David Williams[6]
Lord Dunrossil[7]
Sir John and Lady Cox[7]
Mr and Mrs Repetto[8]
Grand Turk[9]
Cricket on St Helena[10]
Manager's House, Boddam Island[11]
Diego Garcian islander[12]

ACKNOWLEDGMENTS

1. Peter Marlow/Magnum
2. Cindy Buxton/Annie Price/Survival Anglia
3. British Antarctic Survey/C. J. Gilbert
4. Richard Davies
5. Joanna Barlow
6. Patrick Ward
7. Frank Fournier
8. Simon Winchester
9. Laurence Burns
10. Rory Coonan
11. Dr Charles Sheppard
12. John Madeley

ONE

THE PLAN

Like most long journeys into the unknown, this one began with an idea – an idea that was triggered by a strange story I read one wet Sunday afternoon in a recent early spring, on the front page of a London newspaper. It was all about the alleged 'invasion' of an island known as Southern Thule, which was said to be 10,000 miles away from England in chilly wastes of the Southern Ocean.

The island of Southern Thule is quite barren, windswept, bitterly cold, uninhabited and, to all intents and purposes, useless. The Admiralty's *Antarctic Pilot* says that it is part of an old sunken volcano, and is covered with ash and penguin guano. There are seals, a variety of petrels and a bank of kelp weed a few hundred yards offshore, especially around a small inlet called Ferguson Bay. Of other possible delights the *Pilot* is silent.

The central fact of this curious tale is that Southern Thule belongs now, and belonged at the time of the 'invasion', to Britain. It was, and is, a part of a British Crown colony – one of the South Sandwich Islands, which are themselves dependencies of the Falkland Islands. Southern Thule was, indeed, part of the British Empire. It was given its name because it must have seemed to its first finders at very much the extreme end of the discoverable world.

Some time during the November of 1976 – no one is certain of the exact date – a party of fifty members of the Argentine Air Force landed on this remote British rock and, with neither notice, permission nor publicity, constructed a small military base. They built barracks, and a small concrete landing pad for their helicopters. They set up weather-recording machinery and a radio station. They built a plinth, and erected a flagpole, and they flew their flag – the blue and white *bandera* of the Argentine Republic. So far as they and their commanders were concerned the island, hitherto British, was now an integral part – *de facto* if not *de jure* – of Argentina.

It was a month before the British Government discovered what had happened. Ham radio operators on the Falkland Islands, a thousand miles away to the west, heard chatter between Argentine naval vessels and the Thule air force detachment. On the orders of the Ministry of Defence the local Royal Naval guard ship – HMS *Endurance* – was sent down to investigate. Five days before Christmas a helicopter from the ship spotted the Argentinians, and the extraordinary news of what was at the very least an act of the most immense cheek, was flashed to London.

But what initially intrigued me about the story is that London did almost nothing about it. More than a year was to go by before word of the seizure was to leak out to the British public – via the Sunday newspaper – or to the British Parliament. The then Prime Minister, James Callaghan, admitted to a House of Commons that was by turns amused and outraged that yes, he had known all about the affair and that no, he was not planning to send in the Marines to dislodge the Argentinian trespassers. Patient negotiations would continue, he said, to try to persuade them to go away, and in the meantime the interests of regional serenity, diplomatic practice and protocols would be better served if everyone remained calm, and made light of the incident.

The Argentines remained on Southern Thule until six days after the Falklands War was ended, on 28th June 1982. The same HMS *Endurance* that had first sighted the men six years before, turned up with a recovery party. HMS *Yarmouth*, a frigate, dropped a salvo of shells on to a bluff not far from the Argentine base. A Royal Naval tug and a Royal Fleet Auxiliary stood by, giving the whole exercise a properly Imperial appearance. And the Argentines, outnumbered and outgunned, surrendered and handed over their weapons to the Royal Marines.

The Union flag was hoisted, and everyone – British victors and Argentine vanquished – sailed away and left Southern Thule to a customarily lonely winter of gales, ice storms and blizzards.

The story did not quite end there. Six months later a passing British warship noticed, to general astonishment, that the Union flag had been taken down from the jackstaff and the blue-and-white Argentine flag run up in its place. Wary sailors clambered on to the island, finding it deserted, but noticed that whoever had taken the British flag down had folded it with commendable neatness and stuffed it under a nearby boulder. There was general agreement that the new invader was a wit, if nothing else.

The sailors' amusement was not matched back in London: a signal was sent to HMS *Apollo* ordering its men to destroy all buildings on Southern Thule, leaving none fit for prolonged habitation. Demolition crews moved in with plastic explosive, and by Christmas 1982 every barrack block and mess room and met station was reduced to a pile of concrete rubble.

Only a tiny refuge hut was left, stocked with rations, in case a British survey team should ever find itself benighted on the island. And to give such stranded men solace, a Bible, presented by the Scottish Commercial Travellers' Christian Union, was tucked in with the food. As a final act the helicopter crew from *Endurance* raised yet another Union flag, though since the halyards had been destroyed it could only flutter at half mast, where it possibly remains to this day, whipped by the freezing winds, to declare to all the world that this minute speck of worthless land is British, and that, as stated in the best-known of all British Imperial axioms, 'What we have, we hold.'

The story intrigued me, for one reason above all. I had thought – to the extent that I had ever thought about the matter at all since schooldays – that we had no longer had an Empire. I had watched so many television newsreels, I thought, about this place being made independent, and that place, and this island, and that peninsula, with this member of the royal family going here, and that one there . . . surely, I had said to myself – surely it was all gone. And yet, if this story were true, we still had some sort of an Empire out there, and what was more, it was still big enough and complicated enough and still so far-flung and unruly and unmanageable that we occasionally misplaced, misfiled or plain forgot some of its more remote members, and didn't worry too much if someone else took a fancy to them, invaded them, and took them away.

What others did we have? How, as King George V is believed to have inquired from his deathbed – how is the Empire? And not just how – what was the Empire, and where, indeed, its members?

Here came the fateful step. I had raised the question in a roomful of friends: which – it was rather like one of those baffling queries from 'Trivial Pursuit' – which were the colonies still run, at heaven's command, from London? No one was quite sure. Fiji, someone ventured – wasn't Fiji 'one of ours'? And what about Tonga, and the Isle of Man, and didn't we still have Christmas Island? In fact weren't there two Christmas Islands, and didn't both belong to us?

Then someone remembered she had an uncle who worked on a cable station that was still British – Assumption Island, she said, a name like that. No wait, Ascension, that was it! 'Gibraltar!' somebody else piped up. 'Malta – and Cyprus!' said a third.

To the atlas, but the maps had been drawn in the early Seventies and were long out of date. Thin red lines were etched under some dozens of mid-ocean islands that I knew – even if my visitors did not – had long since become free of what their islanders had come to regard as the British yoke. The tides had ebbed from the high-water mark of Empire far too rapidly for the cartographers at Bartholomew or Oxford to capture, and so their maps, while no doubt topographically accurate, were monuments for the nostalgic, tempting us to assume that our Imperial manor was far grander than reality allowed.

It was *Whitaker's Almanack* that finally did the trick. There were just eight pages, sandwiched between the statistics of cattle ownership in Zimbabwe and the name of the Chancellor of the University of Adelaide – for how, indeed, had the Empire faded away!

They were in alphabetical order, the forgotten names of Imperial might. There was Anguilla, set in the shallows of the Caribbean Sea. There was – the visitor had been quite right – Ascension Island, tucked into the fold of Africa in the equatorial Atlantic. Bermuda still belonged, and had like most of the others a colonial governor, noted by the *Almanack* as being a peer of the realm. British Antarctic Territory was still ours, though only penguins lived there full-time, and there was no native population, and no government. We had a curious entity known as the British Indian Ocean Territory, and another, less curiously named, and more Imperially enticing in the British Virgin Islands.

There was the Crown colony of the Cayman Islands – these three clumps of coral had, at the zenith of the Empire, been mere dependencies of Jamaica, but Jamaica had gone her own way now, and the Caymans stood colonially alone, their islanders proud to be British in the Caribbean Sea.

The Falkland Islands we knew a little about: the son of the Port Stanley harbourmaster had been in my class at school, and he used to tell me stories of the storms and the moorland and the sheep, and how he longed to go back to the peace of it all during the summer holidays, even though it was winter 'down there'. He had not spent an Easter or a Christmas in the Falklands since he had been sent off to England for his schooling, and that bothered him, as I remember.

There were the Falkland Islands dependencies, too – memories of stamp collecting, and the Stanley Gibbons Catalogue, the thickest book a schoolboy ever owned, came flooding back. The dependencies had always issued colourful stamps, with maps outlined in orange, and sketches of seals and enormous polar birds.

But there were still more. We ran Gibraltar and Hong Kong. We administered Montserrat and the Pitcairn Islands, as well as the exile-island of St Helena, where Napoleon Bonaparte spent the last six miserable years of his life. We had charge of the volcanic morsel of Tristan da Cunha, which had been evacuated in the 1960s when one of the cones suddenly erupted. The islanders, who knew little of 'civilised' life, were all brought to Britain, but loathed the place, and eventually decided that, volcano or not, they would all go back home.

And finally, in this alphabetic list, one colony of which no one in the room seemed to have heard: the Turks and Caicos Islands, utterly overlooked and puzzlingly named, and set in the pleasant waters of the western Atlantic, not far from the Bahamas, 200 miles from Florida.

So, from Anguilla to Grand Turk, just sixteen groups of rocks and atolls and ice-islands were still officially classified as ours, as dependent territories of the British Crown. Not a massive Empire, maybe, but an Empire nonetheless, and more than any other Imperial power of the past had managed to cling on to, were that anything of which to be particularly proud.

But there are lesser islands, too – chunks of rock and ice and coral not large enough to be listed in the gazetteers of the relict Empire, morsels and specks found only on the maps, in the charts, in the sailing directions and in the catalogues furnished by the Directorate of the Overseas Survey, and the Defence Mapping Agency of America, who keep tabs on all the world's dry land, and who, from day to day, claims to own it. So there are many such – many more than even the keenest student of political geography might suppose.

At the time of writing it seems that Her Majesty's writ runs in some 200 named islands of any size, and a thousand smaller rocks and skerries besides. But it is in the fine print of the gazetteers that the true extent of Her Majesty's realms becomes clear. 'Citizen of United Kingdom and Colonies' say the blue-and-gold passports. How many bearers are aware that they are, by virtue of holding such a document, subjects of the British Crown and, technically, proud citizens also of an Empire that includes the island of Zavodovski, the rock of Stoltenhoff, of Elephant Island, Junk Island, of Spectacle Reef and Prickly Pear Cay?

Tireless administrators can still, if their tasks allow, outline in Imperial pink the perimeters of two Dogs, a Swan, a Hen, a Parrot, an Eagle, a Bosun Bird, a Sealion, a Rabbit, a Nightingale, a Shag, a Carcass and a Rat. There are islands called Alpha, Gamma and Lamda; there are skerries named after Robert, George, Peter, Norman and Nelly. London salutes in islet form the memories of Nelson, Henderson, Livingston, Hawkins, Golding, Willis and Pickersgill. Union flags can still, in theory and in good weather, fly proudly over Coronation, King

George, English and St George's. The Royal Navy may by right lie less than three miles off Inaccessible, Astrolabe, and Shelter.

There is an Isle Parasole that is British. There are two islands of the Empire, rather inconveniently close to each other, both named l'Ile Anglaise. Westminster presides in ultimate authority over Three Brothers, a Necker and a Virgin, one Lively, one Barren, one a Danger. British civil servants in Whitehall have technical authority over the fates of places with the unfamiliar names of Po Toi and Shek Kwu Chau, Jost van Dyke and Visokoi, Takamaka, Beauchene and Providenciales.

And, in a serried line stretching through the freezing seas from fifty-six degrees south to the formal boundary of the Antarctic, at latitude sixty, the rocky outcrops of South Sandwich – Leskov, Candlemas, Saunders, Montagu, Bristol, Cook and, most vulnerable of all, the dependent colonial Island of Southern Thule.

We still had, it seemed, dominion over palm and pine.

No, not a bad collection, someone said. And was it not true – yes, it was! we discovered as we studied the maps – that thanks to happy coincidences of history and geography the islands and peninsulas that Britain had not given up were still draped around the oceans and the time zones in such a way that it was still technically correct to say that the sun never sets on the Crown dominions. While it was sinking into the sea over one island in the West Atlantic so, at that same moment, it was rising to a bugle call and a flag-hoisting ceremony half a world away, in the Indian Ocean, or the China Sea.

It was a small and ragged sort of Empire now, no match for that great assemblage of peoples and races – a quarter of mankind, a quarter of the land surface of the globe – over which Victoria had reigned with such supposed benevolence and wisdom. Four hundred million people were, at the moment of Victoria's Jubilee in 1897, subject to her whim and fancy (tempered by English law, proud tradition and good, old-fashioned common sense). Great nation-states, or nations-in-the-making – India, Canada, Australia, South Africa – were governed from Whitehall by her servants, in her name. Oscar Wilde had noted that England was a land 'Before whose feet the world divides' and few could be found who would quarrel with the notion.

But today none give the Empire, even though it exists in shrunken form, so much as a thought. No world divides before Britannia's feet. The United Kingdom, mighty though she sounds, commands little might, wields little power, can number only a few subjects in her sovereign territories. I thumbed through the *Almanack* and did a little mental arithmetic – at the time of the last colonial census, in 1981, there were 5,248,728 people who could justly be called citizens of the Crown colonies – an eightieth of the number noted just fifty years before. And 5,120,000 of those lived in Hong Kong. The remaining fifteen possessions held just 128,000 colonials.

Might it be possible, I mused, to visit all these places and catch, possibly for the very last time before progress and political reality snuffed it out for ever, something of the spirit of the old Imperial ambition – to see what remained, and find out what it had all been like, and why it had been so grand, why it had lasted so long, why it had died so quickly, but yet had seemingly refused to die completely?

Were there really still governors out there somewhere, with their blanco'd topees and plumes of goose feather in white and scarlet? Did British civil servants still look after our far-flung dominions with a sense of romantic fascination, privilege and pride? Was there a little of the colour and pomp and swagger and – dare I say it – the *style* of the old Empire to be found in these forgotten specks left scattered through the seas? I had been in India, and had sensed the Empire in the cool marble of Curzon and the bold sandstone of Lutyens. I had felt it in the echoing halls of Ottawa's parliament, in great cathedrals in Africa, in fretworked bungalows in jungle hill stations from Malaya to Guiana.

From one end of the world to the other railway stations and dockyards and libraries and botanical gardens and Jubilee Memorial Halls served to remind us of what the Empire had given to her subject peoples. (And there were historical tracts by the ton reminding us what the Empire had taken from these same peoples, and how barbaric and wicked an arrangement it had all been.)

But these were all memories of the thing, reminders – premature, maybe, but reminders of a sort – that the Empire had quite passed away. Only, as *Whitaker's* had so concisely shown, it hadn't, quite. Perhaps, I fancied, the still-living, just-breathing Empire was to be found in these sixteen distant dots. Its life might be drawing peacefully to a close, but it might yet be possible to capture one last vision, hear one last remark, sense one final exhalation of pride, watch one small finale to the glories that once had been. I made up my mind to go, to make what in Victorian times would have been called 'an Imperial Progress, an Inspection Tour', to check up – half for the memory of old King George – exactly how was the blessed Empire, what was the state of the fragments that remained.

Out came the timetables and the shipping calendars and the Cook's *Continentals* and the Admiralty *Pilots*. I pored and checked my way around the Imperial world, working out how it might be possible to make a single journey that would take in every colony that remained. It became clear uncomfortably quickly that the journey would not be easy.

Some colonies were not blessed with aerodromes – not St Helena for example, nor Tristan da Cunha. There was no simple way of getting to the Pitcairn Islands, in mid-Pacific (population forty-four), and it was strictly forbidden for anyone to go to the Chagos Islands, the sole members of the high-falutin' arrangement known as British Indian Ocean Territory.

Ascension Island was similarly difficult to reach – it belonged to the military, was administered by – of all people – the BBC, was on part loan to the American Navy and was loaded to the gunwales with secret electronics: strangers were discouraged, though not absolutely forbidden.

But my first draft plan disregarded the Cassandras. I felt that, with some perseverance and a great deal of good fortune, I might girdle the world and take in every British possession inside six long months. I would fly from London to Bermuda – no problem here, since British Airways transports thousands of sunbathers there each year. Then I would fly on to the nearest neighbour-colony, the Turks and Caicos Islands; thence to the other Caribbean possessions – the Virgin Islands, Anguilla, Montserrat and the Caymans. Next – and here was a cunning move, easy to formu-

late at an Oxford desktop – I would travel from the Cayman Islands
to the one-time colony (but now no longer) of Antigua, and catch
the once-weekly American Navy plane that I knew took supplies
across the ocean to the forces on Ascension.

Now I was on the eastern side of the Atlantic, and fully able
to wander down at will, aboard such ships as might tramp by,
to St Helena, Tristan, the Falkland Islands, South Georgia and
the Antarctic bases. I would, of course, be sure to set out from
England in the winter: not only would the West Indies thus
provide a welcome relief from the cold, but down in the southern
latitudes it would be summer, and there would be no problems
with bad weather, or with ice.

From Antarctica it would be but a short step to Chile, to an
airfield where I could catch a plane to Panama. A passing
freighter would then whisk me smartly to Pitcairn Island, and
would take me on to Fiji from where I could take yet more
planes to Hong Kong. Down then to Singapore, on to another
American warplane – how very generous these Americans were
going to be! – to their Chagos Island base on the atoll of Diego
Garcia – and then, via their good offices once more, on to
Bahrein and Tangier. And at Tangier, as every traveller on the
north African coast knows well, a plane of Gibraltar Airways
waits to carry travellers to the Rock. From there, finally, to
London. I would have flown and tramped 40,000 miles; but in
six months the Empire would be mine.

In reality it all turned out a great deal more complicated. What
I had hoped might occupy six months, in fact took three years.
For 40,000 miles, read 100,000. And my fond belief that it might
be possible to include all the remains of Empire in one eccentric
circumnavigation turned out to be the most wishful of thinking.
To make all the right connections, to find yachts, cargo boats,
air force jets, scheduled air services, railway trains, open border
gates, hydrofoils and ocean liners that went to these tiny blotches
of pink that were by now outlined on a map I had pinned to the
kitchen wall – to find these, and to organise them, to beg
permissions and to seek new friends, to get time off and to delay
deadlines (and to wait for three months while I was let out of
prison – that story, which belongs elsewhere, inevitably intrudes

into the narrative of one of my visits) meant that, aside from making what an American would call 'a considerable logistical complexity' of the whole affair, also forced me to return many times to London. So I would sally out to the West Indies and then, rather than try to travel from the Cayman Islands to Ascension Island, would return home, repack my bags, write more letters, cadge more favours, and set out south again.

And in the end, I made it. The entire British Empire – or at least, the entire populated Empire that was still governed by resident British diplomats – was duly visited. The Imperial Progress was duly accomplished. All governors were visited (save one – an old boy from my school, who was away on furlough when I knocked on his door at Government House in Montserrat); all seals inspected, mottoes read, legislatures (where such existed) visited, lighthouses noted, hills climbed, birds photographed, islanders (for most of the colonials lived on islands) engaged in conversation.

There were also some slight problems with definitions and remits – for in strict truth there are more islands that are dependent territories of the Crown, and which are not normally counted as colonies. The Isle of Man, as that other teatime visitor had suggested, is indeed a territory dependent upon the English Crown, and it is not a part of the United Kingdom. And it has a governor. The Channel Islands enjoy an almost exactly similar standing, too. Should I visit these, and include them in the Progress?

I decided, after some debate with friends and diplomatists who know the details of such things, that to visit Man and Guernsey and Sark and the other islands and rocks nearby would be to introduce red herrings into the story – if only (for there is no *logical* argument for excluding them) because these were places that had been so closely interwoven with national British life for so many centuries that they were wholly free of any feel of Empire about them. True, there was a governor in a large mansion outside Douglas – but he and his predecessors never carried the swagger and the style of true Imperial governors about them, and his tiny territories never felt sufficiently foreign to be classed as colonies.

My biblical authority on these questions was to be found in a delightful set of little books I discovered in the Codrington Library at All Souls College, in Oxford. (An appropriate library for colonial research, though rarely used as such: Codrington gave it to All Souls essentially as a means of salving his conscience, since he had made his fortunes slaving and sugar-dealing in the British West Indies.) The books, published in 1903, are the four volumes of C. P. Lucas's *Historical Geography of the British Colonies*, preceded by Hugh Egerton's monograph on *Colonial Origins*, in which I found the paragraph that settled my mind about which I could visit, and which I would not:

> First, then, what is a Colony, according to the common usage of the word? The term, by the common consent of modern nations, includes every kind of distant possession, agreeing herein with the Interpretation Act of 1889, under which the term colony includes every British possession except the Channel Islands, the Isle of Man, and India.

That settled it – almost. One small but important question remained before I wrote to my first friend and booked my first passage. What to do about Ireland? There had been no doubt – Act of Union or no Act of Union – that the Ireland that existed before 1921 had the *feel* of Empire to it. The Irish were a subject people, their status reinforced by the lowering presence of British soldiery in barracks around their country. They were subject, and then they threw off the British chains, and freed themselves, and turned their collective backs on both the Empire and the Commonwealth that took its place. Yet six counties remained, by the choice of most of their inhabitants, held by the British still: Northern Ireland has much the same legal and constitutional standing today as all Ireland did six decades ago. It is a part of the United Kingdom. It sends Members to Westminster. It is not a colony.

But I had lived three years in Belfast, and knew reasonably well that many Ulstermen and women felt, rightly or wrongly, that the British hold on those six counties had *something* of an Imperial feel to it, and that to understand the dying days of the remnant Empire it would be right and proper to make a brief visit to the last Imperial remnant in Ireland. And so, after argument and hesitation, I decided to go there too – to try to weave a course from Anguilla to

Ulster, in other words, and try to discern a common pattern to them all. It was, as I have said, a long and complicated venture.

What follows would have a pleasant neatness were it arranged logically, ocean by ocean, marching down the lines of longitude and along the lines of latitude according to some obvious plan. But my journeys were not like that, and so nor is this account like that. And it begins, not with the colony that is closest to the mother-country – that would be Gibraltar, which a jet can reach in little more than ninety minutes from Gatwick (though in fact I walked there) – but with the colony that is, if not the most distant, then certainly the most remote.

There are islands in the Empire that are themselves more removed from civilisation. Some of those I mentioned at the start of this chapter – Elephant Island, or Zavodovski Island – are merely notations in a colonial clerk's ledger, and a matter of brief excitement only for oceanographers or the authors of *Pilots*. There is no argument that the four Southern Pacific islands of the Pitcairn group – Pitcairn herself, and the coralline knolls of Ducie, Oeno and Henderson nearby – are the uttermost parts of the populated Empire. But they have no governor, nor an administrator, nor any visiting outsider who serves to remind the forty-odd inhabitants of their colonial status.

No, the island group that seemed to me, from my maps and charts arranged on tables and walls and on door-backs in every room of the family house, to be most precisely an *outpost* – a remote colonial settlement, detached, lonely, and tragic – was sited in the very centre of the Indian Ocean, three thousand miles from Africa, eight thousand miles from home. Moreover, this one colony was, because of the dark secrets buried there, a place you weren't allowed to visit. I had asked, and had been turned down – and the refusal rankled. So one blazing May afternoon I packed my bags and sea-sick pills and set off for what the Government, in their current Imperial despatches, refer to as the Crown Colony of British Indian Ocean Territory. The rest of the world knows it by the name of the largest of its myriad islands – a fourteen mile long strip of sand and coral and palm trees named after the Portuguese who first set eyes upon it four centuries ago – Diego Garcia.

British Indian Ocean Territory

15c TIGER SHARK

BRITISH INDIAN OCEAN TERRITORY

BLENHEIM REEF

PEROS BANHOS

SALOMON ISLANDS

BODDAM ISLAND

NELSON ISLAND

0   5   10   15 Kilometres

0   5   10 Miles

INDIAN OCEAN

THREE BROTHERS

EAGLE ISLANDS

DANGER ISLAND

GREAT CHAGOS BANK

EGMONT ISLANDS

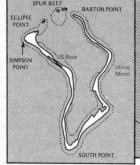

SPUR REEF

BARTON POINT

ECLIPSE POINT

SIMPSON POINT

US Base

Minni Minni

SOUTH POINT

INDIAN OCEAN

N

DIEGO GARCIA

TWO

BRITISH INDIAN OCEAN TERRITORY AND DIEGO GARCIA

The storm had died during the small hours, and when dawn broke the skies were clear enough for the sextant. We were rolling cumbrously in the long, slow swells. During the gales, which had blown for the three days since we crossed the equator, we had taken down the sails, and for this warm winter's night we were hove-to, under bare poles.

It was 200 miles or so since we had last spotted the sun. I had only the vaguest idea of where we were. I knew it was still the Indian Ocean, of course, somewhere well south of Addu Atoll in the Maldives. But the storm might have blown us anywhere. We might even be back north of the line; it might be summer all over again.

I squinted into the sun, and took three sextant readings, sliding the sun's lower limb as gracefully as possible against the grey plane of the horizon. Slowly I worked on the figures: Greenwich hour angle; local hour angle; declination; azimuth. I was tired, and the swell rocked me back and forth against the chart table. A pencil snapped. I cursed it then, and once again as I managed to get a piece of simple addition wrong, and had to rub out a whole column of figures. Then I remembered that the clock was eleven seconds fast and the sextant had an error of two minutes of arc, and worked anew to build these into the ever-more-entangled filigrees of arithmetic. Eventually, though, a pattern of angles emerged. Out came the plotting chart and the parallel ruler and the dividers, and I traced three parallel

lines towards three dots, and drew more lines at right angles.
They were, I noted with some pleased surprise, pretty close to
each other: the sights had been good: now I knew where we were,
to within a mile or so. (To be pedantic, and given that the mysteries
of navigation are what they are, I knew that we were at one of two
points on the surface of the globe – either here, or at a place on
precisely the opposite side of the globe, somewhere off the coast
of Ecuador, not too far from the Panama Canal. But as the boat
had been in India only a couple of weeks before, deductive logic
suggested that we could hardly already be anywhere near Coto-
paxi, the Galapagos Islands, or downtown Quito. We were still
very much in the Indian Ocean, no doubt about it.)

I ran the rule along from the dots to the latitude scale:
five degrees, twelve minutes south. Then again, down to the
longitude, which read seventy-two degrees, thirty minutes east
of Greenwich. I pulled what my faith suggested as the appropriate Admiralty chart – Indian Ocean, Southern Portion – from its
drawer, and found the point where five degrees thirty minutes
south coincides with seventy-two degrees, fifteen east.

Here in the heaving middle of the Indian Ocean, we were in
British territorial waters. After ten days of sailing, after a
thousand miles of doldrum, gale and trade in the highest of high
seas, we had made it to one of the most remote and least
remembered areas of British property anywhere on the face of
the globe. A relic of the greatest Empire ever known. A tiny,
blighted, forlorn morsel of dependent sea upon which swam a
score and more islets still reckoned as Her Majesty's domains.

Soon, if we sailed further west, and if the charts and my
reading of them were adequately accurate, the seas should
shallow, turn green and translucent, and there would be birds
and the smell of land again. We were, I reckoned, but a few
miles – a few hundred cables – from the possession that once
was known as the Oil Islands, one of the lesser dependencies
of the Crown colony of Mauritius. A generation ago this was a
cheerful and prosperous little gem set in the diadem of Britain's
Imperial might. Today, under the name of British Indian Ocean
Territories, and a new function (the need for the coconut oil
having long since vanished, the street lamps of Mauritius now

being powered by electricity), the colony lingers on, just an outpost, a faraway memorial to an extraordinary time.

Ahead of us, if my navigation had been halfway reasonable, stood the morsels scattered at the very northern tip of the Territory – Speaker's Bank, Blenheim Reef, Salomon Atoll and Boddam Island. We set three sails, swung the tiny schooner westwards and, with freshening trade winds off the port quarter, made a course for this speck of Britain's former glory.

Sailing is not, perhaps, as noisy a means of transport as some, but it is not quiet. The halyards creak, the sails slap, the bows hiss as they cut through the waves, and a hundred unsecured bits of would-be jetsam bump and jostle below with the endless movement of the sea. These are familiar sounds, and before long they fade into a kind of silence, noticeable only if they change in pitch or rhythm or volume.

After three hours of this muted concert, a new sound suddenly intruded. At first it was like a distant train, rumbling through a marshalling yard at night, its power magnified by the prevailing breeze. As the miles fell away it became ever louder and changed, until it was like a dull, deep-throated growl, as though some gargantuan beast were lurking in the waters ahead, full of menace. I peered into the distance, but saw nothing, just a whirling flock of petrels.

From twenty feet up the mainmast ratlines the picture was very different. The birds were flying above a long and almost unbroken line of white foam, stitched on to the horizon itself. As my eyes became accustomed I could see huge ocean curlers throw themselves on to the ragged line, breaking and hurling spray and spindrift high into the air, and booming with raw power as they did so. We edged closer and closer to the reef. Occasionally, behind the white, boiling waters, we could spy a flash of coal-black coral and, oddly vertical in this domain of the horizontal, the remnant skeletons of steel ships that had driven on to the razor-wall of rock, and had long ago been ripped apart and had died where they so unexpectedly stranded.

Below us the water was still two miles deep. A mile ahead, rising sheer from the abyss, was Blenheim Reef, 'drying', as the appropriate volume of the Admiralty *Pilot* puts it, 'very rarely, but breaking always'. This, whatever the romantic attractions of discovering a monument to the Duke of Marlborough's great victory so far from home, was a place to avoid, and I swung the boat hard south. The reef became a slim white line on the starboard horizon, more and more broken as we sailed along its length, until just a pair of tiny rocks remained, and then it was gone, with only the growling boom evidence of its sinister existence.

But now, in its place ahead, a smudge of green. It uncoiled before us, became two smudges, then three distinct patches, then five. The green patches became trees – coconut palms, heeling over in the wind. A new line of boiling reefs appeared below the palms and, as we closed to within a mile of the shore, there were sand beaches, and, half-hidden by the barricades of palm trunks, huts of grey wood, with verandahs from which, we mused, old men sucking on their pipes were even now watching us dipping lazily through the waves towards them.

That was a fancy, we knew, having some idea of the strange history of this corner of the British Empire; but the mere presence of the old houses, brooding in the afternoon sun and yet, as I well knew, quite empty but for a few rats, crabs and rhinoceros beetles, cast a chill of sudden excitement. We rounded the reef entrance – the island at the atoll's northern tip is called Ile de la Passe, as is the island at almost every reef entrance in every atoll in the Indian Ocean, thus making it one of the commonest of our Imperial names – and made our way, with infinite navigational caution, into the lagoon itself. Blenheim Reef may have always been a vacant plot in the Imperial landscape; Salomon Atoll, until very recently indeed, was a lively home to 300 thriving and happy subjects of the British Crown – perhaps the most isolated of all the outposts London had ever sought to control.

The lagoon was mirror-calm, and cool green. The charts showed innumerable hazards – a sandbank here, a coral head there, a channel barely a yard wide leading to this island, another ending in a cul-de-sac beside that. The dolphins cared not one whit, of course: a score of them swam out to meet us, and chirped gaily as they leaped and dived alongside, or played under the bowsprit. I had become accustomed to their habits in recent ocean nights: they would sidle up to the beam, leaving yellow trails of phosphorescent fire, and listen – I could swear it – to our soft conversations in the cockpit. If we moved up to the bow flat, and talked there, the swimmers would edge alongside; if we stopped talking, or if only one of us stayed on deck, they would become bored with the lack of discourse, and slip away in a flash of irritated tedium, an illuminated harrumph! and try again later. If these dolphins were the clubbable beasts from the ocean then, I promised, I'd have a word with them, later.

They led us in – or so it appeared, as they were always a few inches from the bow, no matter which way we turned. As we nosed more deeply into the lagoon, and the boom of the surf quietened behind, so the scale of the atoll began to appear. Eleven distinct islands: the Ile de la Passe now a little behind on the port side; English Island on the starboard quarter; Shearwater, Jacobin, Salt, Hen, Cemetery, Devil's, Mapor and Tatamaka Islands on the atoll's gently curving flanks and then far ahead, at the southern tip, Boddam Island, the half square mile of territory recognised by those faraway administrators in Downing Street as being the atoll's tiny capital.

From here Boddam looked no different from her neighbour islets – a high horizon of palm fronds, the irruption of the leafy mass of giant breadfruit trees, the occasional glint of an orange flower, or a banana fist, or a *ficus*. The beaches were short and steep, littered with branches and fallen coconuts, and with occasional outwashes of black sand where some root had become dislodged and spilled humus into the sea. Dead corals – all in a spectrum of reds ranging from the palest of pinks to the richest of carmines – lay half-buried in the shell sand, tugged at gently by the ever-lapping waters of the lagoon.

But then I began to see that Boddam was not quite the same. There was a small wooden pier jutting from a mass of bushes; a tall Calvary, overgrown with greenery, stood behind, as testament to the evident faith of the islanders; and, deep in the interior gloom, the outlines of a grand *petit château*, all fretwork and wrought iron, and seemingly brought here from the Loire a century back and left to decay among the steam and the ants of mid-ocean.

We anchored in two fathoms – a mooring accomplished only after we had hit, and briefly stranded upon, a head of brain coral that rose unpredictably to within a yard of the surface, and of which even the dolphins were ignorant. We were not entirely alone: a small sloop from Marseille lay off the dock, and a catamaran registered in San Francisco bobbed at anchor half a mile off. The skipper rowed across to say hello: he was a postman from the suburb of San Mateo, and had left home – wife, children, dogs – to sail around the world.

'Figured it'd take me five years to go right round,' he grinned. 'Only managed to get halfway, and I'm eight years behind schedule already. So damn pleasant, places like this.' He asked how long I was staying, and when I told him a week, give or take, his grey beard shook with amused outrage. 'Chrissake! A week! I've been here three months so far and I've only been to half the islands. This is undiscovered territory here, friend. You stay a good long time!' And he rowed his dinghy away at a furious pace, stirring up the water and alarming small schools of silvery fish.

He stayed on his boat for the rest of the week, as did, for most of the time, the young couple from France. They had some mysterious problem with their engine, and laboured all day, covered in grease and sweat. The man rarely swam over to the island – though the girl, a lithe and dusky creature from Paris, sometimes came ashore for coconuts. I would find her in a clearing, machete in one hand, a fresh coconut to her lips, drinking the milk. She giggled when she saw me, and wiped her mouth with the back of her hand. 'You like some?' she would ask, and offer the green globe, neatly cut at the top. It was very hot, and the liquid was cool and soothing, especially when it spilled from the sides of the cut and down on my chest. 'Feel good, no?' she would ask, and then run back to the tree, and climb the trunk with all the agility of Mowgli, and thwack! and thud! with her knife until a small pile of fresh nuts lay on the sea-grass below. 'Take what you want,' she would offer. 'Now I go to get some limes. Have you found the chickens yet?'

Once there had been chickens on Boddam Island. There had been a great many chickens, and pigs, and donkeys, and people.

Some 289 islanders at the last count, made in 1966. Almost all of them had been British subjects, and loyal subjects at that: a visitor in 1955 noted that the islanders were 'lavish with their Union Jacks', and a choir had sung a ragged version of the National Anthem to him, heavily accented in French.

A long time ago there had been a plan to turn Boddam Island into the greatest free port in the entire Indian Ocean – a port to rival Hong Kong, and where all transoceanic liners would be bound to call so their passengers could buy silks and perfumes and wines – and coconut milk and coir placemats. But nothing came of the plan, and the islanders continued with their unending attentions to the products of the coco palm – oil, copra, milk and wood – and dispatched them all to the north isle of Mauritius, 1,200 miles away to the south-west.

At the end of the Sixties something very strange happened to the people of Boddam Island, and to their neighbours, too. Exactly what fate befell them belongs to a later chapter; its consequence, though, is what now remains – an utterly deserted desert island, yet reliquary to an old town that still clings on, wind-torn and ravaged, but recognisable – inhabitable, even – in the tiny palm jungle.

There is a main street, lined with little cottages. A church, roofless, but made of coral rock and with its stained-glass still in place, stands in a clearing. The cemetery records the deaths of islanders through the two centuries of habitation: a Mrs Thompson died there in 1932, though in what circumstances her tomb does not record. There is a small railway, and a couple of little trucks I found I could just push through the shards of accumulated rust. A long warehouse, lined with jars and hooks and old tin boxes, stands at the end of the track.

And, behind a low wall, ringed by flower beds that had long since resumed their feral patterns, a mansion. This was clearly where the man who ran the island – or woman, it being a woman who had the idea of turning Boddam into a free port – made his home. It was once a rather splendid place: three floors, verandahs, balconies, shuttered windows, a pergola by the lawn. Now the whole place sagged at an alarming angle; when I climbed up the main staircase the house shook, and when I climbed down the stairs collapsed with a roar and in a cloud of grey wood-dust, and I had to jump the last six feet.

Not long ago a family had lived here. It had been a simple life, undemanding, pleasant. There had been no grand balls or diplomatic receptions at this corner of the Empire; but no doubt they had raised a glass on the occasion of the Queen's birthday. Once in a while there was a radio message from London; and a ship would come every couple of months to collect the oil and the copra; and perhaps every three years His Excellency the Governor would come in his launch, and the children would be lavish with their flags and sing the one English song they knew to him.

But there was little evidence of that today. Tacked to the wall of one cottage I found a photograph of a debutante that had been cut from a copy of *Country Life* – a rather stern-looking girl from Wiltshire. And in another bungalow, four volumes of *The Times History of the War*, mildewed and yellow with age, but readable still, and with portraits of Kitchener, and stirring accounts of the Somme.

Boddam was always a small cog in the Imperial machine – one of the least islands of a lesser dependency of a colony whose best-known inhabitant – the dodo – had become a symbol of the extinct. And yet the island, though apparently dead and inhabited by ghosts, still remains today in London's charge, still vexes the occasional civil servant. One might suppose it does not vex him much, since it has no permanent inhabitants, and thus neither products nor needs; but it is, incontrovertibly, a piece of British territory for which the Crown is responsible and which ultimately, one might suppose further, a government in London would still wish to protect and defend with a degree of passion, verve and style.

In fact, in the specific case of Boddam Island and her neighbours – and in particular one neighbour a few hours' sailing time away to the south – London wishes rather more than that. The colony of British Indian Ocean Territory, which spreads in a wild profusion of atolls and lagoons and reefs over twenty-one thousand square miles of ocean, is at the same time one of the least-known, and in many ways the most important of those that are left. It is a place of great beauty, and until recently it enjoyed the perfect peace of a tropic backwater, unremembered, but unencumbered. However today it is all very different. It is a place of considerable and unnecessary sadness – a territory wrapped in official mystery and internationally directed secrecy, its people and its history victims of a wretched and all-too-little-known scandal. Although its official title is the British Indian Ocean Territory its repute stems from the name of one very large island at the southern tip of the colony, a hundred miles from Boddam, and first discovered four centuries ago by a Portuguese sailor who gave it his name: Diego Garcia.

It is the only colonial possession which it is not legally possible for ordinary civilians to visit – unless they have government permission, which is seldom given. To get there I had to sail for some three weeks in a tiny and comfortless schooner. When I arrived I was brusquely shown the door, and only managed to stay for a few hours. It is not a place whose charms and problems Britain wishes to have advertised around the world. And small wonder, for the history of Britain and her Indian Ocean Territory is an unattractive story at best, and to many critics is a saga of terrible cruelty, best forgotten and wisest ignored.

The background is more complicated than it ought to be and involves, initially, the two large Indian Ocean islands of Mauritius (famous for the dodo) and the Seychelles (best known for a remarkable type of coconut which is formed in the shape of the female buttocks). Both islands were made British colonies in 1814 under the terms of the Treaty of Paris; at first the Seychelles was a dependency of Mauritius, and then, in 1903, it became a fully-fledged colony in its own right.

The two colonies also looked after a number of distant barely populated tropical islands as dependencies. The Seychelles Governor had under his wing such obscure Imperial particles as Desroches Island, a sandy spit planted with 800 acres of coconut palms; Aldabra, known for its giant tortoises, frigate birds, and sacred ibises; and the Farquhar Group, just to the north of Madagascar. Mauritius cared for the minute rock of Rodriguez, 200 miles to the east; and the Chagos Archipelago, known by the more Imperial title of the Oil Islands, and which the Colonial Office List described as being 'four days' steaming' from Mauritius.

Such was the situation in early 1965, when Mauritius was beginning to make noises about becoming independent. A Labour Government was in office in London (nearly all the protagonists in this story are members of the Labour Party, the significance of which will become clear later), and its then Colonial Secretary, Anthony Greenwood, flew to the Mauritian capital with some startling news. The islanders, he said, could indeed have their independence from Britain, but only on condition that they gave up their claim to the islands of the Chagos Archipelago, 1,200 miles away, and in perpetuity: Mr Greenwood gave no reason, but offered three million pounds in compensation, which the local politicians eventually decided to accept.

This accomplished, the Colonial Secretary then flew north to the Seychelles, and informed the Colonial Government there – which was not yet thinking of independence – that its three principal dependencies of Farquhar, Desroches and Aldabra were also being removed from the bailiwick, and the sovereignty of these scraps of sand and coral and giant tortoises was being passed back to London herself. No one knew why, until November, when a brief announcement was made in the House of Commons. The four island groups were to be made into a brand-new colony, to be named British Indian Ocean Territory; they would be administered by a Commissioner, who would be based at Victoria, in the Seychelles; they would use the currencies of the Seychelles and Mauritius and the stamps of Mauritius; and they would be run according to British colonial law 'unless modified by the Order in Council of 8th November 1965', the document that formally established this new, self-standing possession.

It was more than a year before anyone realised why London had gone to the time and trouble to set up a new dependent territory that was so scattered and so seemingly useless. On 30th December 1966, all was answered: Britain and the United States signed an Exchange of Notes 'concerning the availability for Defence Purposes' of the islands. The Notes were voluminous – eleven main sections, and two annexes with more than fifty sub-paragraphs (which covered all known contingencies, including a specific ban on the United States executing anyone on the islands) – but essentially said one thing. America was given permission to lease the islands for fifty years (with an option on a further twenty) without payment, and to build a defence installation there, to suit such needs 'as might arise'.

Lord Chalfont, another Labour minister, signed the Government's acceptance of the Notes (on behalf of his Foreign Secretary, George Brown) and the matter became law – without even the most perfunctory debate in Parliament, and with virtually no publicity. It was in any case generally accepted that to have some Western defence outpost in the region was prudent: the only other bases in the Indian Ocean at the time were the RAF base at Gan, an atoll in the southern part of the Maldive Islands chain, and Aden. Even the least prescient Imperialist would realise that these would eventually be abandoned (as indeed they were: the British were forced out of Aden in November 1967, and voluntarily left Gan in March 1976). Given the general instability of the region, and the absolute necessity of guaranteeing the free flow of Gulf oil, Washington and London seized on the notion of keeping the islands of BIOT for their very own, in case the need arose.

Inexorably and, perhaps, inevitably, the forces moved in. First there was an agreement signed in 1972 (under a Tory government – the only publicly admitted deal that involved a Conservative administration) to allow the US Navy to erect 'a limited communications facility' on the island of Diego Garcia, at the southern end of the Chagos island group. Then, two years later another deal was signed, for expansion of the facility – but it was still only to be what the then Labour Defence Secretary, Roy Mason, called 'very austere'. Indeed, so confident was Mason of the unimportance of the island that he publicly assured the Mauritians, who were by this time becoming rather exercised at the idea of a large superpower fortress being built in their neighbourhood, that 'Diego Garcia will not be used as a military base'.

The most charitable explanation is that Mr Mason simply did not know what was in the Pentagon's mind. Two years later another Labour politician, Roy Hattersley, signed the most crucial of all the many agreements that record the saga: the 'limited' communications facility was now to be allowed to evolve into 'a support facility of the United States Navy . . . the facility shall consist of an anchorage, airfield, support and supply elements and ancillary services, personnel accommodation and transmitting and receiving services. Immovable structures, installations and buildings for the facility may . . . be constructed.'

The United States was, in other words, establishing a base on Diego Garcia. Sailors who were posted there, and who loathed its isolation, came to call it 'the Rock'; the naval authorities put up a water tower near the harbour entrance and emblazoned it with the words 'Welcome to the Footprint of Freedom' – the island, a long and narrow curve of coralline limestone, has the appearance of a child's foot, heel pointing south, toes to the north.

The final purely administrative note in the story took place in June 1976, four months after the Hattersley Agreement was announced. The Seychelles won their independence, and were allowed to take with them three of the four island groups that had been made part of BIOT in 1965. They won back Farquhar and Desroches because the British Government decided it had no use for them; and they were given back Aldabra because, although the US Navy thought it a suitable spot for a base, a number of the world's wildlife organisations had complained that the giant Aldabran tortoises would be disturbed by aircraft noise and construction work, and the pentagon wisely decided not to pick a fight with the tortoise lobby. BIOT, from 1976 on, was limited to the Chagos Islands only, and was administered from London by the diplomat who was also head of the East Africa Department. He seldom visited his charge, though one Commissioner did have a governor's hat made, just in case. The day-to-day running of the island was left to a resident Administrator, arguably one of British diplomacy's least enviable postings.

All of the foregoing would be unremarkable, if regrettable, had the Chagos Islands been but a group of uninhabited tropical atolls upon which the armed forces of the Western Alliance had decided to build a fortress. Perhaps some conservationists would have grumbled at the despoliation of some thousands of square miles of virgin wilderness; and perhaps pacifist groups would have condemned the extension of war-making powers into an ocean hitherto untroubled by the superpowers. But there would have been no exceptional reason for controversy, and the word 'scandal' would probably not have been applied to the case.

But it has been, and with good reason. It turned out that the Chagos Islands were not, and in recent history never had been, uninhabited. There was a flourishing, contented and permanent population on Diego Garcia and on half a dozen other islands in the group besides. There were towns, churches, shops, schools, prisons, farms, factories, docks, playgrounds, warehouses and a light railway. People had been living on the islands for the previous two centuries; there were graveyards, with stones inscribed in Creole and English and telling of a tradition of community and comradeship.

On the day that British Indian Ocean Territory was formally established as a colony the Chagos Islands were peopled by some 2,000 islanders – more than there were in the Falkland Islands at the same time, as many as there were on Tristan da Cunha, Ascension and Pitcairn put together, half as many as on the island of Anguilla. They worked for a French-run copra and coconut oil company known as Chagos Agalega, and their little oil factories were fairly prosperous. 'There were touches of old-fashioned ostentation' a visitor reported in the late 1950s. 'There was a *château* . . . whitewashed stores, factories and workshops, shingled and thatched cottages clustered around the green . . . lamp standards and parked motor launches . . .'

And the inhabitants were all of them British subjects, citizens of a Crown colony, entitled to the protection and assistance of the Crown and, in the early days of their new status, governed on behalf of the Queen by the Earl of Oxford and Asquith, the colony's first Commissioner.

But they were to be given no protection, and no assistance, by the Earl, the Crown, or anybody else. Instead the British Government, obeying with craven servility the wishes of the Pentagon – by now the formal lessees of the island group – physically removed every man, woman and child from the islands, and placed them, bewildered and frightened, on the islands of Mauritius and the Seychelles. The British officials did not consult the islanders. They did not tell them what was happening to them. They did not tell anyone else what they planned to do. They just went right ahead and uprooted an entire community, ordered people from their jobs and their homes, crammed them on to ships, and sailed them away to a new life in a new and foreign country. They trampled on two centuries of community and two centuries of history, and dumped the detritus into prison cells and on to quay-sides in Victoria and Port Louis, and proceeded, with all the arrogant attitudes that seemed peculiar to this Imperial rump, promptly to forget all about them.

Or would have done, had not David Ottaway, an enterprising reporter from the *Washington Post*, travelled to Mauritius in September 1975 and discovered, in a slum close to the Port Louis docks, an abject and indigent group of more than a thousand islanders from the Chagos Archipelago. They called themselves the Ilois, and they told a horrifying story: they had been kidnapped, *en masse*, and turned out of their homes, to make way for the American forces who, they understood, now had control of their islands.

Only a few months before the United States Senate, which had been inquiring into the need for establishing so costly a base (or 'facility' as the British insisted on calling it: even today the Foreign Office refuses to acknowledge that there is a base), was assured by a senior official of the State Department that 'there are no inhabitants on Diego Garcia'. He was right. Such inhabitants as there had been had all been shipped out, were now a good 1,200 miles away, and had been strictly forbidden from ever trying to return home.

The process had started almost before the ink on the BIOT Order in Council had dried. In late 1965 – after BIOT had been created, but before Lord Chalfont had agreed to allow the Americans to use such islands as they wished for defence purposes – a small group of islanders arrived in Port Louis. They often went: a little cargo boat, the SS *Nordvaer*, and a smaller craft called the *Isle of Farquhar* used to make three-monthly voyages around all the atolls, and the Chagos islanders, whenever they could afford it, would make the four-day trip to the Mauritian capital to buy clothes and radio sets and fresh vegetables and toys for their children.

But on this occasion the islanders were given a piece of unexpected and shattering news. They were told they could not go back home. No ship, it was said, was available to take them back to Chagos. They would have to remain in Port Louis, and fare for themselves as best they could. They had been turned into exiles, at the express direction of the faraway Earl of Oxford, who was acting on orders from London.

Over the next eight years the islanders were systematically removed from the Chagos atolls. The Pentagon had been told that only 'a small migratory population' existed on the islands, and that to all intents and purposes the archipelago was deserted – which was just as well, since the US Navy had insisted that the area be made 'sterile', and that even the islands a hundred miles north of Diego Garcia had to be 'swept clean'. The Foreign Office kept insisting there was no problem – only some 'rotating contract personnel' were ever present on the islands, and they would be 'resettled' on the termination of their various contracts. And to assist in speeding up the process the British Government bought out the Chagos Agalega Company for one million pounds, and summarily closed it down.

The islanders now had no jobs; there was no longer any need for the food supply boats to call, since there was no working population, and no money to pay for food imports. So more islanders were persuaded to sail to Mauritius, with promises of work, and an altogether better life.

Paul Moulinie, the Franco-Mauritian whom the British Government entrusted with the winding-down of Chagos Agalega's copra operations, was to say later that it was 'never pleasant' to have to tell the islanders to get out. 'It was a paradise there. We told them we had orders from BIOT. We just said – sorry fellows, but on such-and-such a day we are closing up. They didn't object. But they were very unhappy about it. And I can understand this: I'm talking about five generations of islanders who were born on Chagos, and lived there. It was their home.'

Slowly, steadily the 'small migratory population' was cleared.

'All went willingly,' the Foreign Office said. 'No coercion was used.' (An American congressman snorted incredulously on hearing this remark. 'No coercion was used – when you cut off their jobs? What other kind of coercion do you need? Are you talking about putting them on the rack?')

Then, in March 1971, the first American troops arrived. They were Seabees, marine construction workers, and they had come to rebuild the old RAF runway on Diego Garcia, which had been built during the Second World War, and at the end of which were still two wrecked Catalina sea-planes, damaged in a hurricane. There was an old ops room nearby, and the Americans found RAF emblems and pin-ups stuck to the walls, mouldy after twenty years of neglect.

The last islanders were evicted over the next two years. The British had always said that troops were not used; and indeed the only time soldiers did become involved was when one of the evacuation ships broke down, and the troops gave the departing islanders some of their rations. Otherwise the pathetic became the routine. An islander said: 'We were assembled in front of the manager's house and informed that we could no longer stay on the island because the Americans were coming for good. We didn't want to go. We were born there. So were our fathers and forefathers who were buried in that land.'

Some of the voyages must have been cruelly uncomfortable. One woman reported seeing the *Nordvaer*, which normally carried a dozen passengers, arrive in the Seychelles with 140 islanders aboard, sheltered by tarpaulins from the scorching sun. Some families were given a brief extension, with officials moving them off Diego Garcia and on to one of the island groups to the north, where it was still possible to fish and grow a little grain and fruit. But the Americans demanded that everyone be cleared off every atoll and every island, and so these last few were herded on to a final supply vessel, and carted off, like so many cattle.

Once the dispossessed and ragged Britons had been discovered in Mauritius, the world's attention became briefly focused upon them and their fate. The Senate held hearings; lawyers demanded compensation (and won, four million pounds);

editorial writers expatiated ('this act of kidnapping', said the *Washington Post*; 'this clear lack of human sensitivity', said Senator Edward Kennedy; *'La Grande Misère des deportes de Diego-Garcia'*, fulminated *Le Monde*); civil rights organisations wrote reports ('depressing reading for anyone who wants to believe in the essential decency and honesty of the British Government', wrote *The Times*, reviewing one such); television films were made; the British Government was forced, briefly, to hang its head. A small party of American and British defence writers were flown to Diego Garcia, and were allowed to stay for five hours, and wrote about the island's 'incalculable strategic significance', and compared it, as one American admiral wrote, to an earlier Imperial fortress. 'This is the Malta of the Indian Ocean,' he said.

There was some further editorial and parliamentary bluster when it was discovered (by me: I was working as a reporter for the *Guardian* in Washington at the time, and stumbled on to the story by chance) that Britain had done a secretive financial deal over the islands: the American Government could lease them 'without charge', so long as Britain was given a fourteen million dollars' discount on the price of Polaris missiles it was then buying for its submarine force. The discount was managed in such a way – research and development costs were cut, rather than the missiles themselves being offered at bargain-basement prices – that no one realised what was happening until eight years after the deal had been concluded. And when someone found out the 'price' included money for 'detachment costs', and that the Americans had probably known all along that there were islanders on Diego Garcia and that British officials would have to shift them off, there was even more anger. But, like all stories, this one waned over the months; the court cases were quietly abandoned; the passion was spent; the islanders were paid off and resumed a relatively untroubled life on Mauritius; Diego Garcia came to be regarded as truly essential for Western well-being, and the saga was tucked into the recesses of public conscience, and more or less forgotten.

Except there were some people who cared. A middle-aged English teacher from Kent named George Champion was particularly outraged by what he had read of the islanders' fate. He changed his name to George Chagos – an eccentric idea, but Mr Champion felt that by eccentricity he might attract custom for his cause – and began a monthly vigil outside the gates of the Foreign Office, trying to awaken customarily moribund Londoners to the scandal. People would come up to him and ask, 'Who is Diego Garcia?'; the Methodist Church picked up the case and donated money to help the islanders' community-in-exile.

And there were others: John Madeley, editor of an obscure journal devoted to Third World agriculture, took up the cause, and in 1982 wrote a lengthy report for the Minority Rights Group – a report that won, if briefly, plaudits from almost every serious newspaper and journal in Britain. But soon there were other crises, other tragedies to consider – and Britons soon forgot the case of the faraway Indian Ocean islanders once again, and not long after even the few activists fell silent.

One Saturday afternoon in the spring of 1984 John Madeley telephoned me at home in Oxford. He knew I had long wanted to try to get to Diego Garcia, and he had an idea of how I might do it.

He had just received a letter, he said; it had been written in South India, posted in Australia, and had a return address in Wollstonecraft, New South Wales. It was from a woman named Ruth Boydell who said she had a small yacht, was just then planning to go cruising in the Indian Ocean, and had heard of the case of the dispossessed islanders. She thought she might try to sail her yacht into at least one of the atolls in the Chagos group – could she have a copy of the Minority Rights Group report, and would the enclosed few dollars pay the costs? John wondered if I knew anything about sailing, and whether I felt bold enough to try to hitch a lift.

I called Directory Inquiries, and found the Boydells' number, and called: it was dawn in Australia, and a sleepy-sounding voice told me that yes, Ruth was at that moment in Cochin, in South India, and gave me the name of an hotel, and a telephone number.

That was the moment I very nearly abandoned the chase. It was a Saturday morning, I was just home from one trip, was tired, hardly felt like going on another. I assumed, from all my experiences of the Indian telephone system, that it would be impossible to get through to a small town in southern Kerala; to heck with it, I said to myself – and anyway, I'd never been sailing.

But then, one of those chance decisions that seems to change a life. I peered at the phone number I had been given. It had nine digits, and the first three looked like an area code. On a whim I punched in the India code, and then the possible Cochin code, then the number. There was a pause, a thick hissing noise, and then, quite distinct, the familiar double-purr of an old British Strowger exchange, ringing out the number. Ten seconds later Ruth, clear as a bell, was on the line, and I explained what I wanted. She said her yacht, a thirty-foot schooner with the extraordinarily unattractive name of *Sketty Belle*, was currently moored in the Maldive Islands; she planned to spend the next six weeks touring India with her parents but would then go back to the yacht, and would be delighted at least to talk about going to the Chagos Islands. Had I done much sailing before? I mumbled something about a Sunfish in Martha's Vineyard, and left it at that. We agreed to speak again in two months' time; and I promised I would contrive to get myself to the Maldives a few days later on.

I embarked on a marathon trip: I managed to find things to do in Oregon, California, Hawaii, Hong Kong and Kuala Lumpur, and eventually, and after eight weeks' travelling, fetched up in the Joseph Conrad Suite in what had once been one of Empire's most notorious watering-holes – but which was now a rather seedy tourist-trap – Raffles Hotel, in Singapore. I set out to make contact with Miss Boydell.

It was not easy. Cruising sailors are rarely where they say they'll be; plans change with the wind and the tide, a whim is a better guide than an engagement book. I made a trunk call to the Maldive Islands to the yacht basin where she had thought she might be – the little schooner was indeed there, and the man who answered the telephone said he could see it, 'right pretty she is too'. But no skipper. I was passed from office to office, eventually finding myself talking to the local Cable and Wireless satellite station manager, with whom, it turned out, I had gone to school thirty years before. Old Hardyeans sticking thus resolutely together we managed, jointly, to track down the missing lady, and I arranged to fly to the Maldives the next day.

I spotted the boat first – a sleek, bottle-green schooner, her cream upperworks streaked with rust, her two masts covered with chipped white paint, her three sails wrapped in orange covers. She rode at anchor in ten feet of pale blue water, looking as though she had needed the rest. She was, a sailor remarked, a good little sea-boat, sturdy and well-found. Yellow fish nibbled at the weed that had grown on her waterline. A slim black man lay asleep in the cockpit. Ruth, said a note, was shopping.

She arrived later in the afternoon – a strong, handsome Australian girl, blue eyes, a deep tan, and a glowing smile a yard wide. She was twenty-seven years old, with all the wisdom of a seafarer. Her story was a true contemporary romance: she had run away to sea nine years before: she had found herself in Port Moresby one summer, met an English sailor who suggested she might like to go cruising, and embarked on an eighty-eight-day voyage across the Indian Ocean which finished in Cape Town. By then, she laughed, her teeth were loose in their sockets and she had all the symptoms of incipient scurvy – but she had discovered that she loved sailing more than anything else in the world, and vowed to herself she would do anything to buy herself her own boat. So she went home to Australia, worked as a cook for a seismic crew in the Northern Territories outback, did six months as a jillaroo on a Western Australian sheep station, washed dishes, waited at table, skimped and saved and in five long years found for herself, and bought, this home-made, steel-hulled, gaff-rigged little beauty of a boat with its monumentally but unforgettably ugly name. A Queensland railwayman had built her in his back garden, and had inscribed the bill of sale in the fine copperplate of a Victorian: she was, he promised Ruth, a proud little craft, she would go anywhere, take on any weather, anywhere in the world.

And so Ruth had begun to sail little *Sketty* around the world – she had left from a small gypsum-mining town by the Gulf of Carpentaria, had sailed up to Christmas Island, then on to

Cocos-Keeling, the old cable station and private fiefdom of the Scots Clunies-Ross family, up and across to Galle, at the southern tip of Sri Lanka, then north once more to Cochin and finally down to Male, the capital of the Maldives. Her plan from there was to go down to the Chagos Islands, across to Mombasa, past Aden to the Red Sea, via Suez to the Mediterranean and to sidle through the French canals, over the Channel, and up to London. From there a quick run down to the Caribbean and Panama, a long trek over to Tahiti, and then finally via Tonga and New Caledonia back home to Sydney, then to North Queensland, and the Gulf of Carpentaria once again. Five years should do it, she thought; and then she would get a job.

I liked her from the start. She was generous, sweet-tempered, enthusiastic, but cautious – an excellent sailor, an adventurer, an amiable soul. (She had been particularly, and characteristically, kind to the man I had seen on the boat: he was a Turk, a *Gastarbeiter* from Hamburg whom Ruth had met on the plane. He had nowhere to stay, and so Ruth gave him room on the boat, until it was time to leave for the south.)

There was some opposition to our plan from among Ruth's fellow yachtsmen. They knew I was planning to write about Diego Garcia, and feared that by going there I would cause them needless trouble. A Frenchman named Ivan, who had been sailing a big catamaran around the world for the past three years, remarked that the Chagos Islands were among the most beautiful and unspoiled places on earth, and there seemed an unwritten and unspoken assumption that the yachting community could visit the northernmost atolls, and bask in the peace and loveliness of it all. My trip, he was afraid, might well bring down some ukase from the British Government, forbidding any more visits, and enforcing the prohibition with naval patrols, and visits from the troops. He said he understood that it was right for the plight of the islanders to be written about, and that he knew he was expressing a selfish desire, to keep the islands pristine for the visiting cruising yachts. 'All you say may be true, but you have to remember one thing, Simon,' he kept saying to me one evening, as we sipped Ricards and watched the sun slip down behind the reef. 'These islands of the Chagos – they are our diamonds, Simon. These are our diamonds. Don't make them take our diamonds away.'

But Ruth and I left one evening a week later, and the yachtsmen's grumbles faded into the booming of the surf. *Sketty* settled down to a steady four knots, stretching her legs in the north-east trades, and loping down to the equator. We passed Addu Atoll, where Gan airfield had been, six days after leaving; we ran into the typical equatorial calms, and were blown about wildly by storms for three days and nights. But ten days out of the Maldivian capital, after we had skirted well to the south of a ragged and ugly-looking reef whose white razor-edge showed the black remnants of hulls that had come to grief, we spotted palm trees and coral and sand: Salomon Atoll, the most northerly inhabited island of British Indian Ocean Territory – a place where, just a dozen years before our visit, there had been a thriving little community of (the census reported) 289 men, women and children.

This was the legendary land of Limuria – the relict peaks of that huge southern supercontinent of Gondwanaland, left floating in mid-ocean long after India and South America, Australia, Africa and Arabia had split away, and so tiny and so remote that for many years they were supposed only to exist in the imagination of the cartographers. A British sea-captain, James Dewar, is said to have first spotted the Salomon Islands from the bridge of his cutter, *The Speake*; then Captain Bourde of the French merchantman *Salomon*, who was on the trade run between Port Louis and Pondicherry, stopped by for fresh fruit and gave the islands a name and inscribed them on the chart. A second Frenchman named Dufresne marked them down for settlement; but he was eaten by cannibals in New Zealand, and the plan was abandoned.

We eased our way through the reefs and into the lagoon. Ten of the eleven islands of the atoll had never been inhabited, according to the chart and the *Pilot*; Boddam Island, the most distant from the reef entrance, had a pier and a clutch of buildings. When Salomon sported its tiny industry, and its village-sized population, Boddam was the capital, and so it was there that we anchored, fifty feet from the shore. The old pier, warped and sagging, jutted from a wild mass of sea-grape trees, and a batten of timber clacked rhythmically against one of the old pilings. The moon rose, the sea darkened, the palms turned silver-grey, and there was a glint from a window-pane in a building I had not seen in daylight. This was an island ghost, with the feel of ghosts still very much about it.

Next morning I rowed ashore. I beached the dinghy in a tiny bay, and stepped through an archway of palm leaves, and into an old back garden. Here was a greenhouse, with a few dozen panes still in place; there a brick outhouse, an old bicycle, some rusting tins, a garden fork. The lines of flower beds could still be made out, and the pattern of a lawn. At the top was a cottage, its roof broken, its floors rotting. I poked around inside: there was an old copy of a novel by Pushkin, in German, and a great number of shards of broken glass. Hermit crabs scuttled around on the floor, leaving trails in the dust as they heaved their shells to safety in the dark corners of the room.

I found a narrow railway track, and then, hidden under the fronds of a dead palm, a small and rusting wagon. Then a long warehouse, and a collection of knives that the workers must have used to cut the coconuts. They were thick with rust, and insects seemed to have burrowed into their handles. Nearby, half-buried in soft tropical humus, were the great iron vessels and wheels of the industry – the very reason why these were once called 'the Oil Islands', and the machines from which came the oil that lit the fancy Regency lamp standards in the streets of Port Louis.

I had read an old account of how the islanders had made the oil. They would spend their days gathering the nuts – climbing the great trees, hurling the nuts down to the collectors below – cracking off the husks, splitting the nuts and lying them, flesh-side upwards, in the drying sun. They would arrange them in blocks, eight yards square – 3,000 nuts in each square. After a weekend in the heat the flesh would peel away from the shells, and the women would strip it away, rather in the same way women in the Arctic strip the flesh of a seal, and leave the meat for the men to prepare.

Here in Boddam the men, working under shelters built of

palm fibre, would pile the coconut flesh into flame-hardened wooden vessels, each one shaped like an hour-glass and sunk deep into the ground. A teak pestle, case-hardened by baking over endless campfires, would then be thrust into the soft pile of flesh and, using island mules, would be turned, hour after hour, squeezing the rich oil down into the hour-glass neck, and via a network of pipes and runnels, into a collecting vat. Six hours of mule-work would crush four hundred pounds of copra, and an average of seventeen *veltes* of oil would drip into the tanks to be taken off by lighter to the waiting freighter. The islanders put much of their oil aboard the 'floating charabanc', as they liked to call it, the SS *Zambezia*, which could reach Port Louis in four days.

But the relics that I found, under a huge airy roof of palm, were more modern: they hadn't used mules and hardwood pestle-and-mortar sets on this estate for many years. These ruins were of a vast steam engine, with boilers and cast-iron crushers and a cog wheel ten feet tall. I was told later that the machinery had been imported from Ceylon. They must have been making hundreds of *veltes* of oil on Boddam when the Foreign Office decided to close the island down: it seemed to have been quite a prosperous little place.

There was the ruin of an old shop along one overgrown street: scraps of paper showed they had once sold trousers, mirrors, bottles of claret and tins of sardines. There was nothing left now except for the cracked marble gravestone of the woman named Mary Thompson, who had died on Boddam in 1932. The walls were covered with the graffiti of ten years of visiting yachtsmen, and someone had drawn a map showing where the orange trees were, and the breadfruit, and the fresh water wells. Someone had found some chickens a few months before, and there was an earnest plea, in French, for visitors to feed them; we left plenty of bread and peelings for them, but never saw them. It is said they had gone native, and lived in the palms, pecking at the hermit crabs as they scuttled by below.

I found the melancholy of this deserted paradise beguiling, and we stayed for many days, exploring the long sweeping coastline, wandering through the dozens of empty buildings, watching the sun drift down through the magnificent surfstorms on the ocean-side of the island. I loved the grand old French colonial house that had been built for the Administrator – balconies and fretwork, carved stairways and a broad verandah for the evening Gitane and the glass of marc. Although this has for the last two centuries been – and of course is still – a British possession, Boddam and its few hundred islanders thought and behaved as French men and women. The French had discovered and named the islands, the French had started the copra industry, the French had colonised Mauritius. It was only the provision of the Treaty of Paris that spoiled matters. 'His Britannic Majesty engages to restore to his Most Christian Majesty the Colonies, Fisheries and Factories possessed by France on 1st January 1792 in the seas and on the continents of America, Africa and Asia with the exceptions of Tobago, St Lucia and the Isle of France and its Dependencies, especially Rodriguez and the Seychelles, which are ceded to Great Britain . . .' But for that, Boddam and Diego Garcia might today be under the command of Paris, with all the benefits and evils that might confer.

And I loved the little church. There was no roof – probably never had been. The altar was gone, but the heavy old door still swung slowly open, and inside there were a dozen pews, and a window of blue stained-glass, and a candleholder, and the notice-board that gave the hymn numbers and the psalms. The acoustics were perfect, and one evening I stood at the spot the old priest must have liked, and listened to the boom of the surf and the whisper of the wind through the palms above, and wondered how on earth the bureaucrats 8,000 miles away in London could ever have used such phrases as 'rotating contract personnel' to describe the people who had lived and loved and worshipped here. This was a community, without doubt. The church had been built in 1932 – a slab of stone by the west door said so. There was a little schoolhouse, and the shop, and the warehouse and the manager's mansion. There was said to be an inn, where the workers bought their rum and their coconut toddy; and a small hospital, where the doctor prescribed medicines with names like 'Eau de Saturne', 'Onguent de la Mer' and 'Pierre Infernale'. This was an island of labourers and millmen, rat-catchers, toddy-makers and fowl-keepers, where wives worked on the copra dryers and the children went to school, and the whole island went to church on Sunday. And now, thanks to a sale and a deal and a handshake and the exchanges of Notes between politicians in Whitehall and Foggy Bottom, this community was smashed and wrecked for ever, and the island was forcibly stripped of its people, to lie empty and half-silent, echoing only to the memories, and with the shuffling and scraping of the hermit crabs, and the endless sounds of wind and ocean.

And then the plane flew over.

It came suddenly out of a silent sky – a low hum, then an ominous growl, and a fierce roar as it swept overhead, no more than 200 feet above. It had four propellers, a bulbous nose and a trailing tail – I had seen just the same type of plane a few weeks before, on Bermuda. It was a Lockheed Orion anti-submarine reconnaissance aircraft, belonging to the United States Navy. On board would be twelve men: three in the cockpit, six hunched over screens and dials and gauges in the mid-section, one preparing to drop 'ordnance' – detection buoys, flares, transponders – one manning a camera deep in the aircraft belly, and one man waiting in reserve in the galley, cooking hamburgers for his companions.

The cameraman spotted the yacht, and the plane began a low and lazy circle, dipping down to examine us on each pass, waggling its wings when we waved up at him. After half a dozen times it straightened up and flew around the other ten islands of the group, checking each one for intruders. But there were none: Dog Island, Ile de la Passe, every tiny circle of palm and sand was utterly empty, and the plane soon tired of looking. It flew back over Boddam, roared so low the tops of the Afzelia trees rocked in its slipstream, and then soared high over the ocean and headed due west, for the next atoll of the colony.

The oceanic quiet resumed; but the sense of utter isolation did not. We had been spotted. Our plan had been rumbled. The Americans knew we were in the vicinity, that the area they demanded be 'swept clean' was now contaminated by – I could read their report in my mind's eye – unauthorised civilian personnel. When, we wondered, would the little gunboat appear over the horizon, and order us off?

We stayed four more days on Boddam, pinned down by storm waves crashing deafeningly against the reef wall, and by the sight of thick, molasses-black clouds welling up from the south. A small cutter sailed into the lagoon one afternoon; it, too, had come from the north, and had been battered in a terrible storm; his batteries were soaked and his engine would not seem to work. He was French, and imperturbable, and he and his girl-friend swam, brown and naked, in the clear waters, caught fish and baked them, with freshly made bread, on a palm-log fire they built on the beach. They said it didn't matter how long it took for the battery to dry. 'I 'ave no work in Paris,' said the girl, who was called Emanuelle. 'So I am in no 'urry. This is ver' lovely, no?'

We walked together, silent and content, along the old island paths. The plane came by twice a day, morning and evening, circling, taking more pictures, reporting the various arrivals and our various doings. I built a fire one evening, and banked it with leaves and old breadfruit and coconut husks, and a thick plume of smoke rose over the island. The plane scented it within moments and roared in from the west, radars locked on and engaged. I began to feel the plane was hovering over my right shoulder, watching my every move. If I undid my shaving kit and boiled up some water, there was the Orion, swooping in to have a look; if I read a book somewhere deep in the shade, a black insect-like shape would appear on the far horizon and buzz towards me and dive so low its crew could read the page number. 'Unauthorised civilian reading Pushkin', would go the message, back to the Pentagon. Obvious Commie ploy.

One evening I stumbled on a tiny steel plinth set into the ground. '512 Specialist Team, Royal Engineers' was engraved on the top. 'May 1984–Survey Mark'. The Army had been on Boddam Island only a few weeks before. They might well be back. The weather was better outside, and we realised we had taken to calling the island 'Goddam Boddam' because of the heat, and the mos-quitoes, and the arrival of yet more long-distance yachts. We decided to weigh anchor, and set sail for Diego Garcia itself, little more than a hundred miles south. Emanuelle could not understand why we were going. 'Stay for a little while more!' she pleaded, swimming behind us. But we waved our farewells, and swung and weaved our way out of the lagoon between the shallows and the coral-heads. The dolphins joined us near the lagoon mouth, and leaped and twisted under the bows as we started to pitch gently in the swells. I hoisted the mainsail and Ruth hoisted the head and the foresails, and we butted through a sloppy sea and into the night and a rising full moon.

The principal feature of the Chagos Archipelago is under water. The islands, such as Boddam, and Peros Banhos, the Eagle Islands and Diego Garcia may all be, in a political sense, important; but to the geographer they are almost irrelevant. The Great Chagos Bank is all that really matters – an immense circle of ocean, sixty miles across, where the water can be as little as six feet deep, which is affected by bizarre currents, strange waves, peculiar fish and birds and animals. It is a frightening place, if only because it is so unexpected. There is no land in sight, and the great glassy swells of the deep sea have given way to the riffles and chops of the shallows; this water is not blue, but light green, and coral-heads of pink and orange suddenly thrust upwards from the sand, and scratch ominously against the hull. Most ships give the bank a wide berth; the currents are unpredictable, the air is filled with crowds of birds, the sea heavy with bonito and flying fish, and an occasional white breaker suggesting a reef that could tear your hull in two. We kept to the eastern edge of the bank, with the echo-sounder on, and every time the dancing lights of the display showed less than a hundred metres below the keel, we steered further eastwards, to keep ourselves in the comfort and security of the deep.

It was shortly before dawn on our second night out from Boddam that we spotted the loom of lights of Diego Garcia. Ruth, who had an infallible eye for such things, saw it first – a vague, pale discoloration of the night horizon, the yellowish blur from a thousand lights of a small city. Otherwise the sea and the sky were black – the moon had set – and the loneliness of the setting was profound. I unwrapped the direction-finding radio and tuned in to the Diego Garcia beacon – a faint bleeping pattern of morse sounded from a few points off the starboard bow. We sheeted in the sails, edged a few degrees closer to the breeze, and made directly for this most secret of British islands.

When dawn came up, and the lights went off, so the loom of the colony vanished. But the beacon kept sounding, and by breakfast-time I could pick up a radio signal which was unmistakably American. It was Sunday morning. 'Hi everybody!' said the voice, crackling and fading as we dipped into troughs between the swells, 'Hi! This is Reverend Harry of the God Squad wishing you-all a very Happy Sunday!'

And Reverend Harry, with his Oklahoma accent, his fervour and his enthusiasm, went on to catalogue the miseries and pitfalls of modern service life, and how best to avoid them. Only snatches of his sermon filtered across to us. 'Let's all pray for Marion, of Waxahatchie. She's sick – and I don't mean no cold or headache, folks. I mean major-league misery.' 'And now folks, don' any of you get into drugs, d'you hear? 'Cause you drug-users are gonna die – no doubt about it. And when you die, well, man – that's for a long, long time . . .'

And just in case we had any doubts, the station broadcast its identification, over and over again. 'Yessir, this is Radio Fourteen-Eighty-Five – the American Forces Radio and Television Service, Diego Garcia, in the big wide wastes of the good ol' Indian Ocean.'

We had gone below for breakfast, leaving the boat to steer herself. The water rumbled and chuckled under the hull – we were making good progress, and we had been doing so for about an hour when I decided to go above, and check the horizon. I very nearly fell overboard. The sea, which had been quite empty when I went below, was now seething with ships. Two long container ships were bearing down on us from the east; there was a strangely shaped vessel, painted a brilliant white, about five miles ahead; two destroyers sailed away northwards; and heading on a direct collision course for us, and no more than a mile away, were the black, weed-covered bows of a massive ocean-going tug. A dozen men clustered around the wheelhouse, all apparently staring in our direction.

She bucked and reared in the swell, passed on our starboard quarter, and made a wide turn behind us and came alongside.

She was called the *Robert W.* and was registered in Seattle. I
imagined she was on charter to the Navy as the base perimeter
patrol ship, and that this was as far as we were likely to get. I
cursed silently. Three weeks at sea, to be turned away within
sight of the place. Bloody bad luck. Ruth looked glum, too; I
suspected she thought the same.

'Where you from?' barked a voice from the wheelhouse. We
yelled our reply, and saw the entire audience react with stunned,
but friendly, disbelief. These were big-ship sailors, and our little
schooner must have looked too tiny to accomplish a passage
across the average lake, let alone an ocean as wide and difficult
as this. 'For Chrissake! All that way in that tub!' exclaimed the
skipper. 'You wanna beer?' And almost as he said this, two cans
of Olympia Lite Beer whistled across the green and heaving
gap, each from a different member of his crew. I stopped mine,
and Ruth caught hers, the tug erupted in a burst of wild applause,
and we began a fifty-decibel conversation as both boats struggled
to keep on course, and avoid a collision.

No, they were not on patrol; they were simply taking a group
of sailors on a Sunday morning fishing expedition. As far as they
were concerned we could go and crawl over Diego Garcia about
as much as we wanted. 'It's not us who give the trouble,' the
skipper explained, with a sympathetic grin. 'It's the bloody
limeys here. They run the place, and they're mean as hell. But
you want to get in to Diego? Well, we got a plan.' And he went
on to tell us to fake a mild emergency – 'appendicitis, engine
trouble, something like that – in fact, why not throw out all your
water? They're sure to let you in if they think you're out.'

We had taken on six jerrycans of fresh water at Boddam –
most of it not so fresh, in fact, and alive with wriggling red
worms – and had plenty of spare in the bilge tanks. So we
opened all the deck containers and dribbled the water out into
the sea, to the ironic cheers of the tugboat crew. When the last
one was empty, the skipper disappeared, and could be heard
chattering on the radio. Finally he appeared again and gave a
thumbs-up. 'They'll let you in to fill up – so come on in. Follow
us!' And he turned south, and roared off at ten knots, the skipper
obviously delighted with the success of his small deception. We

fell in beside his wake, let our sails fill out, cranked up our tiny Lister diesel engine to give us the extra knot or two, and made passage for Diego Garcia.

It came into view after only a few minutes, though the first sight was not of a dusting of green palm trees, but of a single white tower, and a cluster of ships' masts. The tower was marked on the chart – 'Wht. Twr. Conspic.' – and as we came closer, and began to see the lines of palms heeling over in the wind, and the upper-works of a veritable flotilla of vessels, we could see it was a water tank, and had words stencilled on the side: 'Welcome,' it said, as we expected, 'to the Footprint of Freedom'.

The reef entrance was marked by lights and buoys, and we passed two islands where there had been a leper colony a century ago. Inside, the channel was deep and wide – no danger of running aground on a coral-head, as we had with such ignominy up in Boddam. The channel had first been widened a hundred years before, when the Orient Steam Navigation Company decided to abandon Aden as a coaling station, and make Diego Garcia the main refuelling stop between the Red Sea and Cap Leeuwin.

Messrs. Lund and Company worked the coal bunker, employing forty Somalis and seventeen Europeans to operate the depot and its 15,000 tonnes of Welsh steam coal. It took about forty-eight hours to coal a liner, and the passengers were asked not to disembark, because of the 'lack of facilities' on the atoll. A Lund and Company official once reported great excitement among the native islanders when the liner *Lusitania* called; generally, however, coaling staff and copra-gatherers kept themselves apart, and there has never been any persuasive evidence of Somali blood in the Diego Garcian stock.

The *Robert W.* led us to a buoy in Eclipse Bay, just beneath the water tower and no more than a hundred yards from the shore. There was a satellite dish and cluster of domes and aerials and a café, with people sitting on a verandah out over the water. They waved and I thought I heard someone inviting us over for a beer.

The tug meanwhile had tied alongside, and the cook was busily passing over to Ruth a bewildering and wonderful assortment of food and drink. For the last two weeks it had been lentils and corned beef; now we had legs of frozen pork, fresh orange juice, beer, strawberries, tinned peaches, fresh pears . . . until suddenly the buzz of friendly American voices gave way to the stern and unmistakable accent of a British Government official. 'Break away, please! Break away! Her Majesty's Government orders. Break away!'

The two men, both in khaki shorts and shirts, with their epaulettes emblazoned with the letters 'BIOT', stepped off a power boat and on to the tug. The crew members took immediate fright: water pipes were disconnected, hawsers were undone, springs released, bowlines untied and the *Robert W.* and *Sketty Belle* began to drift apart. The two newcomers jumped nimbly aboard the yacht and signalled to the tug to move well away. Her skipper waved to us and grimaced at the back of the two, who were now arranging themselves, and opening their government-issue briefcases, in our main cabin.

Neither man smiled. One was named John Eddington, the other Jan Gover, and they had no interest in small talk. Passports were produced, forms were pulled from cases, and all the usual questions were asked – what firearms did we carry, did either of us suffer from malaria or measles, what duty-free alcohol was on board, were we carrying cocaine or marijuana. And then Mr Gover assumed an even more stern expression and asked my profession. 'Representative,' I said, since that was the word on my passport. 'Of what?' he asked. 'Publishing,' I replied, thinking that sufficiently anodyne. 'Oh yes,' Gover scowled. 'Publishing newspapers, by any chance. You wouldn't be a journalist, would you?'

The game was well and truly up. Yes, I said, I was. ('He's admitted it!' Gover whispered into the microphone of his radio, as though, after grilling me for three days, with liberal use of the thumbscrews and the rubber truncheon, he had finally heard me tell him where the gold was hidden.) Then Mr Eddington, the senior man, intervened. He waved a piece of typing paper, and became more formal. 'Last January, Mr Winchester, you wrote to the Foreign and Commonwealth Office, requesting permission to visit this territory.' I nodded mutely. I had indeed written to the Commissioner, Nigel Wenban-Smith (who combined his somewhat less-than-onerous job with that of being head of the East African Department), and had received a polite, but firm refusal. Under the terms of the 1966 agreement with the United States, he said, no civilians, except those working for the Government, could travel to any of the islands. He promised to put my name on the list of applicants, but held out rather little hope.

'Why,' Mr Eddington thundered, clearly quite angry, 'did you disregard the instructions of Her Majesty's Government?' I stifled a chuckle. It all seemed so very comical – this utterly serious conversation taking place in so tiny a cabin, piled high with frozen pigs' legs and cartons of strawberries. I stuttered a reply. I had wanted to see if the Government's assurances that only 'rotating contract personnel' lived on Diego Garcia were in fact true. I wanted to see if the graveyard still existed at Minni Minni, or if the wild horses from the islanders' old stables still ran on the beaches by East Point, and if there were any remanent members of the clutches of Muscovy ducks and Buff Orpington chickens that some islander set free on moving day ten years before, and I wanted to see if the hibiscus still grew by the manager's house, and if the pier still stood, from where the manager's wife once watched 'a giant ray, moving through the water like an animated army blanket'. I wanted to know, in short, whether our Government had been telling the truth when it took over the islands for the American forces to use, or whether the politicians had lied to the world, and dismissed the demands of the islanders like so much chaff in the wind.

All this cut no ice with Mr Eddington, and Mr Gover looked frankly contemptuous. 'You'll have to go,' he said. 'Right away.'

But Ruth had some shots left in her locker. No, she said, she was not prepared to go. As skipper of the vessel, she had a duty to see that neither it nor her crew were likely to be in any danger at sea. There were problems with the boat. The autopilot was not working. The stern gland on the propeller shaft was leaking, and needed to be repacked and tightened. The diesel tanks were almost empty. One of the sails was badly torn and needed patching. All this would take time, she said, and a brief sojourn in a British colony would be most convenient.

The officers left to seek instructions from the island Administrator, a Foreign Office man named John Topp. (The Administrator presides over surely one of the most curious assemblages
of Imperial rulers ever – Naval Party NP 2002, with a lieutenant-
commander, twenty sailors and six female cipher clerks; a
magistrate and a doctor; and six Scotland Yard policemen, who
are permanently occupied trying to investigate the innumerable
cases of narcotics' use among the 2,000 Americans who live on
their side of the cyclone fence. This may be an American base;
but British justice rules, and so the Foreign Office has to see
that the island does not succumb to utter lawlessness.)

While we waited, we watched the vast panorama of the
American war machine. Ahead, directly under the bow, was the
runway – nearly three miles long (and being extended on stilts
into mid-lagoon), and the best equipped between South Africa
and Australia. There were six of the silver Lockheed spotter
planes parked on the apron, and two more roared in as we
watched; ten white-painted fighters, quite probably from a carrier lurking somewhere nearby, were clustered by the control
tower; and at the far end, near the storage tanks and some
ominous-looking mounds of earth, the gun-grey bulk of a B–52
bomber, all the way from California by way of Hawaii, the
Philippines and Guam, and there to show the Middle East that
America had the strategic ability to drop atom bombs, or launch
cruise missiles, at a whim.

The base – and indeed all of the Indian Ocean, right up to
Mombasa and Kuwait – comes under the command of the C-in-C
Pacific, who is based in Honolulu. He remarked to me once that
having a forward line as far away as the Persian Gulf, which his
bombers took nearly a day to reach, was inconvenient, to say
the least. If the Commander of US Forces in Germany wanted
to know how it felt, the Admiral remarked, he should be based
in St Louis, Missouri, and try to run a European war from there.

But the real impression of power came from the lagoon, and the
gigantic assemblage of naval power and supplies. I could count
seventeen ships riding at anchor. Thirteen were cargo vessels,
stuffed to the gunwales with tanks and ammunition, fuel and water
supplies, rockets and jeeps and armoured personnel carriers, and

ready to sail at two hours notice. There was an atomic submarine, the USS *Corpus Christi* – a batch of crewmen were even now sailing by in their liberty boat, off to see the delights of the Rock and, presumably, to ferret out some of the eighty women assigned to the base; there was the submarine tender USS *Proteus*, which I had last seen in Holy Loch, in Scotland, and which was packed with every last item, from a nut to a nuclear warhead, that a cruising submariner could ever need; and there was the strange white-painted former assault ship, the USS *LaSalle*, now converted into a floating headquarters for the US Central Command, and in the bowels of which admirals and generals played 'Games of Survivable War in the Mid-East Theater', with the white paint keeping their electronic battle directors and intelligence decoders cool in the Indian Ocean sun.

But then Messrs. Eddington and Gover swept back in the *Dunlin Express*. Their faces were set. No, we could not stay. London had directed that we leave the Territory forthwith, and the Royal Navy would tow us out to sea if necessary. If we had any repairs we would have to do them at sea.

But we formally refused to go, and said quite plainly that we were within our rights, could claim Diego Garcia as a port of refuge under an international convention to which Britain and her colonies were signatories. Off roared the *Dunlin Express* once more; Mr Topp was consulted, London was telephoned, and back came the boat, with another one, the *Montrose Express*, in tow. Four khaki-shirted men stood in the background as their senior stood to make an announcement:

'I, John Winston Eddington, Marshal of the Supreme Court of British Indian Ocean Territory, do hereby request and require you to remove yourselves and your vessel . . .' And at this point I suddenly realised we weren't playing games any more. We were going to lose – we could have the boat seized, enormous fines levied, possessions confiscated, charges brought under Secrets Acts. So, craven and briefly humiliated, I interrupted. We would go, of course, I said; but we were tired, the weather had been bad up north – could we perhaps stay until daybreak? There was some hurried consultation by radio, and John Eddington nodded his agreement. Till dawn, he said; no hard feelings – a drink in London one day perhaps? Only doing my job, y'know. And off the *Expresses* buzzed, leaving us bobbing in their wake, and then alone in the upper part of the lagoon, in a strange and quarantined kind of peace.

The nights on Diego Garcia are brilliant affairs. The ships are festooned with riding lights and deck lights and illuminations. The airstrip glows with sodium vapour lamps, and the satellite dishes scan the skies bathed in a soft white glow. Aerials wink red and white, strobe lamps flicker, the barrack blocks and the security fences are bright in the blue of the kliegs. Someone ordered that searchlights be directed at us, presumably to make sure we didn't try to swim ashore; and throughout the night aircraft returning from patrol swept above us, colouring the water with their landing lamps. Kipling may have thought Calcutta was the city of dreadful night; this was the colony of perpetual day.

We didn't wake at dawn, and by eight the *Express* boats were back, and people were yelling through megaphones at us, telling us to move. We took our time, and ate our breakfast while the patrol boats circled us, like sharks; finally we slipped the buoy lines at noon. As we hoisted the sails we turned south, into the lagoon, and sailed around the *Corpus Christi*, and under the bows of the *Proteus* and the *LaSalle*, while a party of Royal Navy men in a rubber boat escorted us to the lagoon mouth. They waved us out and turned back to base; we felt the pleasant calm of the shallows give way to the slow swell of the ocean once more, and then the wind took hold, and a strong current, and we were swept away from Diego Garcia for good.

Three hours later I heard a plane above us, and saw the familiar shape and the flash of silver. I turned to see if I could spot the Wht. Twr. Conspic. – but the island had vanished below the horizon. That night the glow was easily visible, and lasted until just before dawn, but it was missing the next night out, and the skyline was uniformly dark. Only the radio told of the American presence – Radio Fourteen-Eighty-Five, blaring its advice on aerobic workshops and US Savings Bonds and drug abuse programmes until it, too, faded in a crackle and a hiss of static, and the island disappeared back into the ocean-bound anonymity it so keenly savours.

It still dismays me that so little anger has been generated inside Britain about the sad saga of the Chagos Islands. It might have been different, of course, had the Labour Government not been the one to initiate the tragedy. We tend to associate the Labour Party with the gentler principles of humanity and human dignity – it is a party that purports to stand for civil rights, self-determination, freedom from colonial tyranny, a slowing of the arms race. And yet it violated all of these precepts by its decisions over the Chagos Islands in 1965 and 1966, and by the actions its officers directed in the late 1960s and the early 1970s.

Had these things been done by a Tory administration, as one would perhaps have more easily accepted, the Roy Hattersleys and George Browns would no doubt have pilloried the decisions, condemned the Government for its barbaric cruelty and inhuman devotion to the arrogance of Empire. But, unhappily, it was these very politicians who directed the tragedy, and so are unable to criticise it in the political arena today. There is a time, of course, when expediency takes precedence over principle; and when that happens, as it clearly did over the formation of BIOT and the expulsion of the native islanders, there is a general understanding that not too much will be made of it all, and people will gradually forget.

And so they do. We reached Mauritius two weeks later, and found the islanders from Chagos assimilating themselves – with resignation, but without resistance – into their new home. They had been offered compensation, had accepted, and were moderately well off. They were beginning to forget that they were British subjects in an alien land; and the world was beginning to forget as well.

But those who run the colony are an unforgiving breed. A few weeks later I heard that the skipper of the *Robert W.* had been called back home, had been stripped of his command, and fired, for giving us help, advice and frozen strawberries out there in mid-ocean. He had helped us briefly delve into this most secretive part of the Empire; and the Empire, irritated and angered, had struck back.

TRISTAN
DA
CUNHA
1d

"LABRICHTHYS ORNATUS 17 CMS.
CONCHA FISH

SOUTH ATLANTIC OCEAN

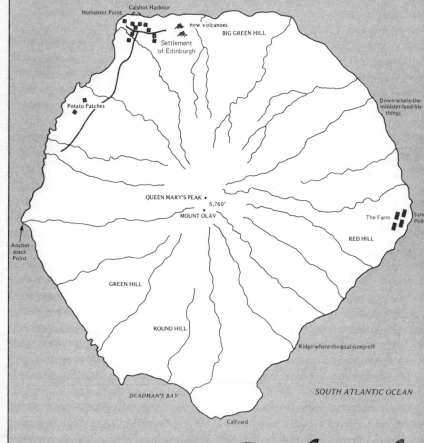

Hottentot Point
Calshot Harbour
new volcanoes
BIG GREEN HILL
Settlement
of Edinburgh

Down-where-the-
minister-land-his-
things

Potato Patches

QUEEN MARY'S PEAK
6,760'
MOUNT OLAV

The Farm
Sand
Point

RED HILL

Anchor-
stock
Point

GREEN HILL

ROUND HILL

Ridge-where-the-goat-jump-off

DEADMAN'S BAY
SOUTH ATLANTIC OCEAN

Calfyard

0   1   2   3 Kilometres
0   1   2 Miles

Tristan da Cunha

THREE

TRISTAN

It was an early November morning at the Zululand Yacht Club. The sky was pale blue and cloudless, and there was the feel of spring in the air. A fresh wind was blowing up from the south-west, and from the nine boats beside us came the familiar sounds of small craft in a port: the clinking of wire halyards against metal masts, the whirring of windvanes and the earnest slap of the tiny waves against well-anchored hulls.

The shipping channel was a hundred yards away, and, though this was a Sunday, the port was busy. The club is at Richards Bay, which the South African Government has decided is to be the pre-eminent bulk cargo terminal between Cape Town and Suez, and that Sunday, like any other day, the approach channels were alive with huge bulk carriers sliding to and fro, arriving empty from Japan and Korea, from Seattle and Valparaiso and Darwin, and leaving full of aluminium, or grain, or copper ore from the mines of the Rand and the Veldt.

Every few moments a funnel would appear above the harbour wall and a long steel prow would ease its way between the buoys and down to the cranes and hoppers of the loading bays. And every other few moments an exactly similar funnel and steel nose would, with even greater solemnity and gravamen, lumber its way, fully laden, out into the long sea. These were not pretty ships: they were quite characterless, immense steel boxes with prefabs for bridgeworks, a few contortions of pipes and a clutch of well-greased winches. Designed solely for the efficient transport of the world's raw materials – and fed not by stevedores, but by moving belts and computerised cranes – they had no evident concessions to maritime grace or beauty. And Richards Bay was the same: stark, modern, bright, efficient, and with none of the dirty charm and roguery of an old town by the sea.

Ruth and I had been stuck there for a week. The south-westerly wind, which all those unlovely bulk carriers could ignore and drive into with aloof impunity, was, for so small a schooner as ours, wickedly dangerous. So long as it was blowing, we had to remain in port. Tristan da Cunha was only 3,000 miles away – a month's steady sailing, if the wind was fair. But with the south-westerlies relentlessly piling up from the Antarctic, Tristan might have been three million miles away, and after this first week in Zululand I was beginning to fear that my trail to the most remote of Britain's colonial outposts might never even begin.

The charts and the *Pilots* had warned us. The eastern coast of South Africa, from the Mozambique border in the north to the rocky headland of Cape Agulhas – which, contrary to the popular assumption that the Cape of Good Hope is Africa's most southerly point, is itself the part of Africa closest to the Pole – has a fearsome reputation. Large, well-found ships have broken up and vanished without trace in the seas beyond these harbour walls. Yachts that risked the coastal waters between Richards Bay and Port Elizabeth, 600 miles away, have, in their hundreds, been driven on to wild cliff-bound shores, have lost masts and sails, have turned turtle, have had great holes gouged in their hulls, or have never been found again.

The coast's reputation arises from an unusual combination of circumstances. A powerful and very fast warm current – the Agulhas current – flows parallel to the coast, from the north-east to the south-west. In places it runs at five knots: it creates huge eddies and whorls in the water, and navigators can detect its malevolent presence simply by dipping a hand into the sea: if it is unusually warm, then that is current water, swirling and streaming south-westwards towards the southern cape. The current itself might not pose problems – except for ships wanting to drive against it – were it not for the certainty that, for at least two spring days out of five, the prevailing wind that blows above is *from* the south-west. A huge body of water is thus running down towards the south-west, and a huge body of air immediately overhead is running the exact opposite way. The charts, in a box outlined in red and displayed at intervals along the coast, explain what happens: 'Abnormal Waves' a warning declares. 'The coincidence of contrary wind and current patterns beyond the one-hundred-metre line can produce abnormal waves, with very steep leading edges and exceptional strength. Mariners are advised, in the event of winds from the south-westerly quadrant, either to remain within the hundred-metre contour, or remain in shelter, where available.'

I had read a little of these legendary waves. Other yachtsmen in the club bar added their own warnings. No one – not even the most carefree of the sailors who came in here – underestimated their power. There were magazines strewn around the bar, their pages opened to terrifying accounts of recent experiences. 'These waves are like nothing anywhere in the world,' one American magazine quoted a Dutch tanker captain as saying. 'They are not only enormously large. They are incredibly steep, so that when you reach the crest of one you tip down into what looks like a great black hole in the ocean, you slide down and down, and as you do so the next crest of the next wave breaks down on you and hundreds of millions of tons of water smashes on to your deck and drives you deeper still. Even the most well found steel ship can find it hard to survive an onslaught like this for long.' The master in question had suffered damage that looked more appropriate to a naval battle: his entire bow section had been ripped away, and all his deck equipment, his foremast and his capstans, had vanished. He had arrived in Durban a sober and frightened man, and, the magazine said, had been flown back by his owners, and was recovering from his ordeal, far from the sea.

And so we stayed in port, day after tedious day. Each morning we would walk to the public phone booth at one end of the dock and call the airport for the weather report. Each day the man on the other end would report back that low pressure zones at this point, and at that point, were causing strong south-westerly

winds from Port Elizabeth north to the Mozambique Channel.
He came to recognise my voice after a few such morning calls.
'Bloody frustrating, isn't it? Best to keep out of the water, I
think.' One day we did set out: the winds had died, and the
coastal radio station thought we might have twenty hours of
calms, enough time to get down to Durban. But within an hour
after we had cleared the harbour entrance buoys I saw a long
black line of cloud ahead of us, and a ferocious mass of dark
water roared towards us, and within minutes we were plunging
deep into troughs of sea and gales were howling through the
shrouds. We dropped sails, turned about, and fled for home and
the tedious comfort of our mooring.

After ten days, though, we had some success. One good day
took us down to Durban, where we met a young sailor who was
able to give us good advice for the next leg of the trip, to East
London and Port Elizabeth. His plan, which he had followed on
more than a hundred southbound ventures, was to wait until a
stiff south-wester was blowing, and leave after it had been
blowing for twenty hours – while, in other words, it was *still*
blowing. That way, he assured us, we would have an uncomfortable first few hours, would then run into a day of calms and light
airs, and would then pick up the north-wester that inevitably
came after the southerlies.

He came down each morning with weather charts and new
advice. One day we told the port authorities we would leave at
four that afternoon, and the immigration and customs men came
down and checked us, and stamped us out. But we were then
told it might be better to leave at eight, and the customs and
immigration men insisted on coming a second time, and charged
a fistful of rand for the privilege. Finally, we left at midnight, on
the tide: the men with their briefcases and sealing-wax
embossers and lead-clamps – for the South African bureaucrat
is a great one for paraphernalia – came down a third time, took
another ten rand from us, and waved us off into the night, and
watched us as we hoisted sails for the 300 miles ahead.

'Between Durban and East London there is nowhere to run,'
we had been warned a score of times. The coastline – the 'wild
coast', as the tourist brochures charmingly call it – has no safe

harbours to run to in the event of trouble. The coast is, indeed, a fine example of the iniquity of the South African regime: most of it belongs to the Transkei, an artificial homeland for the blacks whom the whites don't wish to have living alongside them. And yet the coastline of the Transkei has no port: there is no way the Transkeians – who, the South Africans insist, are an independent people, with all the privileges of nationhood open to them – can fish, or trade, or develop useful harbours. There are South African ports to the north of the Transkei – Durban is one – and there are South African ports to the south – like East London and Port Elizabeth. But the land that has been given to the blacks is, from a maritime point of view, quite useless.

It was an uncomfortable journey, but a safe one. There is a point, off a small bluff known as Port St John's, where the hundred-metre contour comes to within five miles of the coast, and scores of ships eager to keep out of the way of the dreaded waves were crammed into the passage, making for an unpleasant degree of congestion. But once past that, the fair winds and a current that added its five knots to our four of sailing speed pushed us down to East London in two days. It was three weeks since my plane had touched down at Durban: we were just 600 miles down the coast, Tristan was more than 2,000 miles away, and Christmas was looming. I had brought Christmas post for the islanders: I began to wonder if I would be able to deliver it on time.

The winds were against us for four days in East London, though it was sunny enough, and warm, and the time went pleasantly as we idled in the sunshine, painting and varnishing, repairing the headsail that had torn, lubricating the gaff rubbers with neatsfoot oil, reordering the charts, cleaning the autopilot and generally preparing the boat for the long run ahead. One Saturday afternoon I saw a man sitting on the quayside with his small son, and begged a lift to a petrol station so that I could fill the carboy with fuel for our little Lister engine. He was an electrician, Martin Smyth; his son was Ralph, eight years old. The two came down to the docks every Saturday afternoon 'just to look at the boats, and dream a little'.

I told him where we were going, and his eyes widened with delighted envy. He had wanted to visit Tristan all of his life – 'leastwise, ever since that volcano that went off – when was that, '61 wasn't it? A most fascinating little place. I hope you'll write and tell us what it was like!' And he began to explain to Ralph, who wasn't bored at all, and shared in his father's very keen enthusiasm, precisely where Tristan was. He knew all about it: he knew the names of the other rocks in the group – Inaccessible, Gough, Stoltenhoff and Nightingale – and something of the names of the seven families who lived there. (He remembered Swain, Glass, Repetto, Lavarello and Rogers. The two he couldn't recall at first were Green and Hagan, but when I reminded him he then told me that Green was indeed a corruption of the Dutch surname Groen, and that the ancestral Tristan settler of that name was a crewman on the American schooner *Emily* from Stonington, Connecticut, which was wrecked in 1836; he had been Pieter Willem Groen, and had come from the North Sea village of Katwijk aan See: when he decided to settle on Tristan and take British nationality he changed his name to Peter William Green. He became mildly notorious some fifty years later when a parson named Dodgson – Lewis Carroll's brother – came to the island and recommended evacuating the entire community for its own spiritual good. Green wrote a long letter to the Admiralty protesting at Dodgson's plan, and was allowed to stay on.)

I spent the rest of the day with the Smyth family. A small daughter was collected from the local cinema, and the children spent hours clambering in the rigging while we sat in the cockpit, drinking tea, and listening to their father's dreams. Ruth mentioned that once our voyage to Tristan was over she might be selling the little yacht, and she named a price: Martin fell to counting his assets, and wondering out loud if it might not be an admirable idea to leave his electrician's job and sell his house in East London, and take his wife and children around the world, and to all the little islands – like Tristan – about which he had read. He knew something of sailing: he had owned a small dinghy which he sailed at weekends on a lake in Rhodesia – he refused to use the more modern name – and he imagined he could handle this neat little schooner at sea. He called the children down from the mainmast, and the three went off happily, talking animatedly about what they might do.

We made the boat ready for sea shortly before sunset, and were about to cast off when there was the toot of a car horn, and the entire family – Mrs Smyth as well, on this occasion – arrived to wish us well. They had brought cakes and bottles of beer for us, and Mrs Smyth had made egg sandwiches. 'You wouldn't believe how excited they all were when they got home,' she said. 'Virginia came dancing in to the kitchen shouting, "Daddy's bought a boat! Daddy's bought a boat!" He knows as well as I do that we could never afford it. But it has made them all very happy. It's been a Saturday afternoon like no other.'

They stayed for tea and then, as the sun began to slope down behind the lighthouse bluff, they said their goodbyes and waved us off from the quayside. We chugged slowly down the Buffalo River, past the rusting freighters and the derelict tugs – for East London is not the port it was, and handles only a few hundred tons of grain and ore each month – and past the yacht club and into the harbour mouth. There is a green light mounted on a tall steel pole on the end of the north mole, and as we rounded it and hurried to raise the sails to catch the evening breeze, so we spotted a familiar car under the flashing lamp. Four tiny figures – two tinier than the others – were waving sadly, and I heard one voice blown thinly by the gathering breeze, 'Say . . . hello . . . to . . . Tristan!' Then the darkness enveloped them, and I thought I saw the pinpricks of the car lights as it drove away to a quiet evening at home. I felt suddenly very forlorn, and I daresay they did, too. The children would be bouncing in the back of the car, talking at school next Monday about the boat that they were going to buy and the islands they were going to visit. But in the front seat there would be an uneasy silence, for the Smyths well knew the grim economics of it all, and how they would be bound to his job as an East London electrician for many years to come. But still, we said to one another as we rounded out into the rowdy ocean, they had had an afternoon of dreams.

We spent only three days in Port Elizabeth – a dirty dockyard, though with a collection of magnificent old steam engines which clanked and puffed their way between ships and warehouses all hours of the day and night. A bracket on the autopilot had snapped within hours of leaving East London, and I had to find a mechanic to machine a new one. But we left at the end of the week. By Monday night we were rounding Cape Agulhas, leaving the treacherous currents and the south-westerly winds behind, and entering the fresh south-easters that should blow us up to Cape Town. And we had left the Indian Ocean, too: the blue waters of the tropic isles were behind us, the grey and chilly waters of the South Atlantic ranged for thousands upon thousands of miles ahead. This was Tristan's Ocean, and according to the Admiralty *Pilot* the island was but 1,800 miles ahead. The worst part of the trip was abaft; South Africa was still abeam; our goal was a little way ahead.

We put in to Cape Town the next day, revictualled, washed clothes, took advice from the local seamen on how best to approach the island. There were three ships in Cape Town that went with some regularity to the Tristan group: the *Tristania* and the *Atlantic Isle* took supplies to the island, spent three months fishing in local waters, and then took their fish, and such Tristanians as wanted to visit the Cape, back to port. The *Agulhas*, a South African boat, travelled twice a year to relieve the meteorological station on Gough Island – a British possession, but unpopulated save for the South African met men – and then took freight on to Tristan if it were needed. The skippers of the various boats were stern in their warnings to us. Go to Tristan at your peril, they said with one voice: it is difficult to find, often shrouded in mist, has nowhere safe to anchor, is prey to sudden and ferocious changes of weather, and has just one landing beach from which the islanders are only able to set out on sixty days each year. A tiny harbour had been built in the mid-Sixties – named Calshot Harbour, in memory of the military camp at Calshot in Hampshire that housed the islanders for their year's exile after the volcanic eruption – but it was too shallow for a boat like ours. We drew about six feet: the harbour was perhaps four feet deep, and there was a bar to cross which shallowed to perhaps half of that.

It sounded an uninviting prospect. There was a band of kelp weed around the island, and it was strong enough to tie a small boat to, the skippers agreed. No good for big boats, which might get their propellers caught in it, but strong enough for us to lash a hawser to, so long as we dropped an anchor as well to limit our circular movement. But one warning dominated all the others: if the wind began to blow from the north-west – and gales from that quarter would arrive with precious little warning and at devastating speed – then move the boat into the island's lee. No matter how much kelp and how many anchor chains might try to bind us to the spot we had chosen as our mooring – a Tristan nor'wester would tear us away from it and hurl us on to the rocks. We were in a small office when the skippers told us this: a picture was brought out from one of the desks – a picture of a wall of sheer and jagged black cliffs, streaming with falling water, and at their base, patterned with vast lumps of broken stone, a hundred feet of wildly raging foam, blown into sheets by the downdraughts and whipped into a maelstrom by the gales. 'That,' the men said in an uncomfortably smug harmony, 'is what you'll hit if you forget.'

Although Tristan da Cunha is 1,800 nautical miles west by south of Cape Town, thanks to the meteorology of the South Atlantic Ocean and the patterns of currents, a sailing vessel cannot point its prow to a heading of two-sixty degrees and expect to fetch up at Edinburgh-of-the-Seven-Seas (Tristan's 'capital', named after the first Duke in 1867, visited again by the second ninety years later) after fifteen days. Would that matters were so simple. In the centre of the ocean – and the centre of the North Atlantic is similarly endowed – is an enormous, and very stable area of high pressure. No wind blows there – the charts indicate that totally calm weather prevails for at least one day in ten in December, and that light, variable and navigationally useless winds puff fitfully and occasionally. Of all the hours spent in a yacht, those spent becalmed are the most likely to induce madness. The boat lurches randomly, going nowhere; the sails bang and crump as they catch a molecule of breeze, and the booms swing idly and lethally with the swell. You come to loathe sails and all they stand for: you want the luxury of an engine (but hardly dare use yours for fear of wasting fuel) to take you to a strong and steady breeze; the fish dip cheekily up through the hot mirror of the still sea, as if to remind you that they are fine, and cool, and can propel themselves at will. To sail straight from the Cape to Tristan would be to risk a week – maybe a month – stuck in such unpredictable regions of the sea. We were already running late, and wanted none of that.

So we planned a longer, though more traditional route, which took us in a great loop, following the winds that blow anticlockwise round the high. For the first 300 miles we would follow the South African and Namibian coasts, driven north-westwards by the cold current that sweeps up from the Cape (and is the oceanic opposite of the terrible Agulhas current on the other coast), and by the prevailing December winds, from the south-east. We would then head up towards St Helena, where the winds begin to turn to easterlies, around the top of the high. We would pass a hundred miles south of St Helena – Imperial remnant herself, and one I would visit later on – heading westwards, until, two thousand miles shy of the Brazilian coast the winds would begin to turn into the northerly quadrant, and the current would too, and we would sweep down in their train.

The winds would become steadily stronger, with more of a north-westerly heading, driving us straight towards our goal. The seas would get grander, the waters colder, the skies greyer. After 4,000 miles – more than double the length of the direct route, and nearly twice the distance of the great circle route taken by motor ships making the passage – we should be able to see Tristan beyond the bowsprit. If, that is, our boat held out: she was a sturdy little steel schooner, 'a good gunwales-under performer' they said of her – she liked strong weather, and ploughing through heavy waters with the seas lashing over the guardrails, and with the mainmast boom dipping into the ocean. But she had her limitations. She was steel, and uninsulated, and would be very cold. Her mainsail and foresail were canvas, not too well-stitched in places. There was a small but annoying leak in the stern gland, where the propeller shaft left the hull for the water outside – the gland was lubricated by water, which dripped into the bilges in tiny amounts; here, though, the drip occasionally became a steady stream, and we had to pump the bilges hourly, or else the boat became heavy and more sluggish than usual. The autopilot, too, was giving problems: it was a British-made device, used by weekend sailors in the easy waters of the Channel; out in the big ocean, where the rudder took continual pounding, and the winds blew strongly and unpredictably, the steel arm – we knew the device as 'Betty', and so worried ourselves over the fate of 'Betty's arm' – did strange things, and had given up completely on a journey through another ocean some months before. We were concerned, in other words, that we might not make it to Tristan, and wondered how wise we were to press on any further. My inclination – one more motivated by stubbornness than good sense, I came to think – was to carry on; we had already been five weeks in the getting there. To abandon the venture at this stage would sadden me.

So, in the pleasant fastness of the Royal Cape Yacht Club's little harbour, we waited for the wind to swing to the south-east. Table Mountain gives the first clue: when the wind is from the right quarter a low white cloud, one which almost seems to stick to the flat mountaintop, appears. Locals call it 'the Table Cloth', and as the wind begins to blow it starts to fall off the mountain in a wide sheet of whiteness, descending towards the upper suburbs of the Town. It was early on a Monday morning when the cry went up: 'Table Cloth's coming off!' – and we stowed our gear, untied the springs, cast off and said our farewells to Port Radio. 'Whither bound?' they asked. 'Tristan da Cunha,' we replied, cockily – knowing full well that most yachts leaving the Cape in December aim for St Helena, Brazil and the Caribbean, and only the boldest and the bravest made for the wild waters and dreaded anchorage of Tristan. We felt a stirring of pride as the radio operator wished us well, a safe voyage, and urged us to take good care. Our expedition, we knew, was more valorous than most that left this port.

By nightfall, our pride had turned to ashes. We were back in port, the trip abandoned, the five weeks of sailing all wasted. There had been many problems. The autopilot had, indeed, begun to behave erratically, and we balked at the prospect of steering by hand over 4,000 miles of ocean. Keeping watch, turn and turn about, was tiring enough: to have to handle the tiller at night and through heavy seas would be utterly exhausting. The waters off the Cape were miserably cold, and we were chilled to the bone: the prospect of many more days and weeks spent shivering, above decks and below, suddenly seemed more miserable than it had from the warm bar of the Cape Yacht Club. The stern gland leak had been more serious than we feared, and the bilge was seriously awash after only a few hours' sailing. And it was brutally rough out there: the south-easterly had piled the waters up into lumpy, icy swells, and we slammed against them, making the slowest of progress.

It was the timetable that finally decided it. It was early December: if I was going to be home for Christmas I would have only twenty days to do the crossing, and get back. At the rate we were going on the first day out there was no possibility we would make Tristan by the New Year, nor be back before the end of January. And so, with more sorrow than reluctance, I swung the boat's head round and steered to where the coastline of Table Bay – the Lion's Head, the Lion's Rump, Table Mountain and the Twelve Apostles – had just vanished below the horizon. Robben Island light soon came on, and guided us in: by midnight we were passing the outer markers, and reported, shamefacedly, to Port Radio. 'Difficult trip, that,' commented one of the wireless operators as he tore up our exit card. 'Thought you were being a bit optimistic.'

I was back in a dank and grey London a week later, certain now that Tristan was beyond my grasp. I felt wretched about it. True, we had made a vague promise that we would meet in South Africa later in the summer and try again. But it seemed more navigationally prudent to try to attack the island from the South American coast – from where you get a straight run, without having to bother about the high. But I had no friends with yachts in Montevideo or Rio, and spent the Christmas holidays morosely coming to terms with the fact that Tristan, for the next few years at least, was to remain a dream. I had wanted to go there since long before the 1961 eruption: the new Imperial Progress was but an excuse to fulfil a long-held ambition. I was cast into the deepest gloom.

But January brought an unexpected letter. Andrew Bell, who ran one of Britain's most enterprising little shipping lines, Curnow Shipping, based in deepest Cornwall, wondered if I knew that his flagship was making a first-ever journey to Tristan da Cunha, leaving from Bristol in early March? He knew I had been trying to get there: would I by any chance care to go? I was on the telephone within seconds: my cabin was booked, my leave extended. This time I really ought to make it: the only warning came from an item I read in the paper a week later. The Royal Mail Ship *St Helena* had caught fire off the coast of Senegal. She had drifted, powerless and without steering, for four blisteringly hot days before a German salvage tug had towed her into Dakar. The passengers, who had spent some time in the lifeboats, were flown home, and the *St Helena* limped down to Cape Town for repairs. The RMS *St Helena*, of course, was Curnow's flagship: she was the vessel due to take me to Tristan da Cunha in eight weeks' time.

In the event she picked up her schedule quickly enough – by dint of cancelling one complete voyage, to the inconvenience of the population of the colony of St Helena, for whom she is the single lifeline to the outside world – and I arranged to meet her on her southbound voyage Number Thirty-Eight at the port of Santa Cruz de la Tenerife, in the Canary Islands. She swept in past the moles just after dusk one mild March Thursday: at four the following morning, after loading some ten tonnes of assorted cargoes and five passengers, she slipped her moorings and rumbled out into the ocean, and the southern seas. I was in the company, I soon found out, of a strange assortment of travellers.

There was the lawyer from Akron, Ohio, named Parke Thompson who was listed in the American edition of the *Guinness Book of Records* as 'the World's Most Traveled Man', and who was to break into a hysterical fury when told it would not be possible for him to set foot upon Ascension Island, even for the 'single split second' he considered sufficient for his next record attempt. There was David Machin, England's greatest expert in the feeding of pigs, and who had developed a diet of mashed fish heads and minced flax leaves, upon which the average porker apparently feasted with Caligulan abandon. There was a very dour man who ran the Rapid Results College, and turned out to be dour because some crane driver had seen fit to drop the Rapid Results College car into the depths of Number Four hold, and it was sitting down there all the while, a mute reminder that the first job he had to undertake when the boat arrived at the Cape was to spend hours waiting on the services of a panelbeater, when he could have been driving to the vineyards of Stellenbosch.

There were also six Cheviot rams – immense beasts hauled down from Coquetdale to inject some life into the forlorn ewes of Tristan. They sat in cages on deck, nibbled grumpily at pieces of lettuce, and sweated in fleeces that must have been a foot thick until a shepherd from an island we passed came out and sheared them. One of them managed to escape from its pen and leaped around the deck, cornering the captain near the anchor winches and charging him, until the bosun got near enough with a hawser and looped it around its leg. For the rest of the voyage they were more peaceable, glumly contemplating the wearying duties of their calling on the island far ahead.

Our cruising speed was fourteen knots. Three hundred miles of white foam unrolled beneath our stern each day, and on all sides the lonely sea stretched far away. Occasionally we glimpsed another ship – once it was a British tramper, and one night a squadron of six vessels, all moving very fast along the same course and keeping strict radio silence. But generally there was nothing to see but the bulging swell in the daytime, the empty green eye of the radar screens by night.

The chief officer taught me how to navigate by the stars – I already knew how to use the sun, but the stars, he promised me, were much more accurate, and considerably more satisfying. Soon I could repeat the mystic astral names by rote – Procyon and Regulus, Achernar and Betelgeuse, Sirius and Rigel and Zubenelgenubi: within a week I could find them all; and tried gamely to plot a position on the sheet which bore an approximation to what the satellite navigator told us was precisely correct. But my seven position lines from my seven stars invariably formed themselves into some weird kind of parallelogram on the chart, with our good Royal Mail Ship somewhere inside the boundary, give or take five miles or so. It was only after a great deal of practice that the lines began to form themselves into the famous 'cocked hat' of more competent navigation students. But I was never able to match my tutor, whose lines would all, as though by magic or by cheating, converge on a single spot, and he would write our longitude and latitude on to the chart to the nearest quarter-minute, and sniff with haughty disdain at the unwinking electronic eyes of the satellite that had dared do him out of his job.

We crossed the equator after a week. The World's Most Traveled Man had crossed it before, naturally, and was not obliged to suffer the ritual humiliations that mariners inflict on those who have not. But the ever-alert purser discovered a Whitehall civil servant aboard who had never been south of the line, and the poor man was smeared in treacle and flour and had herrings stuffed into his bathing trunks before being dunked in the swimming pool by an officer dressed up as a bear. 'Wish we could do it to the lot of them,' remarked the officer of the watch, as he peered down idly from the bridge. He had just been in trouble with the tax men, and had no particular fondness for Whitehall.

The days bled effortlessly into one another as the routines of shipboard life took over from the concerns of the far-distant outside. True, the BBC World Service was broadcast every afternoon, for the benefit of those who cared about Beirut's collapse, the dollar's rise and fall, the doings of Charles and Diana and the assortments of famines and earthquakes and typhoons that make up what we call 'news'; but fewer and fewer people seemed to listen each day, and after two weeks at sea I came into the ship's lounge at five o'clock to find only a single passenger, fast asleep. The ship's interests centred on the deck quoits contest and the chess game, on the fate of the engine (which stopped one night, leaving us drifting aimlessly in the swell while mechanics swarmed over a leaking valve), and on whether or not we would be able to land on Tristan da Cunha. Only one day in six was fair enough for a landing: we heard on the radio that the *Queen Elizabeth 2* had been standing off the island a week ago, between calls at Rio and Cape Town, but that the swell had been too bad for anyone to be brought ashore.

This dire intelligence brought a cloud of dismay to the brow of the World's Most Traveled Man who was, he insisted on telling the captain, very eager indeed to land. Having failed to trot on to the cinder beaches of Ascension, he was grimly determined to step ashore at Tristan, 'only for a second, even if it kills me'. His dutiful wife, who was called Babette, showed me a bulletin from something called the Century Travel Club of Los Angeles, which prepared lists of 'all the World's Countries, Sovereign and Non-Sovereign States and Islands', and had a motto about 'World Peace Thru World Travel', and urged its members to underline every country they had visited, send photostats of the appropriate passport stamps and receive Handsome Certificates by return. The WMTM, said Babette, had now visited 298 of the 307 possibles – Tristan would make it 299. It was rather like train-spotting. I would ask Babette what Midway Island or somewhere similar had been like, and she would invariably reply that, as far as she recalled, she had only been in the transit lounge for fifteen minutes, 'but this darling little man had stamped the passports, so we have been there, you know!'

She had no notion of what Tristan might be like. The only man who might was a birdwatcher from Los Angeles with whom I had an uncertain first conversation. I had offered him milk in his coffee and he replied, with stern gravity that, 'No, I never take lactates. I have Grave Internal Problems,' and I decided not to pursue further inquiry.

But he knew his birds. There are, he reported, fourteen different types of petrel on the islands, with names like the great shearwater, the Cape pigeon and the snow petrel. The islanders, he said with obvious disapproval, like to catch the shearwaters and boil them down to make cooking oil. There are rockhopper penguins, which are tiny and have wild tufts of hair sticking from above their ears, making them look like small and most eccentric black men. The islanders also boil down the penguins to make oil for waterproofing their famous longboats, which are made of canvas. The mollymawk (the name comes from the Dutch word meaning 'stupid gull') lives on Tristan: it is properly known as the yellow-billed albatross, breeds on one of the island group, and would probably pick us up five hundred miles north of Tristan, to where it ranges, eternally vigilant, like an aerial sentry.

And, the grave American said, there was the wandering albatross, perhaps the most revered of all the world's birds, a rival in popular esteem to the Californian condor and the golden eagle. Huge, pure white, magnificent, the great creatures of the species *Diomedea exulans* soar for years at a time in the ever-blowing gales of the roaring forties, ranging tens of thousands of lonely miles from their breeding grounds in South Georgia and in Tristan. (I tried to joke that this made them British subjects, but the remark fell uselessly by the wayside.) They never range north of the thirtieth parallel, he said; once south of that line one should join us.

Everything changed at the thirtieth parallel. On the pilot charts for the South Atlantic the wind roses show that the trade winds cease, and that northerlies begin to blow as prelude to the westerlies of the roaring forties. There is an easterly current, too, bringing cold Antarctic waters up to mix with the warmer seas of the tropics. We crossed the parallel at noon, sixteen days out from Tenerife, and it was like passing into another world.

I was on the after deck at the time. On either beam, and to astern, the sea was calm and blue, and the sun – behind us now, since we were in the southern hemisphere – was deliciously warm. But then there came a familiar click, and the ship's tannoys began squawking. Not, this time, a message about boat drill, or a request for the bosun to check on number three ram, which was becoming rather seasick, but something rather unusual. 'Passengers are advised that we are about to pass into a heavy rain squall,' said a voice from the bridge, and we looked ahead and saw, in place of blue skies and calm seas, a ragged line of black cloud, and grey razor-edge to the sea, behind which white horses dashed with silent fury as the wind whipped across the swells.

It was upon us within seconds. The sun was blotted out. It became strangely chill and damp. The silence on deck was broken by the furious lashing of halyards against stanchions, and the crack of pennants. And the ship, until now so still and level, began to move, slowly at first, as though waking from a deep sleep. She was starting to roll, and her bows plunged into a wave and threw a curtain of spume over the foredeck. And then the rain began to spatter down, and most of the passengers ran inside, bewildered that the benignity of the ocean had so suddenly turned to malice. 'Welcome,' said one of the deck officers, as he dived for cover, 'to the Southern Ocean.'

The next morning four birds were gliding beside and behind us. Three were mollymawks, and the fourth, aloof and higher than the rest, was pure white, with wings each as big as a man: the wandering albatross, guiding us with stately precision on to Tristan.

We made our landfall at dawn on a showery, windy southern autumn morning. At first, there was a patch of settled grey cloud on the far horizon; then, as we rolled nearer, a shape became distinct – a huge cone, its flanks soaring out of the depths with an abruptness that looked almost unreal, as though a child had daubed its idea of an island on the canvas. It had all the appearance of exactly what it was – a vast submarine volcano, poking up from the mid-Atlantic cordillera, and so tall that its summit pierced the sea and rose 6,000 feet into the sky. There was a ring of cloud 3,000 feet up, which girdled the cone like a starched white collar; and then the slope continued, up to a peak that was dusted with early-season snow, and which gleamed in the rising northern sun.

We radioed the island. 'Hello, *St Helena*,' said a voice, neither awed nor surprised by our arrival. 'You'll have be waiting a whoil. Harbour's closed. Swell too bad. Might take a day or some. We'll let you knows soon as we can.'

A wave of disappointment swept the ship, and for the first time I began to wonder if the damnable 'Tristan luck' they had told me about might keep me off the island still. But no, I reasoned: we had the Colonial Governor of the island of St Helena aboard, making an official visit to his tiny southern dependency; we had the rams; we had a new island doctor; and we had the World's Most Traveled Man, who had a look of acute anxiety about him, and seemed quite unable to tackle his breakfast. He even swore at his bloater, and ordered the waiter to remove it. No, I decided, we would land, sooner or later. I would get to this outpost, now so tantalisingly close.

As the ship neared the northern coast so the island's only settlement, and thus the Tristan capital, Edinburgh-of-the-Seven-Seas, swung into view. It was just a hamlet, sprawled on a wide expanse of grass at the foot of sheer walls of rock. It looked a neat and tidy place, the houses gaily painted, the little gardens full of flowers. I could see two Union flags streaming south in the breeze – one was over the Administrator's office, someone said, and the other flew over his house.

But there was no great monument to might or power here. No castle stood in Edinburgh, nor any battlement or cathedral or cenotaph or statue – not that I could see through my glasses, at least. Tristan was first settled by British soldiers stationed here to prevent any French attempts to free Napoleon from St Helena: but they seemed to have left no obvious relic of their stay, visible from the sea. This was the gentler side of Empire and if our motto was 'What we have we hold', it was more strongly stated in the guns of Singapore and the forts of old Bermuda than here, where we had just built an English village, and had come to live in peace and quiet comfort.

No one seemed to be around. From here Edinburgh looked a ghost town, as though its people, who had all been evacuated to England when the volcano erupted in 1961, had never returned. (In fact all except five did come back, and more islanders live in Edinburgh today than before the eruption.) The illusion was reinforced when a rain squall swept across the island: two twin cones of the new volcano, which sits brooding on the hamlet's eastern edge, began to steam and sputter. Wisps of smoke began to blow from a yellow-lipped crater, and I half-expected a stream of magma to snake down towards the sea, and a shower of red-hot boulders to thud down on the terrified villagers, just as it had done all those Octobers ago. The new lava field, under which the old crawfish cannery had been quite buried, and beneath which lay the longboats' old landing place, stretched black and ugly towards us, ending in a sudden line of cliffs.

The breeze was blowing steadily from the north, and the captain was a little uneasy, lying off these cliffs now less than half a mile to the south. He decided to look for the island's lee – logic dictated it was around on the southern side – and so we set off, engines half ahead and ship's head turned to the east, to work our way clockwise around the colony.

The tannoy squawked the strange names of the little headlands and cliffs and bays we passed: Pigbite, Noisy Beach, Deadman's Bay, and sites that commemorated noted events, and which the ordnance surveyors and the naval hydrographers engraved on their maps without demur – Down-where-the-minister-land-his-things, Down-by-the-pot and Ridge-where-the-goat-jump-off. There was a pine forest at Sandy Point, and we could see a tiny hut in a clearing. It belonged to the island's agriculture department, and was used by Edinburghers when they wanted to go on holiday. It was four miles away from the capital, and you went there by dinghy.

Back in Cape Town, when we had been contemplating sailing to Tristan, the old mariners had warned us severely of one stark fact: the weather can change in an instant. Never, never leave the yacht unmanned, they all said. If a north-wester blows up it may do so without any warning at all, and a yacht lying off the island's northern coast would be dashed to pieces on the lava within minutes. I had good cause to remember the advice as we were passing Sandy Point Gulch, and the wind suddenly rose, and all the world went mad.

It had been blowing a steady Force Six – thirty knots of half-gale that kicked up a moderate swell. But, with a rumbling howl that rose steadily to a shriek, the wind began to blow more and more strongly, Force Eight within five minutes, then Force Ten, and then, before a quarter of an hour was up we were in a Storm Force Twelve and the ship was blinded in a rage of white spray, the anemometers had blown off scale and the barograph was recording the pressure dropping a millibar a minute – all the characteristics of a Pacific typhoon, or a West

Indian hurricane. None of the deck officers had seen anything like it in their careers – the gale slammed and battered the little ship, heeling her hard over into the sea, pounding her with mountainous green seas which poured over her decks in thunderous eddies.

Bows down and shoulders hunched, *St Helena* rammed her way around the island, which was illuminated by sudden shafts of sunlight, instant rainbows, and over which streamed veils of cloud. We reached the southern edge – a cape where the three-masted barque *Italia* had been wrecked in 1892, bringing the surnames of Repetto and Lavarello to the island, where they still survive – but the wind refused to calm. In fact, as we pummelled our way further and further around, it became clear that this, unique among all islands I have known, is a place without a lee – there is nowhere to shelter. The gales either blow around the island in some devilish spiral, or else pour as a katabatic torrent up and over the mountain, striking anything below, no matter at what quarter of the compass.

Without doubt the little green schooner in which I had been planning to make the voyage would have suffered terribly in the storm. Had we been under sail, and north of the island, we could barely have escaped destruction; had we tried to run downwind we would have been blown miles away, quite possibly dismasted, probably overwhelmed. The only escape would have been to hack the halyards with knives and get the sails down in an instant, and run before the weather under bare poles. But I fear we would have reacted too slowly: Tristan weather has a speed and a force to it that is terrifying, and even the old master of our ship, well-found and solid though the vessel was, scratched his head in disbelief and wonder as the winds began to die and the barometer to climb back. Even he had never seen anything like it.

We spent the remainder of the day tacking gently to and fro off the Edinburgh coast – coming in to the anchorage, steaming ten miles out to sea, returning to home waters, and back again. We had a couple on board, the Robinsons, who were hoping to see how their son David, the island doctor, lived, but who now knew they would never be allowed to land, since Mr Robinson was too old, and his wife had her leg in plaster. The islanders had radioed across that only those who were fit and fleet of foot could hope to make it safely to shore, if the swell ever did die down; the couple called their son on the radio, and he promised to stand and wave to them from the green in front of the Administrator's house. But they never saw him: whenever he was waving, the ship was steaming the wrong way, and during those moments the ship was close enough and pointing in the right direction their son was on the radio, or dealing with a patient. 'Everyone here's got a cold,' he explained. 'It must have come from the *QE2*. Some of our people went aboard her, and once one brings a germ ashore it goes round like wildfire. So I'm pretty busy, like it or not. I sometimes wish ships didn't call at all. They may bring the mail, but they bring all sorts of illness, too.' But he added that he was, after all, being paid to deal with illness, and a good epidemic kept him from being bored.

The replacement doctor, Paul Kennaway, with whom I was sharing a cabin, had brought along the Medical Research Council papers with the results of the detailed studies of the islanders that had been made during their exile in Britain after the eruption. Nearly half of them had asthma – 'hashmere' being the local word – and almost as many had a plague of parasitical worms. There were signs of inbreeding, too – there had been no new blood injected into the island stock since the early part of the century, and there were problems with eyes, for instance, that owed much to the too limited genetic pool. Asthma was still a serious illness on Tristan, it seemed. Few of the men left home without a Ventolin 'puffer' – even the hardiest of seamen were afflicted – and when the wind was from the east, and sulphur fumes from the volcano were wafting over the settlement, the sound of wheezing and coughing drowned out even the crash of the surf and the howling of the gales.

The night passed quietly, and the wind dropped to the merest breeze. The settlement was a cluster of lights until ten o'clock exactly, and then the generators at the crawfish factory were switched off, and every light died. I thought I could make out a few windows lit by flickering oil lanterns and by candles, but it might have been imagination: the community seemed to have been snuffed out of existence, and all around was the impenetrable blackness of an overcast night at sea.

Next morning the surf was still running high between the tiny moles of Calshot Harbour – great breakers would regularly crash between them and wash right over the masses of concrete dolosse blocks (said to have been shaped after the design of a sheep's anklebone, and at the core of all new harbours constructed in the southern hemisphere, and to have made their South African inventor millions of rand). But the islanders seemed to think a landing might be possible later in the day, if the weather held. By nine, with the wind now just a gentle and fitful wafting from the south-east, we heard the putter of an old Lister engine, and a blue-and-white boat, flying the Union Jack defaced with the great seal of the colony of St Helena, made its way out towards us. A few minutes later the Colonial Administrator, and the first seven Tristanians to be permitted out of harbour, were standing on our foredeck.

The islanders were tall and tough-looking, with long-jawed faces and olive skins, tanned by years of exposure to the winds and the sea. They wore identical blue boiler suits, and though some were blond and Nordic, and others dark and Mediterranean, their faces all had a strangely similar look, as though they might be close cousins. Their similarity – of dress, of face, of mannerism – they were all given to broad smiles, to courtly politeness, and to an air that managed to be at once proud and deferential – was vaguely frightening, as though these were aliens from a different planet, making their first contact with what they called 'the houtside warl'. One, an immense man who was known to all as Lofty, had an oddly deformed left eye; but he had an almost childlike air of fun about him, and was joking and laughing with all around so that I was minded to compare him with Lenny, in Steinbeck – a gentle giant, slightly out of step with the rest of humanity.

All these islanders, indeed, seemed to step to a subtly different drum – they spoke a pure, though oddly inflected English, they flew the colonial flag, and they carried pictures of the Queen and her children. But there was a difference about them, as though they were detached by more than mere distance and stormy sea from the mainstream of human society. They were British in name alone: before all else they were, without a doubt, Tristanian.

The Administrator, in sharp contrast, looked as though he had stepped out from the members' enclosure at Cheltenham racecourse. Roger Perry, a naturalist, a writer, a specialist in llamas, the flora of the Falkland Islands and the animals of the Galapagos, had been on Tristan for six months. He had come out for the morning's journey, and the first formal greeting with his Governor, in classical British dress: a brown trilby, a tan suit, stout and brilliantly polished brown shoes, a silk tie and a silk pocket handkerchief. He needed only a pair of binoculars and a form guide to complete the picture.

The Governor stepped into the waiting boat, was joined by two Whitehall officials, the Administrator, the seven Tristanian boatmen, and I climbed in just as Lofty cast off and we were whirled out on to the waves. We chugged towards the harbour and waited, the boat turning in small circles until one huge wave raced in towards the land: the steersman, his jaw set firm, his hand clamped on to the tiller, gunned the engine, rode on to the crest of the wave and shot through the harbour entrance six feet above the levels of the moles.

It was all over in five seconds. The water was still and calm inside, and there were dozens of helpful hands reaching down to haul us up. A minute later and, my legs unsteady from all the days at sea, I was standing on Tristan soil, watching an Imperial ceremony of great familiarity, played out in touching miniature. The Tristan Boy Scouts and the Tristan Girl Guides, dark youngsters in the brown and blue uniforms sent down from Buckingham Palace Road, stood at attention. A bugle was blown, a banner was raised, a salute was made, an anthem was played – and the Colonial Governor of St Helena was formally welcomed on to the tiniest and loneliest dependency in the remnant British Empire. I found I was watching it all through a strange golden haze, which cleared if I wiped my eyes with the back of my hand: the children looked so proud, so eager to please, so keen to touch the hand from England, from the wellspring of their official existence.

They all looked as though they were trying so very hard to be British, out here in the middle of nowhere. I found it deeply affecting. I wasn't alone. I looked around, and saw a young woman behind me, wiping her eyes with a tissue. She was a teacher's wife, she said later: she had never seen anything quite so touching in all her days. It was proof positive, she said, that there was some good in the old country yet, if the youngsters were still so keen, and had arrived on the quayside without being told, or ordered. 'They just knew they had to come down and salute him,' she explained. 'They've been looking forward to it for ages.'

Ahead of me stretched the village – a cluster of houses, some roofed with tin, some thatched, all with gable ends of soft basalt. All of them had a split front door, the upper half open, the lower half shut to keep out the chilly breeze. The small number of expatriates sent out to help run the island – two teachers, the doctor, the South African padre, the Colonial Treasurer and the Administrator – lived in wooden prefabricated houses, painted black with creosote. There were hedges of flax on all sides, which helped break up the wind, though the Union flags fluttered briskly, and it was better to keep walking than to stand around in the cold.

But the village was clinging to the edge of a monster. Behind, like a stage set, was a sheer wall of grey, the great basalt cliffs rising to the island summit. The wall was 2,000 feet high, and it was evident that stones were falling with terrible regularity – indeed, one massive section of the cliff had broken away at the time of the eruption, and the pale grey scar, with millions of tons of debris spilled in a fan below, served as a potent reminder of the power of the land, and the weakness of those who dared cling to it. Wisps of cloud floated along the upper reaches of the cliff, and all above was invisible, cloaked in thick grey mist, wet and inhospitable. A few sheep clambered up the crags, and cows wandered on the village outskirts. Once I saw an old woman sitting sidesaddle on a donkey, riding back along the colony's only road from the Potato Patches, two miles from Edinburgh to the west.

I walked through the village towards the new volcanoes,

towards the house I had been told was home to a middle-aged
lady named Emily Rogers, about whom I had once read a
touching story. Derrick Booy, who had served on Tristan as a
naval radio operator during the Second World War, and who has
written perhaps the most sensitive of all the few accounts of
Tristan, fell briefly, but hopelessly under the spell of a girl then
called Emily Hagan:

> The night air was an enveloping golden presence as we stood
> at the break in the wall. I was conscious of bare, rounded
> arms, and the fragrance of thickly clustered hair. The lingering
> day was full of noises. As the sky darkened to a deep
> umbrageous blue, speckled with starlight, and the village was
> swallowed by darkness at the foot of the mountain, from
> somewhere in that blackness came the throaty plaint of an old
> sheep, like a voice from the mountain. From that other
> obscurity, silver-gleaming below the cliffs, came the muttered
> irony of the surf.
>
> The girl waited only a few minutes before her full lips
> breathed 'Good night' and she slipped towards the house.
>
> 'Shall I come to see you again?' I called softly.
>
> She may or may not have answered 'Yes'. If she did, it was
> probably from politeness.

Derrick Booy saw her many more times, and they held hands
before the fire in the Hagans' old house, Emily's face bright in
the guttering light of a bird-oil lamp. And then, as war so often
demands, the young sailor had to leave, suddenly, and with no
notice and no alternative. A ship arrived to pick the party up,
and the pair – if such they ever could be called – were forced to
say farewell:

> The watchers on the beach were all very still, the women
> sitting again in their gaily dressed rows, as if waiting primly
> to be photographed. None of them waved or cheered. They
> just sat watching. All looked very much alike, young and old.
> But there was one at the end of a row, in a white dress with
> a red kerchief, bright red, over smooth, dark hair. She sat

perfectly still, staring back until she became a white blur. Then her head went down, and the woman behind her – a large one in widow's black – put a hand on her shoulder.

Emily Hagan married Kenneth Rogers ten years later, and the BBC once broadcast a programme from the island, and included her voice – a woman with 'a nice face', the interviewer remarked. I wanted to complete the story by talking to Emily, and made my way to her house. Kenneth, a bluff, kindly man who pours beer in the island's only pub, knew what I wanted the moment I stepped up to his neat, fresh-painted door.

'You'se wanting our Hem'ly,' he said. 'Well, I don' wish to be unfriendly, sir, but I'd be grateful if you'd respect our wishes and forget all you'd read in that book. It hurt us all. It was all a long while 'go, and we'd jes' as soon fergit.' He was gracious and polite, but firm. And other islanders told me the same story – about 'our Hem'ly', and about themselves. They did not care for people writing about their private lives, and publishing the detail in 'the houtside warl'. They – the 300 Swains and Hagans and Rogers, Greens, Repettos, Lavarellos and Glasses – were an intensely private people, who wanted their privacy protected. There was no hostility towards the curiosity of outsiders – far from it; the friendliness of the islanders is memorable, their hospitality to their tiny annual crop of visitors has become an ocean legend – but they all wished it would never happen. And they knew I was there to write: there are two ham radio operators on Tristan, and they knew all about me and the purpose of my voyage, long before I had even flown to Tenerife. 'Mr Winchester – you'll be careful with us now, won't you?' one man said, when I recounted Mrs Rogers' reluctance. 'We'll have to live with what you write for years to come. We'll read your words a thousand times. So be careful, for our own sakes.'

I went back aboard the ship that evening to collect some night things, and had a brief encounter that reinforced the notion that the Tristanians are a uniquely private group, uneasy with too great an outside interest. I had arranged to spend the night ashore, and was about to climb down the pilot ladder into the dinghy, when a powerful arm stopped me. Albert Glass, the chief islander and the colony's only policeman – though he is unneeded as such, except for ceremonial tasks, since there is no crime on the island – wanted to know where I thought I was going. Ashore, I said. 'Oh no,' he said. 'I'm not letting anyone ashore. We have limits. We have rules.'

I was dismayed. All this way, and not even a night on the island! And yet he was so reasonable and kindly about it, I felt I had no option but to do as he had said, and try and get back the following morning. But at that moment there was a strange interruption of the Fates. A strangled cry came from the dinghy below, and a shout went up, for the doctor.

One of the islanders, it seems, had drunk a few beers too many, and had staggered backwards off the gunwales and into the freezing sea. I started at this news, since only a few minutes before I had seen a hammerhead shark cruising hungrily around our ship, looking for such morsels as a six-foot Tristanian in non-resisting mood. The man had been crushed briefly between dinghy and ship's side, and was unconscious when they hauled him out of the water and dumped him on the decking.

The ship's doctor, resplendent in what the daily circular had called 'Red Sea Rig', with black tie and black cummerbund over a crisp white shirt, was down beside him in an instant, pumping his chest, clearing his throat, resuscitating, injecting, bandaging, warming. I passed some things down for him into the heaving dinghy, and got a grin of thanks for my little help – and Albert Glass suddenly relented. 'Hall roight,' he said. 'Foine for you'se to go. But make sure you'rs careful with us. No nonsense. We won't forget you, you knows.' And off I went, thumping over the swells in the night, visiting the drowned rat in hospital (he had no more than a couple of cracked ribs, and a stiff warning not to drink again while on such seas as this), taking drinks with the islanders at the Prince Philip Hall, and listening to the padre and his wife, and the teacher and his, recount innumerable tales of Tristan life. No one, it seemed, had a harsh word to say.

Tristan makes a profit – and a very handsome one indeed.

The crawfish, frozen and sold to the Americans as rock lobster – fetch more than two hundred and twenty dollars a case, and with sixty fishing days a year, and eighteen boats that go fishing, and each boat pulling in a hundred pounds of the crustaceans a trip, money comes flooding in to the island.

Two islanders meet each morning at the pier head to look at the weather and decide if this is, or is not, a fishing day. If it is, they ring the 'bell' – an old gas cylinder suspended from a gantry near the village hall – and all those men who are designated fishermen take the day off whatever other work they may be doing, and set out with the longboats for the fishing grounds. If that makes for some inconvenience to those islanders who remain behind – perhaps a plumbing job goes unfinished, or a vital letter passes untyped – no one seems to mind. The crawfish bring in the money, and money, despite the isolation and other-worldliness of the place, is a much-respected commodity in the colony.

Perhaps the most unexpected – and, I have to say, most dismaying – result of the comparative wealth of the island is that, since 1984, there is an island television service. Most houses have a cable providing them with programmes from a small video tape centre (our ship was bringing a new amplifier, which was greeted with considerably more enthusiasm on the dockside than were any of the visitors, rams included), and at seven each Tuesday, Thursday and Sunday evening the cas-settes begin to unroll, and the delights of the 'houtside warl' begin to pour into the little Tristan houses. At seven each Sunday the island is quite immobilised: *Dallas* is being shown – and the islanders watch every frame with adoration, amazement and delight. (There is even less worthy fare than this: the proud, private, fearless Tristanians, heirs to the traditions of egg-gathering on Inaccessible Island, and bird-collecting on Nightingale, now watch shows like *Mannix*, *Jabber Jaws*, and *Fraggle Rock*. To that small extent Tristan Island is beginning to resemble Staten Island, and it somewhat saddened me to find no real opposition, anywhere, to the trend.)

But there are other, less questionable benefits of the wealth. Every islander is allowed to keep, and slaughter, two cows a year, and ten sheep, and so there is fresh meat, and lamb, and milk the whole year round. Tristanians, however, have a loathing for fillet steak, and any new expatriate finds himself weighed down by pounds of prime fillet given free in exchange for chocolate, or cigarettes, or tumblers of brandy which some island women drink during colder weather as though it were lemonade.

Women have an unusually prominent role in Tristan society. True, they spend much time in the traditional island pastimes of carding wool, knitting 'ganzeys' for the fishermen, or socks (adorned with bands of colour for a man to give the girl he is courting, the more bands signifying the more ardour), or mittens. But the island shop manager is a woman, and the day I arrived it was announced that Jean Swain had been appointed Colonial Treasurer – one of the few 'natives' anywhere in the remaining Empire to hold such a post, and certainly the only woman.

There is, I was assured by one of the island men, a rational explanation for the influence of the women. All office jobs on Tristan are classified by the Government as permanent, which means that men who regard themselves as fishermen are not allowed to take them, lest they have to drop pen and paper and take off in the longboats every time the village bell is chimed. Most office jobs are thus held by women, who can assure the Government they will remain in harness, whatever the weather, however low the swell.

But for all the slow changes, the introduction of television, the peculiar division of labour between the sexes, the introduction of money to the colony (thirty years ago all trade was by barter, and the local stamps were given a value in potatoes), the temper of Tristan life remains unaltered and, I would like to think, unalterable.

The size of the population remains much the same: in 1984 there were four births, and three deaths. There are almost exactly 300 islanders. In 1961, when the volcano forced the evacuation of the entire island, there were 264 of them. As an embarrassed Britain well remembers – and much of the rest of the Western world too – all but five of them eventually decided to go back to Tristan. They didn't care for the pace or the style of 'civilised' life; as the *Daily Mirror* was to remark as their ship pulled away from the quay to make the long journey home, their decision was 'the most eloquent and contemptuous rebuff that our smug and deviously contrived society could have received'.

There was, however, a coda to that story. The majority of Tristanians did, indeed, go back to Tristan in 1963. But over the next ten years a number who had evidently found a taste for a faster life during their sojourn in Britain, left Tristan again and headed back up north. About fifty have abandoned the island at the time of writing, although some of those have indeed returned yet again, an ebb and flow of humanity – now little noticed by the press, to the islanders' relief and delight – that displays the uncertainty and indecision that exposure to the 'houtside warl' brought in its train. A sociologist, Peter Munch, has noticed that many of those who returned to England had the surname Glass, and speculates on the possibility of an unspoken schism between the Glasses (not that all people called Glass belong to the same family) and the other leading island group, the Repettos. But whatever the reason for the tidal movement within the community, the total population – 300 – remains fairly constant. This ebb and flow, which was a feature of the late Sixties and early Seventies, can no longer continue, however. The British Nationality Act, passed in 1982, saw to that. Tristanians, like St Helenians and Bermudians and Anguillians and all the rest (but not, as we shall see later, like the people of the Falklands and Gibraltar) are barred from permanent residence in the United Kingdom. A Tristanian who arrives at the immigration counter at Southampton docks might, for all his loyalty and distant patriotism, be a Mongolian, a Uruguayan, or a Turk. Any man from Tristan who feels like a spell in the industrialised world has only South Africa for a temporary home; and then, to his certain dismay, he will find himself classified as coloured, and will suffer all the indignity and ignominy of being on the wrong side in the system of apartheid.

Their language remains strangely accented – a sonorous amalgam of Home Counties lockjaw and nineteenth-century idiom, Afrikaans slang and Italian. 'Gie us a pound o' happles,' a

woman will say. 'I gone done shopping today, Harn'ld,' she will
report, when back home. They may eat 'German's nuts' – a kind
of potato pudding – drink 'Old Tom', a rough cider made from
the apples they'll pick round at Sandy Bay, and finish off with
'pot-of-all-kinds', a fruit salad. They will wear 'ammunitions',
or heavy boots, upon their feet, 'ganzeys' – pullovers – on top,
and hope to keep 'fresh', and free from 'brocks' – healthy, and
with no broken bones. 'Hashmere' is still the main ailment;
even a young man, a 'blow-up' as he is known, may be sus-
ceptible, especially when the volcano is puffing out its sul-
phurous fumes.

The old *Tristan Times* appears a few times each year, usually
to coincide with the boats that arrive three or four times a year.
There are messages from Buckingham Palace, notes from the
Administrator, and small items of news that will almost certainly
have become established gossip for many weeks before: thirty
people went on a bird-collecting trip to Inaccessible Island;
the radio station (from which the island sends a daily signal
to Cape Town by morse code, assuring the world it and its
people are still there) needs a new roof; a cattle egret has been
spotted on the cliffs near Hottentot Point; the newspapers for last December have just arrived in the library (it
is now April); the swimming pool is well under way, and children are warned not to play near it until it is filled with water;
the cost of hiring the government launch goes up by forty per
cent.

The St Helena Governor brings two pieces of legislation with
him: a constitutional amendment allowing for an election for chief
islander, to be held in three months' time; and the new motor
vehicles law, which calls on drivers of all cars to keep to the
left on the only road – the law had to be introduced since,
a few weeks before, a new car was landed on the island, bringing the total number to two, with the possibility of collision.
Rules, the British believe, are the essentials of an ordered
society.

There is a message from the ship: bad weather has been
forecast, the harbour will be closed by eleven, and the anchor
will have to be weighed at noon. Those few islanders who are

leaving Tristan begin to scurry down to the quayside, carrying cases and boxes, and talking excitedly of the first visit – perhaps for years, quite probably the first time ever – to the outside. The post office opens, and a last few letters are posted, and sacks of mail are tied up and bundled on to the back of the island tractor, to be trundled down to the dinghies for transfer to the waiting ship.

Morning service at the church of St Mary the Virgin is taken this day, as it has been every Sunday for the last two years, and will every Sunday for the next two, by David Pearson, the bluff, bearded padre who gave me dinner the night before.

The church, a long, blue-and-white painted hut with a tin roof, is the repository of many of Tristan's most cherished mementoes. Here is the picture of Queen Victoria, signed personally by her and given to the islanders' chieftain in 1896, as a tribute towards the Britons, surviving in so merciless an environment so very far from home. There, beside the altar, is the island flag, 'presented to HMS *Leopard* for the safe keeping in the evacuation, 19th October 1961, returned by HMS *Apollo* to the islanders of Tristan da Cunha, 13th April 1973.'

The organ, upon which Mrs Repetto plays so very nicely, was given by our present Queen. The Bible was given to the island by the son of a woman wrecked on the good ship *Blenden Hall*, wrecked on Inaccessible Island in 1821. There are plaques to missionaries and other worthies, including the Rev Dodgson, who served in the late nineteenth century, and memorials to those who died – nearly all the island men – in the great lifeboat disaster of 1885.

The congregation is all women, aside from Johnny Repetto, that fine-faced man who, when finer and younger than now, came back with five others in 1962 to make the island habitable again after its desertion, and has been regarded as a hero ever since. All the women wear headscarves and long skirts, and sing and pray fervently, especially when they intone the customary requests for the protection and preservation of Her Majesty the Queen and all the royal family, for Her Majesty's ministers in London, and for those who, like all their husbands and brothers and sons, go down to the sea in ships and conduct their business in great waters.

And then it is time to go. The sun is shining outside, and the women hurry back to their homes, and their Sunday lunches of roast beef – the like of which few in the mother country can now ever afford. I walk back down to the harbour, past the canvas longboats – the *British Lion*, the *British Trader*, the *British Flag*, each painted white, with blue and red stripes, symbols of the membership of an ancient and a proud Empire.

I say my farewells to the islanders who are at the quay, and to a young British couple, Richard and Margaret Grundy, who stand, windswept and bereft and tearful, knowing it will be fully four months until they see outsiders again, or hear first-hand news from their homes. There are no flags, nor Scout parades. The cliffs loom behind, sturdy in their grand indifference. The mist is swirling in fast-flowing ribbons, and fresh swells are crashing between the piers. I jump into the boat – Lofty is at the tiller, smiling warmly – and we roar out into the sea. Within seconds the water is too deep beneath the prow even to think of a return: it took months to reach here, it will take years before I could ever think of coming back, and I feel a sudden stab of sadness.

And then we bump against the rusty hull of the RMS *St Helena*, and clamber up the ladder, and the dinghy turns away with a whoop and a wave from the men aboard. And, with a speed and a suddenness that is as kind as it seems brutal, we sound our valedictory sirens, the telegraphs clang to full ahead, and the island, a tiny cone of rock set in a wild and heaving sea, recedes to a mere shadow in the sky, and then a speck on the horizon, and then but a memory.

Behind us, night and day, gale or calm, for a thousand miles and more flies a great white albatross, a bird that was probably born in the Tristan islands, and is amusing herself by following us, her adopted, sea-bound friends below. But then as we draw near the African coast she suddenly turns and wheels away, and soars up into the leaden skies, back to the lonely mysteries of the South Atlantic, to her companions of the colony set far from everywhere, and utterly alone. And when she has vanished in the great empty skies, I know all my links with Tristan have been severed, and that the most difficult and longest of the journeys is done.

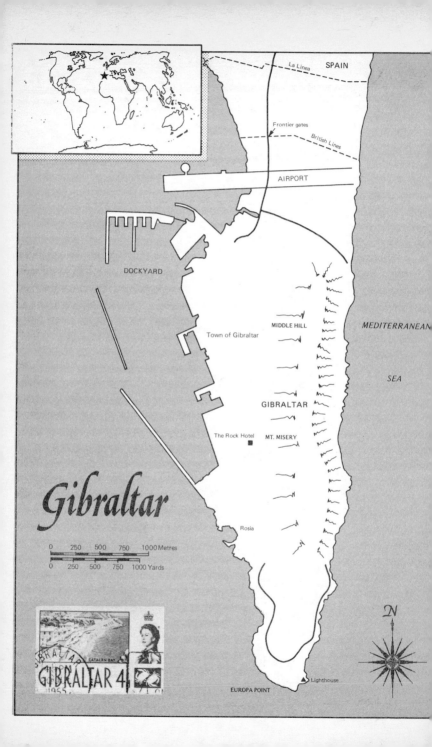

SPAIN

La Linea

Frontier gates

British Lines

AIRPORT

DOCKYARD

MEDITERRANEAN

SEA

MIDDLE HILL

Town of Gibraltar

GIBRALTAR

The Rock Hotel   MT. MISERY

Gibraltar

0   250   500   750   1000 Metres
0   250   500   750   1000 Yards

Rosia

GIBRALTAR 4

▲ Lighthouse

EUROPA POINT

N

FOUR

GIBRALTAR

'This dark corner of the world', Lord Nelson had called Gibraltar. It was a prophetic remark, for it was to Gibraltar, and to the old circular harbour at Rosia at the southern tip of the peninsula, that the Admiral's body was carried after Trafalgar. He had been pickled in cognac, because there was not enough rum on the *Victory*, and the barrel blew up in the October heat: so at Gibraltar the Navy repaired the damage and loaded his remains back on board his flagship which then, to the beat of muffled drums, set sail again for the sad passage to Greenwich, and the January funeral and the burial in the crypt of St Paul's.

All the elements of the Rock's use and meaning are encapsulated in this sad vignette from Imperial history. Gibraltar was, and is, a naval base. Without Gibraltar Britain would quite probably have lost Trafalgar, and Napoleon might have made the British Isles a part of his own French Empire, and never been forced to the ignominy of exile on St Helena. It was, and is, a place for repair, for the treatment of injury, the destination of the dying and the dead. It was, and is, a place of miserable weather, of heat and humidity, of distemper and ill-health. It was, and is, a place of necessity rather than of glory, a place to use rather than to like, a symbol of might and power and domain and steadfastness, a place all utilitarian, and not at all romantic.

And above all, as Nelson scribbled in his log, and as others have noted since, it is a brooding, frowning place, its character delineated and dominated by its towering atmosphere of darkness.

Laurie Lee had it perfectly. He had walked there in the Thirties (all the way from the Cotswolds, in fact) and first saw Gibraltar from the top of a hill behind Algeciras.

> Africa, Spain and the great sweep of the Bay all shone with a fierce bronze light. But not Gibraltar; it lay apart like an interloper, as though it had been towed out from Portsmouth and anchored off-shore, still wearing its own grey roof of weather. Slate-coloured, aloof, surrounded by a scattering of warships and fringed by its dockyard cranes, the Rock lay shadowed beneath a plate of cloud, immersed in a private rainstorm.

One recent summer's day I made my own plans to visit the Rock, which involved approaching it over much the same route, through the hills and on the clifftops of Andalucia. From London I telephoned the Governor's office at the Convent, Gibraltar (the exchange was called, appropriately, 'Fortress'). A date was suggested, teatime said to be most suitable, punctuality said to be important since the Governor was a navy man. I flew to San Pablo airport in Sevilla, drove to Cadiz and, after arming myself with a compass, a sheaf of Spanish army maps, a canteen, a stout hazel stick and a foot repair kit, set off to march around the most southerly bastion of Europe to see Britain's only remaining colony on the Continent. (Britain's European possessions have never been numerous, despite convenience and closeness. She had Heligoland in the North Sea, and from Port Mahon in Minorca the Royal Navy ran the Balearic Islands. There were the Ionian Islands, and Malta, of course, and Cyprus (though hardly a European possession). And the Channel Islands and the Isle of Man, which are not colonies, but direct dependencies of the Crown and lie outside the United Kingdom. Gibraltar is the only unquestioned European colony that remains, and is definitely the only British Imperial possession that there ever has been on the continent of Europe itself.)

It took the best part of a week to climb up from the valley

of the Guadalquivir to the limestone mountain chain of which Gibraltar was an outlier. I had to pass through tuna-fishing villages, where I would sip ice-cold *fino* and discuss the price of albacore; I stopped for half a day to inspect the great lighthouse at Cape Trafalgar – where it turned out that only one of a dozen Andalucians I questioned had ever heard of Nelson, or Villeneuve, most Spaniards evidently preferring to linger on Spain's victories rather than her defeats. I climbed to the Moorish town of Vejer de la Frontera, and looked down across the fog-filled Straits to see the brown rumps of the Rif mountains, in Africa; and then came closer still to the great continent by marching along the mole in Tarifa, and thus becoming briefly the southernmost inhabitant of Europe. But then I was stopped and turned back by a menacing-looking Spanish soldier; the Campo de Gibraltar, along with the Balearics and the Canaries, is one of Spain's three principal military zones, crawling with soldiery who are there to show Spain's determination to protect the vital Straits, and to remind the British that the Crown colony of Gibraltar long has been, still is and always will be claimed by the people of Spain. I was sorry to have to leave the quayside, for there was a most dramatic illustration of the separation of the waters of Atlantic and Mediterranean; on the western side of the mole the water was green and wind-whipped, rose and fell with a long oceanic swell, and looked quite cold; on the eastern inner side the sea was blue and calm, looked warm, and was littered with all the floating debris of the little town.

It was before dawn – deliciously cool, and the best time for a summer's walk through Andalucia – when I breasted the hill above Algeciras. The old port's lights twinkled and blinked below, and there were pricks of riding lanterns on the ships at anchor in the Roads. The bay, I could just make out, was a vast semicircle, the lowlands and the refineries to the left, the open sea, and a dusty glimmer of Africa, to the right.

And on the far side, rising like a long and ragged wall of steel, battleship-grey and ready for war, was the Rock. It was indeed, as Laurie Lee had noted, dark and separate from the land beside – rather sinister, rather magnificent. And then, just at that moment, sliding up and over it like a Barbary corsair's scimitar, was the morning sun. As it rose so the colours changed, from deep burnt orange through gold to the brassy yellow of a Spanish summer day. And as the sunlight became ever more intense, so Gibraltar faded into a rising heat haze, her grey and forbidding aspect becoming muted and pale, and then vanishing altogether into the background blue.

It was a little after seven, and tea at the Convent was at four o'clock sharp. I marched down into Algeciras, crossed the two small rivers, de las Cañas and Guadarranque, hurried under the belching pipework of the refineries at El Mirador and, with the immense wall of the Rock rearing white above me – a Union flag fluttering, proud and familiar, from a summit pole – walked past the shops of La Linea to the frontier.

My watch said almost three, the sun was very hot. But by my reckoning I was now only about two miles from my destination – the old Franciscan friary that had been counting house and Governor's residence from the first days of Imperial occupation. (It is called 'the Convent', but has never housed nuns. King Edward VII thought it an undignified name and had it changed to 'Government House'; but in 1943 his grandson, George VI, ordered it changed back.) It should have been no problem.

But the couple of miles turned out to be considerably longer, and more costly, than I had supposed. The eccentricities of global politics took over at this point, and what I had expected would be simply a matter of frontier formalities turned into a protracted and amusing farce.

The border was marked by a gate – two pairs of gates, actually, parallel, policing the same entrance, and no more than three inches from each other. The inner gate was clearly the British gate – it was made of black iron, and had limestone pillars, topped with cannonballs. It was wide open.

The other gate – the nearer to Spain, and thus nearer to me – was more modern, made of green-painted steel. Festooned with a ganglion of bolts and padlocks, it was very firmly closed. Beside it was a platoon of Spanish soldiers, and a detachment of the Policia Nacional.

Beyond the two gates lay a territory that was manifestly British. There were two policemen, kitted out exactly as their colleagues in Kensington and Chelsea. The Gibraltar Police, I had read, are the oldest colonial force, formed soon after Robert Peel raised the Metropolitan in London. They have been quite severely criticised by the Gibraltarians for being too timid and gentle. There was a flagpole with a large Union flag, lazily undulating in the warm breeze. Beside it were two brass cannon, and polishing them a group of half-stripped British infantrymen – members of the Duke of Wellington's Regiment; a couple of their colleagues, in full uniform and holding rifles, stood to attention outside the sentry-posts. Every few moments one would stamp about loudly, and there would be great clatter and drama as he paced out his brief ceremonial route. Then the site would fall silent, except for a murmur of grumbles from the soldiers polishing the guns, and the distant whine of jet engines as a fighter, or perhaps a civil airliner, readied itself for take-off from the runway close behind.

Teatime was near, and I beckoned to one of the policemen. I gave my name, explained that I had an appointment with His Excellency in half an hour, and suggested he might check. He disappeared into his blockhouse, and returned a moment later with a grin. Yes, he said, the Convent was expecting me; the kettle, he implied, was on. Fine, I said – can I come in?

There was a cough, and an embarrassed silence. Policemen looked at soldiers, at me, at the Spanish soldiers – who lounged around, stretching and scratching themselves, and yawning, until every few minutes, when an officer would bellow some unintelligible order and the squad would fall in, brace themselves and march up and down before the gates, their feet clattering unevenly in amiable disagreements over the step. The constable was indeed both gentle and timid in his reply. Yes, he ventured, I was most welcome, and a car would be provided to hurry me into town. But there might be problems with this gentleman approaching. And as I looked round a tall fellow in the brown and black of the National Police was advancing; he smiled warmly, and begged my pardon (he had trained as a hotel manager in Brighton, it seems, before joining the force), but could he possibly have the pleasure of seeing my passport?

Since my arrival at the gate and the attempt to pass through had been in the nature of an experiment I cannot say I was surprised by what happened, though, since I was quite footsore and eager for a cup of tea, I was irritated. The policeman told me firmly that as a British passport holder I could not, he was sorry to say, cross into the colony by road. If I wanted to visit this charming corner of Spain – he would not accept that its occupation was anything more than temporary – I would have to trek back to Algeciras, take the next hydrofoil to Tangier, and take another similar (in fact, as it turned out, the very same) craft back from Tangier to Gibraltar. In other words I could travel the three inches with pleasure, but only after having made brief obeisance in a third, neutral country, in Africa. It all suddenly seemed rather ludicrous, and I was cross that I was going to be late for tea. (Afternoon tea is not the only British custom still rigorously maintained in the colony. The author Nicholas Luard once met a formidable British nanny near Algeciras. In spite of the heat she was dressed in a severe grey coat and skirt, and wore a grey felt hat, and very sensible shoes, in which she was clumping towards La Linea. Luard offered her a lift, and asked where she was going. 'Gibraltar,' she replied, in tones impeccably Home Counties, 'to buy a reliable kipper.')

In the event, the excursion was pleasant enough, even though the bullet-like craft only narrowly escaped being run over by a tanker in the thick fog – the cotton-wool-like *taro* – that hangs almost perpetually over the Straits. Our captain, a fat and unshaven Moor, weaseled his machine deftly under the approaching bow, and let fly a string of colourful imprecations at the wall of rusty steel above us. The fog thinned, the roar of the motor settled to a dignified chug, and out of the haze ahead, below the crouching-lion shape of the Rock herself, was the stone magnificence of the old dockyards – the former home of the Royal Navy's Atlantic Fleet, built for the Admiralty by Messrs. Topham, Jones and Railton, to be the undisputed and ostentatious guardian of the Straits, the Mediterranean, and the route to the Orient. While Bermuda guarded the Atlantic, Simonstown and Trincomalee – 'Trinco' to the sailors – looked after the Indian Ocean, and Singapore, Hong Kong and Weihaiwei were home to the China Squadrons, so Gibraltar, Malta, Alexandria and Aden preserved the integrity of the most vital of all Imperial waterways – the route to India. Small wonder, then, the sound of bugles from the dockside barracks sounded like a declaration of Imperial intent to any passing strangers: What We Have, they seemed to say, We Hold.

From Trafalgar to the Falklands, from the Malta convoys to the Suez invasion, the dockyards of Gibraltar have long been vital for naval assembly, organisation, coaling, victualling, the loading of munitions and the making of war. Every fleet and every warship of naval note has been there – the *Hood*, the *Nelson*, the *Rodney* and, of course, the *Victory* on her mournful mission. When the Home and the Mediterranean Fleets met in the harbour in 1939, as they would do for spring manoeuvres every year before the war, the bay was an almost solid mass of grey steel, and 200 funnels belched smoke into the sky.

But on this summer morning I could only see the funnel of a single frigate, and the upperworks of another naval vessel, even tinier, buried deep in one of the drydocks. A fellow-passenger, a Gibraltarian, told me that the fleets made little use of Gibraltar now ('though it was very exciting during the Falklands War. Just like the old days!') and at the beginning of the Eighties the Admiralty, in a decision that had caused bitter anguish among the Gibraltarians, had decided to sell the dockyards. A private firm, which had promised to employ most of the workforce, was going to try to turn a profit from commercial ship-repairing, but no one was very optimistic. (Gibraltar is now suffering the consequences of a 'one-crop' colonial economic policy, common to so many parts of the Empire. The sea lords stopped having their ships mended in the Mediterranean, and the economy, not being based on anything else, went to pieces almost overnight. How much more generous, and how wise it might have been for the home Government to have developed an alternative – some kind of engineering, perhaps. Colonial government, however, is not generally blessed with either generosity or wisdom, and never with foresight.)

The dockyard – protected by the north and south moles, and the long and crucial 'detached mole' – slipped astern, and we berthed close to the airstrip (built where the racetrack used to be, just inside the frontier) and the Royal Gibraltar Yacht Club, the oldest outside Britain (it was founded in 1829, and its members regularly race against Spanish sailors from La Linea Yacht Club, making the border regulations seem all the more needless).

The customs and immigration men were as bleakly unwelcoming as in any British possession, and searched diligently for any illicit imports of the products for which Morocco is well known. A thump of rubber stamp and, some twenty-four hours, 200 miles and one extra continent after being turned away at the double gate, here I was in the Crown colony itself – a red telephone box on one side, a pillar box labelled 'ER' – for Edward VII, not Elizabeth – on the other; policemen in shirt-sleeve order, soldiers in khaki drill, customs men in tropical shorts, advertisements for Watneys and Hovis, Rocola shirts and Tootal ties, and fleets of Morris Minors, Austins and Land-Rovers on the roads. (But there is one signal difference: in Gibraltar, alone of the remnant colonies, traffic drives on the right.)

Gibraltar is, and long has been, Britain's smallest foreign possession. (Ignoring, that is, such infinitesimal outstations as Diamond Rock, near Grenada in the Caribbean, granted in the Napoleonic Wars and given the preface 'HMS'; the next smallest inhabited colony is Pitcairn, two square miles, compared to the Rock's one and seven-eighths. Pitcairn, as we shall see, belongs to the Crown still.) Gibraltar is three miles long, three-quarters of a mile wide and, at the Rock Gun, a third of a mile high. As perhaps the only colony it is practicable to express in terms of its weight – about 1,500 billion tonnes of Jurassic limestone, plus a few million tonnes of shale – it looks almost identical to that odd-shaped protuberance on the Dorset coast, Portland Bill, and geologically, it is.

It is the only present British colony that was known to the ancient world. The Romans called it Mons Calpe; it was twinned with Mons Abyla – the Mountain of the Apes – on the African side of the Straits, and the pair were known, so it is generally accepted, as the Pillars of Hercules, the limits of the known and navigable world, and beyond which lay Atlantis. It was a part of the Gateway of the Hesperides; and some scholars will claim, rather more fancifully, that Gibraltar was Scylla, and Abyla was Charybdis, and the Straits of Messina had nothing to do with the story at all. (Since there is no whirlpool in either Strait, Charybdis remains very much a mystery, amenable to all sorts of claims.)

Tarik-ben-Zayed, Moor and Mussulman, brought Islam into Europe and gave Gibraltar its name – Jeb'el Tarik, or Tarik's Rock – in AD 711. He snatched the Rock, without being noticed, from the Visigoths (though for good measure he went on to kill their king, Roderic, near Tarifa, and began a march of Mohammedanism that was to trundle northwards for 400 years and reach almost to the gates of Paris). He was a military man of considerable prescience, and realised at once the strategic importance of his peninsular conquest – the keystone, as it were, to Spain. But neither he nor his successors, who ruled Tarik's Rock as an Islamic extension of the Moroccan Rif for the next six centuries, laid down constructions to denote their rule: today there are the ruins of a wall, fragments of two mosques, and the keep of the Moorish Castle, part of which is now used as the Gibraltar Prison, and which the Howard League for Penal Reform have denounced as 'grotesquely primitive', and its inmates as 'zombie-like'.

The Spaniards briefly regained Gibraltar in 1309, when the Archbishop of Sevilla, his soldiers armed with catapults, drove the thousand Moors of the garrison back home to Morocco. The Moors recaptured the Rock soon after, and the Spaniards attacked again soon after that; over the next century and a half of the slow and painful – but never-to-be-forgotten – *Reconquista*, Gibraltar changed hands eight times; Don Alonso de Arcos, who finally succeeded in stamping out the Moor for ever, marched across the isthmus in 1462: his tomb in Sevilla, which every Briton and modern Gibraltarian should perhaps take trouble to see, records the fact with due eloquence: *'Aqui yace sepultado el honrado caballero don Alonso de Arcos, alcaide de Tarifa, que gano a Gibraltar de los enimigos de nuestra Santa Fe.'* ('Here lies buried the honoured knight Don Alonso de Arcos, Governor of Tarifa, who wrested Gibraltar from the enemies of our Holy Faith.') It would be as well for Whitehall to remember that in Spain's eyes, today's occupiers – the Protestants of England – are every bit as noisome and villainous a bunch of usurpers as were the Moslems of Fez; the spirit of the *Reconquista* is still a powerful motive force – some might say the only motive force – in the continuing diplomatic wrangle over when Britain will abandon her own claims to sovereignty.

Spain managed to hang on to Gibraltar for only two and a half centuries, and her invigilation was neglectful, if not downright malign. The place went to ruin: nothing of note was built, it was peopled by convicts whose sentences were suspended while they lived there, it was a hotbed of religious intolerance (the Jews were all thrown out in 1492), it degenerated into a dreary wasteland of wrecked buildings and wharves, where undisciplined soldiers waited for a Moorish attack that never came – and for pay that never came either – and watched without understanding the steadily increasing number of ships from other nations that sailed on trading missions between the Atlantic and the Mediterranean.

The British had their Imperial eyes upon it from early on. Cromwell lusted after it as fortress and strategic base. 'Gibraltar, if possessed and made tenable by us,' he said, 'would be an advantage to our trade and an annoyance to the Spaniard.'

And yet when finally it did fall to British guns, and to the naval cannonade of Admiral Sir George Rooke, it did so not precisely on Britain's behalf, but rather on behalf of the Hapsburg Pretender to the Spanish Throne, Charles, the Archduke of Austria. And to add further complication to the story, Rooke was aided in his conquest by the Archduke's agent, the Prince of Hesse-Darmstadt, who is still remembered with affection by Ulster Protestants for having been wounded at the Battle of the Boyne by the same ball that hurt King William.

The cannonade must have been terrifying, and overwhelming to the Spaniards, who could muster only eighty trained soldiers, 470 peasant militiamen, 1,000 civilian territorials and twenty working heavy guns. Rooke's forces, which he deployed over the first weekend of August 1704, included seventy-one warships,

26,000 artillerymen, 9,000 infantrymen and 4,000 cannon. His attack, which began at dawn on Sunday, 4th August, needed only a few hours; he poured 15,000 balls on to the tiny city, clustered above the docks and on the comparatively gentle slopes of the Rock's western flanks. Barely a building stood the onslaught – one reason why so little of historical importance remains in the colony today.

Rooke's men landed at daybreak, and by midnight the last of the Spaniards emerged from their foxholes. The Spanish Governor, Diego Salina, surrendered and marched the remains of his garrison and almost the entire population of 6,000 civilians northwards, and to La Linea and San Roque. Gibraltar was now, in fact if not in law, British. In fact the Prince of Hesse, installed as first Governor, first raised the Spanish flag, on behalf of his Pretender's claim; and even when Rooke tore this down, and protested that the peninsula was British, a second Governor was installed who was most definitely Spanish – a General Ramos. Then Archduke Charles himself was brought to Gibraltar in 1705 and formally declared King of Spain, which must have seemed very odd, given that there were no Spaniards there at all except Ramos, and a population of what were called 'shacombe filthies, raggamuffings and scrovies' from Rooke's seventy-one warships.

Total British dominion began in 1707, when Colonel Roger Elliot took office as Governor; and finally, on 13th July 1713, the document that confirmed it all – or didn't confirm a thing, depending upon your nationality and persuasion – was signed by Queen Anne and King Philip, and a host of other European monarchs besides, in the small town of Utrecht, on the banks of the Crooked Rhine, in central Holland.

The Treaty of Utrecht, which brought to a formal end the War of the Spanish Succession, spread Europe's Imperial tentacles across the world. It dealt with Newfoundland, Nova Scotia, Hudson's Bay and the island of St Kitt's (with France handing them over to Britain); it recognised Frederick of Prussia's claim to Neuchatel; it said that the Duke of Savoy could rule Sicily and Nice, permitted Portugal suzerainty over the banks of the Amazon, and cut back French territory in Guiana. Spain gave to

England the exclusive right to supply her colonies with Negro slaves; and it gave her Minorca, and, in the famous Article X, it gave her Gibraltar, too.

The first paragraph is crucial, because it is said to be ambiguous. Interpretations of it by scholars, lawyers and historians, together with ever more subtle interpretations of other paragraphs of the massively formal document, have led to the perpetuation of arguments between Britain and Spain over just who actually owns the peninsula – and not over just who ought, by rights and tradition, to own it. The claims have led to not a little violence, but more often to acts and decisions of sheer lunacy. One recent example is said to have befallen a Spanish painter who was applying green gloss to the gates on his side of the frontier. He dropped the brush, and it fell through the gate and into Gibraltar. According to the tale, which I suspect to be apocryphal, he was told that to retrieve it he would have to travel via Tangier, just as I had done. It is difficult to imagine that he supposed the brush worth the time and money, or that he didn't just search out a convenient coathanger, and pluck the brush back to safety.

The supposedly ambiguous first paragraph of Article X reads as follows:

> The catholic King does hereby, for himself, his heirs and successors, yield to the Crown of Great Britain, the full and entire propriety of the town and castle of Gibraltar, together with the port, fortifications and forts thereunto belonging; and he gives up the said propriety to be held and enjoyed absolutely with all manner of right forever, without any impediment or exception whatsoever.

The lawyers argue that, watertight though the paragraph may seem, the use of the word 'propriety' is ambiguous, and does not necessarily constitute complete title to Gibraltar. The Treaty is wheeled out on almost every public dispute over the matter: it has been suggested, for instance, that by placing soldiers on the peninsula Britain was violating one of the Treaty's cardinal provisions. Since there is no other reason for Britain being in

Gibraltar – the civilians of Gibraltar have always been thought of by the colonists as second-class, tiresome types who get under the feet of the soldiers and the matelots – this particular grumble was, certainly in the heyday of Empire, met with a weary and sardonic shrug of the Imperial shoulders.

The Treaty came after the Spaniards had tried to prise the British off the Rock by laying siege; they failed then, and failed twice more, once in the spring of 1727, and again – for three years and seven months – beginning on 11th July 1779. This latter, the Great Siege, was from the Spanish point of view a monumental waste of time and money.

In one six-week period in 1781, for example, the Spanish artillerymen hurled 56,000 shot and 20,000 shell into the fortress, but managed to kill only seventy men. The following year they held a contest for the best way of subduing the British on the Rock, and came up with the superb folly of the floating batteries, great stripped-down ships roofed with nets and hides and crammed with guns of the heaviest gauge. Dozens of them were hauled out into the bay, and began firing a wild cannonade at the British forces on the west flank from a range of half a mile. The British were serenely undismayed, and fired down at the batteries with red-hot cannonballs, which set the juggernauts on fire, sinking them and drowning 1,500 crew.

When it was all over someone calculated that one ball in 2,000 killed a Briton, and scarcely an excavation made in Gibraltar today fails to come up with at least one of the tens of thousands that failed to connect. The Spanish – and actually the besiegers were a mongrel army, with three Walloon battalions, one from Switzerland, some from Flanders, Ireland and Savoy – never tried again. Diplomacy, tempered by occasional excursions into mild forms of violence, has dominated the argument ever since.

The Great Siege has left many legacies – not least the indomitable spirit, or obtuse cussedness, of the Gibraltarian, and his professed loathing for the Spaniard. 'There are two kinds of apes on the Rock,' remarked a taxi driver, a Mr Ferrary, as his old Ford Prefect laboured up the hill to the place where he promised I would be able to see the famous monkeys. 'Yes, two kinds – the animals, and the Spaniards.'

It left more practical memorials as well. One emerged from the simple difficulty the British artillerymen experienced in defending their fortress. What would happen, one of them mused, if a cannon perched high on the cliff were fired horizontally, its ball going out into space? Ballistics was evidently then an imperfect discipline, since the conventional assumption had it that the ball would proceed outwards in a straight line until the force pushing it diminished to nothing, whence it would plummet, suddenly, like a stone. No truck with parabolas in those days: a cannonball would be like a waterfall, going straight out and straight down, its course impossible to aim, its consequences impossible to predict.

Naïve – and plain wrong – though such wisdom was, it set the gunners' brains to work. One of their number, a Lieutenant Koehler, found the answer: the gun should be pointed downwards so that it could be aimed at the enemy below, and a clever device (which Koehler patented) would stop the ball rolling out before the powder charge went off. Moreover, a cunning recoil system had to be devised so that the gun wouldn't rupture itself every time it was fired in this highly unnatural position. Koehler came up with the recoil mechanism too, and the two devices became standard equipment on British heavy guns for generations to come.

To get the guns into position – specifically, up to a projection known as the Knotch, from where a blind spot on the Mediterranean side could be covered – required still more imagination; this was provided by another of the Rock's favourite sons, a Sergeant-Major Ince of the Military Artificers. He, and fifty stone-cutters, masons, miners and lime-burners, drove a tunnel behind the Rock's northern face, along which the cannon could, it was thought, be trundled. On their way they punched a number of fresh-air vents through the face itself, and then made the discovery that they could poke the cannon through these portholes, and command huge fields of fire while remaining more or less invulnerable. And so the frustrated Spanish Army – including the Walloons (and Maltese cavalrymen, who occasionally charged towards the British lines) – watched while great black holes opened in the white cliffs, gun barrels were thrust out, and withering fusillades of shot flew down at them.

The tunnels – galleries, as they came to be called – were the first of a vast subterranean network. Today there are more than thirty miles of them, some carrying roads, thirteen specially designed as cavernous reservoirs to hold drinking water, some protected by steel blast doors and containing secret communications equipment and, by reliable though unconfirmed accounts, atomic bombs, and some put to even stranger uses. An entire Northern Irish village was built in one very big tunnel; it had a Roman Catholic church (St Malachy's), a pub (the Hope and Anchor) and a fish-and-chip shop (Tom's). British soldiers, some kitted out as IRA men, others as Irish civilians and still others in their usual battledress, would make war on each other, practising for Ballymurphy and the Bogside. It made a fine irony, I thought, for the interior of one British colony to be used to learn how to subdue the post-Imperial wrangling in what some regard as, strictly speaking, another.

By 1784, British rule in Gibraltar was unquestioned, and the Rock had become, in Britain and across much of the world, a monument to tenacity, grace under pressure and bull-doggishness in general. Before the siege there had been many plans to dispose of the colony, or to use it as a diplomatic bargaining chip. Lord Stanhope had offered Gibraltar back to Spain if Madrid would relinquish her claims in Italy; the French had offered Martinique and Guadeloupe in the Caribbean if Spain could be given back Gibraltar; and there were other trading schemes advanced besides. But after 1784, after the failure of the Great Siege, it was clear the British public would have none of it. 'Safe as the Rock of Gibraltar' was the phrase invented at the time, and variants of that most thunderous Imperial assertion have determined British policy towards the Rock ever since.

It was a squalid possession in those early days. The garrison was largely composed of ne'er-do-wells, drunkards and smugglers; the civil population, ignored and despised by the military establishment, was Genoese, Maltese, Moorish, Portu-

guese, British and – despite a specific provision of the Treaty
of Utrecht barring them from settlement – Jewish. (Spain points
to that provision, coupled with a ban on Moors living in the
colony as well, as yet another indication that her cession of
the peninsula was temporary and conditional.) And while the
Genoese and the Maltese attended to the more mundane duties
of urban life – though the Genoese fished, grew vegetables on
the neutral ground between La Linea and the Rock's north face,
and dealt in tobacco, as they still do today – the Sephardic Jews
attended to the essentials of Empire – they lent money, opened
trading houses and warehouses, had no overweening pride to
prevent them from the vulgar business of trade, and thus
managed swiftly to dominate the colony's commerce. The result
was their early prominence among the successful – if not social
– élite of the colony, and their continuing power today. 'Gibraltar
is full of Jews,' people will tell you as you step on to the plane
at Gatwick; well, it is not, but occasionally it feels as though it
might be, or might once have been. Spain rather likes to note
how the British have pointedly ignored the Treaty of Utrecht's
ban on Jews and Arabs by occasionally, and mischievously,
reminding the world of the name of the present, and seemingly
indomitable Prime Minister of Gibraltar. It is Sir Joshua Hassan.

The social élite – the Governor and his entourage, the senior
soldiery and admiralty, the British nabobs – generally kept aloof
from the noisome and mongrel crew down in the town. To
them, Gibraltar town was dirty and smelly, ill-constructed and
primitive, cursed with disease and vagabondage, and they rarely
ventured from their elegant mansions up on the hillside, or from
behind their barrack walls. Except, that is, in matters of sport:
the élite and the more skilled of the native Gibraltarians played
polo, and the British and the Spanish, whatever their politically
inspired loathing for each other, rode to hounds.

The Calpe Hunt, one of Empire's oldest and oddest, still
exists, or at least is revived from time to time, and gentlemen
in hunting pink can still be seen driving through the boundary
gates for a rendezvous with their hounds. But no one is quite
sure how it all began: some say, a little improbably, that a
foxhound couple was actually kept on the Rock, and that foxes

were to be found on the scrub on the slopes of Mount Misery and Middle Hill, scurrying among the apes.

Others say the first hounds were kept in San Roque under the mastership of one Reverend Mackareth, and that more hounds from the Duke of Wellington's pack, stationed near his great estates around Cadiz, were brought down in 1817, given to the interested officers of the 29th Regiment, and named after Gibraltar's classical title. By the end of the nineteenth century Colonel Gilbard was able to say that the hunt was 'the' great institution on the Rock, 'and a well-conducted establishment at the North Front gives accommodation to the huntsmen, hounds and their attendants'. The hunting was no longer confined to the peninsula's slopes, but had extended to the hills and meadows of neighbouring Andalucia, with the local landowners gladly allowing the Englishmen to ride their 'little coarse-bred Spanish horses' in pursuit of the exceptionally cunning native foxes.

The colonel saw his sport as an antidote to diplomatic disharmony. Were the Spaniards themselves to follow the pack 'this would wonderfully smooth the difficulties which occasionally crop up and threaten to spoil sport, and the members of the hunt would gladly welcome the Spanish officers, gentry and farmers joining in the sport in friendly rivalry'. Which is exactly what happened; and grandees of both English and Andalucian parentage rode together and once went over to Tangier 'where a wolf gave an excellent run of over forty minutes and a distance of nine miles'.

The garrison's élite may have rid the Rock of its foxes, and there may well now be fewer hares and rabbits on the upper slopes; but the Rock apes are still there, and in abundance. As well they might be: Spanish legend holds that when the apes go, then the British will surely follow, and British Governments and Imperial representatives have striven mightily – and seriously – to ensure that the animals remain healthy and numerous to this day. The serenity and fecundity of the apes is of great moment to both the Convent and, as a symbol, to Downing Street.

The little gang of Rock apes – *Macacus inuus* – are the only monkeys to be found in Europe. Theories about their having

swum across from Africa, or having arrived drenched, clinging
to Moroccan logs, have long been discounted; zoologists believe
these are the relict clan of a great tribe of Macaques which once
frolicked in Germany and France, and came as far north as
Aylesbury. The last Ice Age forced them steadily southwards:
Gibraltar was their final peninsular refuge, the closest they
ever would come to their native home. Had the blizzards and
hailstorms swept through Spain they might have been driven
into the Straits, and drowned.

But here they still sit, begging for food on the Monkey's
Alameda, swinging from wall to tree to tourist shoulder, spitting,
lunging, hawking, puking and displaying their unpleasant and
oddly tail-less backsides to the daily busloads of the curious.
They are truly loathsome creatures, in a state of permanent
distemper, ogrous packages of green and grey fur, all teeth,
stale fruit and urine. How little these true barbarians know
of the solicitous *tendresse* to which they are subject, or
of the colonial telegrams that have passed to and from the
Gibraltar cable station, attesting to their contentment, or their
decline.

Decline, strangely portentous, does seem to have been
invariably linked with periods of British misfortune. In 1910
there were 200 apes, so many that they split up into two gangs,
battled bloodily with each other – and by 1913 only three female
apes were left. The war that began the following summer was
thus not unexpected by the ever-superstitious Spaniards.

London was alarmed. It told the Royal Regiment of Artillery
to look after the remainder, and offered a grant to buy them
olives, locust beans and green figs (though not loquats, which
make them vomit). For a while, under the paternal invigilation
of the gunners, the apes went forth and multiplied; but by 1931
– the start of the Great Depression – they had fought so much
and so wildly with each other (they like to bite each other's
spines, which can be disabling and fatal if the bite is deep enough)
that only ten remained.

The Colonial Government, earnest and determined, stepped
in. The Governor, Sir Alexander Godley, a man who had commanded the western defences at Mafeking, had been staff officer

to Baden-Powell and had raised an army in New Zealand, was put in overall charge of this crucial Imperial task. He imported two male apes from Morocco, and then five more. But they refused to breed, and murder and mayhem kept the numbers down. At the outbreak of the Second World War only eleven were left, and by 1943, just seven.

The crisis needed a solution of Churchillian dimensions, and it was the Prime Minister himself who issued the order that finally turned the tide. More apes, hand-picked for their fertility and energetic application to their conjugal duties, were flown in from North Africa – and, to the blessed relief of all concerned, they bred, the numbers increased, and the base of today's tribe of fifty-three of the dreadful animals was laid.

Sergeant Alfred Holmes, who was deputed to look after the apes' welfare in 1962 – and who sends them for treatment in the Gibraltar naval hospital should they fall seriously ill – reported during my last visit that the colony (of apes, that is) was very healthy indeed. Eleven had been born during 1984, and one had been named after Princess Alexandra. (Tradition has it that apes are named after prominent Rock politicians; the one called Joshua Hassan dropped dead in 1964, and Lady Hassan sensibly refused to have anything to do with the beasts, which is presumably why the royal princess came to be so dubiously honoured.) Fecundity and serenity thus assured for some while to come, superstitious fears about the future of this tiny colony have, for the time being, been allayed.

A short while before I arrived on the Rock a young man named Allen Bula had created a small sensation by leaping over the steel border fence, into Spain. He was arrested by the Policia Nacional, and taken (via Tangier, naturally) back to his colonial home. Someone asked him what had prompted the gesture, and he replied, in tones of profound misery, that he was simply 'tired of seeing the same faces, and always having to walk the same streets'. A faint rumble of mute sympathy could be heard from every corner of the colony, for few would take issue with the heresy that Gibraltar has become – perhaps always has been – a prison, comfortable enough in a dingy sort of way, but its charms rendered utterly disagreeable in a matter of a very few days.

And it does have charm, especially to the British. It has a suitably reliquary appearance and feel to it. Where other than in a British colony could one find, peeking from behind orange trees and palm fronds, Mess House Lane, London Pride Way and Drumhead Court? What sweet relief, after all the bullfight posters and the cheap white wine and the guards in their silly tricorn hats, to see discreet notices advertising Wally Parker's XI versus the Garrison B Side (weather permitting) after lunch on Sunday, cups of Typhoo and Shippams-and-Sunblest sandwiches on the terrace of the Rock Hotel, and policemen in dark blue serge who will gladly tell you the time, in English, and the directions to the Angry Friar, where they have Bass and Whitbreads and Tia Maria and onion-flavoured crisps, and where one of the customers is sure to know the latest plots of *The Archers* or *Coronation Street*. You can buy the *News of the World* in Gibraltar late on a Sunday afternoon, and all its tales of cheerful scandals back in Britain will be common currency in the colony's buses the next morning as they grind up and down the slopes in clouds of diesel smoke, and dirty rain.

It rains a lot in Gibraltar, particularly when the due easterly wind, known as the Levanter, is blowing, as it does one day in two. Wet Mediterranean air is hoisted up over the colony's summit, forming a plume of cloud which hangs heavily and damply over the western side of the Rock. In the town below it is smotheringly hot, humid, dull, and there are fitful showers.

The streets are choked with people – army wives from Aldershot and Catterick in cotton tee-shirts and jeans and high-heeled shoes, pushing prams and getting in each other's way; old Spanish women in black, shuffling along slowly and silently, looking unhappy; women from Morocco, appropriately veiled, who look away from any male glance; Indians stretching and scratching and spitting into the gutters; swarthy traders of Genoese or Maltese cast beckoning you into their little shops to buy curios and postcards and fizzy drinks.

Outside the Convent a troop of British soldiery, glittering and crisp in their brass and white duck summer uniforms stand guard

for Her Majesty's Governor; and each Monday morning the
prams and shopping carts make way for a parade, all screamed
commands and polished toecaps, and over which the Governor
and Her Ladyship preside, beaming, from the balcony of their
residence. And inside the Convent the splendour of Empire
gently reasserts itself; thick red carpets, a leather-bound visitors' book with an embossed crown, portraits and flags and
banners, polished oak dining tables, a private chapel (with a
soldier-organist practising a fugue for a concert the following
week), smooth young diplomats and ADCs, white-coated servants, tea from Fortnums, Bath Olivers and Tiptree jam. There
is even a pretty indoor garden, with jacarandas and roses and
lilies; and the Governor keeps a cow in his orchard – the only
cow permitted in Gibraltar, which provides properly English
milk for the gubernatorial Weetabix.

But the Imperial splendour here is all illusion. True, the
Gibraltar Conservation Society makes an almighty fuss whenever a new block of army flats or a multi-storey car park
threatens some of the magnificently immense fortifications – the
great gates and bastions and casemates and galleries, the mighty
limestone blocks and rusty iron stanchions, bolts, hasps,
anchors, cannonports, naval guns and sea walls – which are
undeniably grand reminders of such splendour. The fortress and
all it's remnant bits and pieces tell of Trafalgar and Cape St
Vincent and the wartime convoys, of heroism and valour and
tragedy, and there is the whiff of convict ship and merchant
venturer, the memory of sail and steam and majesty and power.

And true, there is a flourishing democracy here, though of
recent invention, and of limited democratic ability. Until the
Thirties the only form of local government was the Sanitary
Commission, run by a cabal of traders and lawyers, and which
was set up in 1865 after an epidemic of plague which killed nearly
600 people. The commissioners had powers that extended well
beyond a purely sanitary remit; in 1920 they were able to report
that a poor law was unnecessary in the colony, and there was
no one to suggest they should stick to the study of tuberculosis
(which was then raging) rather than poverty. The Legislative
Assembly, which gave a semblance of power to the Gibraltarians,

was opened in 1950 by the Duke of Edinburgh; it became an even more powerful House of Assembly in 1969, though the Governor – who is also Fortress Commander – still has very considerable powers.

But the glorious ruins of yesterday and the laudable institutions of today cannot disguise the fact that Gibraltar is, above all, a garrison town, with all that implies. Its function is precisely that of a Tidworth or a Fort Bragg – it supports and supplies a military function, and its civilian servants exist only in a symbiosis with the forces, with no real function other than to service the machinery of war.

During the Falklands War Gibraltar was of major importance – a fact that nearly led to one of the more daring undercover operations of the century. A team of Argentine frogmen arrived in Spain with plans to swim over to the Rock and blow up the Royal Naval ships in the dockyard, and then lay charges inside the more important of the tunnels, and blow the entire Rock up, too. But the Spanish police, tipped off by British intelligence, arrested the quartet at San Roque, just a few miles from the border. The Spanish Government, which despite its antipathy to Britain wanted membership of the Common Market and had good reason to want to stay friendly, deported the men and sent them back to Buenos Aires. I was told the story in Hong Kong, which was ordered to keep on guard in case the plucky Argentines tried to pull a similiar stunt there. People on the Rock knew nothing at the time; on the day the men were detected a parson friend of mine was sailing back from a day's shopping in Tangier, and remembers 'sitting on the boat as we rounded Europa Point, shelling Moroccan peas so they were ready for the deep-freeze the moment I stepped ashore'.

Today the Rock draws its military significance wholly from its membership of NATO (of which Spain is a member, too). America, in particular, regards Gibraltar as crucial, for though her own submariners use the port of Rota, just a few miles westwards, for their nuclear patrol boats, there is inevitable doubt about Spanish stability, and thus no long-term certainty inside the Pentagon that Rota will be perpetually available, unlike Gibraltar, which will so long as it remains British. Washington regards the defence of the Rock with almost as much passion as do the politicians in London. The Pentagon counts the apes as well.

No garrison town holds many attractions, and Gibraltar is not an exception. Though geologically interesting and thus topographically unforgettable, it remains, as Jan Morris noted in 1968, 'only a fly-blown, dingy and smelly barracks town, haunted by urchins fraudulently claiming to be Cook's guides, or Spanish hawkers wandering from door to door with straggly flocks of turkeys'.

It was grander once. You could, on a day when the fleets were in, stand under a palm tree on the terrace of the Rock Hotel and gaze down with wonder and amazement at the glittering array of grey steel and holystoned decking, at the signal flags and the jolly-boats, at the jackstaff ensigns waving lazily in the air, arrogantly proclaiming raw and unchallengeable British power. But now there is no Orient route that needs guarding, nor any fleets of substance with which to do it. Gibraltar, so far as the British are concerned, is a pointless sort of place: we hang on because the Gibraltarians want us to, because we have a certain haughty pride about the Rock's impregnability, and because the Supreme Commanders of the North Atlantic like us to act as proxy for them in this convenient corner of a geopolitically important inland sea.

Britain has offered a special gift to those whom we regard as of such special military significance – even if we have no further grand wars to fight, and even if the natives of the Rock are mere supporters, not participants. In gratitude for all their help the British Government has made the Gibraltarians, unlike most of their colonial colleagues, full-blown British subjects, able to come and live in Britain with no restrictions at all. They were given the privilege in 1981, when the House of Lords voted that they should not be treated like Bermudians, the Pitcairners, or the Hong Kong Chinese, who would no longer be allowed to enjoy full citizenship of the motherland. (The Falkland Islanders were not given citizenship either on this occasion, though after the war the Government changed its mind. The Gibraltarians and the Falklanders are thus unique in two respects – unlike all other British colonial citizens they can come and live in Britain at any time they wish; and unlike all other British colonial populations, they are overwhelmingly coloured white. Any connection between the two is not, as one might suppose, rigorously denied. The British Nationality Act, the basis of all this complicated regulation, was specifically designed to minimise racial disharmony by keeping the number of yellow and black colonials out, while letting whites of British ancestry come home if they wished. The Genoese and the Sephardim of Gibraltar have much to be thankful for.)

And, like the apes, so the British Gibraltarians cling on. At the last count, just forty-four of them thought it a good idea to join back with Spain. Twelve thousand voted for Gibraltar to remain a member of the Empire. So every night the fortress keys – cast iron, weighing ten pounds, and kept by some of the more nervous governors under their pillows, it is said – are handed into safe keeping by the sentries who still yell out the Imperial formulae of three centuries' continual use:

Halt! Who goes there?
The Keys
Whose Keys?
Queen Elizabeth's Keys
Pass, Queen Elizabeth's Keys. All's Well.

All illusion, though. From the Rock Hotel, with no fleet in view, and no reliable kippers available, and Brown Windsor soup and rolls served at nearly every meal, and the same faces passing along the same streets, the same soldiers inviting you to the same drinks parties, the same films on at the same cinemas, and the same awful weather and the same awful apes, I, too, felt like Mr Bula, trapped and claustrophobic, wanting to get off to the apparent freedom of Algeciras, whose lights twinkled invitingly from across the bay.

The terminal was crowded with servicemen bound for home leave; few Gibraltarians were planning to desert the peninsula this particular Saturday. I sat on the right side of the aircraft, and watched with a mixture of awe and some relief as we rose beside the mighty white cliff, dotted with its cannonports, topped with artillery and radio aerial and the Union flag, and headed back home to England. As a structure, it had been an impressive place, all right; but when a soldier caught my eye and grinned and said how glad he was to be getting away, I knew exactly how he felt. The Rock, he remarked, as he tucked into his first beer of the holiday, was also the name they gave to Alcatraz.

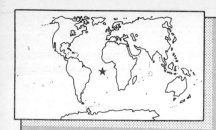

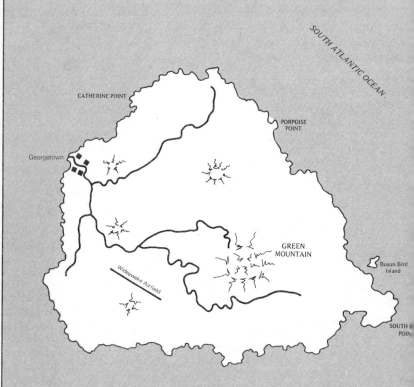

CATHERINE POINT

PORPOISE
POINT

SOUTH ATLANTIC OCEAN

Georgetown

GREEN
MOUNTAIN

Bosun Bird
Island

Wideawake Airfield

SOUTH
POIN

Ascension

0   1   2   3 Kilometres
0   1   2 Miles

FIVE

ASCENSION ISLAND

One of the more eccentric practices of the Empire was to decide that certain of the more remote island colonies were not really countries at all, but ships.

There was, for example, a tiny morsel of granite in the Grenadines that was taken over by the Royal Navy in Victorian times and commissioned as HMS *Diamond Rock*; then again, during the Second World War the Navy possessed a craft called HMS *Atlantic Isle*, which in more peaceful times was the four-island group of Tristan da Cunha. And in 1816 a Mr Cuppage, a post-captain of the Cape Squadron, took command of a brand-new 'stone frigate', as the Lords of the Admiralty liked to call it: the thirty-five-square-mile, oyster-shell-shaped accretion of volcanic rubbish that was assumed into the service of the Crown under the title of HMS *Ascension*.

I first saw the vessel – 'a huge ship kept in first-rate order', Darwin had recorded – from the flight deck of a Royal Air Force VC–10, one steaming day in late July. We had flown from a base in Oxfordshire to Senegal, and I had become rather bored by the curious Air Force practice of putting its passengers facing backwards. (They say it's safer.) So I asked to sit behind the pilot for the next leg; and as we reached the equator, and summer became technical winter and in a million bathrooms below the water began to swirl down plugs the other way, so the loadmaster called me forward, unlocked the door to the cockpit, made a series of perfunctory introductions to the crew, asked me to avoid sudden movements and unnecessary conversation, and strapped me into the jump seat.

Ascension Island came up on the radar a few moments later. A tiny pale green dot, lozenge-shaped and utterly alone – it might well have been a ship adrift in the sea below. We started to go down for the approach. The orange numerals of the satellite navigator showed our position six times a minute. We were at fourteen degrees west of Greenwich, seven degrees south of the equator, somewhere in the hot emptiness of the sea well below the bulge of West Africa. The dot on the radar was bigger now, and we were low enough to see the white curlers on the swell.

And then the pilot muttered softly into his microphone, 'Island in sight. Ahead fifty miles. Plume of cloud.' And on the curved line of horizon a patch of cloud appeared, like a ball of cotton wool on a glass ledge. Beneath it, and speeding nearer at six miles a minute, was a patch of reddish-brown land, tinged with dark green and ringed by a ragged line of surf. 'Wideawake Airfield in sight, sir,' sang the co-pilot – and there, on the southern side of the island was the aerodrome, its straight runway undulating over the contours like the final run on a roller-coaster. A smooth American voice came on the line. 'Ascot Two zero one niner – good day, sir. Welcome to Ascension Island. Wind eight knots. Clear skies at the field. No traffic. Come right on in, and have yourselves a nice day!' And so we slid down the glidepath to this loneliest of ocean way-stations, until with a bump and puff of iron-red cinder-dust we touched down on board and I, who alone in the cockpit had never been here before, thought we had landed on the surface of the moon.

Ascension is indeed an eerie place. It is a volcano, placed on the very crest of an abyssal suture line, the Mid-Atlantic Ridge, and is in consequence very new. (St Helena, which lies some miles off the ridge, but is one of its products, is one of the oldest oceanic islands known. Geologists explain it by asking one to imagine a mid-Atlantic conveyor-belt moving islands out and away from the ridge. Those on it – Tristan, Iceland, Ascension – are still being formed; those away from it – the Azores, Jan

Mayen, the Canaries – are old, and have drifted miles since their formation.)

Ascension looks as though it should still be smouldering. 'Hell with the fire put out,' someone called it – and it looks rather like a gigantic slag-heap, with runs of ashy rubble, piles of cinders, and fantastically shaped flows of frozen lava. Nothing – at least, not among the peaks and plains I saw as I drove from the airport – had been carved by weather, nor has anything had its outline smoothed by millions of years of erosion. Ascension is the earth in its raw state, unlovely and harsh, and grudging in its attitude to the life that clings to it. It gives uncomfortable seismal shudders from time to time, and lets out puffs of sulphur gas and gurgles of hot water and mud, as if to warn those who have dared make this a colony of the British Crown that the lease is far from permanent, and the titanic forces beneath the rocky skin are merely slumbering, biding their time.

Ascension – which is very much an island of the space age today, festooned with aerials and chattering with computers and radar domes – was classified as a ship for rather more than a century. The Navy took it over in 1815 once it had been decided to exile Napoleon on St Helena, 700 miles to the south-east, and the Admiralty feared the French might try to take Ascension and use it as a staging base for helping the Emperor escape. (A garrison was established on Tristan da Cunha for the same reason.) It became a ship of the line a year later, with those few who lived aboard subject to the same rigours of 'rum, sodomy and the lash' as on any of Her Majesty's vessels. One captain was sent a report to the effect that a member of his crew – a lady – had given birth to an infant. With mirthless propriety he jotted one word on the announcement – 'Approved' – and added his initials. (For years afterwards any children born on Ascension were officially deemed to have been born at sea, and registered according to custom in the London parish of Wapping.)

The Crown took charge of the island in 1922, and made her what she is now – a dependency of St Helena. There is an Administrator, who lives in what was once the sanatorium high up among the clouds on Green Mountain; and there is no permanent native population. There is, however – and has been for many years – a very considerable clutch of transients – people whose nationalities and trades vary according to the use to which Ascension is being put at any one moment. At the time I arrived, in the aftermath of the Falklands operations, the island was crawling with Royal Air Force men and their planes, and all the paraphernalia needed for keeping the garrison in the far South Atlantic equipped with all it needs; but there have been at one time and another a bewildering variety of 'users' of Ascension. (The place is essentially run by a body known as the London Users Committee, who, since there is no native to inconvenience, do with the island more or less as they like, so long as they all agree it will do the users some good.) There have been missile-testing engineers, satellite trackers, radio broadcasters, spies (there are still lots of this particular breed) and those most indomitable guardians of the distant rocks, the men of the cable terminals.

Ascension Island was one of the great cable stations of the Imperial universe. The Eastern Telegraph Company arrived in 1899, bringing the free end of a cable that its ships had laid from Table Bay to Jamestown, in St Helena. Within weeks, after the repeaters and amplifiers had been built on Ascension, and a staff left behind to maintain them in working order, so the line was extended – up to the Cape Verde Islands, and then on to England. More cables were fed into the sea – one from Ascension to Sierra Leone, so the Governor in Freetown could send messages to Whitehall without having to wait if a camel had munched its way through the line across the Sahara. A fourth was sunk to St Vincent, a fifth to Rio, and another to Buenos Aires. By the time of the Great War Ascension sat in mid-ocean like a great telegraphic clearing house, the hum of generators and the clack of the morse repeaters echoing across the silence of the sea. (Ascension had always had associations with communication. As soon as Alphonse d'Albuquerque discovered it, on Ascension Day, 1501, sailors travelling past in one direction started a custom of leaving letters there, for collection and onward transmission by ships sailing in the other. There still is a letter-box where passing vessels may drop notes; when someone looked in it recently there was a note dating from 1913.)

Lonely places, cable stations. Islands like Fanning, in mid-Pacific, notable only because 'it was annexed by Britain in 1888 as the site for a trans-Pacific cable relay station'; or Direction Island, on Cocos-Keeling, 'administered by Britain for a cable relay point for the Indian Ocean'; or Ascension. The British saw cables as the vital synapses of the Imperial nervous system. They had to be utterly reliable. They had to be secure. And they had, all of them, to be British. (To illustrate the point it is worth noting that when the time came to construct a cable from Hong Kong to Shanghai the cable engineers built a relay station on a hulk in the middle of the Min River, rather than risk placing so critically important an Imperial nerve-ending on Chinese soil, where anything might happen to it.) The ultimate purpose of the cables was, of course, the unity, and thus the unassailability of the Empire, a theme Kipling was quick to recognise:

Joining hands in the gloom, a league from the last of the sun
Hush! Men talk today o'er the waste of the ultimate slime
And a new Word runs between: whispering, 'Let us be one!'

And so between them the sailors and the cable men built a society on Ascension, and a tiny Imperial city, which they called Georgetown (though it was always known as Garrison). A tradition grew up that every sailor – and later every cable man – brought something to render the moon-scape a little more like home. The Royal Navy and the Royal Marines, who from time to time were also posted aboard HMS *Ascension*, carried in scores of tons of earth and thousands of sapling trees (yews from South Africa, firs from Scotland, blue gums from New South Wales, castor-oil bushes from the West Indies); marines built a farm and brought a herd of cows (the milking shed, robustly Victorian and made from stone, has a crest and the letters 'RM', which the lowing herds blithely ignore); sailors dug a pond at the very top of Green Mountain, and stocked it with goldfish and frogs; and they built greenhouses and a home garden, and grew bananas and paw-paws, grapefruit, grenadillas and tomatoes, roses and carnations and all the familiar vegetables of an English Sunday luncheon.

Over the years the colonists have tried so very hard to impose the contented ways of a London suburb on this monstrously ugly pile of clinker and baked ash. There was probably no place on earth that can have seemed less like home, no atoll or hill station or desert oasis that can have been less sympathetic to the peculiar needs of the wandering Englishman and his family. But, like the good colonist that he was, he did eventually manage to fashion the place into an approximation of Surrey-in-the-Sea. The little houses each have a neat garden and tiny patch of lawn, most of them with a round plastic swimming pool, a child's swing and a snoring dog ('we inherited the old boy from the Parker-Bruces, you know. Eats us out of house and home. Can't think why he doesn't roast, with all that hair. Goodness knows what will happen when we go. He's getting on a bit. I suppose he'll just go to whoever takes our place. Poor old devil. Lucy's quite attached to him now. But then she was positively transfixed by that old mutt we had in the Seychelles. Got over him in time, of course. But it can be tough on the kids . . .'). There is a library and a hairdresser for the wives, and there are drinks parties most evenings – a lot of drinks parties, a lot of drinks, and the usual alcoholic haze of tropical solitude.

The *Islander* newspaper has been coming out each week, thanks to the labours of any number of Our Lovely Wives, since 1971. Take a riffle through the pages of one recent March issue. There's old Brian presenting a teak tray and a couple of tankards to Margot and Dennis, who have just left after their two-year stint; Pearl Robertson has won the whist competition up at Two Boats, yet again! (The road up to Green Mountain has sawn-off gigs stuck into the clinker to act as milestones – One Boat is lower down, Two Boats is up at the 700-foot mark – and small communities, and telephone exchanges, have grown beside them. The boats act as splendid shelter from the occasional violent rainstorms.) Now, what else? Margaret Lee will give a manicure demonstration on Wednesday at the Two Boats Club. Suzanne will host a Tupperware patio sale in Georgetown on Saturday. Communion will be at nine thirty this Sunday at St Mary's. Novice bridge players are welcome at the Exiles Club library every Wednesday at 8 p.m. Irene Robinson wrote to say she was leaving the island and would miss the Church, the Scouts, the Gardening Club and the Tennis Club. A vote of thanks had been organised for Ernie Riddough, who was also leaving: his term as public health officer had been a great success, and 'the island had not suffered from plague and pestilence'. The Messmen would play the Supremes in the island darts league on Tuesday, and there would be a soccer match, Georgetown versus the Forces, the day after. And – best news of all – the Ascension Cricket Association has just received two dozen balls from St Helena, the cricket league can now get under way, and a meeting would be held on Tuesday night beside the Volcano Radio Station to discuss the season's fixtures.

There is no hotel on the island. Visitors are not encouraged – the lack of hotel room being the official excuse. I have stayed in a variety of places. The Americans have huts they call 'concertinas'; they are shipped over quite flat, like sandwiches, and then the ends are pulled apart and a fully-equipped room appears, with mirrors on walls, lights in ceilings, tables clipped to floors. Each time I slept in Concertina City – which was difficult anyway, because of the heat – I started to wonder if the whole room might revert in the night, and I would be flattened out of all recognition, as though I had been trapped in the boot of a car sent to the crushers.

My happiest nights were spent at the old Zymotic Hospital. It had been built by the Navy more than a century ago, perched on a cliff of slag, facing west; it has thick stone walls, and gently turning fans, and the windows and the doors are always open. It is perfectly cool, and I would sit there with the crews of the transport planes, sipping whisky and watching the sunsets, and listening to stories of airborne exploits in every Imperial corner of the world. I found one pilot whom I had known at school; another who had once given me a lift during the rescue operations following a hurricane, from British Honduras to Costa Rica; and a third who had been a member of the Queen's Flight and had spent the last summer shuttling the Queen Mother back and forth from Windsor to Glamis.

One day I flew with my schoolfriend to the Falkland Islands. He was the pilot of a Hercules carrying several tons of freight and fifty Fusiliers down to Stanley. We rose at three – it was still hot, and a warm wind stirred the ash beside the roads – and had breakfast in a tent by the runway. There were innumerable briefings, weather checks, radio messages, orders. At five, while it was still dark, we clambered up into the aircraft.

Two Victor jet bombers, old-fashioned, strangely shaped monsters, zoomed into the air a few moments later; and when they were safely airborne we lumbered off and into the twinkling dawn. The bombers were the first of our refuelling tankers. They met us out in mid-ocean, after we had been going for three hours. One fuelled us, the other fuelled him, and both then turned away for home. Six hours further south, when we were well down in the latitudes, and the sea below was covered by low storm clouds, the bombers met us again – three of them this time, one for us, one for him, and the third to top up the second. Then they wheeled away and back up to their cinder-topped base, and we trundled wearily on to Stanley. It took nearly fourteen miserable hours to get us and our cargo from Ascension to the Falkland Islands; five refuelling tankers had been needed, and a small army of logistics men and planners; and had the British not been able to use Ascension the operation would not have been possible at all. I was not entirely convinced the effort on this occasion had been entirely worthwhile: one of the objects we were carrying was a fan for the desk of an army officer – a man who might have thought he was being sent out to deal with an insurrection in the Sudan, but was in fact stationed in one of the coolest, and windiest, parts of the Empire ever known.

Since the Falklands War the island has become furiously busy. Planes howl in and out every day, at any hour. The mess at the American base serves gigantic meals – steaks, jello, milk, instant potatoes – to pilots and technicians all day and all night. Generators rattle, bored soldiers shine machine-guns, warships slip in and out of harbour, replenishment vessels come and lie at anchor two miles offshore, and let a litter of smaller craft suck hungrily at their nozzles of petrol, or water, or aviation spirit. Up on the volcano-sides radar dishes and strangely shaped aerials whir and nod; and wherever the clinker is nearly flat there are graders and bulldozers levelling it still further to make way for yet more new housing, new headquarters buildings, new mess centres. There has never been anything like it – except that there is no one who has lived on Ascension long enough to be able to compare the daily rounds of 1984 with those of the time before April 1982, when the colony underwent the greatest sea-change of its short career.

Away from the military operations centres, though, much is unchanged. The cable operators still have an office on Ascension, though they run the world's conversations through satellites today, and the dozens of men who were needed to maintain the circuits of old and keep each other company have dwindled to a very few. In their place there are the men with the very ordinary names – Mr Dunne, Mr Turner, Mr Evans, Mr Davies, Mr Little – who have a very extraordinary job: they work for what is called the Composite Signals Organisation, a secret British Government organisation that makes it its business to find out what other interesting traffic is passing through the satellites and around the ether, and which may be of some use to the West. Messrs Dunne, Turner, Evans and their scores of colleagues, who maintain a polite but scrupulous guard on everything they say, are electronic spies, and Ascension is full of them. There are American spies too, working for a much bigger organisation called the National Security Agency. But while the existence of the British CSO staff is officially acknowledged, the American technicians are not admitted to being on the island, not by anyone.

I toured around the island by helicopter one day – buzzing the lush slopes of Green Mountain, the satellite station on Donkey Plain, the tracking station on the Devil's Ashpit, the strange volcanic rings of the Devil's Riding School. We arrived above a cluster of white aerials on the eastern side of the island, near a cliff called Hummock Point. I pointed down, and asked the pilot what they were – and he started, and whirled his craft away, and we roared back to the north of Ascension, leaving the aerials to their secrets. It is said – but then it is always said – that there are vast underground bunkers, crammed with electronic code-breaking machines, and staffed by pale-skinned troglodytes who rarely surface into the sun. All that can be said with certainty is that Ascension is an important little island, and that it derives its importance for more than being a convenient staging post, halfway between the training grounds of Salisbury Plain and the fighting grounds of East Falkland. It is manifestly not an island that Britain – or America, for that matter – would abandon without a struggle. Happily no one – least of all the island population, which comes on short-term and highly lucrative contracts – wants Ascension to break away from the motherland. (Some of the more radical St Helenians, however, wonder why Britain cannot persuade the Americans to pay rent for their bases on Ascension, and thus help the crippled St Helena economy. Britain refuses even to discuss the matter.)

But HMS *Ascension* is not all warship. It is a floating radio programme, too. On the northern tip, beside one of the few bays that is protected from the man-eating sharks that roam the coastal waters, is a smart white office building with a tall white warehouse next door. This is the Atlantic Relay Station of the BBC; the office teems with administrators, the warehouse with transmitters, and the men sent out to keep them running. There are six short-wave transmitters which broadcast the World Service and the various foreign languages of the oceanside countries (Spanish and Portuguese for Latin America, Hausa, French and Swahili for Africa). I had expected the transmitters to be compact, rather unimpressive machines, all solid-state and disc-driven; instead there were six monstrous grey cabinets, which looked like refugees from a Victorian power station, and which opened to reveal a mass of hot, humming valveware, with long and curiously shaped horns that snap in and out depending upon which frequency band the Corporation wishes to use for transmissions that day. Some of the valves are two feet tall, weigh a hundred kilogrammes, cost thousands of pounds each and put out showers of vivid blue sparks and flames while they are busying themselves with getting the *News in Swahili* to the far side of Africa, or sending *Calling the Falklands* to the sister colony halfway down the same cold ocean.

The last time I arrived in Ascension I came by boat. A school of dolphins had joined us two hours before, and had played joyously under the bows as we ploughed ponderously towards the small speck of Imperial volcano. We dropped anchor in eight fathoms, a mile off the Georgetown jetty; for fully five minutes I stood enthralled at this strange sight – this mass of reddish-brown rock, rising abruptly from the ocean, its peaks festooned with delicate filigrees of radio masts, with globes and radar dishes and odder, inexplicable devices for talking and listening to the outer reaches of the cosmos. The additions had made the island look unreal, as though it were an outlandishly shaped submarine that had briefly come to the surface to take on air, and would soon sink into the depths once more and sidle off on some mysterious mission.

But I went ashore – nearly drowning myself as I leapt for the rope at the bottom of the Tartar Steps, missed, and slipped on the slime – and took a car to the Residency, up on the slopes of Green Mountain. (It was not always so easy. The wife of a resident naval officer once arrived at the same jetty and haughtily demanded of a rating where on earth Government House might be, and where was the carriage she had expected would be awaiting her pleasure. 'There's the captain's cottage, ma'am,' returned the sailor, 'and this here is the island cart.')

The Residency here was once the Mountain Hospital, for as soon as Napoleon had died Ascension was turned into a huge sanatorium, dotted with hospitals and sick bays where men of the West Africa Squadron could be taken if they fell sick while on anti-slaving duties off the Guinea Coast. It was used as a coaling station, too – yellow-fever and coal being the principal colonial 'industries' until the cables came at the end of the century. To get to the Residency involves a long climb – I went past One Boat, past Two Boats, past a water tank called 'God-Be-Thanked' and up a helter-skelter of ramps and slopes and hairpins more fearsome than any this side of the Alps.

It would be idle to pretend that the man who fetches up as tenant of the Residency, Ascension, is likely to be a figure on the cutting edge of British diplomacy. It was always one of the least favoured posts in the remit of the Colonial Office, and remains as unpopular today. The Administrator himself has very little to do. He looks after the police force, sets the weekly exchange rate for the St Helena pound, and issues instructions about road closures and sittings of the magistrate's court. Meanwhile the civil administration of the island is now actually carried out by the BBC; the Royal Air Force and the various American agencies run the military side.

But assuming he is able to cast off his memories of ambition, the Ascension Administrator can savour a place of unusual loveliness. His house is more beautifully sited than any other in the remaining Empire: its gardens sweep down to cliffs from which most of the island can be seen, and the ocean stretches to the horizon on every side. At night the sky is ablaze with stars, and the island below pricked with the golden oases of light among the black volcanic shadows. There are wonderful vegetables and exotic fruits; and up here, on the high slopes, the weather is pleasant all the year round.

I walked up from the Residency one afternoon, through the groves of trees the sailors and the cable men had brought – eucalyptus, juniper, monkey-puzzle, acacia, Port Jackson willows. Then, as the road wound higher, so the hedges became as tall and as fragrant as any in Devon in summertime. The old farm, with its stables and milking halls and clock tower (where the naval rum was issued), came into view – a granite testament to the amazing energies of the Victorian sailors and marines. The very thought of building a Sussex farmhouse, with a clock, 2,000 feet up the side of a volcano in the middle of the equatorial Atlantic!

Up here was a world quite different from the harsh clinker desert below, where there was no grass, and just a wretched collection of beasts that included spitting wild cats, land crabs, goats and donkeys, and massive Brazilian turtles clambering wearily on to the blazing beaches to lay eggs. Up here there were palm groves and banana clumps, gardens with raspberries and ginger, and fields of grass and gorse. The trade winds, cool at this altitude, swept in across meadows where dairy cattle (administered by an official of the BBC in London, no less!) grazed contentedly. I climbed a stile, and headed on upwards into bamboo forest, where it was dark and cool, and the path was thick and slippery with clean brown mud. I took off my shoes and socks, and waded ever upwards, to the summit of Green Mountain.

At the top, in the tiny old crater, was the dew pond – made by the Navy to catch water, stocked by the Navy to be beautiful. There were blue lillies in flower the day I was there and large goldfish swam lazily through the dappled waters. The remains of an old anchor-chain lay beside the pond, and I had read somewhere that it was the custom to hold it, close your eyes, and wish . . .

At the far end of the pool, on the topmost point of the island, 2,817 feet above the sea, was a wooden box, with a visitors' book inside, and I signed it: the last climber had been a wing commander, from Northumberland. Most, indeed, had been military men: two years before the entries were by young soldiers trying to keep themselves fit for war; now they were officers, curious, and with time on their hands. They had come striding up stick in hand, pipe clenched between teeth; in 1982 the men had come running and puffing, with a drill sergeant in hot pursuit, and no doubt they hated the summit, and cursed the slime and the knife-edges of the bamboo leaves, and the crazy accidents of creation that put such ghastly hills out here in the tranquil flatness of the sea.

But this afternoon no one else was in sight. I had Green Mountain all to myself. The only sound was the sighing of the trade winds through the bamboos, and the occasional quiet chatter of canaries down in the meadows. Truly, I found myself thinking, of all the forgotten corners of the Empire this was both the most lovely, and the most strange. Below me was all the machinery and technology of war, and the encrypted chatter of half the world's spymasters. Down there – and I could glimpse the wastes of lava, and catch the glint of a radar dome – was that hell with the fire put out; up here, where the sailors of Admiral Fisher's grand Imperial Navy had built a farm and a water supply, and had planted some trees, was something close to heaven. This, these few forgotten acres of hillside, showed to me what the Empire really could be when it tried – Rosebery's great and secular force for good, which left memorials behind of which everyone could be proud, and for which everyone could be thankful.

SIX

ST HELENA

It had been another blazing day on the limitless wastes of the South Atlantic Ocean. The rusty little freighter was three days out from Ascension Island, heading to the south-east. The sun, harsh and brassy and hot, glared down from a brilliant sky. The trade winds, always like the breath of a furnace, always from the south-east quadrant coming at us from over the port bow, wafted by at their customarily languid six knots. The sea looked like hammered silver, and we rolled almost imperceptibly on a long swell. Once in a while a bird appeared from nowhere and hovered and arched in the eddies round our masts and our rigging; once I saw a plastic bag and a beer bottle float past; and the night before a ship passed by on the starboard side, but no amount of calling her on the radio could win a friendly response.

'This is the Royal Mail vessel *Aragonite*' we would chant over the long-range radio, and the little VHF. But the ship never answered. We watched her slip past, her stern light winking and fading in the night haze, the faint throb of her motor a muffled beat across the sea. She was northbound, and she was probably Royal Navy: her radio silence suggested that, our radio operator said.

Once she was gone I stood at the taffrail gazing over the empty immensity of the sea. The night was starlit. This seemed just then such a lonely place. The Admiralty's *Ocean Passages for the World* had a thin red line etched on the map, heading south-east from Ascension, and claiming to be the shipping route from New York to Cape Town. But it must have been a very minor route, or else it lay many miles to the side of us; we saw nothing, except the silent and nameless warrior-ship sliding by on our starboard flank. (The Farrel Line used to take Canadian flour to St Helena. But then the Government found another source a farthing a pound cheaper – and the Farrel Line lost the contract.)

But that was the night before. Now, with the sun going down on the third day, we were expecting a landfall. All the officers – only three, the *Aragonite* being such a tiny tub – were on the bridge, and the purser was on the forepeak, and such passengers as were well enough (there had been a depressing degree of *mal de mer*) were standing up on deck, straining their eyes for land. You could smell it, or you thought you could. The breeze came from almost ahead, and once in a while, especially if you were near enough the bow to escape the diesel-and-cooking-oil-and-tar smells of the ship, there was a momentary wafting of some familiar smell of land. Pine trees, perhaps, or seaweed, or grass. It might have been memory playing tricks; but noses become very sensitive at sea. I knew of a cat that, after three months on an ocean passage, would stand on the bows lashing her tail and sniffing in the direction of Madagascar, which was 200 miles away: she could smell that far. Now we could smell the island that lay ahead of us.

And then, with a whoop of triumph, a cry from the bridge. 'There she is! That's her! Right ahead.'

At first there was nothing, just the endless steel edge of the Atlantic horizon, pinkish in the early evening, touched by a small patch of settled cloud. But then, slowly, from within the cloud a vague darkness took form and shape – a grey, shadowy thing with straight, steep sides. It was the island: some of our passengers, standing mute, gazing at her gradually spreading bulk, were weeping. They were almost home.

The ship rolled closer and closer. Grey became brown, and patches of green mottled the upper slopes. The steep sides became sheer cliffs, rearing suddenly out of the empty sea. Seabirds came wheeling at us now in great clouds. As the sun slipped away so lights twinkled on the island ahead. I could see the crawling firefly of a car moving high up on the mountainside.

The master, a quiet Scotsman for whom this was a final voyage – he was about to retire to his house many thousands of miles away in Milngavie, and make a living in the bed-and-breakfast trade – rang down to the engine room. 'Half ahead!' The bells jangled. 'Slow ahead!' Then 'Stop!' The anchor chain rattled away in a cloud of iron dust. We came to a firm and definite halt, and a dozen small boats began lashing towards us, their occupants waving and cheering at our passengers, who waved and sobbed back. 'Finished with engines' the master telegraphed, with a tired smile. The Royal Mail Ship *Aragonite*, 682 tonnes, and of Glaswegian registry, had arrived at last at the loneliest major outpost of the British Empire. 'This most solitary island,' as the Edwardian writer E. L Jackson began her classic book, 'of St Helena.'

If we can agree that in the ragged spectrum of the current Empire the islands of Bermuda sit firmly at one end – important, prosperous, by and large contented and assured of a reasonably stable and secure future – then the colony of St Helena, sad to relate, lies foursquare at the other. This 'pinpoint of inaccessibility, unbelievably remote' was once a place of significance; it is now, to Britain, of no consequence whatsoever, is steadfastly ignored and neglected by a mother country to whom her natives look in vain for succour and friendship. It has been turned, in consequence, into what one recent visitor called 'an Imperial slum'. '

One cannot come away from St Helena without shaking one's head and muttering that something must be done; but nothing has been, nothing is, and nothing ever will be done – under the suzerainty of Britain, at least. The story of St Helena is a tragedy of decay and isolation, poverty and ruin, and all played by a principal cast of proud and enchanting islanders, and in their home of magical beauty. (But a recent decision taken in London, taking the daily running of the island away from the Foreign Office, may yet improve matters.)

Jamestown, the capital, provides the first indication of the charm and loveliness of this forlorn little island. There is no harbour, and I was puttered to shore in a tiny dinghy, and had to step on to dry land by way of a slimy, sea-washed step. The legendary Atlantic rollers – long swells born in Newfoundland storms, six feet high in the inner bay, and booming ashore every half-minute or so – make any landing perilous in the extreme, and there are stout ropes hanging from a stanchion for nervous visitors to grab. I most certainly did; and so, on his visit there in 1984, did Prince Andrew. But his host, the Governor of the day, did not, and half of him vanished in the sea, spoiling his white duck trousers and splashing his Imperial jacket. The dunking, recorded for British television, remains about the only popular vision Britons have of their far-away possession. (The Governor left soon afterwards, and was offered a posting in a considerably drier segment of the former Empire, in Guyana.)

The quayside was jam-packed with islanders – 'Saints' as they are known by outsiders, 'Yamstocks' as they call themselves, a nickname supposedly derived from the diet of yams on which the island slaves were once fed. Ships are infrequent callers at St Helena these days – the island was for many years on the Union Castle main line, and there would be a liner a fortnight – and any ship, even so small and undistinguished a vessel as a former North Sea dynamite carrier, brings out the crowds. People were jammed up against railings, perched on parapets, shinned up lamp standards, sitting on the old stone walls. There was a buzz of excitement in the air, and many of the eyes shone with tears. Every so often a cheer would go up when a relation or a friend would step on to shore – everyone would cheer, since everyone was a relation, and all were friends.

For all the shortcomings of their isolation in mid-ocean, the Saints are a home-loving people. They loathe the year-long contracts they have to work on Ascension 700 miles north or the four-year scholarships their students take up in Cheltenham, or Southampton. Few places can feel with such intensity the unalloyed pleasure, after years away, of just coming home.

'Three weeks I been away,' said one young man whom I met, and who told me he had been working for the Americans at their base on Ascension. 'Not a long time, I know. But too long for me. I give it up. I miss my brother and my mother. I miss home too much.' He had been a good companion on the boat, had taught me a new card game and had helped me rig a hammock on deck. Now he was back on his beloved island. He vanished into the thickets of friendly brown arms, and it was three days before I saw him, happily nose down in a pint of beer at the Consulate Hotel, surrounded by his workmates. He vowed he would never leave home again.

For him, as for many another islander, St Helena is a place 'with only one entrance, and no exit'. And it feels like an entrance, what is more – you walk along the seafront for fifty yards, then turn inland, cross a narrow bridge over the dry castle moat and pass through a portcullis'd gate, and a wall a dozen feet thick. Inside, to the wonder of all who first enter this unique little ocean city, is the eighteenth century, preserved by happy accident, in every last detail.

'Lifted bodily from Tunbridge Wells,' wrote one visitor, on first seeing the square called Lower Parade. 'A bright-looking tree in the centre . . . but still the capital of a second-class Imperial coaling station,' said another, less kindly, at the turn of the century. '. . . the town resembles St Peter Port, the capital of Guernsey . . .' according to Mrs E. L. Jackson a few years later.

Two rows of Regency houses, all bright paint and high dignity, iron trellis-work and sash windows, look at each other across the main street. In the square there is a castle – whitewashed stone walls with the coat of arms of the Honourable East India Company in red, white and silver, and all enclosing a little courtyard with shade trees and cobblestones and worn stone steps leading to the old offices of the present Governor. There are courts, and the library, and an exquisite public park with peepul trees brought from Hindoostan by John Company's brigantines as they stopped at the island for fresh food, or by the warships back from the India station, and who called for water and coal.

There is a zig-zag path above the park – Governor Patten had it laid out for the pleasure of his two daughters at the beginning of the last century, and it is now called the Sisters' Walk. It was probably the first view of the island seen by the island's most famous resident, Napoleon, and leads to a not insignificant tale

– as does so much in a town that, as the South African writer Lawrence Green suggested, 'holds more of the strong meat of history than any other town in Britain's colonial possessions'.

Napoleon had arrived on the evening of 17th October 1815, to begin his exile (an astonished St Helena had learned about the plan to keep the defeated Emperor on the island only a few days before, when he and his court of twenty-seven French men and women were but a few days' sailing away). The Royal Navy – he had been brought from Plymouth aboard HMS *Northumberland* – decided to bring him ashore at night, to avoid the crowds. Sir George Cockburn, whose flag *Northumberland* flew on this most splendidly Imperial voyage, decided to put the Emperor up – for the first night, at least – in a pleasant Georgian house at the side of the park, and where the government botanist, a Mr Porteous, supplemented his meagre India Office wage by taking in lodgers.

But there was a coincidence, though whether Napoleon was told about it that night, and whether his sleep was thus disturbed, we do not know. It turned out that only a few months before Mr Porteous had rented the very room he now gave to Bonaparte to the man who met and savaged the Emperor at Waterloo – Arthur Wellesley, the First Duke of Wellington.

A few months after Napoleon had arrived – and was by now settled into a very grand mansion in the cool island interior – Wellington learned of the coincidence, and wrote to Admiral Malcolm, who then commanded the naval garrison on the rock of exile. And what is more, when Wellington wrote, he did so from Paris.

'You may tell "Bony",' the Iron Duke scoffed, 'that I find his apartments at the Elisée Bourbon very convenient, and that I hope he likes mine (in St Helena) . . . It is a droll sequel enough to the affairs of Europe that we should change places of residence . . .'

It sometimes seems as if there is more history and a greater fund of anecdotes squeezed into the tiny city of Jamestown than in any other place on earth: it is, after all, a very tiny place indeed, with only 1,500 people jammed into a maze of lanes at the base of a narrow valley, its craggy walls given to collapsing with calamitous regularity.

The monuments tell of real local heroes, like Dr W. J. J. Arnold, whose obelisk stands in the very centre of the parade ground, and which is convenient to read as you step out into the sunshine from the old Consulate Hotel, and take a short walk after breakfast. 'The best friend St Helena ever had,' says the inscription.

He was an Irishman, colonial surgeon, and Acting-Governor for a few weeks before he died in 1925. He, unlike most of his peers, loved the islanders, and did all he could to help. He recognised their poverty and their need. And in turn the island poor worshipped him. He is said never to have charged those who couldn't pay, and would buy medicines for those who couldn't afford them. 'He knew the heart of every poor person on St Helena,' a boatman reminisced to a visitor in the Fifties. An old woman added that, in her view, 'a shiver went through this place the day the doctor died'.

Dr Arnold is one of the few colonial figures the islanders remember with affection: as we shall see later, the British sent to run the colony, and those officials back in London who administered its fortunes, have never been liked or admired by the Saints themselves – except, it seems, Dr Arnold and a very few recent Governors, who seem game to stand up for the islanders' cause, no matter how eccentric the notion seems back at head office.

The Jamestown church – St James's, though presumably not named after the James who was Duke of York when the East India Company annexed the island in 1651 – stands on the right of the parade ground, opposite the castle, beside the tiny prison. It is an unlovely church, with a white stone tower, and, when not blown off by a storm, has a weathervane in the shape of a fish.

Most of the Jamestown aristocracy is buried here, and the same names recur. Benjamin, Thomas ('Throw a stone and hit a Thomas,' the islanders used to say, there were so many of them), Hudson, Young, Green, Yon (descendants of the indentured Chinese workers brought to St Helena by the

Company), Moyce, Maggott, Youde, Jonas. And a batch of classical names, plucked from scholarly memory and given to the freed slaves who arrived here in the mid-nineteenth century, and which exist still as memorials to Victorian enlightenment: Plato, Caesar, Hercules, Mercury. (A Mr Jeff Scipio was enjoying congratulations when I visited the island: he had just repaired a stricken cargo ship by fashioning a new shaft bearing out of eucalyptus wood. The ship managed to get across the Atlantic to Recife, still going strong.)

There is a tablet in St James's to one of the island's great dynastic figures, Mr Saul Solomon, who died in 1892. His ancestor, who was also called Saul, was put ashore, gravely ill, from an India-bound merchantman, in 1790; he recovered, persuaded his brothers Benjamin and Joseph to come down from London and join him in business – one of the very few to have enough confidence and imagination to try to make money in St Helena. (Some would say his considerable success was a testament to his Jewishness, though the family later became Anglicans.)

The first Saul Solomon is said to have tried to help Napoleon escape by smuggling a silken ladder to him, hidden in a teapot. The plot evidently failed, but Solomon's admiration for the Emperor was recognised by the French, who made him French Consul, and gave him a medal when they took Napoleon's body away to be buried in Paris. The dynasty dominated St Helena for generations; it is still barely possible to get by on the island without doing business with Solomon and Company, who brew beer, run a banking service, sell Carnation milk and act as sole agents for the shipping line that is the Saints' only means of escape to the outside world.

Jamestown lies at the base of a valley between two immense ridges of basalt. On the eastern side is Munden's Hill, with the ruins of two batteries; the western side is Ladder Hill, where the old fort, the barracks, the observatory and signal station were built. There is a road that winds and twists its way dangerously along the valley sides, and must be two miles long. But there is also a stairway – a remarkable, unforgettable stairway of 700 stone steps each eleven inches high. (The lowest one is buried, so you only count 699.) The 'Ladder' thus formed must surely count as one of the most extraordinary and breath-taking structures to be found anywhere.

I could hardly believe my eyes when I first saw it. I hadn't read about it in the guidebooks, and the name on the map – Jacob's Ladder – meant nothing. It was the first morning; I was waiting for an appointment to see the Governor, and was mooching about in the square, admiring the tiny fire engine, chatting to the prison guards (only one inmate that day in Empire's tiniest gaol, as 'we normally let our guests out each afternoon to have a swim') and peering behind the minute city power station. It was then that I noticed a flight of steps, flanked on each side by black iron railings, running up the mountainside.

But they didn't end at rooftop height, nor level with St James's steeple. I had to crane my neck right back, until it hurt. The steps went up and up, their steepness apparently increasing as they did so, so that they seemed to curve outwards and become vertical, like a rope ladder into the sky. They went so far and so high that they and their guard rails vanished into a single line, and were just a faint black etching as they reached the lip of Ladder Hill and the fort. It looked like a trick, painted to amuse passing tourists; and for a second I thought it was a cunning piece of *trompe-l'oeil*, until the first schoolboy hurtled down, breathless and grubby, and landed at my feet.

The boys' slide was, a hundred years ago, said to be 'a feat most indescribably terrible to watch'. It began in the days when soldiers from the Ladder Hill barracks had to be on sentry-go down in Jamestown at lunch. The steps had been built, along with a pair of tramways, to help carry ammunition, stores – and, in particular, manure – between fort and city: the soldiers decided it could be used to bring their lunch. Boys were thus directed to climb the stairs – which rise at an average angle of thirty-nine degrees, enough to give most first-time climbers severe vertigo – and fetch tureens of soup. The boys, deter-mined to serve the soup hot, devised a perilous-looking descent: with shoulders over one rail, and ankles over the other, and arms spread along the bars to act as brakes, they would slide

down, tureens balanced on their stomachs. The average time
from taking a squaddy's orders, running up the stairway and
returning with a bowl of steaming mulligatawny was eight
minutes.

And down the boys – and girls – still come, their satchels
where the tureens once were, their mission simply to get out
of school, and back to their homes in Jamestown, as quickly as
possible. Terrible though the slide may be to see, only one
person is said to have been killed on the Ladder, a sailor who
tried the climb after a night in one of the Jamestown pubs. (A
retired colonel lived in the old signal station during the 1950s;
he had perched his bed against a railing overlooking a thousand-
foot drop and, had he rolled over in his sleep, would surely have
fallen. He said he had lost his breakfast cup of tea more than
once, but had never fallen over the edge himself. He died,
peacefully, in his bed, in 1982: he had moved to the Isle of Man.)

Like so many of the great Atlantic rocks, this forty-seven square
mile confection of basalt and banana trees was first glimpsed,
its mist-topped mountains surging theatrically from the warm
seas, by the Portuguese, in 1502. They named the island after
Hellena, mother of Constantine the Great, upon whose birthday
the discovery was made; the spelling was modified on the second
map, and has remained thus ever since.

But despite the evident pleasantness of their find, the Portuguese made no attempt to colonise it. They left some animals
and planted some trees; and eleven years later they called back
on their way home from India, and left behind a nobleman named
Fernando Lopez, who had been mutilated, in Goa, for desertion,
and who had stowed away on the ship. The Goanese magistracy
had cut off his nose, his ears, his right hand and the little finger
of his left – so it was perhaps hardly surprising he decided,
rather than carry on home to meet Mrs Lopez, to stay alone on
this charming, if deserted island. He hid in a cave until the ship
had left, only to find that his shipmates had taken pity on him,
and left him a barrel of biscuits and a fire, which he kept alight
for months.

A year later a southbound ship stopped by; a terrified Lopez fled into the jungle. When he emerged, and the ship had gone, he found more food and clothes, and a letter telling him not to be afraid, but to present himself next time his countrymen turned up. But he wouldn't. For a decade he would run and hide whenever he sighted a sail. A letter from King John III offering him a free pardon and safe passage back to Lisbon had no effect.

But then a ship was wrecked and its sole survivor, a Javanese slave boy, came ashore to join Lopez. Romantics might wish the boy to have been Friday to Lopez's Crusoe, but in fact they loathed each other; and when the next Portuguese ship stopped in the bay, the child betrayed Lopez, and led the sailors to his hiding place. He agreed, eventually, to come back to Europe. He was a great celebrity; he was seen by the King and Queen, and went on to Rome to confess his sins before the Pope who asked him – according to this most charming of St Helenian legends – what his greatest wish might be. 'I yearn to go back to the peace of St Helena,' he is supposed to have said; and so went back, and lived for thirty further years in the valley where Jamestown now stands. 'He cultivated a great many gourds, pomegranates and palm-trees,' a Portuguese history relates. 'He kept ducks, hens, sows and she-goats with young, all of which increased largely, and all became wild in the woods.'

When I stayed on the island in 1983 I lived with a couple of similar pioneering spirit, keen to return to quieter ways, eager for island solitude. He had been an electrician in Devon; he had always yearned to go to St Helena; when he retired he took a ship there, and bought – for a pittance – a splendid Georgian mansion near a hill called Mount Eternity. Then came his wife and all his worldly goods, his books, his billiards table, his electronic organ; the couple settled there to farm, to read and live out a peaceful conclusion to their lives. They seemed wholly content with their choice, and not in the least concerned with their distance from home, and friends, and intellectual stimulus. I used to waken every day at seven when the flock of geese began to cackle madly; when I went down into the garden that was cool and fresh with dew I would find him, picking each goose up in his arms, cuddling it, and kissing it lightly on the beak.

The Portuguese managed, more by luck than judgement, to keep their discovery of St Helena totally secret for nearly a hundred years. Luckily – and rather oddly – no other nation's ships strayed close to the island; and it was not until the English sea rover, John Cavendish, captured and looted a Spanish galleon and carefully read the ship's pilot, that anyone learned of the approximate position of the island. He sailed there in 1588, finding 'a valley . . . marvellously sweet and pleasant, and planted in every place with fruit trees or with herbs'. There were some slaves on the island, and thousands of goats, which proved a pest, gnawing everything to pieces. But pleasant as the island was, Cavendish did not colonise it either; nor did any of the Dutch or French or Portuguese or Spanish sailors who stopped by in succeeding years. They simply used it as a watering station, left letters under a prominent boulder (the practice of using remote islands as mid-ocean post-boxes was then well established, with outbound masters leaving mail for homebound ships to collect and deliver at their final port), and collected fruit and vegetables and fresh meat.

The Dutch finally claimed it, in 1633, but never occupied it permanently, and when the Cape Settlement in Africa was established, promptly abandoned it (though they did send expeditions there to look for fruit trees; Cape Town's best-known variety of peach comes from the island, via one of those early Dutch expeditions). But this was, in Britain, the time of the great royal trading companies, and it was not long before the merchant adventurers of the City reached out into the South Atlantic. Armed with capital of seventy-two thousand pounds (more than thirty times the capitalised value of the Bermuda Company half a century before), the East India Company annexed the island, claimed it in the Company's name, and, using the four vessels *Dragon*, *Hector*, *Ascension* and *Susan*, occupied it and set about building a fort.

Within two years the island had a charter; and although it was attacked by the Dutch in 1673, the force was routed in a matter of weeks and guns were erected and batteries installed so that any further attacks would be repulsed. A new charter was issued on 16th December 1673 – it can still be seen at the Castle – and

St Helena was from that day on indubitably, in theory perpetually and, as it has turned out, rather less than fortunately, ruled by the British.

At first it was a happy little place. Posters went up in London advertising its charms, and after the Great Fire in 1666, scores of homeless Cockneys set sail for a new life on the new possession. Their Cockney accent is still very much a part of the strange tongue that is spoken on St Helena – an accent that is part Devon, part Hottentot, part Olde English, and with that curious transposition of v and w so often mentioned in Dickens. The purest form of St Helenian speech, delivered with machine-gun rapidity and intensity, can still be found among the fishermen, and Lawrence Green was able to quote an entire conversation: 'Dere was sumting say bout Govinmint ought to send for nets and men to sho how to ketch fish. Tcha! man, foolish . . . us can ketch fish better den orrer fellers. You know, sir, when us get gude luck and plentee fish and tinks for once will get couple shillings dem wimmin in fish maarket stick up fer price. When peepil see plentee fish and price high they buy little tinking bum-bye cheap. Us poor fishmin get werry little.'

The islanders tilled and planted, raised their cattle and pigs, built their cottages and generally turned the island's interior into the soft, green countryside they had left behind to the north. The legacy of those early farmers remains: for although St Helena, ringed with frightening cliffs and with inhospitable mountains frowning over all, has a wild, prison-like aspect for many visitors, the inner valleys and meadows are as charming and delicate as any in southern England. Those refugees from London soothed and teased all the harshness from the island's rugged topography, and left it a model of what they thought lay down the road from Spitalfields and Lambeth.

(They lived in a time of terrible discipline, though: when a woman named Elizabeth Starling beat up the captain of a visiting ship she was stripped naked and given fifteen lashes, and then ducked three times; thieving slaves had their hands cut off; and when two runaway apprentices stole a gun and shot a pig each had the tip of an ear sliced off, the letter 'R' branded on to his forehead, and a pair of pothooks rivetted around his neck before being flogged from one end of Jamestown to the other.)

The polyglot community filled up with slaves, Chinese indentured labourers, Malays, Madagascans, Indians – and still more Englishmen and Scots lured by promises of comfort and opportunity. The array of inhabitants and visitors produced bewildering complications: there was no island currency, and at one time a treasurer complained that among the coinage in common use in Jamestown were gold dubloons, mohurs from Bengal, moidores, star pagodas, gold gubbers and Venetian sequins, as well as rupees and ducatoons, German crowns, Marie Thérèse dollars, joes from Portugal, guilders from Holland, rixdollars, francs and English shillings.

A steady cavalcade of the distinguished dropped by: Edmund Halley, the astronomer who gave his name to the comet, came to the mountains of St Helena to observe the transit of Mercury; fog obscured his view, and it often swirls over the flax-covered hill that bears his name, and where he mounted his telescope. Captain Bligh looked in, and presented some breadfruit which he was taking from Tahiti to Jamaica. Captain Cook, on his way back from Antarctica, spent a few days on the island, and made some pointed criticisms of the islanders' agricultural methods. HMS *Beagle* stood off for six days in 1836 when Charles Darwin made as near as possible a complete inventory of the unique flora and fauna. (Not all of it home-grown: the British brought in furze and blackberry, frogs and rabbits, and an enthusiastic naturalist, Phoebe Moss, released five mynah birds at a country house in mid-island, and the colony is now thick with them. But the wirebird, a small fat plover which lives in the Kaffir figs, is unique; and the depredations of the voracious native white ant have become a St Helena legend. They had an eccentric liking for theological books, and contentedly munched their way through the entire library, leaving only the bindings. Hardly a house has escaped the attentions of their jaws; the main staircase at the Castle collapsed with a roar one night and had to be replaced by a cast-iron model brought out at great expense from England.)

'Without Napoleon, there would be no St Helena,' the French Consul once remarked to me. And it was, indeed, fortunate for the island that it had so illustrious a prisoner. The other choices for his confinement, according to Lord Liverpool's notes of the time, were St Lucia, the Tower of London, Fort William, Dumbarton Castle, Gibraltar, Malta and the Cape of Good Hope – one trembles to think of the present state of St Helena had the Emperor not been exiled there, and the island had been forgotten by everyone. His six progressively more wretched years – they started well enough, playing whist and blind-man's buff with the flirtatious Betty Balcombe in the house that is now the island's cable station – effectively produced two more colonies for Britain.

A garrison had to be sent to Ascension Island, and another to Tristan da Cunha, to foil any French adventures to free their subject. The houses constructed by the soldiers and marines, and later inhabited by some of them who opted to remain, formed the basis of pioneering colonial settlements; and St Helena, too, benefited hugely from the military interest placed upon her in consequence of her notorious guest. Nearly 3,000 soldiers were camped up on Deadwood Plain, within easy sight of the house eventually chosen for Napoleon's residence (and now, like his empty grave, the property of the people of France, and presided over by a resident consul, complete with tricolour and diplomatically immune motor car).

Such cruise ships as arrive at Jamestown today do so because of Longwood House. Here are the mournful portraits and the billiard tables, the marble busts and the formal gardens where Napoleon walked along deeply incised paths so his hated sentries would not see him. There are the wooden shutters from behind which the Emperor would gaze at the stars – one hole for his telescope when he was standing, another below it for when he sat. Here is Vignali's massive sideboard, used for the celebration of Mass, and there the great copper bath in which Napoleon would lie, soaking gently and dictating his memoirs. The visitors can twirl, if the watchman is dozing in the sun, the globes of earth and sky which still bear the marks of the Emperor's fingernails; and they come to see the deathbed.

And one can scrabble about in the garden to look for shards of glass from old French wine bottles: no greater evidence of British insolence can be found, French visitors believe. For the Governor of the day, the much-loathed Sir Hudson Lowe, had demanded of the Emperor that, after drinking wine, he return his empties to the British Government. Napoleon, not surprisingly, angrily refused, and had his staff smash the bottles and scatter the glass among the roses.

I met a pretty young girl one afternoon at Longwood House, walking around the gardens in a dress that looked uncannily out of date. She was, it turned out, from California, and worked at a dull task, punching out pieces for the insides of a computer. She had become obsessed by the sad story of Napoleon since her childhood, and had vowed to visit the island of his exile. Easier said than done. She worked hard, earned the necessary money to get across to England to catch the once-every-twelve-weeks boat from Bristol to St Helena.

This was her second visit. She had had some dresses made, along the lines of those worn by Josephine. A hairdresser had shaped her blonde hair in ringlets, just like the most famous painting of Josephine. And thus armed and fashioned, this other-wise normal young lady from San Mateo would glide around Longwood, or sit on the empty grave beneath the willows with wildflowers in her hand. She would read, and dream, and compose odd poems about the inhumanity of Sir Hudson Lowe and Britons involved in the defeat and humiliation of her hero.

She had ample reason to dislike the Government a few weeks after I first met her. An order was issued from the Castle dismissing her from the island, and though she hid in a clump of bushes, two policemen dragged her out and forced her on to a ship. I saw her in London a few weeks later: she was deeply hurt, and considered she had suffered as awful an injustice as had Bonaparte. The islanders had a soft spot for her, too, and were sorry to see her go. 'Pretty girl,' said the old man who drove me around. 'A bit touched. But 'armless enough. Very American, I 'spose.'

The Crown took over all the running of the island in 1834; of all the disasters attendant upon St Helena's history, this was quite probably the worst. None of the islanders wanted the change; most were appalled at the cavalier way King William's men dismissed faithful Company servants, slashed budgets, reduced the status of the island to a mere cipher in the grand colonial roll. Hundreds left the island for good, and settled in Cape Colony, or came to England. The Governors chosen to rule on the Sovereign's behalf – no longer, that is, as representative of the Court of Directors – were henceforth the pygmies of Empire, paid less money, and less attention, than any other Excellency in any other colony. (The Governor of Nigeria by tradition always received the highest salary; the man in Jamestown Castle took home about a sixth as much.)

The tradition of exile and imprisonment of Her Majesty's enemies, evidently spurred on by the success of Napoleon's banishment, took hold; the Chief of the Zulus stayed there with his two uncles, and learned to play hymns on the piano; 6,000 Boer prisoners, including General Cronje, were put into huge prisoner-of-war camps up on the high meadows. Both groups evidently loved the island and its inhabitants, and one Boer baker was still alive and working in Jamestown sixty years after the end of the war. There was an elderly Zulu living on the island in the 1980s. The prison industry did brief wonders for the Saints' economy: it was said that during the Boer War the place was crowded, rich and extraordinarily happy. But then the Boers went away, peace returned, and the old habits of neglectful superintendence once more held sway.

There were all manner of brave but brief agricultural experiments. St Helena coffee was briefly famous, particularly as Napoleon had said he liked it. A London firm was sent samples: 'we find it of very superior quality and flavour, and if cultivated to any extent would no doubt amply repay the grower.' It wasn't. Admiral Elliot ordered cinchona trees to be planted, and for a while the island produced quinine. But later Governors wearied of the idea, and the plantation was allowed to run wild.

Only New Zealand flax did well. The huge plants, with their spiky leaves that often grew ten feet long, covered thousands of the island's upland acres. The Colonial and Fibre Company built the first mill in 1874: seven more were put up over the next twenty years, and a rope factory was built in the 1920s. The familiar whine of the flax scutchers, stripping the long fibres from the leaves, echoed across the hills for half a century. At its peak the noble *Phormium tenax* gave employment to 400 men, and the little factories made cloth, rope, tow and hemp, which was sold to the British Post Office to make string for tying up bundles of letters. A fifth of the hemp went to make Admiralty ropes – the *Manual of Seamanship* still quotes the breaking strain of St Helena hemp.

But this reliance on the flax industry proved, ultimately, as injurious to the St Helenian economy as was the making of lime juice to Montserrat or the milling of sugar in Barbados – too much of a concentration in one product meant, inevitably, that the colony became a prisoner of its customers' whims. In this particular case the fatal day came when the Post Office decided it would be cheaper to use nylon twine for its bundles, and abandoned its contract with the faraway Saints. At about the same time the world price of flax and hemp dropped – St Helena's crop no longer had a ready market.

But that was not the only reason. No one disputes that the Colonial Office must take the responsibility for its lamentable decision to turn St Helena into a one-crop island; but its sorry management of the finances of that crop contributed also to the economic disaster that followed, as a brief explanation will show.

Fluctuations in the price of hemp gravely affected the island, and it was agreed after the Second World War that the Government would help. It did so in a cunning manner. If the market price fell below a certain level, the millers would receive a subsidy. If it rose above the level, however, the Government would charge export duty. The net result was that more duty was paid in than subsidy was paid out – so the Government's 'support' was carried out at no effective cost.

Nevertheless, the subsidy was regarded as irksome – not so much by the Castle, who tried to support the sole industry, but by London. On New Year's Eve 1965 the then Governor, John Field, called the two major mill-owners to his office: from the next day the basic wage of government workers on the island would be doubled (to two pounds fifty a week – well below the poverty line, and about a tenth of the wage then paid in England), and to help finance the increase, and at the insistence of London, the flax subsidy would be removed, instantly, and with no right of appeal.

The industry collapsed. The Government had no other ideas for the mills, and one by one, they all closed. The last scutcher sounded its rasping note in midsummer 1966. The Foreign Office, at whose behest the industry essentially collapsed, was accused of 'grave irresponsibility' by one miller; but appeared to show no remorse.

Coffee, quinine, flax – and shipping; a litany of failures and mishaps, poor planning, bad decision-making, the steel-eyed rule of uncaring accounts-men and faraway time-servers. Nothing could be done, of course, to help the island when the Suez Canal opened in 1869 and the steamers bound for India no longer called at this convenient mid-ocean coaling station; when the Navy switched to oil the need for St Helena diminished further, and the last vessel recorded as having taken on some tons of Welsh steam coal for some Imperial adventure, or duty, was in the 1920s. Even before that there seemed to the War Office no real point in maintaining a garrison at the top of Ladder Hill once the coal was gone and the island's strategic value was devalued.

And nothing could prevent the Union Castle line – 'Intermediate Vessels carrying First and Tourist class passengers are despatched at intervals from London for Cape Town, proceeding via Grand Canary and with calls with Mails at Ascension and St Helena' – from withdrawing its service. There had been two cargo vessels, one each way each month. But they were cancelled in 1967, and the final lifeline, the Cape Mail Service, was ended a decade later. Since then a single ship run by a firm in Cornwall, helped by a huge and grudgingly given government subsidy, has provided the colony's only means of physical contact with the outside.

All the enginework of Empire remains on St Helena. In the Castle there are vast airy rooms hung with the oil paintings of past Governors – Robert Jenkins (of the War of Jenkins' Ear – there is a plaque on his cottage at Sandy Bay), Charles Dallas, Sir Harry Cordeaux, Sir Edward Hay Drummond-Hay. There are shelves of leather-bound books of great age, rubbed with beeswax and fragrant still. Clocks tick gently and when they strike, the booms shake the bougainvillaea and the banana fronds beyond the ever-open windows. There are great silver inkwells and blotters to match; in His Excellency's office there is a spyhole so that his assistants – such as the Colonial Treasurer, the last to hold that title in the Empire that remains – can see if he may be disturbed. One expects periwigs and vellum, sealing-wax and quills, and the courtly language of Victoria's diplomats, and the prosy essays to the Court of Directors. If there is a telex (and there must be, since the Foreign Office lists a number, 202) its vulgar presence is well concealed.

Plantation House, where Governors have lived since the East India Company built the mansion in 1792, is a gem – perhaps the loveliest house available for any senior British diplomat anywhere, though it is neither as large, nor as smartly furnished as some of the residences elsewhere, as Paris, Singapore, or Vienna. When I arrived the Deputy Governor was busily moving in; His Excellency had departed for home leave, and his Deputy wasn't going to miss the opportunity to spend a few weeks in the place. 'Best thing about the job,' he said. 'Pay's rotten, as you know. But did you ever see such a perfect place as this?'

Visitors – if invited, and deemed at all important – arrive by black Jaguar (a silver crown in place of a number plate, and a small Union flag with the St Helena arms on the fly), which whispers up the gravel drive scattering the four tortoises which are, invariably, busily munching up the lawn. The tortoises are named Emma, Myrtle, Freda and Jonathan, the last – the biggest – said by experts to be 255 years old. Whether he has attained that great age – and he is blind, and staggers more than tortoises usually do – he is documented as having munched across the lawns for at least a hundred summers, and doubtless did the same on lawns in Mauritius for some years before. A Rothschild tried to buy one to take home, but was refused, whereupon the animal he wanted threw itself over a cliff. But however

Methuselan the qualities of the Plantation House Quartet, they are not, by St Helena standards, as big as some of the local turtles. Many islanders remember an 800-pounder being landed – it provided soup for two regiments for three days, and the shell was used by a soldier as a roof for a new house he was building for his family.

Plantation House, staffed by a dozen servants decked out in starched uniforms of white and sky blue, is quiet and fragrant. As in all colonial government houses there are portraits of the Queen and Prince Philip, and a photograph of the Prime Minister; there are acres of polished oak floors and polished mahogany tables, of silver salvers and Spode china dinner sets, each with a crown and a dark blue rim. The older rooms have brass plaques above each doorway – Governor's Room, Admiral's Room, General's Room – dating from the Company days, and there is one room with a plaque saying 'Chaos' outside, and which is said to house a friendly poltergeist who hurls chairs about at night.

There is also a quite magnificent library, built by Sir Hudson Lowe during Napoleon's stay – presumably to occupy his mind with other than the vexing matter of his dangerous neighbour. Distinguished visitors were often asked to address St Helenian society in the library: Joshua Slocum, who called in on his solo circumnavigation in his tiny boat *Spray*, recalled meeting Paul Kruger in Pretoria. When he told him he was going around the world Kruger snorted and said, 'You mean *across* the world, young man!' The crusty old Boer still believed the world was flat.

Every nut and bolt of the Imperial machine remains in St Helena, preserved in the amber of her isolation. There is a colonial policeman, in charge of a police force known as the Toys. The last chief came from Birmingham, and by marrying a local girl quite scandalised the island Establishment (though the Attorney-General did the same, and promptly took the stunningly pretty Saint off to a new posting on the Caribbean island of Anguilla). One advantage of the chief's marriage is that he became wholly accepted by the island community, to the point of being given a nickname. Islanders take nicknames quite seriously: there was a Conger Kidneys, a Cheese, a Fishcake, a Biffer and a Bumper. The police chief, for reasons perhaps better known to his wife, was called Pink Balls.

There is a fully-fledged bishop, too, and a cathedral that was prefabricated in England and brought out to the island on a ship. The bishop presides over the smallest diocese in the Anglican communion (though the largest in area – it extends all the way up to Ascension Island, and while only having 7,000 souls, looks after an almighty stretch of ocean). He and his priests, who are recruited in England for thirty-month contracts, seem not the slightest bit reluctant to marry off young islanders who quite cheerfully bring a baby or two along to the wedding ceremony. Half the children born on the island are, technically, illegitimate. The islanders who dote upon all children call them 'spares', and if they are old enough to take part in the bacchanal that usually follows an island wedding, are welcomed like old and much-favoured relatives. Since the ceremony legitimises them they, too, have something to celebrate.

Both police and church worry about the growing crime rate. Some blame the fact that many islanders now work on Ascension, and come back full of American ideas (many of the jobs on the dependency being for the US Navy, or NASA, or PanAm). Some say video cassette recorders, of which there are a number on the island, bring evil in their train. Whatever the cause, there has been a dismal increase in misbehaviour. There have been three murders since 1980 (the previous killing was eighty years before; in some intervening years so little crime was committed that the magistrates were presented with white silk gloves as a token of island innocence). Murder trials, almost without precedent in living memory, are major events: a judge has to come from Gibraltar, defence lawyers must be brought out from England, and on conviction the prisoner must be taken to Parkhurst to serve his time – the island prison being too small and insecure. The St Helena Governor petitions the Home Office in London under the terms of the Colonial Prisoners (Removal) Act.

All the institutions that provide a link with 'home' are lovingly nurtured. There are Boy Scouts (the 1st Jamestown Troop, shorts still worn, and socks with flashes) and their Guides, an

Armistice Day parade, an Agricultural Show, a St Helena Band and a specially composed St Helena march. And there is cricket, played on the only piece of level ground on the island, about the size of a postage stamp (one of the island's only ways of making money is through the sale of stamps) and with deep ravines on all four sides. (They say that if they could find another piece of level ground they would build an airfield, which might solve the island's problems overnight.) The ravines have caused problems in the past: during one match a fielder, running backwards for a high ball, fell off the edge and was killed. The scorecard, as laconically as befits the sport, recorded his passing by writing '*Retired, Dead*'. The Governor of the day built a fence along the boundary, and a ball that falls down the cliff scores six.

And along with the trappings of Empire, so also a real affection for its leaders. It is rare to find a house in St Helena, no matter how humble a shack, without its picture of the Queen, or the Queen Mother, or Princess Diana and Prince Charles, pinned over the mantel. Sometimes it is an official portrait, bought from Solomon's store; more usually it is a gravure print torn carefully from the likes of *Woman's Own*. Once I called at a small house on Piccolo Hill and asked the woman, in passing, if she had a portrait. She reddened, and looked briefly terror-struck. 'I'm terrible sorry but I've not,' she stammered. 'I had no idea they'd be sending anybody up to check.' It took some time to convince her I was not from the Castle, testing the loyalty of Her Majesty's most distant subjects.

In every apparent way, then, St Helena is, or seems to be, British. The people, from whatever ethnic origin, all sound like friends of Sam Weller; they have their own version of the BBC relayed down to them each day; they get the *Telegraph* and the *Observer* at the local library; there are still Humbers and Veloxes and Minis parked on the streets; people eat marmalade, and fishcakes, and stop in mid-afternoon for tea.

But there are two signal differences between the citizenry of St Helena and Her Majesty's subjects back home in Britain.

The Saints, first, are poor. There is no work for them, barring a few jobs in the vestigial fishing industry (an industry which by rights should take off – the island is surrounded by rich fishing grounds, and one day I sat next to a man with a bamboo pole and a hook and who pulled tunny out of the sea at the rate of one every two seconds). Almost all capable males, aside from those who go to Ascension, or crew ships away at sea, are employed by the Government – digging holes and filling them in again, in effect.

London complains that its aid to the island amounts to about a thousand pounds per head – more than to anywhere else on earth (except the Falkland Islands since the 1982 war). But in effect most of that money is paid out in wages – and, by British standards, derisory wages they are, too. I spent some time with a man who lived in a tiny cottage overlooking Sandy Bay. His family of ten and his eight cats lived with him. He worked as a labourer for the Public Works Department, and was paid twenty-six pounds a week – 'hardly enough' he admitted. The nearest shop was five miles away, and sometimes one of his daughters walked the entire way barefoot. Living, he said, was 'very hard'.

And yet he was loyal, did have a picture of Prince Charles hanging in the living room, thought the Falklands War was an excellent thing and was sorry not to have gone himself. He would have done anything to fight for Her Majesty, to show how British and loyal he was. The only thing was . . .

And then he raised the second point – a point which came up again and again during my stay. Why – just why – were the islanders not counted as Britons by the Government back home? The Falklanders and the Gibraltarians were: why not the Saints? 'These are not primitive tribesmen or coolies,' as the South African, Lawrence Green, put it two decades ago. 'These are a unique and truly multi-racial community of considerable natural intelligence and loyalty . . .' So why does Britain not take them in – more precisely, why, by the passage of the British National-ity Act, did Britain seek to exclude them from the privileges of Britishness, and yet still rule them?

After all, islanders would keep mentioning to me – the Charter was our guarantee. The Charter promised we would have rights.

I first learned about the famous Charter – famous, that is, to every St Helenian – one sunny afternoon, when I was strolling up Napoleon Street in Jamestown. I was passing a little café, where motherly waitresses bring tea and buns each afternoon (and barracuda fishcakes for supper), and where the customers are slow old ladies in enormous summery hats who look like refugees from a Women's Institute in England, only rather more tanned. One lady stepped out of the shadows as I passed and, with a quick look up and down the street to make sure no one was watching, thrust an envelope into my hand.

Inside was a letter, and a leatherette-covered diary for the year half gone, with more writing inside, and a five-pound note. It asked me to send a copy of my researches to a Saint who now lived in Yorkshire, and to make sure that 'the sad matter of our Nationality is raised back in London. The Charter says we are British, and can come to Britain any time we want. But we can't. The Government won't let us. They won't admit we are full citizens. It is very unjust. We were colonised by British people, from Britain. And now they turn us away. We want to know why?'

The document, preserved in the Castle, is written in the name of King Charles II. It is very long. The section that most Saints know by heart – or have since the Nationality Act was passed in London – runs as follows:

Wee do for us, our heirs and successors declare . . . that all and every the persons being our subjects which do or shall inhabit within the said port or island, and every their children and posterity which shall happen to be borne within the presincts thereof shall have and enjoy all liberties, franchises, immunities, capacities and abilities, of franchises and natural subjects within any of our dominions, to all intents and purposes as if they had been abiding and borne within this our realms of England or in any of our dominions . . .

In other words, the Saints are, by ancient right, as British as had they been born in Sevenoaks, or Knotty Ash. So why have they had their privileges stripped from them? And will they get them back?

A long and energetic campaign has been mounted on their behalf. (The island's Anglican synod sent a telegram to Downing Street, which raised some eyebrows.) Calculations were made showing that even if they were handed proper British passports, and not the half-worthless ersatz papers they have today, only about 800 would ever come to settle in Britain. 'Hardly a flood,' said one islander. 'You've nothing to be afear'd of.'

But the Government seems in no mood to budge. There was a debate in the House of Lords late in 1984, at which friends of the island, men such as Lord Buxton and Lord Cledwyn (who went there in 1958, returned home shocked at the poverty and neglect, and wrote an article in the *Daily Mirror* entitled 'Paradise on the Dole'), spoke with passion and eloquence about the sad fate of this most enchanting island. But Lady Young, representing the polite but unyielding face of Mrs Thatcher's immigration policy, said she had no plans to change the law. Of Britain's remaining colonies only the Falklands and Gibraltar enjoyed the privilege of total national equality; the remainder – Hong Kong, in particular, which promises millions of Cantonese at Heathrow should the strictures be relaxed – are, to all intents and purposes, peopled by aliens. (Unkinder critics noted that the Falkland Islanders and the Gibraltarians enjoy one other unique quality within the Empire – a quality which may or may not have been wholly unconnected with the decision to reserve the privilege of full British nationality to them. They are white. The Foreign Office regards such suggestions as unworthy.)

So – a 'ridiculous dwarf of a Colony'; a 'Cinderella'; 'Paradise on the Dole'; 'Distress on St Helena'; 'Bleak Outlook – Colonial Office largely responsible'; 'Hard Times on Forgotten Isle'; 'Famous Island the World has forgotten'. These were all headlines from the Forties and Fifties. And there were smaller, more human tragedies – like the story of the island's only leper, who lived alone on Rupert's Bay, and who was sent a second-hand gramophone by a well-meaning lady in Eastbourne. The Government charged him threepence duty on every single record.

Or the time there was a bus crash on Christmas Eve, and ten islanders were hurt. The Governor found he couldn't alert anyone in the Foreign Office for seven days, and it took the best part of a month before a doctor came out. The only recorded remark from an island Colonial Service man was that he was sorry for some friends of his, because the crash had meant they had lost a good cook. Delays in answering telegrams are still considerable; John Massingham, a recent Governor, complained publicly of the second-rate clerks who manned the island 'desk' in London, and said it often took months, and several reminders, before a simple request would be answered, or even acknowledged.

Successive British Governments, in short, have little to be proud of in their running of this lovely place. Poor decisions, ignorance, insouciance, obstruction and unkindness have characterised British rule in the past. It seems so unfair a lot for so good-hearted and so loyal a people.

The memory of them that will remain with me for a long, long while is of a Sunday morning at the Sandy Bay Baptist Church, a tiny stone chapel perched on a bluff overlooking the ocean. Twelve people had toiled up the hills to Matins, and the old minister, his ancient and threadbare suit buttoned, his shoes lovingly polished, was leading them in song. There was no organ, nor a piano. Just thirteen devout old islanders, dogged, perspiring in the summer heat. Their thin voices rose out into the valley. 'Lead us, Heavenly Father, lead us . . .' they sang.

It might have been Devon, or Cumberland, or Suffolk, on a summer Sunday morning. When the service was over the people shook the minister's hand and then, in small family groups, straggled off down the hillside, and back for a Sunday lunch of tuna and rice, blackberry duff and island-brewed beer.

Life continues to a noble and unmistakably British routine on St Helena. It has for 300 years. It probably will for many more, though times will get harder, the suits will get a little shabbier, lunches will get more frugal still. As it was for Napoleon, so this island has become a rock of exile for a British way of life – a way of life now only to be found in Britain in isolated rural retreats.

Unwittingly the St Helenians have preserved it and, come what may, they seem determined to preserve it for a long while still to come. Five thousand miles from their imagined home the Saints, forgotten and forlorn, go marching on.

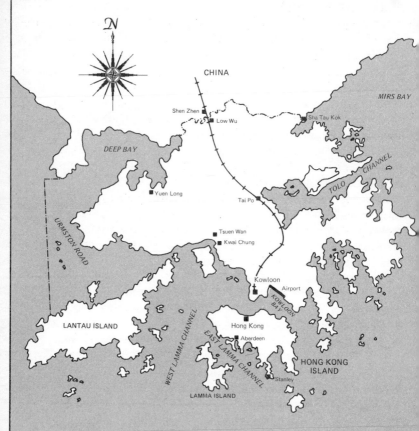

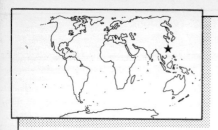

SEVEN

HONG KONG

It was Easter Saturday and there was a watchnight service at the cathedral church of St John, in the part of Hong Kong which the old-timers call Victoria, and which today's millions simply call Central.

It was April, and the steamy heat of South China rolled like a fog through the open doors of the half-empty church, to be beaten down, for the comfort of the worshippers, by the relentlessly thwacking fans. The fans looked as though they had been twirling and swaying away through a million Matins and an eternity of Evensongs, and looked most unsafe, as all tropical fans do; they were suspended on long iron rods from the vaulting, and parishioners would glance up from time to time, to make sure all the nuts were secure, and that decapitation was not imminent.

St John's is a church built very much in the Imperial mould. The foundation stone was laid in 1847, just six years after the colony was established, and the gothic building, with its solid square tower and great stained-glass east window was placed ideally for the spiritual benefits of the colonial servants and grandees. Government House was but a few steps away – though up the very devil of a slope, the locals grumbled – and Flagstaff House, and the Club, the barracks, the parade ground, the cricket ground and the City Hall were all nearby, downhill, towards the harbour and the bustle of the shops.

On the old maps, the cathedral stands squarely and centrally,

in apparently comfortable charge of the colony's purpose and
well-being, as the Church of England so very often was. It is on
Queen's Road (Albert Road is just above and beyond, as we
might expect), and Victorian prints show it rising well above the
mess of vaguely Italianate warehouses. It was, in all the prints,
white-limed and pristine, modelled on the unassuming churches
of the English provinces, those in Cheltenham, or Carlisle,
or Weston-super-Mare. The building was unspectacular and
pleasing, made to reassure rather than to impress, a cosy chunk
of home, out here in the merciless Orient.

Today it is more difficult to find. In all today's classic pictures
of modern Hong Kong – whether they are taken from the Peak,
or from the crowded waterway below – there seems to be no
church. It does, however, still exist, though it is well hidden by
skyscraping monsters of steel and glass, monuments to the
newer religions of the market-place. There is one view, taken
from the upper terminus of the Peak Tram, where you can see
Government House and the Botanical Gardens, and some of the
green of what they now call Chater Gardens (and which was the
cricket pitch, beside the Bank of China, where teams once had
to play beneath huge pictures of Mao tse-Tung, and exhortations
to the Cantonese proletariat). You can see some of the reliquary
pieces of old British Hong Kong – but you cannot quite see the
church. Unless you look very closely; and then, behind the east
wing of the Government buildings and hunkered down under the
glittering slabs of the Hilton Hotel, there is the tower, the
limewash a little faded, the brickwork a little crumbled, but
unmistakably and reassuringly C. of E. Once it rose as the
emblem of all that the Colonial Empire liked to think it stood
for; today it has been utterly submerged by more mercenary
realities.

Similar watchnight services were, no doubt, being conducted
at a dozen other old Imperial cathedrals and chapels in the nearby
time zones. The Archbishops of Auckland and Papua New
Guinea, the Bishops of Busan and Kuching, of West Malaysia
and Riverina, of Gippsland and Wangaratta, would be leading
their flocks in the Nicene Creed and the Eucharist conducted in
a variety of languages and accents. In all those churches, though,

the congregations would, largely, be locals – Malays or Aussies or pidgin-speaking Papuans: only a few expatriates, businessmen on short term assignment, or diplomats, would be there, sharing in the hymns, listening to the sermon.

But in Hong Kong the devout were nearly all Britons. A few Christian Cantonese were there, in pews near the west door; but the cathedral looked that night as though it still was peopled by those for whom it was first built – the governing élite of this most distant, most extraordinary colony. The typical colonial family was at every pew, kneeling on red woollen sacks prepared by the Ladies' Volunteers, reading from prayer books furnished by the British and Foreign Bible Society, gazing up at brass plaques commemorating the passing of the various Governors and Chief Secretaries, Chief Justices and Commissioners who had kept the place ticking over for the century and a half of its colonial existence.

We lit candles, and held them in small wax paper cups; they guttered in the breeze from the fans. Outside the palm trees thrashed as a squall passed over, and the choristers had to work hard to make themselves heard over the jungle noises. The organ – one of the finest in the East, said the old *Kelly and Walsh* guide – squawked and rasped, and as we knelt to pray for Her Majesty the Queen and all her subjects there was a sheet of lightning and a rumble of thunder from a storm coming eastwards from Lantau Island.

With Communion over we strolled out of the cool old building. It was just after midnight – Sunday morning now, and still very warm. Heavy drips of rainwater were falling from all the leaves, the pavements were slimy underfoot, and steamed gently. The Bishop shook hands as we left the porch, and bade us all a peaceful holiday. Down a flight of stone stairs, along a small gorge made of granite blocks, all covered with moss and foliage, and then, suddenly, with a blaze of light, a clatter and a shriek and the urgent banging of a great jackhammer, we were back in the Hong Kong of today.

Ahead was a sea of multicoloured neon – all glaring steadily red and orange and white, for the laws of the colony do not permit neon signs to flash or twinkle. Taxis hooted, trolleybuses clanked, roadside stalls did business to unending streams of passers-by, selling steamed prawns and plastic dolls, small radio sets and diamonds, and all under the friendly hiss of pressure lamps with their attendant clouds of flying insects. Gleaming shopping centres were still open, their escalators lifting the crowds out of the crowded streets into the luxuriant acres where you could still, even at this hour, have a suit made, buy a computer, have your palm read or buy anything up to forty flavours of American ice cream, in any currency or with any small sliver of creditworthy plastic you could name.

Newspaper stalls were on every corner: the first editions of the *South China Morning Post* were out, with the football results from England; there was the *Asian Wall Street Journal*, the previous day's *Melbourne Age* and *Sydney Morning Herald*, and the *Los Angeles Times* and West Coast edition of the *New York Times*. Dozens of papers in Cantonese – and a smaller number in Mandarin – jostled for space, and there were a thousand magazines, most of which seemed either to have something to do with girls, popular computers, horse racing or yachting. The stallkeepers, who also sold cigarettes and matches, chewing gum and trinkets, were yelling the news of the arrival of the *Post*, and were collecting custom, too; business was evidently good this Sunday morning.

The jackhammers thudded constantly. The sound came from a gigantic half-finished building which soared into the dark sky, though great arclights turned every inch of steel into silver, and the workers who crawled and clambered up its spars were like theatrical performers, acrobats spotlit in some magnificent aerial circus. This was the project of which the colony was currently most proud – the new headquarters of the Hong Kong and Shanghai Bank, the colony's largest (half of Hong Kong's total bank deposits are held by the 'Honkers and Shankers' and another third by associate banks), the world's most valuable (in terms of its stock market worth), and the most powerful and influential commercial force in the north-western Pacific Ocean.

The building work, which went on twenty-four hours a day (although the Governor, who lived nearby, had at first asked that no jackhammering be permitted during the night), was once going to create the tallest, most architecturally adventurous and most luxurious building in the East, which would loom above the colony's other skyscrapers and remind everyone of the bank's complete dominance of every aspect of colonial life. But then the Chinese Government hired an even more flamboyant and reputable architect and announced it was planning a new HQ for the Bank of China, which would be even taller, grander and more impressive. And cheaper, into the bargain.

Both banks have outside their front doors a pair of lions – stone ones at the Bank of China, bronze for the Hong Kong and Shanghai. There is something a little peculiar about them. Neither pair, on close inspection, appears to be aligned as perfectly as one might expect them to be if they were in Cheapside, or on Wall Street. They are set oddly, though subtly, on the skew: the effect, to Western eyes, is slightly unsettling.

But they weren't put there for the benefit of Western eyes. They were designed to promote prosperity for the banks, and for all the thousands of Chinese workers inside, and the Chinese customers outside. And so, when both sets of lions were put in place, the bank directors called in the *fung shui* man – that specialist in cosmic alignments whose job it is to ensure, so far as he is able, that all furniture, doors, windows – and sculpted lions outside – are so placed as to command the greatest advantage for all, and so the fortune-bearing winds that blow across and around the great buildings are deflected and diverted in as profitable a way as it is possible for earthbound mortals to divine. A building with good *fung shui* can be expected to enjoy a prosperous existence; one that has not sought the advice and blessing of the *fung shui* man suffers (one big skyscraper on the Hong Kong waterfront, and which supposedly has bad *fung shui*, has experienced severe difficulties in attracting Chinese workers, and has picked up – because of its circular windows – the nickname 'the house of the thousand arseholes', which must be even less propitious).

Two hundred yards, a narrow palm-shrouded alley, and a busy street named after a long-dead Queen-Empress, separate St John's Cathedral from the *fung shui* man's lions at the front door of the bank. At times the distance that separates old Empire from Hong Kong's contemporary reality, or the gulf that divides both Western colonial and Eastern merchant from the ancient principles of Confucius, seems like a million miles. The one seems, on one day, not to understand the other, nor to like the other, nor even to respect the other; and on another day, in another set of circumstances, Chinese businessman, British taipan and every sorcerer and necromancer, priest and divine known to theology will come together for a common purpose. The mixture that is today's Hong Kong is almost impossibly rich and varied, its elements so often in theory repugnant to one another, the potential for explosion enormous.

And yet, *mirabile dictu*, it works – far more successfully than any part of the Empire ever did. No one has yet managed to fathom precisely why this is – why in so small and cramped a territory, so filled to bursting by refugees and immigrants, so corrupt and so cruel, so informally directed and so constantly under threat, so temporary and so little loved – why, despite social ills that make New York, by comparison, seem like a template for the welfare state, this tiny speck of British China is so rich, so powerful and so magical.

Hong Kong is perhaps the only place on earth to witness the vision of what mankind can do if, his talent unleashed and his ambitions unchecked, he sets out quite ruthlessly to manufacture a fortune. Some may look upon Hong Kong as the natural consequence of a classic experiment in the nature of success; others may regard the place as the vision of nightmare. Whichever is likely to be the verdict of history there is no colony like it, nor, after 1997 when Chinese sovereignty is again restored, will there ever be such a place again.

Most visitors from the West come in by air, as I did first in the mid-1970s, from New Delhi. The approach to Kai Tak airfield is unforgettable – though not at first: the plane usually contrives to come in from the western side of the colony, and the last few miles of the journey are over the brown and undistinguished hills of Kwangtung province of Southern China, and the muddy estuary of the Pearl River. (The British have been this way, evidently: even the airline maps show the southernmost point of China, just off to the starboard side, was once called Cape

Bastion, and there is a Macclesfield Bank and a Money Island out in the South China Sea, barely visible from five miles up.)

But then the sea begins to swarm with shipping. Big freighters can be seen lumbering northwards, contained in channels between a clutch of tiny, tree-covered islets. Red and white hydrofoils scurry to and fro leaving trails of white foam, and stately ferry boats plough across the straits. As the plane gets lower still we can see the country boats – skiffs and punts and a few elegant sailing junks, each a superb piece of Eastern imagery with its three lugsails stiffened with long battens, and a lone crewman fishing from the stern.

We sink lower still, and flash over a small island where there seems to be a barrack block, and a clutch of radio towers. And then, in a bewildering rush of concrete and steel and neon, Kowloon is below, and blocks of flats stream past at 200 knots. They say the locals hang their washing out for a warming blast from the passing jets; we clear the roofs by no more than a hundred feet, and then make a sharp right turn and, twenty seconds later, touch down at Kai Tak, on the runway which is built out into the bay, and from which all Hong Kong can be seen, draped like a great wall of whiteness against the lush green foliage of the Peak.

It is a mesmeric, intoxicating sight, a view to make one gasp. A hundred years ago there was almost nothing: just a thin line of warehouses, a few church towers, the mansions of the taipans up on the slopes, and Government House on Upper Albert Road with the Union flag waving lazily in the steamy air. Today a vast white winding cloth of concrete, steel and glass has been bolted on to the hillsides, obscuring the contours, turning a world once dominated by the horizontal and the gentle diagonal into a pageant of the vertical. On the waterfront – on land reclaimed from the harbour – are the glittering towers of the 'mighty Hongs' – Jardines, Swires, Wheelock Marden, the Honkers and Shankers, Hutchinson Whampoa, Hong Kong Land, and all the other guardians of capital might.

'I began to wonder,' Sun Yat Sen once wrote, 'how it was that Englishmen could do such things as they have done with the barren rock of Hong Kong within seventy or eighty years,

while in 4,000 years China had achieved nothing like it . . .'
His wonderment was spurred, no doubt, by the prevailing
contemptuous Chinese view of Western inadequacies. Xu Ji
Yu, a scholar of the nineteenth-century mandarinate, described
Britain as merely 'three islands, a handful of stones in the
western ocean . . . her area is estimated to be about the same
as Taiwan and Hainan.' To both mandarin and revolutionary the
name 'China' meant the same thing – 'the area beneath heaven'.
No other upstart nation – and certainly no mere handful of stones
in the western ocean – could contemplate changing the aspect
of the Chinese island of Hong Kong, even a little.

And how it has changed! Huge tower blocks, with flats costing
three thousand pounds a month to rent; six-lane motorways,
streaming with Rolls-Royces and Mercedes (more Rolls per
head than anywhere else on earth); palaces of gleaming black
reflecting glass, each connected to the other by aerial walkways;
massive housing projects with population densities of up to a
third of a million people per square mile; tunnels, railway lines,
yacht harbours, container ports, ice rinks, roller-coasters, spy
stations, cable terminals, a planetarium, two race courses and
all the paraphernalia of urban life, jammed on to a tiny chunk of
granite once described as 'a plutonic island of uninviting sterility,
apparently capable only of supporting the lowest forms of organ-
isms' but which now (the commentator was writing in 1893)
'stands forth before the world . . . as a noble monument to
British pluck and enterprise.'

The first view of Hong Kong from the air is impressive
enough. But to arrive in Hong Kong from her motherland, from
the mainland China from which she draws her people and her
inner strengths, and to which, it is internationally agreed, she
will return three years before the end of this century, is to see
all the drama of an Imperial extravaganza, and to be allowed to
make comparisons between the two systems under which modern China has been run.

I had flown into Peking with the Royal Air Force, aboard a
VC–10 that was taking Sir Geoffrey Howe, the Foreign Secretary, to the Chinese for another in what then seemed an
interminable series of negotiations over the colony's future. The

journey seemed interminable, too, only enlivened for me by our brief stop in Delhi, where the British High Commissioner's Rolls-Royce was waiting, driven by the Imperial chauffeur, who had the splendidly down-to-earth name of Mr Omo, and whose charge was, naturally, pure white.

We landed in Peking in the mid-afternoon, and everything was strangely silent: no band, no guard of honour, no cheering and no applause. The plane's engines ceased their whining, and the great quiet murmur of China took over, wrapping us all in its strange soft blanket. It was cold, too, and dusty, and the skies were heavy with the fine yellow sand from the Gobi desert. The streets, thronged with cyclists, were quiet and dusty too, and the whole city looked shabby and tired, as though its citizenry and its buildings were emerging from a long sleep, and were blinking their rheumy eyes towards the light.

I took the Canton train a few days later, and experienced one of those intense bitter-sweet moments that becomes ineradicably etched on to the memory. It is not strictly relevant to the saga of Empire, perhaps, but it lies at the centre of my great affection for China, and had something to do with my mixed feelings about Hong Kong.

I had been on the platform at Peking central railway station a few weeks before as a great express, the 3.54 p.m. to Chongqing, pulled out. A young woman, dressed in dark blue Mao overalls, was saying her tearful farewells to a baby, probably her own, that someone was holding at a carriage window. A guard blew on her whistle, the woman began to weep softly but uncontrollably, and the train, with painful slowness, started to move out of the station. But as it did so the loudspeakers on the platform began to sound a melody of wonderful sweetness, a tune so sad and grand and gentle that I knew it had been written especially for a departure platform, and particularly for that young woman and her child.

Some days later I was in Hong Kong, whiling away one late evening in a bar, talking to an old British actor I had met in the lift. He was a forlorn figure, a man for whom his bottle now seemed more comforting than his lines, and who was reduced to playing the Hong Kong hotels in place of the West End theatres he had once known. The Empire takes such people, and makes them briefly feel wanted again.

We were the only ones left in the bar, and ordered a final whisky while the old Cantonese waiters began stacking the chairs, and the girl at the turntable pulled out a last record, sighing deeply as she cued down the needle. The music flooded out into the bar, and my companion's endless conversation faded into a mere hum. It was, of course, the same sweet tune, cascading over this sad old night as though it had been designed for moments like this, too. The girl told me what it was called, 'Fishing Junks at Sunset'. Classical piece, from up there – and she jabbed her thumb towards the harbour, and Kowloon, towards the New Territories, and the fence, and China beyond.

And then I was back in Peking, and down at the station and waiting in the corridor of the 10.43 p.m. from Peking to Canton, while a group of friends stood with a bottle of champagne to wish me God-speed as I set off for the south, and the Imperial foothold. The guard waved her flag and blew her whistle; the train moved slowly away, everyone was waving and then, above the screech of flange against rail, I heard a shout. 'They're . . . playing . . . your . . . tune!' And I listened over the din, and heard its sweetness once again: 'Fishing Junks at Sunset', the perfect music for a melancholy China night, and a piece that has haunted me ever since.

The journey lasted for two nights and three days. My travelling companions were, variously, a Japanese businessman who either bought or sold pig bristles for use in shaving brushes; a welder from Minneapolis who had come to see his son at university in Shanghai; and Professor Yang, who was in charge of the Tungsten, Tin and Bismuth Group of the Chinese Geological Society and, to judge from the number of ballpoint pens in the top pocket of his Mao jacket and the fact that he was travelling Soft Class, was a very senior cadre of the Party.

In Canton station I found a taxi driver who was prepared to take me to the frontier, a hundred miles away across the delta of the Pearl River. We bumped along rutted roads, crossed wide rivers on rickety ferry-boats, and managed to get a speeding ticket from a policeman who jumped from behind a bush and waved a red flag at us, angrily, but then offered us a cup of chrysanthemum tea by way of consolation. He said he was sorry that a *gweilo* – a foreign devil – had been so inconvenienced.

Ten miles away from the frontier, still deep inside a China of timeless rural peace – workers knee-deep in the paddy fields, ducks straggling along the roadside, the occasional bullock-cart lumbering down a muddy lane – we passed two unexpected signs of the new, post-Mao order: a petrol station, run by Texaco (though no cars were taking advantage of it), and a tall, electrified fence, with watchtowers and a massive and well-guarded border control post, such as you might find when taking the autobahn from Vienna to Budapest.

This was not the frontier with Hong Kong, however. It was a new 'internal' frontier that divided the special economic zone of Shen Zhen from Marxist orthodoxies of the rest of China – the zone being a sort of halfway house, an airlock, between the rigidities of the Communist world and the *laissez-faire* capitalism of the Crown colony. It is a frantically busy place, with factories and tower blocks and hotels (most of them paid for by wealthy Hong Kong investors) rising out of the paddy fields, and restaurants jammed solid with a new Chinese élite who are making money on a scale of which Mao would never have dreamed.

And then, dark on a distant hill, the first sign of a familiar Empire: the square and battlemented outline of a fort. I had seen such things on the brown ridges above the Khyber Pass, and in the Malakand Hills near Swat. Both there, and here, they looked as if they belonged on a film set for *Beau Geste*: they are called Mackenzie Forts, after the Bengal Governor who designed them. Elsewhere in the world they are mere relics of a British Raj; they belong now to independent governments, who use them for training, or turn them into museums, or just allow them to fall into ruin.

But on this frontier they are still British Imperial forts, guarding an old British Imperial fortress. A huge Union flag waved from the one I could see from Shen Zhen, and once in a while there was a faint glint as binoculars swept the town, and the border river and the fence. There were British soldiers up there, in their last few years of Empire-watch.

The taxi dropped me at the Lo Wu railway station, where the Friendship Bridge crossed the muddy little border stream. There was a steel gate across the single railway line, and a dozen khaki-uniformed soldiers of the People's Liberation Army stood in front of it, chatting to each other and smoking. They smiled and waved as I walked past them on to the footbridge and into British territory. One of them asked, in sign language, if I had enjoyed the time I had spent in his country, and offered me a cigarette. They seemed genuinely pleased when I told them I had, and they were clapping and laughing when I looked back at them, at the point where the corridor turns and all view of the People's Republic is deliberately blocked. A few days later I thought back to their little group: theirs had been the last gesture of true human friendship from a Chinese stranger that I was to experience for my remaining few days in the East – from now on, in the superheated mercantilism of Hong Kong, civilities and kindnesses were at a premium.

I had breakfast with the British soldiers who hold the line – nearly all of them Gurkhas, members of one of the world's last remaining mercenary armies performing one of Empire's last remaining tasks. They built the fence: it is fourteen feet high, twenty-six miles long, alive with sensors and arclights, but with 150 gates (only three of which are guarded) through which the local Chinese farmers are permitted to wander more or less at will. There is a standard briefing given to visitors: small men from the hills of western Nepal demonstrate high-technology systems, acronyms like CLASSIC (the Covert Local Area Sensor System) and VINDICATOR, maps are drawn showing how many illegal immigrants – or 'eye-eyes', as the troops call them – are seized each month in each of the border's four sectors, slides of helicopters and dogs and tracker-teams are shown with a mixture of pride, puzzlement and embarrassment. The troops have a threefold official role – protecting the 'integrity' of the Sino-British border, collecting low-level intelligence (which means gazing endlessly through those binoculars at the fields and the tower blocks below), and capturing illegal would-be settlers in the colony. But the Gurkhas know that they, as Nepalis, have no business in the matter; the British officers have no real heart for it, now that they know the border will vanish for all time on 1st July 1997, when the lease runs out; and the only pleasure anyone takes in the task is that it is done well, efficiently and, so far as the immigrants are concerned, with despatch and compassion. (The captives – about eleven a day – are given a cup of tea and handed over to the Chinese border guards at a small ceremony each afternoon at three, and are fully expected to have another try at scaling the fence the very next day. Some, indeed, are regulars, and the soldiers hope that before too long the most persistent will evade the detectors and the tracker dogs, and get into one of the crowded slums of Hong Kong and begin to enjoy what is said, by comparison, to be the good life.)

The train from Lo Wu was very different from the slow and rickety antique that had brought me to Canton. No chipped paint and cracked leather upholstery, no lace antimacassars and bed-time tea, no fronded lamps and grime-crusted window; here, instead, was a gleaming steel arrow, silent, cushioned, smooth and very fast. At the first station, in the New Territories village of Sheung Shui, a pretty Chinese girl got on board: she was dressed in white silk, had a Hermès scarf, carried a costly handbag and wore a gold wristwatch as thin as a wafer. She was a picture of perfection – a signal contrast to the last girl I had seen in China, now just a few thousand yards away to the north. She was working at the Lo Wu station, shuffled around in slippers, wore a baggy uniform of rough blue drill, and a flat cap adorned with the red star of the Party. The girl in silk, however, was haughtily disdainful, and shouted at a porter for some unfathomable misdemeanour; the girl in blue drill had smiled happily, and her resignation to her role in the proletariat seemed not to depress her. Whose life, I wondered, was the more fulfilling? Who had the more reason to hope?

And then I was at Kowloon station – the most distant railway station to which it was possible to journey, without interruption, from London. All the chaos and urgency of the colony was here – shouting porters, magazine sellers, hustlers, hawkers, policemen, old ladies with chickens, bewildered American tourists, businessmen being ushered into long black cars, the girl in silk being kissed by an immensely fat Frenchman who whisked her away in a Mercedes to his model agency, or his apartment in Tsim Sha Tsui, or to lunch at the Kowloon Club. And there, across the harbour, was the great crystal wall of Hong Kong herself, with the Peak, swathed in a warm and swirling mist, looming faintly above. It was a month since my Easter visit, and the black framework of the Hong Kong and Shanghai Bank building had grown by another hundred feet, and blocked out yet another view, and another bit of the greenery I had been able to see the last time I had stood here, gazing south from Kowloon at the richest colonial possession on the planet.

Hong Kong is – setting aside Anguilla, and the mid-ocean peak of Rockall – the youngest of Britain's remaining colonies. The Convention of Chuen Pee was announced on 21st January 1841, ceding Hong Kong Island to Britain, and to the Honourable Chieftainess Victoria, in perpetuity; the settlement reached between the British Conservative and Chinese Communist Governments in 1984 established that the Victorian interpretation of perpetuity no longer obtained, and it was agreed that sovereignty would revert to China on 1st July 1997. Hong Kong thus knows precisely the duration of British Imperial dominion: 156 years, five months and eleven days – a great deal less than her three and three-quarter centuries in Bermuda, rather longer than the ninety years during which the Crown administered India.

Of all Britain's innumerable Imperial conquests, occupations and annexations, that which won Hong Kong for England was the least honourable. The 'unequal treaty', to which the Chinese understandably objected almost from the moment they were compelled by circumstance to sign it, had its origins in the mucky trade between British India, and China, in the dried cakes of ooze from the seed pods of the pretty red flower *Papaver somniferum* – opium. Hong Kong, however glittering a prize it has become today, is a colony first established for the convenience of the British narcotics business – a fact the Chinese, despite the diplomatic niceties that attended the signing ceremonies of 1984, are loath to forget.

The Javanese Dutch are said to have shown the Chinese the

delights of inhaling the pleasurable fumes of opium. By the 1830s between four and twelve million Chinese were addicted. The side streets of Shanghai and Peking were thick with furtively run divans, inside which, in an atmosphere of warm, sweet-scented gloom, Chinese men were able to slip contentedly into the untroubled sleep and dreamy fantasies that the opium induced.

But China grew few poppies, and those that were harvested were not for lancing with the opium-knife. The Imperial court had forbidden the practice, and officially discouraged its import. They condemned what they called the 'foreign mud' – and yet, unofficially, connived at the trade. Americans brought in opium from Turkey, and Parsee traders would bring it in from Persia and Afghanistan. But the best opium, guaranteed unadulterated and most competitively priced, came from Bengal and Bihar – and from the British East India Company's headquarters in Calcutta.

The opium trade worked to everyone's advantage – except the Chinese mandarinate. The British had been alarmed for some time that the balance of trade between London and Peking was weighted heavily in the favour of China. The English taste for tea, and the London public's liking for silk and later, more unaccountably, for Chinese rhubarb, caused an enormous outflow of silver from the treasury coffers (the Chinese, mistrusting every barbarian product, including paper money, insisted on convertible silver in payment). The British tried to sell them wool – but poor Chinese wore padded cotton, and the rich wore silk and fur, and the wool project was a fiasco. Only the export of Indian opium, it was swiftly realised, would bring that silver back.

And so, at the great factories in Patna and Ghazipur, opium was made into six-inch-wide 'cakes', placed carefully in crates made of mango-wood, and sent down river to the Company's warehouses on the Hooghly. There it was auctioned to the agents already established on the China coast – of which, pre-eminent, and established since 1832 in both Canton and Macao, was the firm of grocers and traders established by the legendary Scotsmen, William Jardine and James Matheson. If any commercial entity can be said to have created Hong Kong – a classic reversal of the axiom that 'trade follows the flag' – it is the firm that, until 1984, continued to dominate the colony's reputation as dealer and trader – Jardine, Matheson and Co.

The arrangements for getting the illegal Indian opium into Canton were byzantine in the extreme, and depended largely on the assiduous corrupting of the local Chinese officials – in particular the Canton trade superintendent who was called *Hai Kwan Pu*, but whom the British insisted on calling the Hoppo. He, like everyone else, took his cut – the term then was that he 'squeezed' those below him in the trading chain, and was in turn squeezed by those above. So the Hoppo squeezed the Canton merchants (the 'Hongs') who alone were authorised to do business with the round-eyed barbarians; the Governor of Canton squeezed the Hoppo; the Viceroy squeezed the Governor and, it must be assumed, the Forbidden City in faraway Peking squeezed the Viceroy. It was all strictly illegal, of course; but before long British India was selling 50,000 cases of opium a year to the Chinese, and poppy products were providing a healthy ten per cent of India's annual revenue.

The rules were mysterious, and complicated. The East India-men would sail to the mouth of the Pearl River, and to the island of Lin Tin, halfway between Macao and the then barely inhabited (and wholly Chinese) island of Hong Kong. Here a score of floating warehouses were moored for the exchange of the contra-band: opium cakes were taken from the ships, tea and rhubarb were loaded in their place. Barges then took the opium upriver – through a narrow, well defended defile known as the Bogue, to the port of Whampoa, and the foreign factories in Canton.

The factories – warehouses, presided over by foreign factors – were the only places in Canton where barbarians were permit-ted to live, and then only for the trading season of the summer. They lived well, and drank furiously – especially of a cocktail known as Canton Gunpowder, mixed from alcohol, sugar, tobacco juice and arsenic. Jardine's had a factory in Canton, and came to dominate the opium trade into China, and the export of silks and teas to London.

But then the Manchus decided to crack down – less on moral grounds, more for the simple reason that opium imports were

Distant loyalties: a St. Helena family, and the wedding they never saw.

The scale of it all: colonies hot (Ascension, above left) and cold (British Antarctic Territory, below left), enormous (Hong Kong, population five and a quarter million, above) and minute (Pitcairn, population forty-four, below).

The Governor, Admiral
Sir David Williams of Gibraltar,
with the ancient keys of the
great Imperial fortress.

Lord Dunrossil, Governor of
Bermuda, at his swimming
pool, Government House,
Hamilton. The hat was his
father's, when Governor-
General of Australia.

Sir John and Lady Cox of Bermuda – the look is pure Home Counties; to the immigration authorities though, they are Bermudians, not Britons.

Mr. and Mrs. Johnnie Repetto, outside their flax-thatched cottage in Edinburgh-of-the-Seven-Seas, Tristan da Cunha. Mr. Repetto was evacuated to England in 1961, after the volcano erupted, but led the battle to return home.

A resident of Grand Turk, her son and the family pet on Parrot Cay, Turks and Caicos Islands.

Cricket played in every remaining territory of the Empire, is a hazardous activity on St. Helena. The only level ground is surrounded by cliffs, and in the nineteenth century a player fell off and was killed. "Retired dead" records the scorebook.

The decayed Manager's Château on Boddam Island, forcibly evacuated by the British after the American Navy built its base nearby on Diego Garcia.

A Diego Garcian Islander, forced from his home by the British authorities, now living in a slum in Mauritius, 1,800 miles from home. Nearly 2,000 others were obliged to leave home at the same time.

beginning to cause a serious haemorrhage in the Imperial silver reserves. In 1839 a tough, honest opium-hater named Lin Tse Hsu, a man who had already cleaned up the drugs business in his home provinces of Hunan and Kwang Tung, was sent down to Canton: he ordered all opium supplies to be surrendered, and warned that anyone found in possession of the drug or of an opium pipe would be strangled in public. And he tackled his British opposite number, Captain Charles Elliot, recently appointed as Superintendent of Trade in China (and, ironically, as opposed to opium as was Mr Lin). Elliot was ordered to cease all trading in opium, under pain of the most severe punishment.

London was outraged. Whatever Lord Palmerston might have thought about opium itself (and there is no evidence he objected – after all, it was regularly included in medicines available in London, and the only peculiar dimension was that the Chinese smoked it – but didn't they wear pigtails, and write from bottom to top, and do other odd things too?) opium trade was free trade. Protection of free trade had been the lynchpin of British foreign policy for forty years: it was imperative that the trade in opium be allowed to continue. (Palmerston's public stance was actually rather different: he said he understood Mr Lin's objections, but would brook no violence done by Mr Lin's henchmen to subjects of the British Crown, in the event that the dispute over the drug became heated.)

Violence did, indeed, break out. Lin closed Canton to foreign trade; Lord Napier, who was British Superintendent of Trade at Canton, took a pair of frigates upriver, ran the gauntlet of the Bogue (with Elliot on an unarmed cutter, sheltering from the gunfire under an umbrella) but was turned back at Whampoa. Lin then seized 20,000 cases of British opium, and became involved in a furious row about compensation to its owners. Then, while that was under discussion, in July 1839, there was a drunken brawl in Kowloon, and British and American sailors were blamed for killing a villager. Lin demanded a scapegoat for public strangling. Elliot refused. Lin occupied Macao, and threw out all Britons – whereupon they retreated to their ships and anchored in the Fragrant Harbour on the far side of the Pearl River – the harbour of Hong Kong.

Meanwhile, back in London, William Jardine – known in Cantonese as 'iron-headed old rat' ever since he failed to turn around after being hit from behind with a club at the Petition Gate in Canton – was advising Palmerston on just what to do. James Matheson had advocated force once before, but the Duke of Wellington had said no; on this occasion Palmerston agreed that a task force must be sent, to protect the Empire's trading interests, and to ensure the financial stability of the Government of India. By December 1839 Cabinet had concurred: the Jardine paper was an accepted battle plan: a fleet would sail for the East, and rendezvous with Captain Elliot's tiny flotilla, in the harbour at Hong Kong. The mountainous little island, and its sheltered harbour to the north, may not yet have become a British colony. It was, however, a British base.

The task force, assembled in Madras and Calcutta, arrived in Chinese waters in June 1840. It was massive – sixteen men-o'-war, thirty-one other vessels – and it struck fear into the Chinese.

The Royal Navy's demands were essentially Jardine's demands: an apology for the insult at Canton, full payment for the costs of this regrettably necessary expeditionary force, reimbursement for the 20,000 cases of opium seized by Lin, and free trade guarantees at five Chinese ports, and no further dealings through the Canton Hongs. The demands were put, with the persuasive addition of cannonfire, to the Chinese at Amoy, at Ting-hai, and Pei-Ho: within weeks the approaches both to Peking and the Yangtze ports were secured by the British. Troops landed on Chusan, less than a hundred miles from Shanghai, and prepared to march into the mainland. The Navy moved down to the Pearl River and seized the forts guarding the Bogue, thus securing all access to Whampoa, and to Canton itself.

The Chinese had no choice, and capitulated. The Emperor's representative sullenly agreed to the Convention of Cheun Pee – already existing in draft form, so confident were the British of eventual triumph. All of Jardine's demands were met, including the additional humiliation: the island of Hong Kong, and the harbour to its north, were to be ceded in perpetuity to the British.

That was on 20th January. Five days later Sir Edward Belcher and the officers of HMS *Sulphur* landed on Hong Kong Island, and drank a toast on Possession Mount, and gave three cheers for Her Majesty. On the twenty-sixth the full squadron arrived from the north: as a contemporary report put it, 'the Union Jack was hoisted on Possession Mount, and formal possession taken of the island by Commodore Sir Gordon Bremer, under a *feu-de-joie* from the marines and the Royal Salute from the ships-of-war'. Five days later still all native residents of Hong Kong were told that, whether or not they approved, they were now subjects of the Crown, under the benign protection of the Queen of England.

It was still not clear that the island was to be British for ever. The Chinese were still fighting. The Emperor declared that he would 'seek another occasion for attacking and destroying [the British] at Hong Kong, and thus restore the ancient territory'. But a year later, after reverses that rubbed salt into his wounds, the Emperor was forced to a final, abject surrender. Nanking was about to be attacked; Shanghai had already fallen. He had no choice.

The famous Treaty of Nanking was the outcome of this sad occasion. Ratifications were exchanged on 26th June 1843 – the official birth of the colony. It stated baldly that the Island of Hong Kong was 'to be possessed in perpetuity by Her Britannic Majesty, her heirs and successors, and to be governed by such laws as Her Majesty the Queen of Great Britain shall see fit to direct'. (In fact the draft Treaty had left a blank at the name of the island to be annexed. Some in London favoured Chusan, with its proximity to Shanghai. But Jardine and Matheson favoured Hong Kong, and that was the name eventually inked in to the document.) The Chinese were bitterly dejected, and closed the meeting with their conquerors with the haunting words: 'All shall be granted – it is settled – it is finished.'

But it wasn't quite. Two more opium wars followed, and not until 1860 was all the perpetual cession completed. The tip of the Kowloon Peninsula, and the tiny Stonecutter's Island, were given up, for all eternity, when a joint Franco-British force was at the gates of Peking, and had already sacked the Emperor's Summer Palace, and forced the proud and ancient nation to its knees. By the end of that year Britain had absolute control of the finest port in the Orient, the perfect base for trade, for quartering the Royal Navy, and for exerting dominion over all the East.

But it was not enough. Hong Kong Island soon became wretchedly overcrowded, and the paranoia of Empire – the feeling that a piece of British territory was never big enough, or secure enough, and that there was always a mountain or an isthmus or a harbour from which it could be attacked by the barbarian hordes – soon led to demands for its expansion. The Chinese Emperor concurred, though from a position of great military weakness. Not one he was prepared to display to his subjects, though: he ended his address to them with the characteristically Imperial warning – 'Let every one tremble and obey! An Important Special Notice!'

The agreement that was signed in Peking, in quadruplicate, in both Mandarin and English, on 'the twentyfirst day of the fourth moon of the twentyfourth year of Kuang Hsu' (or, more prosaically, 9th June 1898) was designed for the short-term gain of the colony. But unknown to all concerned the agreement held the seeds of the colony's ultimate destruction. It was called simply 'the Convention of Peking, 1898'; it allowed Britain to lease an extra 350 miles of Chinese territory – which the British insisted on calling the New Territories, even when they were quite old – and it can be regarded as one of the most significant and underrated documents in British Imperial history.

It was signed on the one side by two officials of the Tsungli Yamen – which is what the Chinese then called their Foreign Office – and on the other by the great Imperialist figure of the British Minister in Peking, Sir Claude MacDonald, who was known as 'Gunboat' MacDonald and was described by *The Times* correspondent as 'the type of military officer rolled out a mile at a time and lopped off in six-foot lengths'. (His colleague in Peking at the time was another celebrated personage, Mr H. Bax-Ironside, whom everyone knew as Iron Backside.)

But the land was not Britain's to keep. The Convention of Peking was only a lease, ninety-nine years long. It had come into force on 1st July 1898. It was due to expire at midnight on 30th June 1997. The British may have liked to regard the extra real estate as a new possession, an integral part of the Empire on which the sun would never set; some academics said that the phrase 'ninety-nine years' was a cunning Chinese device that meant 'for ever and ever' without actually saying so. The Colonial Office wrote papers insisting that Hong Kong had been expanded in just the same way as any other colony might have been. Territory had merely been added, for British convenience. The New Territories, a memorandum said, were 'part and parcel of Her Majesty's Colony of Hong Kong, in like manner and for all intents and purposes as if they had originally formed part of said Colony'. They may have liked to regard the land as such – but if they did so, they engaged in the most wishful thinking, and were to get their eventual come-uppance. The Chinese are a patient people, and they have long memories.

The New Territories stretch north from Kowloon – they begin, appropriately, at Boundary Street – and up to the Shen Zhen River, where we meet the Gurkhas, the fence, and the soldiers of the People's Liberation Army. They present a marvellous contrast to the overpopulated, superheated dynamo of the harbourside cities – here are wild mountain ranges, remote bays dotted with rockbound skerries, meadows and lakes, paddy fields and forests. This is where the practices of China, ancient beyond the reach of memory, meet the ceaseless rhythms of the Imperial merchants: here are the workers in the rice-fields, the walled villages, the China of willow-pattern and temple-bell, of mao-tai and the courtly bow. It is being developed now, furiously – high-rise flats, fast railway lines, motorways, dockyards – but it is still a remote and peaceful place, with wild birds and animals and room to move, and air to breathe. People stuck in Hong Kong used to complain of a kind of hyper-claustrophobia, as though they lived in a pressure-cooker: the lush tranquillity of the New Territories provided them with a means of escape.

One small enclave has, however, remained resolutely Chinese. The Walled City of Kowloon, neither truly a city, nor having any walls – the Japanese knocked them down in the Second World War – was specifically mentioned in the Convention as the one place that would remain under Chinese administration 'except insofar as may be inconsistent with the military requirements for the defence of Hong Kong'. The British unilaterally revoked that particular clause of the Convention a few months after the lease had begun, and tossed the Chinese officials out. But the Walled City has never accepted colonial rule – it is a teeming, dirty little slum, unpoliced, unorganised, unfriendly and dangerous. There was never any town planning, though the Kai Tak airport authorities insisted recently that some buildings be lowered to an appropriate height, and so police moved in and obligingly lopped some storeys off. There has never been any sanitation, and electricity is siphoned from the main Kowloon grid, illegally. Fifty thousand people live in this single speck of China inside the Empire (which is itself, of course, a tiny speck of Empire inside China); the city is dangerous, stepping to the rhythm of a different drum, and likely to be unchanged by whatever forces come to dominate the future of the colony itself.

The British had few early doubts about the purpose behind the annexation of Hong Kong. The island had been placed there for the exclusive convenience of the British Empire, and its acquisition could only lead to one thing. 'It is a notch cut in China,' it was said at the time of the original Nanking Treaty, 'as a woodman notches a tree, to mark it for felling at a convenient opportunity.' Victoria, Empress of India, might soon add 'Empress of China and Queen of Corea' to her vast string of titles – and Hong Kong would surely be the vehicle by which she might do so.

But it was not to be. China was to be penetrated, but never vanquished. The British pierced the Manchu Empire one other time in 1898, when they forced a leasehold deal for the port of Weihaiwei, which lay across the Gulf of Chihli from the Russian enclave of Port Arthur. The British renamed their possession Port Edward, for the sake of symmetry. The Royal Navy loved the place and its people who were, as a journal reported at the time, 'a comfortable set, easy to deal with'. But Weihaiwei was not to remain in the British Empire for long: the American Government, which disliked the idea of foreigners muddying the western Pacific waters, urged the British to give up the lease. They did, and abandoned the colony in 1930 – the first part of the Empire to be given up voluntarily. (It was almost immediately overrun by the Japanese, and China did not get her little port back until 1946.)

The importance of Hong Kong was at first more symbolic than real. It gave the Royal Navy theoretical charge of the China Sea and, with the battleships and destroyers based at Esquimault on Vancouver Island, the northern Pacific Ocean. It was, as Lord Curzon wrote, 'the furthermost link in the chain of fortresses which . . . girdles half the globe'. Or it was, as that most Imperially minded of admirals, Sir John Fisher, noted, 'one of the keys to the lock of the world'. The ships came steaming in from Calcutta and Sydney and Aden and Gibraltar, the flag flew proudly over the Peak, and a naval cannon was fired at noon each day. And still is: Jardine's got into hot water once for firing a twenty-one-gun salute to welcome home the 'Honourable Merchant', as they call their boss. The Royal Navy set the firm a forfeit: a single cannonshot would be fired each noon as a colonial time signal. Noel Coward records the fact in his ditty about Mad Dogs and Englishmen – 'In Hong Kong they strike a gong and fire off the Noon Day Gun.' Visitors have been recently known to fire the gun. One simply phones up Jardine's, and asks permission.

There is no more potent symbol of British rule over Hong Kong than the existence of His Excellency the Governor. His rule is absolute. His authority is positively dictatorial, deriving from the Letters Patent and Royal Instructions written in 1917, and empowering the Crown's personal factotum to 'do and execute all things that belong to his said office . . . according to such instructions as may from time to time be given to him'.

'What – no one interested in the job?' asked one commentator, when told of some difficulty in finding a replacement. 'Direct personal authority over five million people? Incredible that no one should want it.' Someone – a fluent Mandarin speaker, as it happens – was promptly found.

The University of Hong Kong conducted a study in 1973 of the nouns most commonly used in the colony's daily paper, the *South China Morning Post*. The word 'Governor' came third. (A similar survey of the fifty-four daily Cantonese-language papers would have produced, one suspects, a rather lower figure.) He is omnipresent – making speeches, issuing declarations, presiding over meetings of the ruling committees, flying to London for talks, opening flower shows and concerts and exhibitions, or sidling off for weekends at his splendid country house at Fanling, in the New Territories. (Mountain Lodge, the Victorian grange built to help His Excellency survive the colonial summers, proved unsuitable: it was invariably shrouded in thick mist. It was pulled down in 1946.)

The Governor of Hong Kong has not always been the highest-paid of the colonial chieftains. In 1930 he took home six thousand pounds; the Viceroy of India received three times as much, the Governor of Northern Ireland was paid two thousand pounds more, and he was pipped by all the Indian State Governors, the Governors-General of the Dominions, and the Governors of Malaya, Ceylon and Nigeria (the latter getting an extra ten pounds a week). But regard the list of those who fared less well – Jamaica, Baluchistan, Uganda, Tasmania, the Falkland Islands, Somaliland, and nearly forty others. The Governor of Hong Kong was paid six times as much as his opposite number in St Helena.

Today he is the best-paid Colonial Governor – hardly surprising, since his Chinese charges outnumber all the other colonial citizens by some seventy-two to one. He is driven in an unnumbered Rolls-Royce Phantom, the only Colonial Governor to be thus chauffeured (at least two of his colleagues, in Grand Turk and Port Stanley, make do with London taxis: the remainder tend to Fords. Not even a British government minister rates a Phantom. Only the royal family has that privilege). He is also supplied with a private government launch, the *Lady Maurine* – though one critic publicly voiced the view that some Governors needed neither the *Maurine* nor any other boat for the purpose of crossing the harbour. They behaved, he said, as though they thought they could walk on the water.

Almost every Governor of Hong Kong is favoured by having something named after him. Sir Henry Pottinger has a peak, Sir John Davis a mount, Sir Samuel Bonham a strand, Sir John Bowring a town. There is a Robinson Road, though Sir Hercules Robinson has not endeared himself to Chinese memory: he introduced an early version of apartheid, 'to protect the European and United States communities from the injury and inconvenience of intermixture with the Chinese'.

There is a Hennessy Road, too: Sir John Pope-Hennessy, Governor from 1877 to 1882, decided to give a number of senior government jobs to able Chinese, won all Chinese the permission to visit the colonial library, and ended up with the Cantonese appellation 'Number One Good Friend'. The Colonial Office thought rather less of him for that, and packed him off to Mauritius.

And so the memorials go on: Northcote Hospital, Peel Rise, Sir Cecil's Ride (after Sir Cecil Clementi), and Grantham (who served until 1958, and is quoted as saying that, 'The Governor is next to the Almighty') College. Nathan, Macdonnell, Kennedy, Bowen, Des Voeux, Lugard, May and Stubbs all rated roads as well: and no doubt the final incumbents will be so honoured – though with the colony reverting to the ministries of Peking, their distinction may not last for ever. (Even the most innocent of British Imperialists were seen to wince when they found their High Commission in Calcutta on a street renamed Ho Chi Minh Sarani. Hong Kongers suspect only Hennessy Road will survive the revolution.)

One Governor is not commemorated thus, though he is not forgotten, and in fact has left the most impressive memorial of all. Lieutenant-General Rensuke Isogai was Governor of Hong Kong from 1941 to 1945, when it wearily accepted control by its third Imperial suzerain, Japan.

Hong Kong fell swiftly – though not as swiftly as Singapore a year later. Nor did its occupation by the Japanese Imperial Army cause particular alarm: it seemed to be accepted that since Hong Kong was a part of China, and Japan had occupied southern

China, then it was inevitable – irritating, but inevitable – that Japan should march in. The troops arrived at the colony's border on the day before the Imperial Air Force struck at Pearl Harbor (and on the day that the Hong Kong Chinese Women's Clubs were holding their annual fancy-dress ball at the Peninsula Hotel). At the moment Honolulu was hit, so was the airfield at Kai Tak, and the troops poured in across the Shen Zhen River.

Five days later all British troops were pinned down on Hong Kong Island, and the Governor, Sir Mark Young, was arranging for the storage of his furniture and the more valuable paintings from the Government House collection. Sir Mark then went and hid in a cave, and tried to run his fast-evaporating colony from underground. He finally surrendered on Christmas Day, at a brief ceremony in the Peninsula Hotel, and was led away to prison in Manchuria.

General Isogai turned up his nose at Sir Mark's Government House on Upper Albert Road. For one thing, it was ugly; for another, it was cracked, and looked about to fall down. 'Your Governor must be a very brave man to have lived in a building in that condition,' a Japanese official told one of the British administrators at the prison camp at Stanley (from where, the British insisted, the true colonial government still functioned). He decided to rebuild it. An architect from the South Manchurian Railway Company did the design, and Japanese engineers did the building. The result, Isogai's memorial, is by far the largest Government House still inhabited by a British Governor, and it looks, as might be expected, just like a Japanese Imperial railway station.

Isogai never lived there, though he had equipped the mansion with rice-paper screens, tatami baths and raised floors. The British used it for the surrender ceremony. 'It was a scene,' wrote the *China Mail*, 'etched against the background of a magnificently rejuvenated Government House, which gave the Japanese no opportunity of evading the humiliation of their position, and it was perhaps apt that the ceremony should have taken place in the only building which, judging by the spacious grandeur of its interior, had furnished their high ranking officers with moments of pride in achievement.'

Sir Mark Young came back in triumph: someone dug up a bottle of brandy that had been buried in the garden while the Japanese were closing in: and the Union flag, raised slowly by an able seaman on surrender day, flew over the colony again. Sir Mark tore out the strange baths and edible screens, levelled the floors and ordered old-rose cretonne from the Ministry of Works in London (which, despite wartime shortages, soon obliged; the colonies still commanded some degree of precedence). Hong Kong and the New Territories were, as was to be said of the Falkland Islands four decades later, 'once more under the Government desired by their inhabitants'.

It was a close-run thing, in fact. The Americans had long wanted Britain to give up Hong Kong, as they had abandoned Weihaiwei, to provide the East with a timely gesture of non-Imperial goodwill. At Yalta, President Roosevelt had suggested to Stalin that it be internationalised, like Trieste, and run as a free port. It was only because Franklin Gimson, the British Colonial Secretary, had the wit to make contact with London the moment he was released from Stanley Prison, and accept orders making him Lieutenant-Governor, that British dominion over the colony was assured.

'Astrologically, September 1982 was the worst possible time to start negotiating on anything.' Thus begins the most crucial chapter of a book written by a Canadian named Ted Gormick – 'the first in a series of astropolitical studies' a preface assures readers – about the future, as directed by the stars, of the colony of Hong Kong. Astrology, superstition, augury and omen loom large in the consciousness of the average Chinese, and so Mr Gormick's book sold well, and his words were listened to with some care.

September 1982 was when Margaret Thatcher arrived in Peking, to discuss the status of what the Chinese now called Xianggang, and what many Britons still fondly thought of as the farthest of the far-flung battle-lines. The talks were essential: the 1898 lease on the New Territories was due to expire in 1997, and anyone wanting to buy land there on a fifteen-year mortgage was going to have to be certain (as was his banker) of the ultimate fate of the land. The colony's future had to be firmly established, and for more than mere reasons of pride or nostalgia.

But nothing about the talks was auspicious. Two months before a Vice-Chairman of the Chinese Communist Party had publicly announced that his country intended to make Macao, Taiwan – and Hong Kong – into 'special administrative regions' of the People's Republic, and that the various residents ought to prepare themselves for life under Chinese sovereignty. When the talks began the 'malignant influence' of Saturn was in the air, and in fact had just moved into the transit of Venus, creating what Mr Gormick said was a 'sour' atmosphere, and a time when 'some chickens came home to roost'. And then, when the talks had finished, Mrs Thatcher tripped over on the steps leading down from the Great Hall of the People, and fell on to her hands and knees (prompting the irreverent observation by some of the colony's Cantonese papers that she had decided to perform the kowtow before the image of Chairman Mao). To Britons, the accident seemed of no consequence – President Ford had appeared to fall over almost every week, and President Reagan was not totally steady either. But to the Chinese, and to the stargazers, it was more than simple chance.

There was less than total surprise, then – though there was great dismay – when Mrs Thatcher proceeded to make a diplomatic blunder. She arrived in Hong Kong to tell the citizenry something of the talks she had had in the Chinese capital. She was in a tough mood – possibly she was still flushed by the great military victory in another colony, the Falkland Islands – when she made two declarations: the treaties that had given Britain dominion over these few square miles of China were in her view 'valid in international law', and China's honour would be impugned if it thought otherwise since 'if a country will not stand by one treaty, it will not stand by another'. Britain, she said, 'keeps her treaties'. Moreover, Britain had a responsibility to the people of Hong Kong; and she was proud of what had been achieved by Hong Kong under British administration.

Peking was outraged. As David Bonavia, *The Times* man in

China, was to write: 'Seldom in British colonial history was so much damage done to the interests of so many people in such a short space of time by a single person.' The Hong Kong dollar slumped, and the stock market – and its index, the regionally notorious Hang Seng – went berserk. People began to wonder if the People's Liberation Army would march in there and then, and end what Hsinhua, the New China News Agency, was to call 'British Imperialism's plunder of Chinese territory'.

In the event it was the professional, often maligned diplomats who saved the Prime Minister's reputation. For the next two years a team of Foreign Office men, all speakers of *putonghua* (Mandarin) including a romantic scholar-athlete figure of the old Lawrence school, a man named David Wilson who had climbed in some of China's highest mountains, shuttled back and forth between Whitehall, Upper Albert Road, and the Fishing Platform Guest House in the centre of Peking. Their mission was formidable: they had to accept China's firm belief that the three treaties ceding Hong Kong and the New Territories were 'unequal' – signed when the Chinese were in a position of temporary weakness, and were not balanced by the offer of a *quid pro quo* from Britain; they had to accept that the end of the lease on the New Territories meant, essentially, an end to British rule in all Hong Kong (notwithstanding the terms of the Treaty of Nanking, which gave Hong Kong Island to Britain 'in perpetuity'); and they had to construct a system for Hong Kong that would discharge Britain's responsibilities to the five million people who lived there. Most, after all, had fled from Communist China; they had to be given a firm assurance, internationally respected and underwritten, that their freedoms and their remarkable ways of life would be preserved, at least for some generations.

The result was a document signed in Peking shortly before Christmas 1984, by Mrs Thatcher. Hong Kong would, indeed, become a Special Administrative Region of the People's Republic. There would be an elected legislature (something the colony had not enjoyed under British rule) and perhaps an elected Governor. The legal system would remain precisely as it is. All the freedoms commonly accepted by Hong Kongers – the rights to free speech, a free press, freedom of association and religion and choice of employment – would be guaranteed. Capitalism would remain the economic dogma of the region, provided that was what the local people wanted. The Hong Kong dollar would remain in circulation, and would be convertible. All land leases would be honoured. The citizenry would be able to carry British passports (though of the less-than-entirely-worthwhile kind – they would not enable their holders to settle in Britain, and would to all intents and purposes be regarded by British immigration officers as alien travel documents) and would enjoy some degree of British consular protection, long after Peking took control of the territory.

All these provisions would be preserved until at least 30th June 2047. A Joint Liaison Group, made up of officials from both London and Peking, would supervise the arrangements for the transition; the group would begin work in 1985, and would cease to exist in the year 2000, once Peking was firmly established as ruler once again.

The document was welcomed as a diplomatic triumph. Sir Geoffrey Howe, the Foreign Secretary, a man with a reputation for weakness (being attacked by Sir Geoffrey in the House of Commons was like 'being savaged by a dead sheep', a member of the Labour Opposition Denis Healey once said), was the hero of the hour. At least, he was in London. The people of Hong Kong were told their objections would be noted, if they had any (and a team was set up to note them, and the Whitehall mandarin Sir Patrick Nairne, now an Oxford college principal and head of the Italic Handwriting Society, was sent to monitor the monitors), but that the agreement was not about to be changed. A few did object. Some, who had good cause to appreciate the mercurial nature of the Chinese leadership, said they were deeply sceptical – how, they asked, could the British, in all good faith, negotiate with the heirs to the Cultural Revolution, the practitioners of dogmatic madness? How could anyone be trusted? Others were angry about their own status – why had the Falkland Islanders and the Gibraltarians been admitted to the cosy club of full British nationality, and the Cantonese of Hong Kong specifically excluded, and rendered into some national half-caste status, neither properly British, nor properly Chinese, nor even properly of an entity called Hong Kong?

A few leader writers in the British newspapers agreed with them, and so did a clutch of Members of Parliament, and some in the Upper House, too. Sir Patrick Nairne, with the utmost courtesy and care, took note of all the objections, agreed that they had been considered most fairly by the monitoring team, and wrote a report for Parliament. A Bill was presented, a vote was taken, an Act was passed, the Treaty of Nanking and the Convention of Peking 1860 were each effectively rescinded, and Hong Kong began its inexorable progress out of the British Empire, and into the fathomless mysteries of Special Communist Administration.

The rest of the Empire, and a gaggle of Commonwealth brother-nations, smelled fortune in the air. People would never stay in Hong Kong, they reasoned; companies would bail out, would place their funds in countries that had a guaranteed future (guaranteed non-Communist, that is), send their personnel to more stable outposts under Imperial control or influence. And so, like vultures (or like lifeboat crews, depending on the viewpoint) they flew in to Kai Tak – the Caymanian bankers, the tax-shelter aficionados from Grand Turk, officials offering passports from Fiji or citizenship in Canada or resident status in Bermuda and the Bahamas. There were uncountable billions of dollars in Hong Kong that could well be looking for new homes: everyone seemed, reasonably enough, to want to help find them.

In December 1938, W. H. Auden wrote of Hong Kong:

> *The leading characters are wise and witty*
> *Substantial men of birth and education*
> *With wide experience of administration*
> *They know the manners of a modern city*
>
> *Only the servants enter unexpected*

Their silence has a fresh dramatic use
Here in the East the bankers have erected
A worthy temple to the Comic Muse

The servants, and the bankers. Always the servants triumph in
the end. They are on the verge of doing so now, though the
Europeans – the bankers, the dealers, the merchants, the
taipans – seem to do so for the moment.

It was not so long ago that the taipans, the great men of the
Oriental Empire, really did rule Hong Kong. Their names –
Jardine, Swire, Hutchison, Gilman, Dodwell, Marden,
Kadoorie – really did cause the colony to tremble and obey.
Power did once rest with the Jockey Club, Jardine's, the Hong
Kong and Shanghai Bank, and the Governor – in that order.
Hong Kong Land, China Light and Power, the Hong Kong Club,
the *South China Morning Post* – these were the pillars of
established order, and woe betide any who dared forget.

But behind all these grand panjandrums of the Western Empire
there was always – though not always heard, or recognised – the
dull, thunderous murmur of the Eastern, mightier Empire of the
Chinese. This may have been a British enclave, run by Sherwood
Foresters and Grenadiers, flown over by the Royal Air Force,
sailed around by the Royal Navy (though only in twenty-five-
year-old Ton class minesweepers today), and policed by officers
from Glasgow and Bristol and West Hartlepool; this may have long
been run under the stern authority of the Union flag, all blanco,
brass and tropical whites, goose-feathers and the Anthem and the
Queen's birthday party; this may have been the base for a hundred
thousand temporary merchants with their gin-and-tonics, their
cricket matches, their yachts and their bored wives; but this was
also, irrevocably, unmistakably and magnificently, no other place
than China.

Hong Kong was never separate from China. It succeeded
because the vision and investment of the immigrant round-eyes
was able to marry with the energies, the acumen and ambition
of the refugee Chinese. It was not another Gibraltar, able to
hold itself aloof from its population; nor was it a St Helena or a
Caribbean island, where a small élite kept the native peoples in

subjection, and wondered why there was no progress, and little hope. In Hong Kong the British were past-masters at ordering and directing the irrepressible energies of the mighty crush of Chinese humanity, until the point was reached where the stream became too strong, burst over its banks, and carried the British along in its exuberant fury.

And so today the rulers of Hong Kong – the new rulers – are the Chinese. The drivers of the 600 Rolls-Royces registered in the colony are, invariably, wealthy men from Canton or Shanghai. (There are only fourteen registered rickshaws, also driven by Chinese, but for tourists coming off the Star Ferry.) The big names, the new taipans, are the Run Run Shaws and the Y. K. Paos and the Woo Hon Fais – hard-working, shrewd, ruthless, merchant venturers. And in the background, the Triads – the Chinese version of the Mafia, controlling and manipulating and directing the seamier side of the colony, with all its curious needs and desires. It was a supreme irony, a policemen said to me one evening over a drink in a Wanchai bar, that the British gained Hong Kong as the result of a war that stemmed from British attempts to force opium on the Chinese market; the Triads were now the principal target of the Royal Hong Kong police for trafficking in derivatives of the very same substance, and trying to ship it, and sell it, back to the British.

A few days after the excitements of the signing ceremonies, and once the colony appeared to have accustomed herself to the harsh fact that the British were no longer going to rule and the Han Chinese would be taking over in the Year of the Rat, 5,000 days hence – once all was settled, and the arguments were stilled, I took a morning ferry ride to Lantau Island, on the western perimeter of the colony.

I went with a friend, a beautiful young Chinese girl. We sat together on the prow of the ferry, the early sun warming our backs, and watched the wall of great skyscrapers slip past, and the junks dip through the waves, and the great ocean freighters flying their flags from Panama and Liberia, Greece and India. This was indeed the engine of Eastern commerce, a key to the lock of the world! Sir John Fisher had been right; Lord Curzon was correct in assuming that all foreigners would bow in mute respect at the sight of Hong Kong, this perpetual exhibition of British might and main.

But then the skyscrapers were behind us, and the green hills of Lantau rose ahead, and my friend was chatting to a neighbour in the shrill singsong of her old Canton, and the waters were busy with small fishing boats, and a sort of peace had settled all around. We took a car to the very western tip of the island, and up among the hills and the tea plantations to the Po Lin monastery, where the Buddhists pray and teach and find their sanctuary. I had come because an English friend had a son there. He was learning to be a priest, and I had come to give him his mother's love.

We walked through a different world. The monks, silent and shuffling in their deep brown robes, went about their holy business in a rich silence. The air was heavy with incense, and thin blue eddies of smoke rose from the incense sticks before an effigy of the Lord Buddha. Offerings of oranges and figs, bananas and papayas and freshly gathered tea lay on the altars. Old women would approach the statue, bow, kneel, make wordless prayers and offer silent supplication.

I found my Englishman, shaven-headed and serene, learning to fold a robe made of red silk. He was on a three-day vow of silence; but my friend asked the abbot if he might speak to me for a few moments, and permission was given, with a smile. 'Come to see the real Hong Kong?' was his first question. He said he loved the island, its feeling of one-ness with China, its timelessness, its immemorial qualities. He did not know where the abbot would send him, and he was naturally content to do as he was bidden; but he would love to stay here, among the clouds and the fragrance of the tea bushes, and on the edge of China. And my friend nodded happily, and she was silent on the ferry boat back to Hong Kong Island, and when we said goodbye – for I had to fly on to another country, and another island, even more remote – she said she hoped the Hong Kong that arose after the British left was more like Lantau, less like Wanchai, Central, and the streaming shops of Tsim Sha Tsui.

This is the only British colony of whose constitutional future we can now be sure. It is the only colony that, on being freed from British rule, becomes subsumed into a neighbour nation (Northern Ireland is the single remaining possession that awaits a similar fate). At one second after midnight on 1st July 1997 the Crown colony of Hong Kong will be retitled the Special Autonomous Region of Xianggang – Hong Kong, China.

A few moments before there will have been a sorry little ceremony. A small detachment of British troops, all in Number One dress and gleaming brass, will have wheeled, clattered and saluted, and a blare of trumpets will have sounded the familiar anthem. The Governor, all in white, with the plumes of his hat fluttering white and scarlet in the night-time breeze, will have stepped forward to the dais. Drums will have rolled; the distant chimes from the cathedral church of St John will sound the midnight hour; a marine will have lowered, with infinite slowness, the Union flag from the white jackstaff.

And then, jauntily, up will go the red and gold flag of the People's Republic and, perhaps, a new banner for Xianggang. A small man in a modest brown suit will step forward from the shadows and shake the Governor's hand; the Governor will slip into those same shadows, and be borne off to a waiting warship on which the troops have already started to embark. Someone in the watching crowd will start to sob quietly; another will mutter the line about the captain and the kings departing, the tumult and the shouting dying . . .

And British rule will all be over, just as it is predestined and preordained. That small but precious jewel in the Imperial crown will have passed back to its rightful owners to the north; Hong Kong, China, will stand ready to do business with the world in the name of the massed proletariat of the People's Republic, rather than the House of Windsor and the taipans of Great Britain. Whether or not it will continue to be a success cannot be known; Britons assume that without the wisdom of their direction, the Chinese cannot hope to succeed as they have been allowed to do since Captain Elliot did his deal in 1841. The condition of Hong Kong? remarked a wit – a British, Imperially minded wit – in the Foreign Correspondents' Club one evening. Past imperfect, present tense, future conditional.

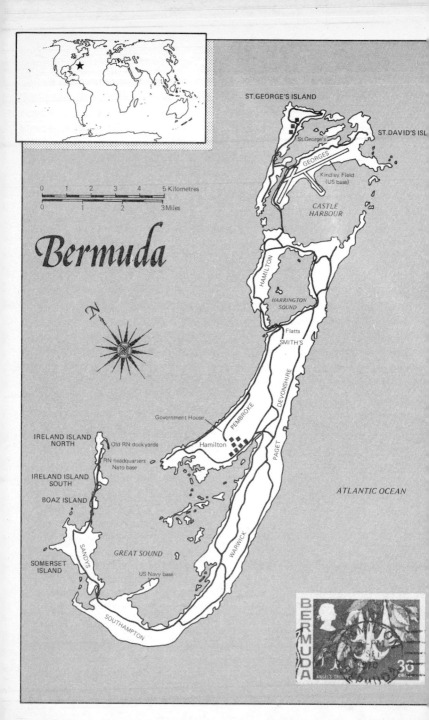

Bermuda

ST.GEORGE'S ISLAND

ST.DAVID'S ISL

St.George's

GEORGES

Kindley Field
(US base)

CASTLE
HARBOUR

0 1 2 3 4 5 Kilometres
0 1 2 3 Miles

HAMILTON

HARRINGTON
SOUND

N

Flatts
SMITH'S

Government House

DEVONSHIRE

PEMBROKE

IRELAND ISLAND
NORTH

Old RN dock yards

Hamilton

RN headquarters
Nato base

IRELAND ISLAND
SOUTH

PAGET

BOAZ ISLAND

ATLANTIC OCEAN

SANDYS

GREAT SOUND

SOMERSET
ISLAND

US Navy base

WARWICK

SOUTHAMPTON

BERMUDA

ANGELS TRUMPET

30

EIGHT

BERMUDA

The telephone rang shortly before six, startling me from what I had supposed the night before would be a long, deserved and comfortable Sunday lie-in. It was March 1973 and I was in Chevy Chase, a pleasant suburb of Washington; the caller was in London, and seemed, through my sleep-fogged mind, to have but a single question: 'Do you think you ought to go?'

He said it again. 'Do you think you ought to go?' I had no idea what the Foreign Editor was talking about, and for a few further seconds I was too fuddled with sleep to care. But then, in a flash of sudden realisation, it occurred to me that my editor in London knew more about something – moreover something that had evidently happened in my parish – than I did. Considering that I was the man on the spot, and had only recently arrived there, such an imbalance of knowledge could prove embarrassing. I muttered something about holding on, shot out of bed, raced to the front door and found outside, on the doorstep, the rolled copy of that Sunday morning's *Washington Post*.

I scanned it with a frantic urgency. Nothing at the top of the page. Nothing below – no, wait a minute, here was a small paragraph, inserted late in the night. 'Governor Shot Dead' read the headline. And underneath, a one-word dateline. 'Bermuda'. This, surely, must be the story – something that had happened while I was asleep, and must have already been broadcast back home, on the BBC.

I hurtled back to the phone. 'Sorry to keep you waiting,' I

said, and then tried to assume a tone of sage and languid authority, as though I had known about the shooting all along. 'Yes – I suppose I should wander over. Could make a decent piece.' 'Fine,' returned the voice on the other end. 'There's a plane from Baltimore in an hour. I've booked you on it already. Should get in to Hamilton by lunchtime. Talk to you later.' And he hung up.

Sir Richard Sharples had been Colonial Governor for six months. He had arrived, in the proper style for an island that makes its living from holidaymakers, aboard a cruise liner. He had made himself reasonably popular – he had the Imperial bearing that Bermudians like their Governors to have, and he gave pleasant parties, and he mixed well. But now, astonishingly, he was dead. He, his ADC, and his dog had all been shot as they walked between the rose bushes after dinner. A state of emergency had been declared. A frigate had been dispatched. The well-oiled machinery for dealing with native insurrections was swung into place, on the off-chance it might be needed, as in Malaya, or British Guiana, or Cyprus, or those dozen other sites of old Imperial trouble.

I remember less than I should. The visit was too hurried, the images too compressed, the story too confusing. No one knew who might have fired the shots, or why. There was a great pall of bewildered sadness over the island, and yet I remember the sun shining and the blue sea looking particularly exquisite, and the tiny pink houses in their neat gardens, and the fields of Easter lilies being picked for delivery to the New York flower markets. I had to hire a scooter to get me around the island – visitors were not allowed to drive cars – and this only added to the strange feeling I had about the place. It should have been grey and stormy, or perhaps steamily hot and crawling with snakes and leeches, and I should have had to make my calls in a black car, being talked to by a gloomily pessimistic taxi driver. Instead I was zipping along narrow lanes between bushes of oleander and bougainvillaea, humming above white coral beaches, feeling fit and well and getting a handsome tan in one of the prettiest places in creation. I was glad to get away, and back to the real world.

Bermuda then gave me the feeling that it was a sort of Disneyland, and that the shootings were the local equivalent of a tourist having a heart-attack inside the plastic Matterhorn – smiling young men with shrouds would clear everything up within seconds and hustle the cadaver away through a back door, and then the whirligigs would start up again and the crowds would re-form, like waters briefly parted, and the music would start, and the smiling young men would resume their cries of 'Have a nice day!' and all would seem well once more. It had all been just a brief interruption to the placid rhythms of paradise.

It was more than a decade before I went back. I seemed to be on opposite sides of the world whenever Bermuda crept into the headlines. The police did, eventually, find the murderers – two young hoodlums – and a jury convicted them. They were hanged, after the Foreign Secretary in London reported that he was 'unable to advise the Queen to intervene'. The hangings triggered riots, and, in true Imperial style, soldiers of the Royal Regiment of Fusiliers were sent in to restore order, and a Royal Commission had to be set up to find out how it had happened. But before long the tranquil blue waters closed over these events, too. The 'still-vex'd Bermoothes' may have inspired Shakespeare to write *The Tempest* – but so far as the public relations firm who acted for the Bermudian Government were concerned the murders and the mayhem, the rioting and the Royal Regiments were as nothing. The islands were delightfully and permanently unvex'd, the atmosphere anything but Tempestuous, and for everyone's sake, long may the cruise ships call, the lilies bloom and the invading armies of suburban Americans come each year from honeymoon to retirement, to enjoy the peace and beauty of it all.

When I next went back to Bermuda it was to see the first girl I ever kissed. Gillian was the daughter of my boarding housemaster at school. I was fourteen and she thirteen when, as I think I recall, we exchanged a tentative brushing of lips outside the fourth form bathroom. Thus committed to one another we had gone for a few walks together in the Dorset countryside, had pledged all kinds of lifetime troths and trysts, but had then parted and, eventually and inevitably, lost touch. I heard that she had moved to Paris, and then to Amsterdam. Rumour said she was in Boston in the early 1980s, and finally a chance letter from her father mentioned that she now lived in Bermuda, married to a man who had made a fortune in computer programs. She was, her father said enviously, 'more or less retired'.

She met me at the airport, and it was both curious and enchanting how little had changed. It had been twenty-six years since we had last smiled conspiratorially at each other across the dining hall – for even the thought of romance was forbidden – and yet we recognised each other in an instant, and by the end of the first day were talking just as we had done on those walks to Beaminster and Upwey all those summers ago. Her husband must have felt a little left out, for the first day of reminiscence; but after a while the pleasantness of the memories became subsumed in the idyllic realities of daily life in Bermuda and that, I confess, began to weary me, and I began to feel left out, a stranger in a place that was in some unfathomable way most peculiar and, as I had felt a decade before, still oddly unreal.

They lived in a quiet apartment two miles away from the capital, beside a small cove where they kept the yacht they were only just learning how to sail. One room was reserved for their computer and its telephone links with the outside world – Boston, particularly, where the wealth from the magic invention cascaded into their bank account in a steady stream, and could be monitored at the touch of a button. There was a collection of other electronic wizardry, and there were soft carpets and soft sofas and cushions, all in pastel colours, easy on the eye, deliberately unexciting, inducing a permanent feeling of relaxation. Once in a while a telephone would purr its summons, and arrangements would be made for a tennis game, or a squash tournament, or a dinner in a nearby restaurant. But otherwise, nothing ever seemed to happen.

Days slipped into nights with measured ease. The weather was sunny, the skies and the seas were blue, the beaches were pink and white, the sunsets were soft and salmon-coloured, people wore cotton clothes that were white or vaguely tinted with lemon or cerise or eggshell. It was like living in an ashram, amid an atmosphere of studied perfection, as though everything that had been created, from the sky to the carpets, and whether natural or made by man, had been designed to promote a feeling of inner well-being among everyone who lived on the island, or had come there for a holiday. It was Disneyland, I was certain – or perhaps it should have been called England-land, a caricature of an always-sunny part of Cornwall, fashioned in polychrome and vinyl, and served up daily for the affluent East Coasters.

And then I began to have a nightmare – that Bermuda was like the village in an old television series called *The Prisoner*, and while everything was perfect and lovely to look at, it was impossible to get away, and you were stuck in its sticky sweetness, walled into a pastel cell and hummed at by the Muzak machine, smiled at and bowed to eternally by humanoids who wished you would have a nice day and wasn't the weather grand and wasn't the sea warm and the beaches pretty and the flowers nice? Sartre had written a play about being trapped in a room in a luxury hotel for all eternity. I had this feeling about Bermuda, and began, after only a very few days, to look around for the way out. And it was only then that I began to discover some of the reality of the island, and found it a good deal more curious than I had ever imagined.

One afternoon I was at the airport. A friend had told me that there were interesting things to see – it was an American military base, for one thing, and probably held some secrets – and so I begged permission for a tour. The control tower, while not exactly an Imperial monument, proved most interesting.

The air traffic controllers who talk down the jumbo jets bound for Kindley Field, as the base is called, are all members of the United States Navy. The ones I met were all attractive young women; for hours at a time each one sits, hunched over the green glow of her radar screen, a half-cold Pepsi-Cola beside her, a half-smoked Kent between her lips, the rasp of fatigue and concentration heavy in her voice, bringing some order to the apparent chaos of the mid-Atlantic flight paths.

Once in a while, if the inbound pilot is a cheery sort, she'll purr up at him, suggesting he may like to take his passengers

along what she'll call 'the tourist route' down to her island.
'Okay, Delta six-five heavy,' she'll say, talking to a Tri-Star
droning in from Atlanta, 800 miles west, 'make a heading of
one-five-zero and come down to flight level five-zero and show
your folks where they're coming for their vacation.'

And down the plane will swoop, a long and lazy right-hand
turn, a slow and gentle dive through the creamy lather of clouds.
The controller, taking another sip of Pepsi, sucking once again
on her crumpled tube of tobacco and murmuring some item of
arcana to a crossbound long-haul plane which has strayed into
her control zone while *en route* for somewhere else, forgets the
Delta Airline passengers, turns her attention to another blip on
her screen, sees that it is an Eastern charter inbound from
Newark, New Jersey, and prepares to say good day to the pilot,
although she well knows that Eastern pilots are a lot less friendly
than the good men from Delta and the Deep South.

Up in the sky, twenty miles west of her and coming down
fast, the Delta passengers – the 300 'souls' reported by the pilot
as being on board and sitting, quite probably entranced, behind
him – are about to get their first impressions of the islands on
which they will probably have spent, in advance, so many dollars,
and for which they have spent so many months awaiting. They
will have heard the pilot's breezy account of the islands' history
and present status ('Her Majesty Queen Elizabeth is Queen of
Bermuda, you know,' he will have announced, to a delighted
gasp from some of the more impressionable members of his
audience), and now they want to see the reality of this little
chunk of Britain set so near to their home.

And yet all they can see down there is the ocean, an unpleasant
greyish-green colour flecked with white streaks, and looking not
at all inviting. It is always this way: the great current of the Gulf
Stream, which coils itself around the atolls and islets of the
Bermudas, wrinkles and contorts the surface of the surrounding
seas as though a storm were always brewing there. It is not a
good advertisement for the delights that lie ahead.

The sea's colour begins to change, quite suddenly, from deep
green to a paler aquamarine when the aircraft is about five miles
distant. The white horses vanish, the water below assumes a

calmer, more friendly aspect. In places there are shallows, with sandbars and spits and ridges of pink and yellow coral, and then, fringed by a line of white foam, the first small island heaves itself out of the Atlantic, showing itself with trees, grass and a lighthouse.

There are dozens of small houses, their roofs pyramid-shaped, and whitewashed, their walls picked out in a variety of soft pastels – lemon, bluebell, lilac, primrose. It all looks very prim and ordered: the lawns look neat, the swimming pools glitter in the late morning sun, the sea is the palest of greens and splashes softly against low cliffs of pink and well-washed orange.

As the plane bumps down on to the concrete of the runway at Kindley Field it will speed past a half-dozen silvery warplanes belonging to the US Navy – nothing too surprising, perhaps, for American visitors, who are accustomed to seeing squadrons of Hercules and Starfighters and Phantoms at their own airfields, and knowing them to be for the use of the military part-timers among them, the members of the National Guard. But perhaps a British visitor might have cause to wonder – what are American warplanes doing on what is, after all, soil that is still technically British? Yes, of course, there were American airbases back home, but he might be a little taken aback, especially since these planes were in the middle of what he assumed was a civil airport. It would be rather like him finding a squadron of Lockheed P–3 Orion surveillance aircraft – which is what these are – at an innocently civil aerodrome like Luton, or Manchester – why here?

He would be even more surprised – perhaps a little dismayed – were he to have noticed a couple of white-painted American aircraft – Lockheed C–130 Hercules transports, specially modified, he might be able to say if he is a student of such matters – tucked at the other end of the runway, close by where his wheels had touched ground a few moments before. These planes, guarded by United States marines and deliberately kept well out of the public eye, are important, in a way that the Orions are routine. The Orions are based in Bermuda for the specific purpose of intelligence-gathering – shadowing the Soviet submarines which lurk in the shallow waters off the American

Eastern seaboard; the Hercules, however, are instruments of total war.

They are known as TACAMO aircraft, and they take off each day for twelve hours of patrolling across the North Atlantic, their crews talking to the American nuclear submarines lurking in the deeps of mid-ocean. TACAMO is an acronym for Take Charge And Move Out. These white-painted Hercules with their black wingtip tanks have on board the go-codes for launching the atomic weapons – the Tridents, the Poseidons, the Polaris – on board the big black subs that cruise endlessly hundreds of feet below the water. Should war break out, or be deemed about to break out, the controllers aboard these planes assume god-like powers, giving the machines below them the orders to destroy half a world. The squadrons of these aircraft are based in two American sites: Patuxent River, Maryland, and the island of Guam – and in one British Crown colony – Bermuda.

With this knowledge – and I knew nothing of it until I visited the control tower, and one of the girls let slip a small morsel about one of the TACAMO planes that was leaving for patrol near Iceland – our British visitor might well begin to ask himself one question. He has heard that the air traffic controllers in Bermuda are women from the United States Navy: he has seen the small swarm of American surveillance aircraft parked at one end of Bermuda's only runway, and he now knows that the third world war may conceivably be directed by aircraft dispatched from Bermuda. And yet he was told by the pilot of his aircraft that Queen Elizabeth, his own Queen, was Queen of Bermuda. Somehow it didn't seem to fit; on paper the place was British – but in reality it sounded very American. His stewardess had mentioned that the drivers preferred the left, and tea was still taken at four, and *The Statesman's Year Book* had said, he was sure, that Bermuda enjoyed the benign presence of a British Governor, and he could well imagine feathered helmets and Queen's birthday parties on the lawns at Government House; and yet there was American nuclear power, and the Stars and Stripes, and a currency tied to the US dollar, and to dial to Bermuda on the phone you used an American dialling code. All of which prompts, perhaps not unreasonably, a question that positively nudges to be asked – Just whose colony really is this? Who really runs it? Who calls the shots?

The same question has been asked many times before. Lady Daphne Moore, whose husband was Colonial Secretary in Bermuda in 1922, declared that 'this place is a parasite of and absolutely dependent upon the States – not a very healthy position for a colony to be in . . .' (The dependence was not exactly discouraged by the then Governor, General Willocks, who invited only Americans to parties at Government House because it was only the Americans, he said, who knew anything about horses.)

Lady Moore was no slouch as a diarist, nor one to mince her words. 'We only ask ourselves in wonder why England should wish to keep this rotten place, from which she can derive no profit and which is more than half American already. The United States could probably be prevailed upon to pay quite a decent price for the place . . .'

Her dyspeptic view of Britain's oldest remaining Crown colony might not be worthy of being taken seriously, did it not find echoes in the jottings of scores of the eighty-five grandees who have governed the place over the centuries. 'The people of these islands are lazy, stupid, obstinate, small-minded and thoroughly objectionable,' reported Governor Bruere in 1763; or else they are, as another official from London had it a century later, 'a lot of close-fisted swindling swine . . . a tight little trade union of thieves and extortionists'.

The combination is at first, quite frankly, puzzling. Here we have a group of coral islands, steeped in a warm sea of the palest green, caressed by trade winds of fragrant serenity (except, it must be admitted, in the summer hurricane season), constructed of rocks in pink, soft white or peach, with streams of bright, fresh water, with oleanders and pineapples and cedarwood groves; and a place, moreover, in which Britain has had a vested interest since the early years of the seventeenth century; and yet a good number of the Britons who stay on the islands – islands that many would think of as being almost paradisiacal – seem to come to loath them, to detest these people and find that while the colony is supposedly and unquestionably British

– notionally, legally, officially – it is in very many senses dominated by the United States, is utterly dependent on the United States and can well be regarded, and not by cynics alone, as the only British colony which is more like an American colony, run by Bermudians, on Britain's behalf, for America's ultimate benefit.

Bermuda's use through all of its 400 years of habitation (it is Britain's oldest surviving colony; Princess Margaret went to help it celebrate 375 years of British rule in the autumn of 1984) has been principally for defence. True, it produces fruit and vegetables for New York, it once dominated the world pencil-making industry, and cedar-hulled yachts with the classic 'Bermuda rig' were for many years the best on the ocean. But once, for Imperial Britain, and now for superpower America, Bermuda, despite her small size, her isolation and her position among evil reefs and evil Atlantic weather, was and is of considerable military importance.

The protection of the shipping lanes was, for nineteenth-century Britain, an Imperial obsession, and dictated Imperial policy – small islands being snapped up, small ports being built up purely as guarantees of the preservation of untroubled passage rights for vessels flying the Ensign. Thus did Trincomalee and Bombay police and service the Indian Ocean; Esquimault and Hong Kong and Weihaiwei looked after the Pacific and the China Seas; Aden guarded the Red Sea; Malta and Gibraltar the Mediterranean; Simonstown the South Atlantic; and Halifax and Bermuda the North Atlantic, the Caribbean and the approaches to home.

Bermuda was, after Malta, the most heavily fortified of the naval stations. (Protection was always overdone in Bermuda: dozens of forts, many of which survive for today's tourists, were erected almost from the first months of settlement, but no one ever attacked. The surrounding reefs, one assumes, were good enough.) The Admiralty bought an entire island from the Bermudian Government (a purchase that serves to underline the fact that Bermuda was master in its own house, and not utterly subservient to the British Crown, as most other colonies were); Ireland Island, at the far western tip of the fish-hook shape of the colony, cost the Navy four thousand eight hundred pounds; some smaller islands with more than 5,000 cedar trees were bought as well; and a programme began in 1810 to build one of the mightiest naval stations the world had ever seen.

An Admiral presided, with the splendid title of Commander-in-Chief America and West Indies Station. (The more pedantic geographers might find this odd, since Bermuda is not, strictly speaking, in the West Indies. For virtually all purposes of Imperial and military adminstration, however, it was regarded as being at one with Jamaica and Grenada, though most certainly not a Caribbean island, having neither Carib Indians, nor a shoreline on the Caribbean Sea.) Splendid names occasionally matched the splendid title: I came across a marble plaque listing past C-in-Cs and saw it had had to be extended a couple of inches at one point to accommodate the name of one Admiral Sir Reginald Plunkett-Ernle-Erle-Drax and his string of appropriate honours.

The old Royal Dockyard, closed since 1951 – the Admiral was first transmuted into a lesser figure known as 'SNOWI', the Senior Naval Officer West Indies, and is now a humble Senior British Officer, based in a shoreside house called HMS Malabar – is a haunting place. Its buildings are vast, with towers and pinnacles, tunnels and embayments, wharves and anchor stands and a chapel and a ravelin tower and a clutch of caponiers, all hewn and blasted from the pink-and-white limestone, and sewn together with plates of rusting iron.

It had a rotten reputation for thievery and idleness. Everything was stolen, it used to be said, except the lavatory seats and the storehouse clock – someone was always sitting on the lavatory, and everyone kept an eye on the clock.

Nowadays it is a museum (although the Casemates, once the ordnance barracks, is now Bermuda's maximum security prison, and where any island murderers are still hanged). The museum's keeper is a merry old Newfoundlander named Doug Little who has a long beard and a wooden leg and looks as though he should have a parrot sitting on his shoulder. His appearance, though highly appropriate to a naval museum, is purely fortuitous: he lost his leg when he was three and a wagon rolled over it near

Gander. He says he wears out his wooden stump in a couple of years; it is made of ash, not Bermuda cedar.

The strategic position of the islands, reluctantly recognised by the eighteenth-century Admiralty, is even more readily accepted today. The Americans came in 1941, building an airfield and an army base which, once the war was over, became the islands' civil airfield. The lease signed in London and Washington guaranteed the American forces rent-free use of the field and one other site at the western end of the colony for ninety-nine years; the United States Naval Air Station, Bermuda, is a crucial link in the anti-submarine 'fence' that now protects the Eastern seaboard from the attentions of the Soviet silent service. (A fine maritime irony has also made Bermuda a convenient hiding place for the very submarines the Pentagon is hunting: on any day, as the Orion spotter aircraft roar out from Kindley Field for their mid-Atlantic mission, three or four nuclear-powered, missile-carrying Russian submarines are lurking off the reefs of Bermuda, poised to hurl their weapons towards Washington, five minutes' flight time to the north-west.)

The matter of the bases is a sensitive one, for it opens up the nagging question of just who runs Bermuda – who needs Bermuda, in fact? The answer, inevitably, is that the United States needs Bermuda, much more keenly than does the United Kingdom; and that the Pentagon's military involvement in and dependence upon the colony ensures that, so far as Russia is concerned, it is a perfectly legitimate target for attack – annihilation, in fact – in the event of an atomic war.

The question of Bermuda's own security became something of an island issue during the winter of 1984, after I had gone back to the island for a third time, and had decided to ask people what they thought about the dominant presence of the American military. It seemed to me slightly absurd that British foreign policy, so closely linked to that of the United States, required a colony whose people are not party to the East-West argument to keep American weapons on their soil and thus render themselves liable for attack, as America's proxy. I came across dozens of young blacks in the seedier parts of Hamilton (for Bermuda does have slums, of a sort, and there are still small riots and strikes, and the place is far from crime-free) who were angry, but whose views never found expression in the island newspapers. There was a clever and articulate trade-union leader, Ottiwell Simmons, who spent an entire evening putting the case against the bases. 'These are our islands. Yet we have no say whether or not the Americans put atomic bombs in their bases. They don't have to ask us. They have to ask the British, and the British say yes. Of course they do. The constitution gives them that right, to decide on Bermuda's foreign policy. But is that morally correct, do you think? If we are made a target for extinction by carrying these weapons on our soil, should we not have the right to say whether or not we want them? I think many ordinary Bermudians would want to keep the Americans at arms' length, but we are never asked, or never listened to. It's not that we are anti-American – not at all. We just want more control over our own destiny, particularly when it comes to things like defence, where all of us can die in an instant.'

To answer this swell of disquiet I went to one of the island's more prominent white citizens, a courtly banker named Sir John Cox, who had represented Bermuda's interests at the Bases Conference, held in London in 1941. We met one afternoon in his sitting room, surrounded by antiques and by old clocks – for Sir John is an amateur horologist – and I told him that I had heard islanders speak critically of the American bases. He was scornful – particularly of the suggestion that his island might, in the event of nuclear war, be a target for attack.

'In the event that there is an atomic war,' he said, 'we may or may not be the unlucky one. It is absurd to believe that an island of twenty square miles, 600 miles from the nearest continental land mass, can maintain its complete independence; but if it did so attempt, and successfully, can we be assured of immunity from nuclear obliteration? In such an event we would be open to being occupied by a power hostile to our present friends, and the latter might then be forced to eliminate us for reasons of self-preservation.' It was difficult to realise that Sir John, with his curious brand of sanguine pessimism, was speaking about a place which holidaymakers are wont to think of as paradise.

The disturbances that followed the hangings have not been repeated, though there are still strikes. There is a growing plague of lawlessness, a rash of drug-smuggling and addiction, and there are occasional demands among the poorer and more radically inclined black Bermudians – who are both in the majority on the islands and, thanks to a highly effective democracy and a manifestly fair constitution, now run the Government – for a greater degree of independence.

Britain's policy, voiced by successive Governors, is essentially that laid down by the Colonial Secretary in 1964 – any territory that wants independence and is capable of sustaining it can have it, without let or hindrance from Britain. But the Bermudians, for all their occasional bouts of grumbling, seem either not to want it, or to regard themselves as not quite ready for it. Sir Edwin Leather, the forceful and eloquent former Tory MP who was made Governor after the murder of Sharples, and who still lives in retirement on the island (cable address Loyalty, Bermuda), pointed out to me one morning over coffee that, 'Black Bermudians hold every single office of importance on the islands, except the Governor, and as the Government and opposition parties know full well, I publicly informed them in 1973 they could have that post too, any time they chose to declare their independence. In two subsequent elections the subject has never been mentioned . . .'

And thus matters stand. The colony hangs on, the majority of its people – all of its whites, and most of its blacks – appearing to prefer to remain under Britain's invigilation, if not under its control; the American Government is eager to see the island remain secure, in Allied hands, with American military needs guaranteed by treaty with a reliable friend. Only a few voices are raised in support of real independence – the matter of freedom from the colonial yoke is not one that appears significantly to interest the islanders, and would not be argued in such terms anyway.

The tourists are as unaware of this as they are of the missions of some of the planes parked at the airport. For them, as they bounce down the gangplank from the cruise ships moored at Hamilton, or as they squeeze into taxis or wobble away on their newly acquired scooters, Bermuda's image is just as Walt Disney might imagine a tropical England, a coral island set in an azure sea.

There are British policemen – they wear shorts. The traffic drives on the left. You can buy tea in the afternoons. Old ladies with rosy cheeks and in Liberty print dresses are much in evidence. There is a Kennel Club, a Croquet Club, a Saddle Club, a Cricket Club, a Rose Society, a Girl Guides Association, a Keep Bermuda Beautiful association and the Meals on Wheels. Two clubs (Bermuda Yacht, and Hamilton Amateur Dinghy) can call themselves 'Royal'. There is a fine cathedral, with a British bishop, and columns carved from granite quarried in Peterhead. There are British goldfinches in the trees, and a shearwater known as a Pimlico. There is a town crier in St George's, and it would seem that every man and woman on the islands has a set of seventeenth-century clothes kept in a chest at home, and which is put on whenever there is a fête to attend or a busload of tourists to entertain.

There was a pretty little English railway, brass bound and chuffing from one end of the island to the other; but it was closed down, and sold to British Guiana in 1947. There is a little Army, too, with scarlet uniforms and bearskins, and which will remind Americans of the redcoats whom they so roundly defeated in the colonial wars. There is the ducking stool (set in a park ornamented by a notice proclaiming 'I am a Park with Feelings; Please do not litter me with Trash and Peelings') and the well dug by soldiers of the Black Watch. The splendid majesty of English law can be seen on an Assize Sunday, when full bottomed wigs are put on, and the judges wear scarlet robes. There is a *Royal Gazette*, which has appeared each morning since 1823; the Queen's head appears on the coins and the banknotes, even though pounds, shillings and pence have long been abandoned and replaced by cents and dollars which are kept at par with the United States currency, to avoid confusion.

The visitor is advised to keep to a simple routine. Step off your liner, pop into Trimingham's (est. 1842) for a pair of Bermuda shorts in a nice classic clan tartan, take pictures of the British bobby directing traffic on Front Street, dunk a Twinings tea bag into a Spode cup of warm water at the Princess Hotel – still painted pink, and proud to remind its customers that it served as the headquarters for Imperial Mail Censorship during the war – buy some Pringle jumpers and Royall Lime aftershave and then spend the evening dancing to Johnny McAteer's Orchestra in the Inverurie Hotel, and looking at the view from the terrace, with all the lights and the fireflies twinkling, and waves beating gently on the coral sand, the faint streaks of phosphorescence in the cool waters . . .

Cynicism aside, Bermuda is, without doubt, a success. It is, generally speaking, a peaceful place – more so than many Caribbean islands nearby. There is no unemployment worth speaking of, and that in Britain's second most populous colony (Hong Kong being the biggest, by far). It is very wealthy – the 55,000 inhabitants took home some nineteen thousand dollars each in 1983 (compared to Britain's eight thousand dollars, and to the two hundred and sixty dollars earned by the natives of Haiti, only a few hundred miles south). And there are no pioneer industries to decay and decline – Bermuda is dedicated almost wholly to the service industries, and is as such a vision of the future to which many countries might aspire. 'The prosperity of Bermuda,' a friend wrote to me once, 'was largely built on the willingness of the British and American aristocracies to pay almost any price for the opportunity to consume alcohol in a congenial warm climate.'

Other writers have claimed that apartheid, of a kind, is rampant in Bermuda; younger people dislike the social exclusivity of the place, and the strict and heavy-handed ways of the Colonial Government; you hear complaints about the Americanisation of the place, the suggestion that Bermudianism is merely an anomalous cultural hybrid, a mule of a culture, attractive in its own way but of no lasting value or use.

And yet it does seem to work; it is rich, it is as content as any place I know, and it is stable. A young black woman I met shortly before Princess Margaret arrived to preside over the anniversary celebrations put it most eloquently: 'I hate to do it, frankly,' she said, in the middle of a dinner party at which all the guests had been arguing for independence, and had been saying fierce things about kicking out the American bases and declaring Bermuda a nuclear-free zone. 'I hate to do it – but when she comes I'll be down there waving a Union Jack as the car drives by and the Princess waves at us all. It is something instinctive. I can't explain it. I want it to go away. But while it's there I'll take part. It just feels good, I guess. But I'll feel bad the next morning.' And everyone at the table laughed, and nodded, and said things like, 'Right on!'

And they were indeed all out on the streets waving their flags when the Princess drove by, and the most militant of them all at that dinner was seen in a white dinner-jacket, happily applauding the Queen's sister as she made her thank-you speech for having been made Colonel-in-Chief of the Bermuda Regiment.

'A place where we have practised cricket diplomacy,' a smooth young man at the Washington Embassy once said of Bermuda. 'A place where we don't intend to pull stumps.' A place that has the feel of a very elegant, British-built film set; a place that is a twenty-square-mile offshore aircraft carrier, crammed with the men and materials for the prosecution of an American war. A place where, though the British may provide the pomp, the Americans, for good or ill – and most Bermudians conclude it is for good – provide the circumstance.

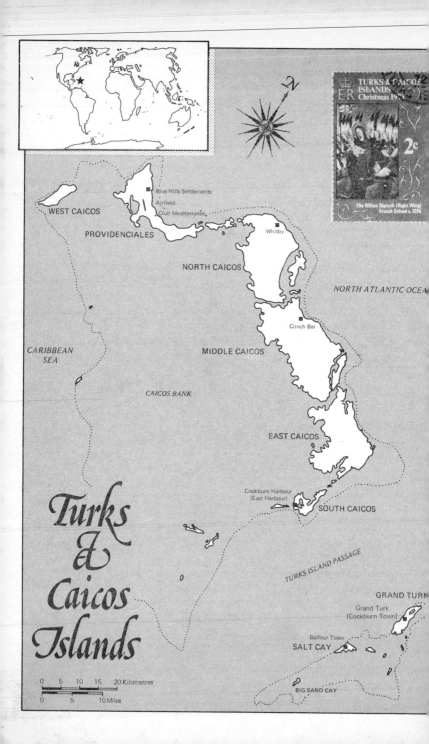

NINE

THE BRITISH WEST INDIES

A free ticket for seat 14 C on the Ryan Air International Charter from Kennedy Airport to the island of Providenciales had been thrust into my hand at the last minute, and so I wasn't about to complain; but my neighbours in seats 14 A and B? After listening to their chatter for an hour or so, they were, I thought, just a little peculiar.

He had something to do with dentistry, came from Bayonne, New Jersey, must have been about sixty and had grey hair that seemed to have been sculpted, rather than merely combed, and was brittle, and of suspiciously perfect trim. The lady who sat between us – she may have been his wife – was about ten years younger, had bleached hair and wore a frilly blouse from Laura Ashley. Both drank from a bottle of Canadian Club whisky and concentrated intently on sex magazines, and carried on a breathless and deeply distracting conversation, ripples from which spread as far as row nine in front and, I suspected, at least to the beginning of the smoking section behind.

It thus proved very difficult indeed to concentrate on Hosay Smith's *A History of the Turks and Caicos Islands*, particularly since it appeared to be written in pidgin. All I seemed able to retain was the fact that in 1893 the Turks Islands Government had raised thirty-three pounds thirteen shillings from the sale of dog licences, but I suspect that may have lodged in my mind because at the time the woman next to me was extolling the virtues of performing what sounded singularly unpleasant and possibly illegal things to her German Shepherd, which I gathered was most definitely not the blond Bavarian who looked after the flock of Merinos she and her dental friend kept in the garden in the back of Bayonne.

So it was altogether a relief when the tone of the engines changed and we began to sweep down through the sky, and glimpsed an island and a coral reef three miles below us on the port side. It was the island of Providenciales (or Provo) in the Caicos groups, on the western end of the oldest remaining British possession in the West Indies. Everyone aboard the plane was about to have a week's holiday in the island's newly opened Club Méditerranée, and they gasped with delight when the captain announced the outside temperature was eighty-five degrees. It had been snowing heavily in Manhattan, and Bayonne, not a pretty place in the best of weathers, must have been one step removed from hell.

The airport at which we landed, brand new, and with the heat wafting in visible waves from its unscuffed runway, was already well-known to most reasonably informed British taxpayers. In 1981 it had been at the focus of a small scandal: the developers of Club Med had promised to build an hotel on the island providing the British Government built an airport, and paved the dirt road leading along the island to their front gate. The British agreed and coughed up five million pounds – only to suffer a torrent of abuse from Members of Parliament who, perhaps rightly, wondered why on earth taxpayers at home were having to finance a scheme on a nearly uninhabited coral island that would make huge profits for Frenchmen and give pleasant holidays to rich Americans and give no benefit whatsoever to Britain. The Government of the Turks and Caicos Islands tried to reply that their airport would bring in tourists for many other hotels, and would help bring revenue to the island coffers thereby helping the colony to become economically independent – but London was in no mood to listen, and has dealt with the colony fiercely, and at arms' length ever since. The day I arrived there had been a message from Whitehall insisting that the islanders all pay their electricity bills immediately, or Her Majesty's Government would want to know why. The Chief Minister was arrested in

Florida for drug smuggling. And in 1986 the entire administration was dismissed by the Governor. Such are the trials of contemporary colonialism.

But the particular trial, so far as the island Governors are concerned, is that – the airport scandal aside – not one Britain in 10,000 appears ever to have heard of the colony of the Turks and Caicos Islands. It is the third largest inhabited colonial possession after the Falklands and the curious scattering of reefs south of Ceylon known as British Indian Ocean Territory (the British Antarctic is of course far larger than all the others put together, and with the British Isles thrown in for good measure, but neither has nor has had a permanent native population); it is one of the earliest discoveries in the New World, and indeed lays claim to having been found by Columbus himself, it is claimed, on his first voyage. Depending on which local account is the less incredible, he landed first on the island of East Caicos, or on the beach beside the present British Governor's mansion on Grand Turk.

Most modern scholarship suggests in fact that Columbus made his landfall either on Cat Island or, most probably, on Watling Island, both of which are in the Bahamas chain, a hundred miles to the north-west of Grand Turk. But one of his ships, the *Pinta*, is supposed to have foundered on a Caiconian reef, and, along with hundreds of other Spanish galleons that also stranded nearby, is regularly explored by treasure-hunters. Conventional belief holds that it was Juan Ponce de Leon, searching for the fountain of youth – which turned up on Bimini – who formally discovered the islands in 1512, nearly a year before he found Florida.

The Turks – named after a local fez-like red cactus, the Turk's head – and the Caicos, or 'Cays', form, with their forty-two islands and skerries, two distinct archipelagos, separated from each other, and from their neighbours (the Bahamas to the west, Hispaniola to the south) by immensely deep channels. To see the drop-off into these much-used shipping lanes is impressive enough from the air, with the water's colour changing abruptly from the palest of greens to a vivid dark blue. But to swim out over the reef edge is a decidedly more dramatic, and a terrifying venture: I tried it one calm afternoon, lying flat on the surface with my face, suitably masked and snorkelled, below water.

The bottom was perhaps ten feet below, with pink and yellow corals and the waving fronds of tropical water plants. Small fishes glittered and glinted in the dappled sunlight. I paddled slowly onwards, out to the open sea, keeping my eyes fixed on the magical display below. The reef was still there, close enough to touch, glistening, gleaming – until suddenly, horrifyingly, it ended. It fell away, downward and vertical, into a bottomless black chasm. In an instant there was no coral, no fish, no light – just the edge, the beginning of the deep ocean. The charts said it was two miles deep here, and I shuddered with vertigo, and swam hurriedly back to the reef edge and to the lagoon beyond.

There had been Arawak Indians on the Caicos during the ninth and tenth centuries, and archaeologists from Pennsylvania regularly find potsherds and fishhooks buried in the limestone gravel. But the Arawaks vanished, inexplicably, and it was not until 1678, when sailors from Bermuda arrived in their fast cedarwood sloops, that the basal stock of today's 7,000 islanders was laid. The Bermudians discovered that the islands, perpetually warm, almost wholly flat, and pierced by small lakes and lagoons that had a tendency to dry in the heat, could produce one commodity of which they had little and which, moreover, they could sell: salt. An annual routine was established: Bermudians from St George's would arrive in March, when the daytime temperatures on Grand Turk, Salt Cay and South Caicos – the only islands where they constructed salinas – were creeping up into the high eighties, and through the summer they would collect the white crystal masses and pack them in boxes. By November, at the end of the hurricane season, they would be on their way back, calling in at Charleston, or New York, or Boston, or Halifax, to sell the boxes of a salt that was said to be particularly suitable for packing beef and pork, its principal use at the time.

The salt industry was to dominate the Turks economy for three centuries. The islanders called it 'white gold', and many fortunes were made – negro slaves from West Africa raking in the crystals, their white Bermudian owners raking in the money. Island time-keeping was ordered by the whistle on the old Frith and Murphy steam-powered salt grinder, which blew at ten each morning and five each night, and could be heard, on a windless day, across the sound that separated Turks from Caicos, twenty miles away.

There were salt piles on the old colonial flag, though one can be forgiven for thinking that one of the piles looks like an igloo. The London flagmaker, as ignorant of the islands then as most Londoners are today, thought the sketches – two white dome-shaped objects in front of a three-masted merchantman – referred to some far-off British possession in the Arctic – Frobisher Bay, perhaps, or Point Barrow. So, without asking anyone, he obligingly touched up the sketch by adding a door to one of the salt piles so that any Eskimo could go in and out at will; the device was duly stitched together and remained the colonial symbol for a century, until someone noticed, rubbed out the door and put two black salt rakers beside the ship to leave no room for doubt.

Salt raking was a risky business in the eighteenth century. The Bermudians were chased away by angry Spaniards from time. to time, and in 1764 kidnapped by the French Navy, who then established a small settlement of their own. They told the rival powers that they had done so to stamp out piracy, and clamp down on the growing local habit of building false light-houses, which caused shipwrecks which could then be plundered. The British would have none of it. The Bermudians were, after all, their own kith and kin, and under the principle of *civis Romanus sum*, whereby any Briton in trouble abroad, particularly at the hands of the dastardly French, was fully entitled to Crown protection. In any case by this time the British Empire itself was already firmly established in the West Indies (of which the Turks are not, technically, a part: they, like Bermuda and the Bahamas, think of themselves as Western Atlantic islands). London was moved to make a tough response, and for what was to be classically Imperial reasoning.

Although the nine square miles of Grand Turk was made merely of mud, limestone and salt and thus of no great economic consequence to Britain, the island and its sister Cays did in theory have one vital function: they commanded the sealanes from the ocean to Cuba, and to Hispaniola, and Jamaica – and control of sealanes was central to the growing Imperial philosophy. George Grenville, the Foreign Minister, complained to the French in terms of unalloyed arrogance: 'The islands must and shall be restored. I shall wait for nine days for your answer. If I do not receive it, the fleet now lying at Spithead shall sail directly to assert the rightful claims of Britain.' The Falklands War thus had its antecedents; in this case, though, after a ludicrous suggestion from the French that the island be governed in a three-way condominium, with Spain, France and England each taking three square miles and building proper lighthouses, Paris capitulated, and Britain took over. A British official was sent out from the Bahamas 'to reside there and by his residence on the spot to insure the right of the islands to His Majesty'.

One might have expected the Bermudians to be well pleased. In fact they were furious. The appointment of Andrew Symmer as representative of the King's Governor at Nassau meant that the islands were now, in effect, dependencies of the Bahamas, and no longer belonged to Bermuda. A century later they became official dependencies of Jamaica, and then when Jamaica became independent switched back to association with the Bahamas once more. It was not until 1973, once Nassau took independence, that the islands became a fully-fledged Crown colony on their own; Bermuda hasn't had any official connection with the islands since 1764.

Up to this point the Caicos Islands had remained uninhabited, but for turtles and, down on South Caicos, the salt rakers who built a settlement called Cockburn Harbour. But the American War of Independence changed that, very suddenly. Flotillas of small boats brought hundreds of Loyalists out from the coast of Georgia: most settled in the Bahamas, but a number, with their slaves, made it out to Providenciales, and to North and Middle Caicos, and farmed cotton; but weevils, drought and, in 1811, a devastating hurricane that destroyed all the plantations, forced them to abandon the islands: only the negroes were left to get on with it, sinking rapidly into what one writer noted was 'a state little short of savagery'. The Caicos Islands remained the poor relation of the group, although the brief prosperity the salt rakers of the Turks enjoyed (at one stage during the American Wars salt was making forty-eight dollars a ton) fell back during the nineteenth century, and the colony subsided gently, an impoverished backwater, overlooked by London, ignored and forgotten.

The islanders, nearly all descendants of the slaves, have tried gamely ever since to make a living. They gathered sponges from the Caicos reefs, helped by divers from Kalymnos, one of the Greek Dodecanesian Islands, who were experts in sponge diving off the coast of Libya. The conch – various varieties, such as the Florida horse conch, the queen conch and the clam eating lightning conch – was harvested, and still is, by divers who can stay under water for two minutes on one breath. Lobsters and crabs, too, provided an income; and today there is considerable optimism that the spider crab, fed on plates of algae, will flourish, and provide crabmeat for the gigantic American market.

The Smithsonian Institution from Washington, using a drug-smuggling boat that was captured by the local police, have been carrying out experiments with different kinds of crabs; the boat is crewed by a posse of girls from the Peace Corps, who seem to prefer the idea of diving off Grand Turk to some of the tougher tasks the Corps hands out.

But generally the islands have suffered – either from neglect, or from that invariable error of the Imperial design, the one-crop economy. Whatever efforts have been made to rear conch and lobster, crabs or cotton, they have been minimal compared to the colony's reliance on salt. And when, in 1964, the Bahamians established a massive, fully mechanised salt plant, mechanically raked, with a deep-water port for the ships that would collect it, the Turks economy collapsed – just as the St Helenian economy collapsed when demand for flax evaporated, just as the Gibraltarian economy did when the Admiralty closed the local dockyard. The islands present a sorry sight today.

I flew from Provo one morning, leaving behind the tourists and the sailing crowd, the rich American investors and the diving teachers, and into another, older, decaying world. Twenty minutes later we bumped down at the airstrip at the colony's capital Cockburn Town on Grand Turk: an ancient Haitian collected me in a taxi, a twenty-year-old Buick that bucked and reared around the potholes like a maverick pony.

Cockburn Town was utterly worn out. The tin roofs rusted and sagged; weatherboards had warped, and flapped in the steady wind; there was barbed wire and broken glass, sleeping dogs, and a clutch of bored-looking donkeys standing in the sun. The sea wall was cracked, and water was splashing on to the front street; the government buildings, creaking venerably, were flyblown and dusty, and the electricity kept failing. And dominating everything, the great Town Salina, where once ten thousands pounds' worth of salt had been raked and boxed each year, and which hasn't produced a cellarful since 1964. The shallow pans are brown with mud today, the low walls between them chipped and broken. A windmill that had once pumped the saline water from pound to pound had broken long ago, and its blades swayed uselessly back and forth, with a screech of rotten iron and a shower of rust.

There were some new buildings, true: a determined effort was being made to turn the islands into a tax haven, and one lawyer I knew had noticeboards outside his office showing him to be the headquarters of some 4,200 companies, mostly American. The Government charges five hundred dollars a year as a registration fee, and my friend takes another hundred or so: the Chief Minister went off to Hong Kong in 1984, looking for firms who are nervous about that colony's reversion to China in 1997, and who might like to set up in Grand Turk. He was optimistic, though some of his colleagues wondered about their pride: the Turkmen and the Caiconians had been fishermen and salt rakers once, he said, and had liked hard work, and sweat; merely to sit back and earn fees from so dubious a business as offshore finance seemed, they said, a little 'undignified'. There was something rather pleasant, an old fisherman said, 'in being the least developed of the colonies. No one comes and bothers us here. That used to be the case, and now it's changing. Once the bankers and the insurance men discover us, and the Americans, we're done for.'

He might have added to his list the drug smugglers. The lonelier islands of the Caicos group, unpoliced, unsupervised, and lying temptingly midway between Florida and the Colombian marijuana and cocaine farms, have become one of the world's great trans-shipment points for narcotics. Billions of dollars' worth pass through each year – cocaine from Bogota to Miami, heroin from Paris (via Haiti) to New York, marijuana from Caracas to Atlanta (via Nassau). Planes fly in and out of the South Caicos aerodrome at night; some are intercepted, most are untroubled. A very few islanders make a few dollars turning on the lights, or turning blind eyes; some of the offshore banks swell their accounts a little with drug commissions. But in general the big money stays away from the Turks and Caicos, and whatever their role in the distribution of the world's drugs, the islanders remain generally poor.

Chris Turner, the Governor, who lives in a wonderful mansion named Waterloo (it was built in the same year), and who drives a London taxi as his official car (its mirrors are gnawed off by the wild horses) can do little – either to clamp down on the drugs trade, or perk up the economy. Like all colonial governors he seems perpetually frustrated by the lack of interest shown in London. When I asked his deputy whether his colleagues in the Foreign Office responded quickly to queries he immediately said, 'Oh yes! very quickly,' and went on to say that his recent request for compassionate leave had been answered on the same day he had asked. But when I explained that I had not meant that at all, but was interested in whether they answered queries about serious island problems – more money needed for a school, perhaps, or a much-wanted scholarship for a medical student, extra medicine for the hospital, he had to change his tune. 'I see what you mean. Well, no, I'm afraid not. It takes weeks, sometimes months. We're at the bottom of every in-tray, I sometimes think. They look after the diplomats all right. We're part of what we call the Coconut Mafia, and they keep us happy. But the island – it seems that London just forgets we exist.'

The islanders, who have known this for many years, now try to make a virtue out of the unpleasant reality. 'Where on earth are the Turks and Caicos Islands?' ask the advertisements put out by the tourist board. 'As close to paradise as this world offers,' comes the reply, meaning Provo, presumably, rather than Cockburn Town. For our friends from Bayonne, New Jersey, the colony probably does appear a temporary paradise; for many of the islanders, forgotten, not paid, it must appear rather considerably less.

The journey from Grand Turk to the next way-station on this Imperial Progress, the Virgin Islands, was not easy. Only a few miles of sea separate the two colonies, but LIAT, the main inter-island airline, does not fly on this route, arguing that those who might want to travel can't afford the fare, and those who can afford it don't want to go. So I had to return to America, wait endless hours in Miami airport, take one aircraft to Puerto Rico, and finally step on to another to the colonial aerodrome on Beef Island. Since the initials LIAT, which officially mean Leeward Islands Air Transport, are also said to stand for 'Luggage in Another Town' it may well have been a blessing.

Beef Island's airport is a travellers' airport, the kind of place where men in bomber jackets and white silk scarves hang round the bars waiting for little men named Nobby or Curly, who have cotton waste in their fists and grease on their cheeks, to tell them that the kite's ready, but go easy on Number Three today because there's a bit of a leak in the pitot head. The first man I met came from Surbiton, was covered in oil, and was asking the black lady at the tea stand if she thought it was possible to die of tannin poisoning, since the cup he was ordering was the tenth of the day, and it was only half past nine.

Air-BVI had a couple of Dakotas parked on the apron; one was built in 1937 and had logged 72,000 hours. 'A little corrosion in places, but basically she's a solid old thing,' said her captain, who had taken her to every Caribbean airport over the last twenty years. 'You should see the log. Must be over five inches thick. It's basically not your one lady driver, not this one!' He climbed aboard and the grease-monkey swung the engines, which poured black smoke for a few seconds before settling down to a sweetly contented gurgle. He took off into the morning sun, to collect an American lady from the island of Anegada up

ANEGADA

The Settlement

CARIBBEAN SEA

British Virgin Islands

VIRGIN GORDA

Spanish Town

GREAT CAMANOE

BEEF ISLAND

Airport

GUANA ISLAND

GINGER ISLAND

TORTOLA

COOPER ISLAND

Road Town

SALT ISLAND

JOST VAN DYKE

PETER ISLAND

GREAT TOBAGO

NORMAN ISLAND

LITTLE TOBAGO

ST JOHN
(US VIRGINS)

UK/US border

DRAKE CHANNEL

FRANCIS

SIR

N

north, an island which, he said, was mercifully quite devoid of hills.

There were other pilots waiting in the bar. One man, from Manchester, had just delivered a second-hand Hawker-Siddeley to the island Government. The trip had taken him the best part of a fortnight: his route had been from Manchester to Stornoway in the Outer Hebrides, then to Reykjavik, then the American airfield at Sondre Stromfjord in West Greenland, Goose Bay in Labrador, and finally Bangor in Maine, and Wilmington in Delaware, before making the crossing to the colony. His co-pilot, a Mr Patel, used to work for a small charter company in Calcutta, and had spent many recent months dropping food supplies to the victims of the Brahmaputra floods in Assam. He was amused, being a good Hindu, to find himself based on Beef Island.

The Queen Elizabeth Bridge, complete with toll-booth and smiling toll-collector, connects Beef Island and its ten acres of flat land (hence the airfield) with Tortola, which is the upper part of a long and very rugged mountain chain, and on which there is no space to stand a pencil, let alone land a plane. Tortola is, thanks to the ever-warm seas, surrounded by coral reefs, but it is not a coral island: the hills are carved from crushed and twisted sandstones, there are peaks of volcanic breccias, veins of coarsely crystalline pegmatite and cliffs of fine grey diorite, and everything is overgrown with deep green vegetation, with frangipani and "ginger Thomas', scrub and palm and patches of rain forest. From the bridge Tortola looks as though a few square miles of the Matto Grosso had been snatched up and crumpled by a giant's hand and tossed carelessly into the dark blue waters of the Caribbean Sea; but there are white sand beaches, banana groves, mango trees and coconuts, and the Union flag flutters from a pole on a small flat building, which turns out to be the local station of the Royal Virgin Islands Police.

Virgin Islands – not 'British' Virgin Islands. There is some confusion over the name of this particular territory, and which will take a little explaining.

Until the Sixties the Virgins were administered as a British West Indian Presidency, a rather anonymous entity that was buried in the complicated edifice of the colony of the Leeward Islands, which had its headquarters on the island of Antigua, and looked after more than a hundred islands sandwiched between Puerto Rico in the north, and Guadeloupe in the south. Until 1917 they had every right to call themselves the Virgins: Columbus, who found them in 1493, was so delighted to see so many little islands and rocks clustered together in the shadow of one great all-protecting mother that he named them after the legend of St Ursula and the 11,000 virgins whom the Huns supposedly murdered outside Rome. Columbus was probably trying to impress his royal Spanish sponsors, Ferdinand and Isabella, by naming his discovery '*Las Once Mil Virgines*': there are only about eighty islands in the group, and he had exaggerated five hundred-fold.

During the seventeenth century the ownership of Tortola and its neighbour islands to the north, up to and including the flat coral island of Anegada and an important little uninhabited rock called Sombrero – it now belongs to Anguilla, and is still very important to some – passed back and forth between Spaniard, Dutchman and Briton according to the byzantine rituals of Caribbean history. But in 1666 newcomers to the region announced themselves: the Danes, buoyed by a wave of mercantile zeal, were busily colonising small morsels of the world, in India, on the Guinea coast, and in the West Indies. They took possession of St Thomas, an island that was technically a Virgin – one of Columbus's 11,000 – and was only ten miles from Tortola.

Stern messages passed out from Government House, Antigua, but the Danes ignored them. The British were not keen to fight, the Danes not eager to conquer any island which the British particularly wanted. They set up indigo and cotton plantations, annexed St John (which was just a mile from Tortola) and then bought St Croix from the Knights of Malta. But they seemed not to have taught anyone Danish: no trace of a Creole Dansk remains today, anyway. And the name of their colony was written in English: the Danish West Indies. The Virgin Islands, in the strict official sense, were now wholly British.

But in 1917 the Danish sold out to the Americans, for twenty-five million dollars, and St Thomas and its sister islands became

an extension of the United States, run at first by the Navy, then
by the Department of the Interior, and finally by the people
themselves. And – the final complication – the Americans
decided to rename the collection of islands 'the United States
Virgin Islands'. Britain grumbled – not too much back in 1917,
since Tortola and her sister islands were but an unimportant
presidency of the Leewards, but much more later, when the
islands began to try to stand up on their own. London suggested,
with great politeness, that the Americans might have inadver-
tently misappropriated the islands' title, and forecast great confusion for anyone wanting to go to the Virgin Islands and turning
up in the town of Charlotte Amalie (which is the capital of the
United States territory) while actually wanting to go to the
Imperial capital, the far less charmingly named Road Town.

The Colonial Office in London might well have swallowed its
pride and renamed the colony, to avoid mistakes of this kind.
But it would not countenance such a thing. It was left to the
islands' tourist board to make the change: in the mid-Seventies
it took upon itself the task of retitling the colony 'the British
Virgin Islands', and adding the slogan 'Yes, we're different', to
show tourists that Tortola offered charms that were not at all
the same as the gaudier delights on show in the US territory.
Informally, London has now concurred, and the Colonial
Governor heads his annual report with the word 'British'. But
legislation continues to be passed under the old name, official
instruments are still issued by the colony of the Virgin Islands
and the police are not the Royal British Virgin Islands Police,
but simply the RVIP, their Britishness unspoken, though undis-
guised.

I came to know something of the Virgin Islands Police on
almost my first day on the colony, when I stepped straight into
what might well one day be called 'the mysterious affair at
Brandywine'.

There was a Canadian woman on Tortola, a wealthy divorcee
whose principal home was on Grand Cayman, where she sold
dresses to passengers on the passing cruise liners. For the past
five years she had also owned a modern and spectacularly sited
house outside Road Town, from where, when she chose to take

a break from the arduous tasks on Cayman, she could come to read and swim, or watch the yachts schooning down the Sir Francis Drake Channel, 400 feet below the cliffs. The house must be one of the loveliest in the Caribbean, and when she was away – which was for about nine months of the year – she rented it, at a premium, to wealthy Americans. On the day we met she was about to take it over after an absence of three months: a young and reportedly delightful couple from Philadelphia had taken it for a thirteen-week honeymoon, and were due to leave on the Wednesday.

But no one turned up with the keys on the Wednesday, nor on the Thursday, nor by the weekend. On Sunday, by which time we had convinced ourselves that the young couple, delightful or otherwise, were clearly no longer in residence, we broke in.

It was like stopping a film in mid-frame. The couple had been there, living a full and energetic life in one frame, and by the next they had vanished. The bed was unmade. There were magazines, open, on the tables. Letters, half-written, were on desks. A can of warm beer, open, was on the kitchen bench. A lipstick, just used, had rolled to the side of the dressing table. A crumpled négligée, a pair of stockings, a tee-shirt lay at the foot of the bed. Someone had been reading Elspeth Huxley's *The Flame Trees of Thika*.

We read their letters, examined their bills, looked at the photo albums. They spoke of 'shipments' which customers were meant to have received in Boca Raton, Fort Lauderdale and Phoenix. They had checked into hotels in Caracas and Bogota, using false names, always paying in cash. They had taken pictures of each other naked, and standing beside the light plane they owned. They wrote that they used cocaine a great deal, and we found several pounds of hashish hidden in boxes.

And they were never heard of again. The Virgin Islands Police inquired. So did the Virgin Islands Governor. And the FBI, and the Drug Enforcement Administration, and the Pennsylvania State Police. Everyone on the island seemed to think they were running drugs, using their little Comanche to ferry cocaine from Colombia to Florida, perhaps even going via South Caicos as so many Americans before them had done. Everyone seemed to think they had crashed into the sea one afternoon, on their way home to Brandywine House. They hadn't looked a very appetising couple, my friend had said, but even so, it was a rotten way to end a honeymoon. 'The main business of the Caribbean these days,' said a policeman. 'Things have changed a great deal.'

My friend never received her last month's rent for the house. Instead a lawyer in Philadelphia offered her all the personal belongings of the vanished pair. She sold the radios and the records, read the books, and tried to sell the girl's clothes to the cruise line passengers on Grand Cayman. Finally she sold the house; it had been spoiled, she said. It felt cursed by a strange spell. There used to be voodoo in Tortola, when the Arawaks were there; some of the older people in Road Town wondered if it had reared its head again, briefly, in the mysterious affair at Brandywine.

The air of somnolent decay which had been so evident in Cockburn Town was very much abroad in Road Town, too. The streets were potholed and dusty, the houses peeling and shabby, with cracked window-panes and broken verandahs. Rusting cars, their tyres long since stripped off by fishing-boat crews, who used them as fenders, were sprawled on the waste land, grass growing up through the seats. There was a clatter of thin applause from behind a small supermarket: schoolchildren were playing cricket in the evening sun, their parents lying on sandy grass, drinking beer and clapping lazily as one child hit a four, and the ball rolled into the ditch.

The smell of the sea was very rich and heavy here, and the cobles bobbed up and down on the scummy water, in a foam of weed and peelings and a litter of styrofoam fragments. Three ancient men sat in the twilight, fishing idly, smoking, talking in low tones. A pair of snappers, still glistening scarlet, twitched on the timbers. One of the men pulled out a piece of crumpled paper and tried to read it in the fading light; it was in Spanish – he was hoping to do some small deal with a man in Puerto Rico – and I had to translate it for him. It had something to do with an ice-cream maker which the man thought he might like to buy.

Up in the hills lights twinkled like fireflies, and there was a sudden burst of distant music as the wind shifted, and blew us a song from a cruising yacht moored out in the Roads. But then it fell silent, except for the water lapping against the pier, and the low buzz of talk among the fishermen. A lovely, sleepy cul-de-sac of Empire, content in its own oblivion.

The dark bulk of the American Virgin Islands could still be made out to the south. The guidebooks spoke proudly of their achievement, and politicians I had encountered there liked to compare the relative sophistication and economic development of the American islands with the insouciant backwardness of their British neighbours. Highest per capita income in the Caribbean! Five hundred million dollars a year from tourists! Three hundred miles of roads! Thirty thousand cars! An elected governor! American citizenship for the islanders!

And it was true, comparing statistic for statistic, that our colony had a forlorn and lacklustre sound to it. Income was woefully low, the islanders lived simply, the yachts and the cruise liners brought in less than a fifth the number of dollars generated across the Narrows. And only seventy miles of road, and less than a thousand cars, and a governor who was appointed by London without any islander being asked what he thought, and a passport that, unlike that issued to the Gibraltarians, gave no right of free access to the mother country, and was regarded by most islanders as almost useless, though handsome. The only statistic about which the British islanders could feel proud was the literacy rate: everyone in Tortola could read, but in the US territory only nine in ten could. The Americans, mind you, had a university, paid for by the Federal Government.

But the figures conceal the reality, of course, and the islanders seem proud of their home. 'Ah born here' is the slogan on many tee-shirts, and, rubbing the point home, the shops sell tourists others with the words 'Ah wish Ah born here'. The American islanders have no such affection for their home. Their territory is a dreadful place, flashy and gaudy, loud and vulgar, with nightclubs and casinos and a thousand profitable diversions for the over-worked young of the Eastern seaboard. The charm went with the Danes, seventy years ago, and not a few islanders wish, for all the

pleasures of owning an American passport, that the cool administrators from Copenhagen would come back and bring some
dignitas with them. In the British territory the *dignitas* – which,
admittedly, buys no bread – is still in evidence. There is silence
and a sort of peace on Tortola; maybe the boardwalks are a little
splintered, and the door of your hotel room does sag from a single
hinge, and the goats wake you up in the morning, and the maid
sings too loudly as she sluices water over the cool flagstones – but
there can be serenity in an undiscovered place, and Tortola still
has serenity in great abundance.

A number of the outer islands trade on the peace. One of the
Rockefellers built an inn on the Virgin Gorda where, he promised, the only strenuous activity was cracking a lobster shell or
pouring a glass of wine. On Peter Island a hotel owned by a
Welshman charges three hundred pounds a day for each guest,
and suggests that they do 'what you've always wanted to do –
nothing'. The scenery is described by one enthusiastic copy-
writer as 'the kind God would have made if He'd had the money'.
Advertisements for the secret hideaway hotels of the Virgin
Islands are to be found in the back pages of the *New Yorker*,
among all those other carefully vetted notices for tie narrowers,
ancestors traced and hand-tooled leather bookbindings. The
customers tend to be an altogether better class – no riffraff from
New Jersey need apply to come to Virgin Gorda.

The long-distance cruising yachts drop in on the Virgins,
which have become one of the West Indies' main sailing centres.
The mountains rearing straight out of the sea provide easy
landmarks – far more visible than the flat coral islets of the
Bahamas – and cause interesting eddies and eccentric winds.
The sailing in Virgin Islands' water is testing, and enormous fun.
Hurricanes are a problem in the summer season. People still
talk with awe about the great blow of 1772, 'the greatest
hurricane in the history of Man', and wonder when the islands
are due for another. Standing instructions to islanders urge them
to remove all coconuts from the trees near their houses: in a
fifty mph gale the nuts can smash through a wall like machine-gun
bullets.

I gave a lift in my car one day to the daughter of a Welsh

Member of Parliament; she was crewing on board a sixty-foot sloop that her boyfriend had been asked to deliver from Auckland to New Orleans. They had already been a month on Tortola, and had just about exhausted their money – 'most of it went on pina coladas and lobster, I'm afraid,' she laughed. The pair were going on an economy drive from now on: only pineapples and papayas, she said, and such fish as they could catch from the marina wall. And draught Guinness, laid on at this particular marina because the Guinness company owned the place.

The smaller Virgin Islands occasionally come up for sale; Lord Cobham, a wealthy Worcestershire farmer, sold Necker Island to a record producer (via a firm in Newcastle upon Tyne which specialises in selling islands); a British businessman bought Anegada and tried to sell it off in square-foot chunks via the personal columns of the *New York Times*, earning him much disapproval from the British Government; but Fallen Jerusalem and Dead Man's Chest and Jost van Dyke have not been recently traded, nor Ginger, Cooper and Salt Islands, which the locals know, because of the initials, as Grand Central Station.

And if not for sale, then the site for a story. Dead Man's Chest is said to have provided inspiration for Robert Louis Stevenson's *Treasure Island* (he never came to the Virgin Islands but his father, the builder of lighthouses, knew the Caribbean well). The island dignitaries make an annual summer journey – under the terms of the Salt Ponds Ordnance, 1904 – to Salt Island, where they watch those islanders fortunate enough to have licences gather their salt for the coming twelve months. A policeman fires a gunshot to start the collectors sifting through the muddy brine.

And Jost van Dyke, now a pretty resort island, is best known to the locals as the island of the fiercest of all planter slave-owners, the Quaker minister John Coakley Lettsom, of whom it was said:

> I, John Lettsom,
> Blisters, bleeds and sweats 'em,
> If after that they choose to die
> I, John, Lettsom.

The British may not have as liberal a reputation as some for ending slavery in the Caribbean (the Danes abolished the practice on their Virgin Islands twenty years before the slaves were freed on Tortola); and they may wince today at papers in the Virgin Islands' library advertising the arrival of a boat at Road Town 'bearing three tons of Negro'. But the fact that they did abolish it remains as one persistent reason for the affection with which Britons are still held. 'Queen Victoria was de bestest of all de kings in de world,' a Road Town boatman remarked to a visitor in the 1940s. He thought, wrongly, that Victoria had freed his great grandfather.

On August Monday – like Britain's summer bank holiday – each year the islanders organise a big parade along Main Street to give thanks for their freedom. They march past the great old prison, built in 1859, and in which murderers are still hanged, and in which prisoners are still flogged (both capital and corporal punishment being on the Virgin Islands' statute book, and used from time to time); they march past the equally antique Government Buildings, where the little elected legislature sits, and from where the British Governor, kitted out in his white finery and his goose-feathered topee, proffers his salute.

By some Caribbean standards the Virgin Islanders may be thought less well-off, or perhaps less free, and perhaps less fortunate; but they are a happy and untroubled people, and believe they have little cause for complaint. Whatever the textbooks and the politicians and the statistics may say, the Virgin Islanders remain proud, indomitably so, of the fact that it is still the Union flag which flies above Government House, high up on the jungle hills, above their dusty and old-fashioned little town.

Until the early hours of 19th March 1969, the eel-shaped sliver of coral limestone known as Anguilla was no more than a footnote in British Imperial geographies. You could rarely look it up in a book without being referred to its colonial superiors of St Kitts and Nevis, or to its mother-colony of the Leeward Islands. It was an utterly insignificant morsel of Crown land, peopled by peasants, covered with scrub, infertile, thick with mosquitoes, rarely visited, unheard of, unremembered and vastly unimportant.

SCRUB ISLAND

LITTLE SCRUB ISLAND 🔔

CARIBBEAN SEA

Island Harbour

ANGUILLA

The Quarter

The Valley

Sandy Ground Village

Blowing
Point
Village

Airfield

SEAL ISLAND

PRICKLY PEAR CAYS

DOG ISLAND

West End Village

0   1   2   3   4   5 Kilometres
0   1   2   3 Miles

But before the dawn broke on that calm spring morning something rather peculiar happened. Two Royal Navy frigates, HMS *Minerva* and HMS *Rothesay*, stole silently into Anguillian waters. They dropped a flotilla of rubber boats, cranked up a helicopter or two and unleashed a force of 315 members of the second battalion, the Parachute Regiment, who landed complete with their red berets, machine-guns and blackened faces and tried to make friends with the local goats. A group of Scotland Yard policemen, some still in their blue serge uniforms, were landed too. For a few moments Crocus Beach, Anguilla, must have looked like Omaha Beach in Normandy: the British forces on this occasion were storming ashore to still a rebellion that had broken out among the 6,000 islanders.

The invasion, planned with deep seriousness by the Cabinet in London, was given the codename Operation Sheepskin. It was probably the last strictly Imperial military task ever performed by the British, it was a total failure, and it made a delicious farce in which no shots were fired, no one was hurt and which the whole world – except the British Government – enjoyed hugely. Its only consequence was that a small cameo of Caribbean history took a sudden and unexpected swerve, and the name of Anguilla has been well-known ever since.

Well-known, but still not easy to reach – at least, not from Tortola, not on the day I needed to travel. Thanks to the caprices of Europe's various West Indian dominions I had to pass through the passport and customs checks of no fewer than three great powers before landing on Anguilla, and had to cross the only land border anywhere in the world that is shared by France and Holland.

The linear distance between Road Town and The Valley – British colonial capitals have the most wretchedly prosaic names! – is almost exactly 100 miles. It took me six hours, via aircraft, car and speedboat. First, I flew from Beef Island to the island of St Kitts, the first West Indian island to be colonised by Britain with, confusingly, a capital with the very non-British name of Basseterre. After a cup of coffee at Basseterre airport matters became more confusing still. The plane, which was so small it looked more suitable for entomology than for aviation, turned back northwards to the extraordinary island of Saint Martin – extraordinary because the island's southern half, where the plane landed, is still run by the Dutch under the name Sint Maarten, and the northern half is run by the French. Technically it is French, an *arrondissement* of Guadeloupe. It sends deputies to Paris, has a prefect, and its *citoyens* are as French as if they were born in Marseilles.

I landed at Queen Juliana airport, was checked by a dour Dutchman who stamped my passport, took a taxi via a dusty little hamlet called Koolbaai – in fine rolling countryside; it reminded me of Cape Province, and the hills near Stellenbosch – and was driven up to the frontier. I would like to have seen a red-and-white pole, members of the *Staatspolizei* on this side, kepi-wearing *gendarmerie* on the other, but there was only a boundary stone and a couple of flags that I had great difficulty telling apart (both having the same colours, the one being horizontal, the other vertical). There was no one to look at my passport, but when, eventually, I was taken to the *quai* at the French capital, of Marigot – after a quick snack, some shrimp, half a baguette, and a glass or two of chilled Sancerre – and found the boat to Anguilla, I was duly inspected, my bags checked and a stamp affixed, all with great Gallic flourish. The boat, driven by a pair of excitable youths who appeared to have had the odd glass or two of Sancerre as well, took off northwards at about sixty knots. We rose out of the water, and seemed to fly. The service, I learned later, was by hydrofoil.

Anguilla lay low and white on the water, like a submerged whale. It is a long, narrow island with no hills, except for a 158-foot peak on the eastern tip, named Navigation Hill because of its use as a sea mark, and a 200-footer in the middle. The island's axis lies parallel to the ever-wafting trade winds, which is said to be the reason there are no forests, and little rain: the winds just divide and waft on, leaving nothing (whereas on Tortola they are forced up, form clouds, and burst out with rainstorms). From afar Anguilla looked strangely empty and lifeless. Sand beaches glittered brilliant white, with a line of low palms beyond. A tiny blue yawl bobbed at anchor by the pier. A Land Rover arrived, scrunching over the coral pebbles. The immigration inspector, wearing the crown of office, welcomed me ashore. 'Not too many people come by sea and stay,' he said. 'Nice to have you here. Rare thing.'

Anguilla is Britain's newest inhabited colony – new in the sense that, while it has been British territory, and in the cadet branch of far grander West Indian possessions for many years, it has only lately been a colony in its own right. (The very last piece of real estate that was subsumed into the Empire was actually the island of Rockall, out in mid-Atlantic, in 1955. London felt it vital to annexe the lonely chunk of guano-crusted rock because, just perhaps, it might have oil nearby; so it ordered out the Royal Navy, and matelots clambered up the slippery cliffs and fixed a brass plate to its granite summit. An expedition went there a few years later, and found the plate had been unscrewed, and taken away. Britain still claims Rockall, though, brass plate or not.)

Anguilla – or 'Malliouhana' as the Caribs named it – was formally made into a Crown colony and given a constitution, and a fully-functioning governor, in December 1982: she thus became the last colony 399 years after Britain took her first, Newfoundland. The reason for the establishment of a new colony – bucking the trend of twentieth-century decolonisation in no uncertain manner – has much to do with Operation Sheepskin, and the events that led up to it.

Anguilla has always been a poor island. The soil is thin, the rainfall scarce, the possibilities for livestock or agriculture minimal. There was precious little that the Britons who settled there could exploit, and very little work that their slaves could do for them. Across in Barbados, or down in Montserrat there was sugar to cut, or limes to pick, or tobacco to cure. In Anguilla there was nothing, and the slave-owners took a decision that was to have far-reaching consequences. They gave their workers four days off each week – the Sabbath, as was customary, and three other weekdays to allow them to cultivate their own patches of thin ground. When the Britons departed, for more fecund islands, and for their old home, the slaves that remained were more accustomed to working their own land, more familiar with the idea of freedom – even if it had only been of the four-day-a-week variety, it was more than their fellow slaves in the neighbour islands.

Thanks to this oddly gifted freedom, the ability to till land that was their own, and finally the hasty departure of the uninterested Britons, so the Anguillians, uniquely among the Leeward Islanders, evolved a rugged kind of independence. They proved awkward to rule, eager to mind their own business, and would brook no nonsense from any colonial master. In 1809 the Government told the Anguillians to build a prison at The Valley; yes, they replied, they would build one if and when they had anyone to put in it. And not before.

They had their own government, known as the Vestry, with four nominated members, and three elected. A dull little place, maybe, but it had rudimentary democracy earlier than most – another good reason for the islanders to feel determined, and a little aloof.

All raiders were repulsed. The French tried twice; the first time, in 1745, they were driven off at the battle of Crocus Bay by sheer mass of numbers, and number of island cannon. On the second occasion, fifty years later, the Anguillians showed gentlemanly restraint: the French powder was damp and, thinking they were out of the islanders' sight, they spread it out on sheets to dry, right along the beach at Rendezvous Bay. The islanders planned to toss burning staves at the powder, and blow it up, but their leader said that would neither be fair, nor British, and so they melted down all their fishing weights, made new bullets and fired away at the French with those, and drove them off, too. A determined, indefatigable people.

The British failed to recognise this 'passionate devotion to independence' when they came to organise the colonial arrangements for the region. No thought was ever given to creating Anguilla as a separate presidency, able to run itself under the general invigilation of the Leewards' Governor. No suggestion was made that Anguilla be linked with Tortola, which was at least notionally in its line of sight. Instead, for some unfathomable reason, Anguilla was formally linked with – and run from – an island a hundred miles to the south, separated from it by four other groups of islands that were run by the Dutch and the French, and peopled by natives whom the Anguillians cordially loathed.

The British, for administrative convenience, chose St Kitts to be the titular head of the presidency – it was called St Kitts-Nevis-Anguilla, and under the new arrangement Anguilla was very much the junior partner. The medical officer now ran the island, and doubled up as the beak; one Anguillian was sent to St Kitts to represent the island on the council; there was never enough money to build proper roads or a decent airfield, and there never was a secondary school, although the other islands shared four.

All this was just bearable so long as the British remained in power. The essential fairness of the Colonial Office and of the British establishment in St Kitts meant that the Anguillians were at least reasonably well provided for. But in 1967, after lengthy negotiations in London, St Kitts-Nevis-Anguilla became an independent nation – day-to-day rule over Anguilla moved from the British to the detested men of St Kitts. The Kittitian who was in the unhappy position of being his Government's official representative in the Valley on Independence Day decided to make as little fuss as possible: he got out of bed at four, raised the independence flag in his living room, saluted it while still in his pyjamas, and then crept back to bed.

One man in particular, the St Kitts' Chief Minister, Robert Bradshaw, became the focus of Anguillian venom. Hardly surprising, perhaps: he had once publicly vowed to 'turn Anguilla into a desert'. The islanders threw out his police force (there was not a single Anguillian policeman) and called in a motley crew of advisers – mostly Americans, and not always men of the most savoury reputations – to lead them to the state that Rhodesia had recently adopted: a Unilateral Declaration of Independence.

The Anguillian leader, Ronald Webster, and a remarkably colourful and patriarchal figure named Jeremiah Gumbs pleaded their case to the world. Mr Gumbs appealed before the General Assembly of the United Nations. Over in St Kitts Mr Bradshaw, who drove around in a vintage Rolls-Royce, appealed to the British to whip the Anguillians into line, and to halt the unseemly rebellion.

A parade of British officials came and went – one of them being brusquely turfed out because the Anguillians thought he was rude. He felt he was in danger of being lynched, so he gave an emergency message to the local Barclays Bank manager, who smuggled it through the islanders' lines in his shoe: the note was addressed to SNOWI – the Senior Naval Officer, West Indies, and asked for help.

In an act which half the world thought amusing, and which to the other half indicated that Britain was still an Imperial bully-boy, London decided to send in the troops. The second battalion of the Paras was alerted and sent to a holding base at Devizes. Forty policemen, members of the Metropolitan Force's Special Patrol Group, were kitted out in tropical uniforms (though not all of them; their leader was reckoned too fat for any of the cotton drills to fit) and joined them.

Fog delayed the group at their airfield in Oxfordshire, and Fleet Street found out all about Operation Sheepskin. Reporters met the plane in Antigua – a foolish place to land, since the Antiguans liked what the Anguillians were doing; they expressed their irritation by tossing out their Prime Minister in the following year's election, saying he had 'connived' with the British.

The troops and the policemen were put on the *Minerva* and the *Rothesay*, and left for the high seas. The reporters chose to invade at greater speed and in greater comfort: they flew across to Anguilla and waited. At 5.19 a.m. on the 19th March the first of the Red Devils landed. A series of blinding flashes greeted them as they reached the beach, and, as per their training, they threw themselves to the ground. They needn't have worried. Fleet Street was merely photographing the landing, for posterity.

Ronald Webster had no idea there would be a landing by British troops. He was in the bath when they arrived, and first got to learn of the invasion from a reporter, who asked him what he thought of it. Others were more prescient. An American lady confessed, with characteristic candour, that she had 'spent the entire night in my brassiere to be ready for the invasion. I never did that before in my life.'

If there were an armed rebellion brewing in a remote British possession, they never found the arms. Four old Lee-Enfield rifles, not very well oiled, and securely locked up, seemed to represent the total armoury. (It was later suggested that the rebel leaders had buried the guns in the mountains of Saint-Martin, but they have never been found.) A few people were arrested and taken off to the warships for a little talk. Some reporters said a shot had been fired at a plane they had chartered, but it was probably the perfervid imaginations of Fleet Street at work. In fact the little war must have been the most peaceful ever prosecuted, anywhere; and it made Britain look very foolish indeed. 'The Bay of Piglets!' jeered one American headline. 'The Lion that Meowed!'

The Imperial power was made to look even more ham-handed a few years later, when Anguilla and her 'rebel' leadership were formally offered every last thing they had wanted. They were not forced to join up with St Kitts and Nevis. Kittitian policemen, and Englishmen who wanted Kittitian policemen, were not foisted upon the islanders. The island was given back its own parliament – larger than the Vestry, and with greater powers. And the British Government happily prised the island away from Mr Bradshaw's clutches by making it a Crown colony (although, with the word 'colony' no longer thought proper, the actual technical term used was British dependent territory). The senior Briton dispatched to run the place was no longer to be called a medical officer, nor a resident, nor a senior British official, nor an administrator, nor a magistrate, nor a commissioner: from 1st April 1982, thirteen years and two weeks since the arrival of the two tiny warships off Crocus Bay, Anguilla could relax under the benign rule of Her Majesty's representative, His Excellency the Governor, complete with white uniform, sword and a splendid hat, gold braid and feathers, all entwined. Nothing so grand had ever been seen.

'Coffins for Sale – No Credit.' The sign was the first I noticed as my car bumped its way slowly up from the quayside, and to the Valley. It was, indeed, another shabby island, its capital another shabby town. Not forlorn, though, in the way that Cockburn Town had been forlorn; this looked like a place that had been overlooked for a long while, but was just being discovered, and was on the edge of better times.

'Bank of Nova Scotia' was the second sign I saw, and notices for banks and insurance companies turned out to be more numerous than any others. Small armies of workers were sawing and hammering away at rows of shops, twenty shops to a row, two rows to a complex. But on looking more closely the shops turned out to be little banks – some of them very odd banks, and from countries a very long way from Anguilla. But the building of them evidently gave the Anguillians work, and the Chief Minister – the same Ronald Webster who was sitting in his bath when the Red Devils burst in – promised me that many more would be invited over the coming years. (Mr Webster was defeated in an election soon afterwards, but the policy of turning Anguilla into a tax-haven was still being pursued with great energy.)

Hotels, too, were springing up. Anguilla's coastline – seventy miles of it, almost untouched – had just been discovered by American entrepreneurs (and by a Sicilian, who had been flung out of Saint-Martin and who was hoping to salt away his millions in a beach under the protection of the British Crown; he was asked to go elsewhere) and by a growing number of wealthy tourists. I fell in with a curious crowd one afternoon: he was a Greek-American, from Boston, and he said he was one of the leading potato brokers on the East Coast. He would keep me in close touch with happenings in the world of American potatoes for months thereafter, going so far as to send me a laudatory book about the Idaho variety, called *Aristocrat in Burlap*. We sat on a pure white beach, under an umbrella, and spent a good hour watching a pelican as it flew lazily over the endless blue rollers. It was a wonderful, faintly terrifying sight as the bird did its trick. It would be flying along, quite calmly, rising and falling in the thermals. Suddenly without warning, it would crumple up, all bones and wings and disordered brown feathers, just as if it had been shot. Down, down it fell, into the sea. At first we thought it had died, but after ten seconds or so it would emerge from the sea with a splash and a shower of spray, like a watery Phoenix, and would fly off in happy triumph, with a blue-and-gold fish clamped in its beak. It repeated its act time and time again, and each time the Greek potato king would laugh till the tears came; and we looked further along the beach and other pelicans – Eastern Browns, the book said – were doing the same thing, raining down into the sea and flying off with their flapping harvest of fish. We wondered who was enjoying the more perfect idyll – we two, or the birds.

I had a friend on the island, a man who had been the Attorney-General on St Helena and who had married a Saint of exquisite and serene beauty, and had then decided to leave and look for work on another colonial possession. They had given him the job of 'A-G' on Anguilla, and he was having a rare old time – no murders on the island perhaps (the only prisoner in the Valley had been sent there for using bad language) but an exquisite dilemma over a drugs case in which he was deeply involved.

Off the eastern tip of Anguilla lies Scrub Island – a couple of miles long, with two low hills, a tiny lake and a rough grass airfield. The latter had no obvious legitimate use, since no one lives on Scrub Island, and hardly anyone goes there (the *Baedeker* lamely reports Scrub Island as having 'much fissured coral rocks' and little else). But the airfield did have an important use for the classic non-legitimate business that has become a mainstay of Caribbean commerce – the trans-shipment of cocaine. A plane would fly out from Florida, empty; another would fly in from Bogota, full; there would be a hurried mid-night transfer, whereupon the two aircraft would return to their respective lairs, and plan to meet again later. Scrub Island, Anguilla, became, in the early 1980s, one of the great unsung drug markets of the Western world.

Until one evening in November 1983. The American drug enforcement agencies got wind of a big transfer plan, and called Anguilla, and spoke to my friend who had just arrived from Jamestown. He alerted the Royal Anguilla Constabulary, advised them to draw guns from the armoury, sailed them out to Scrub Island and hid them behind the clumps of loblolly pine and seagrape that grew beside the airstrip.

A man arrived in a launch, and set about lighting small fires to mark the strip. Then the aircraft arrived, as expected – one from the west, one from the south. Two men climbed from the Colombian craft, one from the American machine, everyone shook hands, and the policemen could see bags being humped from one hold to another. They drew their service revolvers, switched on their arclights – and made the most spectacular arrest Anguilla had ever seen. Four big-time drug smugglers, and a haul of a quarter of a tonne of cocaine – the largest and most valuable capture ever made in the Caribbean. It was worth one thousand million dollars.

The sheer scale of the haul posed one immediate problem. The Governor, a pleasant and very quiet Scotsman who had been brought to Anguilla from a lowly post in the British Embassy in Venezuela, was deeply ˄larmed. What, he wondered, if the Mafia tried to get it back? A billion dollars' worth of drugs would make it worth some gangsters' while to take almost any steps imaginable. They might land in force, at night, armed with heavy weapons. He might be captured, the Chief Minister might be assassinated, the colony might revert to the suzerainty of some Lower East Side *capo*. It was too horrible to contemplate. He wondered whether to ask for a frigate to stand off the coast, but then decided the evidence would be much safer under the care of the Americans, and had it all shipped off to Florida, and breathed a sigh of great relief when it had gone.

The four prisoners, on the other hand, represented a very considerable windfall. All were released, on half a million dollars' bail. They were told to come back for trial three months later, and when I met my friend he was praying hard that they would decide to skip bail – he would take great pleasure in leading their prosecution, of course, but he and the colony would very much like the money as forfeit. And in any case – what if they were found guilty? Where could they be kept? What if their Mafia chums tried to free them? And the drugs would have to be brought back as evidence, too.

In the event they never did show up. The Government of Anguilla made a clear profit of half a million United States dollars, and was able to tell the British Government, which wearily and reluctantly hands out grants to poor islands like Anguilla each year, that on this occasion at least it would need less of a grant than normal. It might even be able to afford a new school, or an extension for the hospital, out of the proceeds. It is, my friend remarked, an ill wind . . .

In one classically Imperial sense, Anguilla is a colony of some importance. Because of where she is, the colony controls – or, put another way, Britain controls – a vital sea lane. And this has come about because of a clever piece of sleight-of-hand which Whitehall played when St Kitts became independent, and Anguilla refused.

Thirty-five miles north-west of Anguilla is a tiny islet, two miles long, shaped like a Mexican hat, and called Sombrero Rock. It has a large deposit of phosphate, and because of that has been visited by quarrymen from time to time, and a few tonnes have occasionally been shipped away. The true importance of Sombrero is that it lies directly athwart one of the busiest deep channels between the Atlantic Ocean and the Caribbean Sea, and it has a lighthouse. The Admiralty bible, *Ocean Passages for the World*, lists Sombrero among the world's great reference points (and gives specific routes from Sombrero to, among others, Bishop Rock, the Cabot Strait, Lisbon, Ponta Delgada and the Strait of Gibraltar).

The light on Sombrero – 157 feet high, visible from twenty-two miles, and exhibiting a white flash every five seconds through the night – has always been British. It used to be run by the Imperial Lighthouse Service; it was one of the final three in use when the Service was abolished (the others were Cape Pembroke on East Falkland, and Dondra Head in Ceylon).

But Sombrero belonged to the presidency of St Kitts-Nevis-Anguilla, and, so logic dictated, should have moved to the newly independent St Kitts in 1967, since it had no population, other than a British lighthouse keeper. But – and here was the cunning move – London decided that Sombrero should remain British, and remain attached to Anguilla. For this one reason Britain was well pleased with the Anguillian rebellion – it enabled her to keep control of a lighthouse, and a sealane, that would otherwise have fallen under the less predictable rule of a newly independent state.

The Board of Trade took over the light, turned it into an automatic station, and brought the keeper home. And then in 1984 Trinity House, which looks after all British home waters' lights, as well as Europa Point off the southern tip of Gibraltar, assumed control over Sombrero, too. Thanks to the existence of Anguilla and her minuscule limestone possession to the north-west it was still true, technically, and on a very small scale, that Britannia ruled the waves, or at least a small portion of them. No ship could pass conveniently between Europe's great ports and the Panama Canal without coming under the unseeing scrutiny of a lighthouse that belonged, firmly and for the foreseeable future, to Britain.

When you arrive in Montserrat they stamp your passport with a shamrock. The signs say, 'Welcome to the Emerald Isle', and the coat of arms has a blonde lady holding a cross in one hand, and in the other a harp. There is a volcano called Galway's, a farm called O'Garra's, a town called St Patrick's and a mountain called Cork Hill. You can be forgiven for thinking that you have landed in altogether the wrong place.

It is even said that the islanders speak with a thick Irish brogue. A story is still told in the island pubs of a man from Connaught who arrived in Montserrat and was astonished to hear himself greeted in his native tongue by a man who was as black as pitch.

'Thunder and lightning!' exclaimed the newcomer. 'How long have you been here?' 'Three months,' said the native. 'Three months! And so black already! Blessed Jesus – I'll not stay among ye!' and he got back on to his boat, and had it sail all the way home to Connaught.

Ireland has the distinction of being known as a redoubtably anti-Imperial nation – struggling for most of her history against the rapacity of the English and the Scots. But early in the

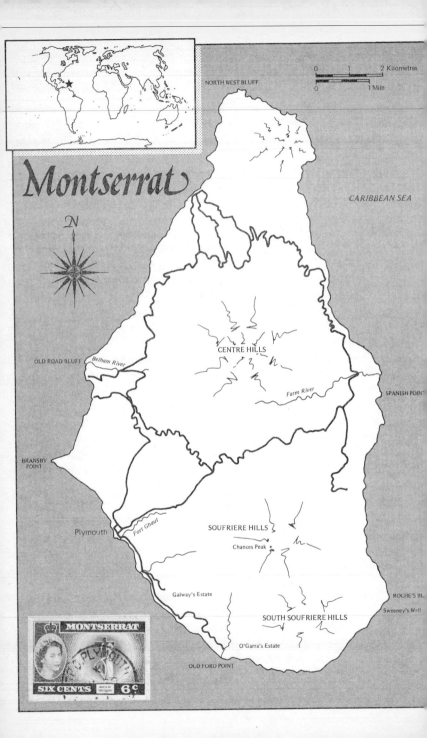

sixteenth century the Irish did colonise the island of Montserrat. They didn't discover it – Columbus did that, in 1493, and named it after a Catalonian monastery, because he thought the rugged hills and the needle-sharp peaks looked similar to the mountains beyond Barcelona. (The monastery of Santa Maria de Monserrate was where Ignatius Loyola saw the vision that prompted him to form the Jesuit movement – the island's name thus seemed an ideal refuge for Catholicism.) But the Spaniards made no attempt to annexe the little island, and it was left to Irishmen, in 1633, to take the place over.

They did so precisely because the name suggested refuge from the intolerance of Protestantism. There were Irishmen in Sir Thomas Warmer's newly growing colony on St Kitts – but Sir Thomas was a bluff Suffolk squire, not particularly eager to mingle with wild Irishmen, and he made life difficult for them. A party left by boat, and were blown by the trade winds to an island in which they saw 'land high, ground mountainous, and full of woods, with no inhabitants; and yet there were the footprints of some naked men'. The countryside was fertile, the weather pleasant, and, best of all, the place even looked like Ireland. So they named their landfall Kinsale Strand, and set about making the island into a new Irish home.

For a while it became a sanctuary. Irishmen arrived from Virginia, where the Protestants were busily establishing an ascendancy in that new colony; and they came from Ireland, too, once Cromwell had started to busy himself there. By 1648 Montserrat had '1000 white families' – all of them Irish. There was an Irish Governor named Mr Brisket, and the islanders were eating Irish stew, which they called – and still call – goatwater. Montserrat goats are said to have flesh tasting like the best of Galway mutton. ('Mountain chicken', another local dish, is actually breadcrumbed frog.)

But charming though the idea of an Irish Caribbean colony might have been – think of the mournful ballads that might have been sung under a summer's moon to the lilting music of the harp and the steel drum, or the sad sagas of the O'Flahertys' sugar mill, the tales of Irish tobacco and Irish rum, the hurricane shelters at the shinty matches – it had not the wit to last. The

Irish tried cunning, and it failed. They formed an uneasy alliance with the French, hoping that they might together drive the English out of St Kitts. But the English kept hold of St Kitts, and drove the French – who by this time had taken over Montserrat completely, having merely made use of the Irishmen – out of the area totally. Three years later, in 1667, the French were back, but then the Peace of Breda was signed, and England was given the island in perpetuity.

The French in *les Indes de l'Ouest* were extraordinarily determined. They tried three times more to lay hands on Montserrat – in part for simple territorial ambition, in part because it was a stronghold of Catholicism, and thus more amiably disposed to the ways of France than the English or Dutch islands nearby. They attacked in 1712, and caused so much damage to British property that a special clause was inserted into the Treaty of Utrecht; and they attacked again in 1782, and captured the island (along with most of the Leewards), but were ordered off under the terms of the Treaty of Versailles. The final French invasion came in 1805, when Montserrat was forced to pay a ransom of seven thousand five hundred pounds. After that everyone left the island alone, and the British ruled untroubled by any foreign rival. Including, of course, the Irish, who by now had been all but forgotten, except in the names of the towns, the stews, the shamrocks, and the strange habit of many Montserratians – which remains today – of adding the words 'at all' to the end of most sentences.

I flew to the island in a very small plane which had taken off from the neighbour-island of Antigua. My companion was a red-headed Scot from Kirkintilloch, a diplomat from the British High Commission in Barbados. He called the island 'Monster Rat', and was going there on a curiously non-diplomatic mission. The Governor's safe had a combination lock, and while he was admitting nothing, it seemed that someone had forgotten exactly what the combination number was. It wasn't written down on any piece of paper to be found, and so the Governor couldn't get at his secret papers (nor his hidden supplies of Marmite, or Glenfiddich, or whatever else this particular expatriate missed so far from home).

My friend, it turned out, had been sent out from Barbados with the specific task of opening His Excellency's safe and changing the combination, and making sure those in line to know it, knew it. The Governor had prudently chosen the time to take his leave, back home. The job only took the little Scotsman ten minutes, and he spent the rest of his diplomatic mission lying in the sun and enjoying the view.

For Montserrat is a spectacularly lovely place. It is a teardrop-shaped island, covered with dense, green rain forest, and dominated by three huge volcanoes (but only one active). The settlements are scattered along the coast, where the land makes an effort to be flat. But scores of little rivers course down from the jungles, and the road crosses dozens of bridges under which fierce torrents race busily down to the sea.

The airport is on the eastern side, with one runway jutting out into the ocean, and the islanders professing themselves certain that before long a plane will end up in the surf. (A Pan Am jet hit one of the volcanoes in 1965, and everyone on board was killed. The volcano, Chances Peak, is the only active one.) I was collected by an elderly driver called Rudolph, and when I asked him where I could hire a car he said he would gladly give me his for a few days, 'and don't you waste your money hiring no car, no suh!' I tried to protest, but he insisted, saying he wasn't planning to do any driving for the next few days. 'I won't need the car. I'll jes' cool my brains for a while.'

The road wound steeply up and over the range of hills, the views becoming ever more spectacular as we gained height. We stopped under a giant tree to let the radiator pressure ease. As the steam hissed from the radiator a pair of hummingbirds were floating in the warm afternoon air, wafting liquidly like tiny, brilliantly coloured kites tugged by invisible twine. Three types are said to live on Montserrat – one that is green with a curved beak, one just the same but with a crimson throat, and one that has a straight beak and a crest of pure emerald colour. These had long, aquiline beaks, and their crests were tiny feathers of deep angelica.

There were butterflies, too, and lush carmine flowers with big waxy petals and leaves that were thick and rubbery, like

great green ears. Rain had just fallen, and the asphalt was
steaming in the hot sun. A rich and humid smell seeped lazily
from the depths of the forest, but it was not a decaying smell,
nor was it in the least bit sinister. This was a friendly, cosy,
manageable jungle: no snakes, I remembered reading, nor any
unpleasant animal or bird. Just doves and rabbits, a type of wild
guinea pig, and a species of yellow oriole. Down in the valleys
I could see islanders picking cotton bolls from the bushes, and on
the hilltops the turrets of old sugar mills, like ancient fortresses
silhouetted against the pale blue sky.

Islands in the northern tropics usually have their principal
towns tucked down at the south-west corner. It is all a matter
of the wind. In the northern tropics the trades blow almost
constantly from the north-east, and the easterly coasts are thus
lee shores, easy to be blown on to, difficult to sail away from.
The western coast, by contrast, is a sheltered shore – sailing
boats can come in to port without danger, and can get away with
ease and speed. And there are always the sunsets – islanders
like the idea of gazing into the setting sun: 'It's like I'm looking
at tomorrow,' one old man said to me on a verandah one evening,
as we watched the sun slip downwards and the sky change
through salmon and orange to purple, and then into night.

While there are exceptions, most Caribbean islands do have
their capital towns down in the south-west, or the west: Antigua,
Grand Cayman, Aruba, Curacao, Dominica, Grenada, St Vincent, Martinique, and Nevis all do – and so does Montserrat.

Plymouth, the tiny Georgian town with well-proportioned
houses made of Portland stone that was shipped in as ballast on
the early sugar boats, is a pretty and dignified place – an Imperial
capital that has been cared for, and of which the local people are
proud. They are forever repairing the roofs and touching up the
pointing, painting the old walls in whites and blues and yellows,
keeping the place cheerful and spotless, even though they have
few visitors and have very little money to spend.

It is a very English town, despite the supposed Irishness of
the countryside. The suburbs are called Dagenham and Amer-
sham and Jubilee Town, and there is a Richmond and a Streat-
ham, and St George's Hill overlooks the place. In the town

centre, where John Street and George Street meet Strand Street and Marine Drive, there is a war memorial. Nearby is the old Custom House, the market, the abbatoir, the post office, the prison and the clock tower. There always is a war memorial, and here in Plymouth it is where the Boy Scouts and the Montserrat Volunteers and the Guides paraded on Empire Day each May, when the schools were all closed and the Governor could be seen in his white uniform and his feathery hat, and when the children sang 'God Save the King' and fidgeted during the speeches and then lined up for sticky buns and lemonade. Empire Day seems less appropriate now, so they celebrate the Queen's birthday instead, in June; but the war memorial is the focus of it all, as it is in every remaining outpost of the Empire. Some memorials are in shabby and forlorn corners; some, like those in Jamestown, the capital of St Helena, and here in Plymouth, the almost-perfect capital of Montserrat, seem more properly Imperial, and the children and their parents seem to have an extra spring in their step and sing just a little more heartily, believing, as they look around at all the lovely constructions of their mother country, that they do in fact possess something of which they can be proud.

The British Empire today sports only two active volcanoes: one, Chances Peak here in Montserrat, the other one is on Tristan da Cunha (it erupted in 1961, sending the entire colony into brief exile). Chances Peak is exactly 3,000 feet high. I walked there one afternoon, past the disused sugar mills of Galway's Estate, towards a long ochre scar of sulphur which smoked gently on the mountain's jungle-covered western flank.

The rocks were soft and crumbly, and there was a smell of cooking and bad eggs, and the place was warm and steamy, like a kitchen in which something was boiling on the range. The river – called the White River where it spilled into the sea, but it was yellow and cloudy where it gurgled here – was scalding hot. From tiny fumaroles that peppered the floors and walls of this tiny, enclosed valley, steam jetted in random bursts, and the sound of a groaning and cracking suggested some fearful being below ground, struggling to escape. Blobs of brilliant purple mud would suddenly erupt from nowhere, and I once set my foot on

what I thought was solid ground and went through the crust into
hot yellow mud, right up to the knee.

High above the valley and its steam and noise and cooking
smell, the jungle was silent. Occasionally a bird, iridescent and
cawing softly, would rise from the trees and flap its way towards
the sea, and once a donkey appeared at the edge of a cliff
and inspected me, chewing disconsolately. Otherwise all was
peaceful on the borders of hell. I suddenly had the terrible
realisation that if I were to fall in one of the pools of bubbling
mud, or became embedded in the hot yellow earth, I would roast
away without anyone knowing, and would be folded into the
bowels of the earth, become a small fixture in colonial geology
and be regurgitated on a tectonic whim many millennia later. So
I clambered, perspiring and panicky, up to the Galway's Estate
road, and made my way back to Plymouth, and the rickety
cosiness of the Coconut Hill Hotel, where I had tea on the
verandah and tried to shake the sulphur out of my jeans.

Few tourists come to Montserrat. The volcano spews black
sand on all the beaches, and those who worship the sun feel that
white sand is somehow better than black, and stay well away.
There is one white sand beach at the northern end, where a
few rich Americans congregate. One British record-maker has
set up a studio above the bay, and rock-music stars come and
live in his house for months at a time, secure in the knowledge
that they won't be bothered by their public, and that the
Montserratians, as a kindly and down-to-earth people, won't
bother them either. Paul McCartney brought Stevie Wonder to
Montserrat, and he played the piano in one of the Plymouth
bars; and Elton John met his wife on Montserrat – so the island
is well-known to students of the pop world, who associate it
wholly with the production of their particular kind of music.

Other generations will know it for its production of limes.
Montserrat Lime Juice was world-famous. *The Lancet*, quoted
by the *India Planters Gazette* of 1885, said: 'We counsel the
public to drink their lime juice either alone or sweetened to taste
and mixed with Water or Soda Water and a little Ice if obtainable.
Care should be taken that Montserrat Lime-fruit Juice only is

used, as it has the delicate aroma and flavour peculiar to the Lime Fruit and found in no other Lime Juice.' One can imagine the burra-sahib planter of Darjeeling, sitting in the cool of an evening gazing at the slopes of Kanchenjunga, a cheroot smouldering in one hand, a glass of *nimbu pani* in the other. After 1885, no doubt, the *nimbu* would have come across two oceans, all the way from Montserrat.

The lime estates were started by a remarkable man – Joseph Sturge, a devout Quaker from Birmingham who insisted he would grow his limes without the use of any slaves and with the hitherto unprecedented policy of 'fair and just treatment of the native labourers' as a spur to profitable production. He loaned money to the freed slaves, helped them pay for school, went to America to agitate for their freedom there. He would describe his principal interests as 'peace, anti-slavery and temperance', campaigned against the Corn Laws and the war in Crimea, and founded the Friends' Sunday schools in Birmingham. The city fathers erected a fountain and a statue to his memory in Edgbaston; in Montserrat, though, there is no memorial, and the lime factories have all but closed down.

In 1885 the island sold 180,000 gallons of juice to Crosse and Blackwell, in 1928 some thirty-five *puncheons* went to Australia. They made lime oil, too, for perfume and soap. But the crop was badly damaged in a hurricane, and by 1931 cotton had taken over as the major commodity exported from Plymouth dock. Sturge's Montserrat Company was sold in 1961. When I ordered a glass of lime juice at the hotel one afternoon there was nothing fresh available. I was given a bottle of Rose's Lime Juice, with a label that said, 'St Albans and the West Indies'; but the company later explained that this was a polite fiction, and that Rose's limes now came from Mexico and Ghana.

The cotton grown on the island is unlike any other. A sample of Carolina Sea Island cotton seed was brought to the island in 1909 and planted in an experimental field. It grew with tremendous vigour, and produced a fibre that was as soft as cashmere and as strong as silk. For a while exports boomed – three-quarters of a million tonnes were shipped in 1938, and Montserrat was second only to Barbados in the Caribbean cotton league.

But then came the weevils, and the rain was erratic for a few
seasons, and another hurricane flattened everything – the sad
story of so many small West Indian islands – and cotton failed,
too. Sugar had vanished from the island economy fifty years
before for much the same reason; the lower slopes of the hills
were, by the 1980s, littered with the ruins of abandoned projects
– empty cane fields (which islanders used to burn by dipping a
mongoose in petrol, setting it aflame and letting it run in between
the cane stands), bedraggled cotton bushes, overgrown lime
plantations.

Just as in Grand Turk, where the islanders feel somehow
shamed that tax-avoidance and tourism have taken over from
salt raking and fishing, so the Montserratians today are saddened
to realise that what they see as the nobler labours associated
with lime, sugar and cotton have been subordinated to ignoble
schemes – the making of pop records, and (the biggest export
at present) the manufacture, in a factory, of plastic sandwich
bags. A Canadian plan to get cotton-growing under way again,
and sell Montserrat Sea Island cotton as a luxury, is breathing
a little hope into one old industry, but no one is very optimistic.

On my last day on Montserrat I came across something quite
unexpected, and quite dreadful. An old resort hotel, built on a
bluff to the north of Plymouth, had been bought by a group of
young Americans who were running it as a clinic for cancer
patients, men and women who were desperate to cling on to life
at almost any cost, and at almost any risk. The clinic, which
charged phenomenal sums of money, offered treatments with
drugs that did not, at the time, have the approval of the American
Government. Laetrile was one, dimethyl sulphoxide the other.
Neither was a proven cure for cancer, but to a patient eager
enough and financially able, they did offer a possibility of life, if
nothing else. The old hotel had truly become, as a cynical
Montserratian remarked, a last resort, and I should go and look
at it.

So I walked up the hill, through the steel gates and the
welcoming signs, and made for the bar. The ballroom next door
opened out on to a terrace, which overlooked a still and silent

sea. Inside the ballroom a band from Antigua was playing reggae music. Its leader, in red-and-yellow blazer, was doing his best to lighten the atmosphere of the place, giving encouraging smiles and imploring some of his audience to come on to the floor and dance.

But no one wanted to dance that night. Nor any night, I suspected. There were about twenty people in the room. Each was slumped back in an armchair, peering wanly at the band through eyes that were heavy with sleep, or narcotic drugs. Behind mos' chairs was a steel rod from which was suspended a bag of saline solution, a plastic tube carrying the liquid to each bandaged arm. One or two tapped fingers, or toes, to the rhythm. There was a strong smell of garlic, and when one of the 'guests', a woman in her fifties, saw me wrinkle my nose, she beckoned, and whispered an apology.

'I'm sorry about the smell. It's the drug – the dimethyl stuff. It goes through you so fast, and leaves this garlic smell. I guess it's bearable if you know the stuff is doing you good.'

And was it? She thought so, yes; she had put on three ounces in the first week she had been a resident, more than she had put on in the last month back home. She was no more than a bag of bones, her face was drawn and grey, her skin was translucent, yellowish, like parchment. She wasn't fifty at all: she was thirty-two and she had had cancer for a year. The visit to Montserrat was costing her three thousand dollars a week, and she was sure it was doing her good. An elderly man – or was he young? – in the next chair nodded his head in vigorous agreement. 'You tell 'em, Sal. You are getting better, sure you are.'

But Sal wasn't getting better. She died two weeks later on her way home. She was an ounce heavier on departure than when she arrived; she had spent nine thousand dollars. Perhaps she had been given a measure of hope, and considered her money well spent. I couldn't help but feel a sense of distaste, even anger; and most Montserratians loathe the clinic, and wonder how the Government ever allowed it to open for business. 'The death house on the hill' was how I heard it described down in Plymouth.

Six years ago the politicians in Plymouth were ruefully contemplating an indefinite future as a colony. 'The Last English Colony?' was the title of a pamphlet published in 1978, and there was a general acceptance that, as it said, 'Montserrat will probably be a colony long after Britain has shed all her other responsibilities.' But after the American invasion of Grenada the perspective shifted. The Montserrat Chief Minister became chairman of a local power bloc, the Organisation of Eastern Caribbean States; he asked if he could send a token force of the Royal Montserrat Police to Grenada, and Britain said no, he couldn't, since Britain was keeping strictly neutral and expected her colonies to do so as well.

That did it. Why, the Chief Minister asked, should Montserrat be subject to 'the overruling and sometimes myopic colonial power' any longer? Was it not embarrassing and degrading? Should not the islanders accept 'the dignity of managing their own affairs'? He said he would be formally requesting independence from Britain; the Foreign Office, with the languid superciliousness for which it is renowned, simply replied that it was unaware of any request, but would study the matter in due course. And there the matter remains.

For the politicians doubtless the independence of Montserrat is of crucial import. For the islanders I suspect it is, and will be for some time, a matter of less immediate moment. They are as unhurried and untroubled a people as any in the West Indies, without much undue passion, without a burning sense of injustice or a pervasive feeling of subjection.

Perhaps it has much to do with their Gaelic spirit. As a local columnist once wrote, from old Sweeney's sugar estate in the north to O'Garra's deep down in the south, this truly is 'our Ireland in the sun'. Every bit as content to be under the rule of Whitehall, or Plymouth, or even Dublin all over again.

There have been many government committees in Whitehall, and most of them have been deservedly forgotten. The people of the Cayman Islands, one of the wealthiest and most successful of British colonies, have good reason to remember, and indeed

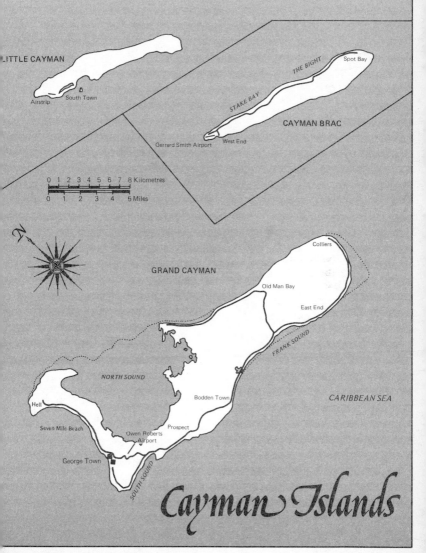

LITTLE CAYMAN

Airstrip   South Town

THE BIGHT   Spot Bay

STAKE BAY

CAYMAN BRAC

Gerrard Smith Airport   West End

0 1 2 3 4 5 6 7 8 Kilometres
0 1 2 3 4 5 Miles

N

GRAND CAYMAN

Colliers

Old Man Bay

East End

FRANK SOUND

NORTH SOUND

Hell

Seven Mile Beach

Bodden Town

CARIBBEAN SEA

Owen Roberts
Airport

Prospect

George Town

SOUTH SOUND

Cayman Islands

raise a glass to one of them – a committee which is generally regarded as having been a total failure, and which only stayed in existence for six years.

The Colonial Policy Committee was set up in 1955, by Sir Anthony Eden. Its avowed purpose was to suggest to the Cabinet how best Britain might accomplish the running down of Empire, and how the country might treat those colonies that remained; it was the body Sir Winston Churchill had meant when, some years earlier, he had said that the Colonial Office would have so little work to do that one day 'a good suite of rooms at Somerset House, with a large sitting room, a fine kitchen and a dining room' would be most suitable for the direction of Empire.

The CPC – with the Colonial Secretary, the Commonwealth Secretary, the Foreign Secretary and the Minister of Defence meeting under the chairmanship of the Lord President of the Council – was a flop. The Cabinet complained that it never got any direction from the Committee; the Committee complained that it was bogged down in sorting out day-to-day problems, and never had an opportunity to make exhaustive analyses of Imperial policy. It was abolished in June 1962, and nobody appeared to miss it.

But lacklustre though its overall performance may have been, the Committee enjoyed a spectacular success in what was almost the last decision it ever took. On 30th March 1962 it accepted the advice of the then Colonial Secretary, Reginald Maudling, and agreed that the Cayman Islands should be detached from the colony of Jamaica, which was then about to become independent, and become a new Crown colony, on their own.

The reasons had a lot to do with geography. The three Cayman Islands – Grand Cayman, Little Cayman and Cayman Brac – are tucked below the Great Antillean island of Cuba, and lie several hundred miles away from the island-arc chain of the Leewards and the Windwards. Jamaica, the Caymans' mother-colony, was in 1962 a member of the Federation of the West Indies, and the Caymans, having nothing in common with the other members of the Federation, wanted to pull out. There is an almost exact parallel between the Caymanian attitude to the

Federation, and Anguilla's hostility to St Kitts – in the case of Anguilla, Britain sent troops to try to stop the impending rebellion; in the case of the Cayman Islands the Colonial Policy Committee agreed that no islander should be forced to join anything he didn't want to. So the recommendation was made that the Caymans become a separate colony, with loyalty neither to Jamaica nor to the West Indian Federation (which in any case collapsed in an ugly shambles shortly afterwards), but only to the distant figure of the reigning British monarch. The full Cabinet agreed with the Committee, and so with cap-and-feathers, sword-and-spurs bought, Government House duly built and a suitable colonial servant duly appointed (at first styled 'Administrator', but a full-fledged Governor after 1971), the colony got shakily under way.

It has proved to be a quite extraordinary financial success – perhaps, in purely monetary terms, the most successful little country in the world. It is a success measured solely in numbers, maybe; the place has little charm, and even less culture; but in numbers – and that essentially means numbers of dollars – its triumph is unchallenged.

The islands are flat and, save for a modest hillock on Cayman Brac ('brac' is a Gaelic word for 'bluff', which on this islet is just 140 feet high), they are utterly featureless. Columbus spotted them in 1503, but decided not to bother landing, as they looked so uninspiring: he named them Las Tortugas, because of the enormous numbers of green turtles in the surrounding seas. They were renamed Las Caymanas because of the similar abundance of sea-crocodiles; but there are no crocodiles left today, and many islanders wish for the old name back, as the place still crawls with turtles.

The islanders – a mongrel mixture of races and nationalities, pirates and deserters, freebooters and buccaneers, a crew who knew no racial divisions then, and, almost alone in the West Indies, appear to harbour none today – built mahogany schooners, fished, and fattened turtles for export. But it was a poor living, and in the early years of this century hundreds left, to go to Jamaica, or even to Nicaragua, which lies temptingly close to the west. In 1948 there was just one bank on the island,

and a collection of shanty towns and peasant farmers: the exchequer took in only thirty-six thousand pounds from the 7,000 inhabitants. They exported 2,000 turtles, at about three pounds a time; the total export income was twenty thousand pounds, and the Administrator had control of a Reserve Fund of thirty-eight thousand pounds, and a Hurricane Fund of two thousand. The soil was too thin to farm; the islands swarmed with mosquitoes, with dengue fever and yellow fever occasionally breaking out as epidemics; there were brackish swamps, acres of scrub and casuarina, and a few thin cattle. The Cayman Islands were a long way from being the brightest star in the Imperial firmament.

But a genius was waiting in the wings. Vassel Godfrey Johnson, a slender, bespectacled Jamaican whose family came from Madras, was a civil servant in the Finance Department in Jamaica. He came to Cayman during the debate over whether or not the island dependency should join the Federation; and, when it was decided that they should in fact become a new colony, separate and self-standing, he hit upon the solution that has since made the Caymans one of the wealthiest places on earth.

He explained that he had a sudden idea: since the islands were too poor to pay taxes, and since they were in the enviable position of being a British Crown colony, with all the stability and protection such status conferred – why not offer freedom from taxes to anyone who wanted to invest money on the islands? Why not encourage businesses to come and place their headquarters on Grand Cayman, and shelter themselves from the burdens of taxation they might face elsewhere? Why not offer secrecy and discretion, and make the islands into a Little Switzerland-on-Sea?

Mr Johnson worked for months, studying legislation and banking regulations, persuading the Jamaican Government, and then the Cayman Administration and the supervisors at the Foreign Office, that all would be well. By the time full colonial status was achieved the legislation was in force. The mosquitoes had been wiped out, too – Vassel Johnson had decided that bankers would not come to Grand Cayman if they were going to be made the subject of a Torquemada's feast as soon as they stepped off the plane – and the colony was ready to receive its first millions.

It all took a little time. Bankers were reluctant to divert their monies from Zurich; American investors were content to keep their funds in Nassau, 500 miles north, in the Bahamas. There was a natural reluctance among this most cautious of communities to set down with funds in a new and untried country – British colony or not.

But then came the independence of the Bahamas, in 1974. The bankers were content with the Prime Minister whom the British left in charge; but within a year there were audible stirrings of Socialist opposition in Nassau, and the back streets were displaying posters calling for the nationalisation of the banks. Caution vanished; alarm took over; and banker after banker packed his suitcase and headed south, for Grand Cayman. Barclays Bank went first; and then a trickle, then a stream, and then a tidal wave. Banks from all over the world, from Winnipeg to Waziristan, set up shop in George Town.

The Yellow Pages in the Cayman telephone book lists six pages of banks, from the Arawak Trust (Cayman) Limited, to the Washington International Bank and Trust Company. Billions of dollars are invested in more than 440 banks registered in the Cayman Islands; and there are 300 insurance companies, dozens of world-class accountants, and more than 17,000 registered companies – one for every inhabitant. Outside the offices of most lawyers in town are long noticeboards listing the names of each and every company registered with the firm: pretty secretaries can be seen every day adding new plates to the list as fresh companies send in their government registration fee (of eight hundred and fifty dollars, minimum) and commence operations under the benign and liberal style of Caymanian protection.

Now, from a sleepy mess of mangrove swamps and seagrape trees, the Cayman Islands have undergone an amazing and breathtakingly rapid evolution. There are now more telex machines per head of population than anywhere else on earth; there were, in 1980, more than 8,000 telephones on the islands – one for every two people, and almost as many per person as in Britain. Satellite dishes have spawned like mushrooms all over the islands – when I met Vassel Johnson we did, indeed, sit under a seagrape tree beside the ocean, and there was driftwood on the beach and the sea shimmered in the late afternoon sun; but beside his house was a great white dish pointed up at Satcom Three, and he could receive fifty-three channels of television, twenty-four hours a day. He had a Mercedes and a motor cruiser, and there was a badminton court next to his bungalow. The standard of living he enjoyed was not, by island standards, particularly remarkable: but there was no poverty on Cayman either, and none of the shabbiness I had encountered on Grand Turk, or on Anguilla, or Montserrat.

But the liberality of the Cayman laws has led, it is thought, to some abuse. The islands are generally thought of as the prime resting-place for some of the world's hottest money – drug money, Mafia money, pornography money. It is rarely provable – the island laws make it a crime even to inquire about a certain bank account. But the island authorities seem to think it is happening, and have looked, without success, at ways of helping the very worried American police agencies who come to trace notorious criminals here, only to find the trail suddenly running cold, as though the fox had dived into the river, and had swum away to safety.

I stayed with an elderly couple in a grand house outside George Town; they were British and had come to retire on Cayman because of the sunshine, and the absolute certainty they felt that, of all places in the world, this would not become tainted by Socialism. They showed me their bank statement one day – a Barclay's International statement, sent from the branch in George Town. It was of only minor interest until, quite by surprise, another statement fell from behind it. The Barclay's computer had folded the statement for the next customer – next in alphabetical order, that is – into the same envelope. The customer was a small firm that hired cranes in a town in Yorkshire; it had more than four hundred and fifty thousand pounds on deposit, and I couldn't help but wonder why. I thought I might telephone when I got home, and pretend I was a detective, and ask why they felt it necessary to keep so much cash in a Caribbean tax haven. But charity, and prudence, prevailed, and I left them alone.

The nervousness of the banking community showed itself after the Falklands War, and the Cayman Islands were briefly worried. There was talk, easily audible in New York and Miami and Houston, that the British might well want to dispose of their remaining colonies, to make sure no such costly embarrassment happened again. It was all rumour, of course – the reworking of a few editorials in the more radical quarters of the British press. But it set the bankers wondering – were the Cayman Islands secure? Should the money go to Switzerland once more, or to Liechtenstein, or Andorra?

The Governor of the islands, an astute Englishman named Peter Lloyd, a man with a long record of Imperial service – Fiji, Hong Kong, Bermuda, Kenya – recognised the danger signs. A royal visit should do the trick, it was agreed; and so the Queen, on her way to Mexico and the American West Coast, was briefly diverted to Grand Cayman in February 1983. It was expensive – two hundred dollars a minute, someone calculated. Her Majesty was given a Rolls-Royce that had once belonged to Mr Dubcek of Czechoslovakia; she unveiled a plaque for a new road, she saw an exhibition of local crafts (which, it must be said, are limited, and tend to involve turtle shells, conches, and raffia work), she made one seven-minute speech, spoke to some elderly islanders, performed one walkabout and lunched and dined with the island grandees. Government House was not reckoned either grand or secure enough for the Monarch; instead she slept at the headquarters of a company called Transnational Risk Management Limited, which everyone agreed had more the ring of today's Cayman Islands about it, anyway.

Brief and costly though the tour had been, it underlined Britain's determination to keep the colony British, come what may. The bankers expressed their relief and their gratitude, and growth resumed, as though the Falklands War had never happened. The islanders had already expressed their own thanks – a fund-raising campaign under the title 'Mother needs your

help' was organised by the Caymanians to help the bereaved
and the injured from the South Atlantic, and the Caymanians
contributed to the tune of twenty-eight pounds each, indicative
both of their generosity, and their wealth.

However, the Caymans are not particularly endearing islands.
There is no scenery (except underwater, where the diving
is said to be among the best in the world); there is a relent-
less quality to the money-making on which the islands seem
so firmly based – seminars on tax-avoidance in every hotel,
beach lectures on insurance, advertisements for Swiss banks
and tax-shelters and financial advice centres. There is little left
which is obviously West Indian about the place: it seems like
an outpost of Florida, rather than of the British Empire, with
a tawdriness, a mixture of the seedy and the greedy that
was less attractive than the shabbiness or the decay of the
other islands.

But that is a churlish judgement. The lives of the Caymanians
are undoubtedly much more comfortable than those of their
brother-islanders up in Tortola, or across in Montserrat. Why
should I deny them a life that gives them such riches? What was
it that bothered me about the place?

Perhaps, I thought to myself in the airport taxi, it was because
one associates British Imperial relics, and associates them rather
fondly, with sadness and decay, with the sagging verandah and
the peeling paint, the wandering donkeys and the lolling drunks,
and with a generally amiable sense of indolence and carelessness.
It was not very laudable, maybe – but it was rather, well,
pleasant, and cosy. Perhaps because of all of that, the discovery
of a colony with 200 telexes and a telephone for every couple
and seminars on investment opportunity, and moreover to discover it in a place like the West Indies where efficiency and
technology and wealth have never been at a premium –
perhaps it was all too much of a shock to the system. I was
not, I must admit, at all sorry to leave. The plane took me
to Miami, and it was full of men in business suits, and they
seemed to be carrying small computer terminals, and read
the *Wall Street Journal*. This, surely, had not been an out-

post of our Empire? Where was the charm? Where was the Britishness of it all? They hadn't even seemed terribly keen on cricket.

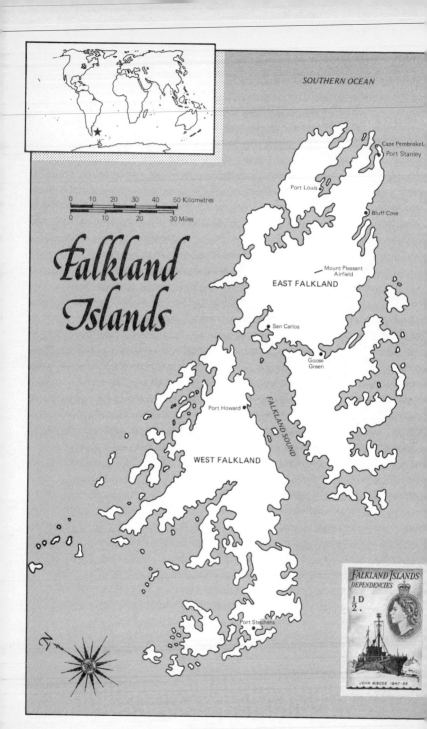

SOUTHERN OCEAN

Falkland Islands

EAST FALKLAND

WEST FALKLAND

FALKLAND SOUND

Cape Pembroke L
Port Stanley

Port Louis

Bluff Cove

Mount Pleasant
Airfield

San Carlos

Goose
Green

Port Howard

Port Stephens

0   10   20   30   40   50 Kilometres
0   10   20   30 Miles

FALKLAND ISLANDS
DEPENDENCIES
½ D.

JOHN BISCOE 1947-52

TEN

THE FALKLAND ISLANDS

It was the first Friday in April – early spring in England, but a crisp clear autumn morning in Port Stanley, the capital of the Crown colony of the Falkland Islands. I was lying wedged under a bed, the Colonial Governor's chauffeur had one of his feet in my left ear, a terrified cat was cowering under a pile of pink candlewick, and the sound of gunfire was everywhere. Britain's very last Imperial war – although I didn't know it at the time – was beginning, and I seemed to be in the very middle of it.

I had arrived three days earlier. This was the first colony I had visited for years, and I had fallen hopelessly in love with the place. Everything, so far as I was concerned, was exactly right. It was a place of islands, and I loved islands. It was cold, and I loved cold places. A fresh, damp wind blew constantly from the west. There was the smell of peat in the air. The grey and purple moors and the white-capped sea-lochs looked as though they had been plucked from the remoter regions of Argyllshire, or Ardnamurchan. The men, slow and deliberate of speech, pipe-smoking, church-going, all dressed in old tweed, oilskins and studded boots, made a modest living as seafarers and farmers; they knew about such things as Admiralty charts and weather and horses and birds and wild animals. They had the old and solid virtues of an earlier age – they were of the same stock as the ghillies and postmen and lobster fishers and shepherds of a seaside town in Northern Scotland, contented

with their lonely living, wanting for little, happy to have been
passed by and forgotten by the world outside.

And yet on this crisp Friday morning the whole unwanted
outside world, with all its awfulness and wasted energies, was
preparing to descend upon the Falkland Islands and their people.
An Imperial outpost that had languished for two centuries in the
comfort of well-deserved obscurity was about to erupt on to
every newspaper and every television screen in every country
in the world. A week from this day it would be on the front
cover, in full colour, of the major American news magazines,
would be the subject of a thousand televised discussions, a
matter for urgent diplomacy and for the meetings of presidents,
prime ministers, generals, admirals and intelligence chiefs in
capital cities on every continent. This morning, at the very
moment I had decided it would be sensible to lie on this strange
bedroom floor, almost no one in the world was even aware of
the existence of these islands, or of this tiny windswept capital
town.

And even as I mentioned this irony to the friend who sheltered
beside me, a tragedy that was to alter the fortunes of the islands
and the islanders for all time was under way, and we were hiding
from it among the feet, the frightened cat and the rattle of
bullets, among the dust balls and yellowing newspapers under a
standard British government-issue bed.

I had come to the Falkland Islands from Simla, the old Imperial
summer capital of India. Just a few days before I had been
strolling through the grand viceregal lodge, up among the roses
and the deodars, with the fine white ridge of the Himalayas in
the distance. Then I heard the BBC World Service tell about
some curious goings-on in the South Atlantic, with scrap metal
merchants from Argentina trying to dismantle an old whaling
station on the Falklands dependency of South Georgia, and the
British Government being mightily exercised about it. I decided
to go home. In the bus that took me from the hills to the plains
I read what little there was in the Indian papers about the remote
turmoil. It seemed that many of the old southern ocean whalers
– and, indeed, the owners of the South Georgia whaling factory
– were Scotsmen; and having just come from a building in India

that had all the appearance of a magnificent Sutherland shooting lodge I was able to expatiate to the Bengali lawyer in the next seat on the theme the Scots as Empire-Builders, which at least matched his sermon on the Patriotism of Netaji Subhas Chandra Bose for length and tedium, after which we both fell into exhausted silences.

The Britain I got home to was more amused than interested in what seemed to be happening on South Georgia. I knew a little about the place, because I had once contemplated applying for a job with the British Antarctic Survey, and had seen pictures of the old granite cross, the memorial to Shackleton, who had died there of a heart attack in 1922. The capital, if such it could be called, was Grytviken, and a small party of BAS men worked there, with their leader nominated as magistrate and representative of the Falkland Islands' Governor. What appeared to have happened on this occasion was that a small party of Argentinians had landed at Leith, twenty miles up the coast, and were busily dismantling the rusting hulk of the whaling station. The problem, so far as the Foreign Office was concerned, was that the scrap dealers had ignored instructions to check their way through British immigration and customs; a Royal Navy patrol vessel had been dispatched to scare them off, the Argentine Navy had in consequence landed marines and sent in two frigates, ostensibly to support their civilian scrapmen, and both governments were angrily sending Notes to one another demanding discipline, respect for sovereignty, and withdrawal of respective threats.

And so, six days after coming home from India, I was aboard another plane, heading south to write about this ridiculous little argument and, as it was to turn out, an unimagined and unimaginable war. It was a Sunday night, we were droning across the Atlantic between Madrid and Buenos Aires, and I was attempting a crash course on Falkland Islands' history.

Few seemed to have cared very much for the islands. To the first navigators they must have been terrifying: huge rock-bound monsters, looming out of the freezing fog and giant waves, bombarded by furious winds that screamed out of Drake Passage and howled unceasingly from around Cape Horn. The seas are almost always rough, the air is filled with flying spray, visibility is invariably poor, and navigators and steersmen on passing vessels always had too many tasks to perform at once to enjoy their leisure of island-spotting – the consequence being, uniquely in British Imperial history, that we have no real idea who first came across the Falkland Islands. The surviving records are confusing – was Hawkins' Maidenland, discovered by Richard Hawkins in 1594, the north shore of East Falkland? Did Magellan's expedition discover them, or are those insignificant patches on Antonio Ribero's maps of 1527 and 1529 records of the Spaniards' having found them at the start of the sixteenth century? The maps certainly give them a variety of names – the Seebalds, the Sansons, the Malouines, the Malvinas; and only when Captain John Strong was blown into the island waters by a mighty westerly gale in January 1690, and landed and killed geese and ducks, did they assume the name by which the British still call them today: Strong named them Falkland's Land, in honour of the Navy Treasurer, Viscount Falkland (a man whose career did not flourish, and who ended up committed to the Tower); seventy-six years later John McBride, who established the first British settlement, officially named the entire group the Falkland Islands.

The jumbo jet thundered quietly on. From the flight deck we heard a hushed voice mention that we were a few miles south of Tenerife, in the Canaries. Dinner was over and the stewards moved silently through the aircraft, dimming the lights for a Spanish-dubbed version of *The French Lieutenant's Woman* to be shown to those few passengers still awake. My reading lamp illuminated the pile of papers I had gathered up before I left London, and I read on.

There were innumerable references to the firm Argentine belief that she had sovereign rights to the Falklands (and persisted in calling them Las Islas Malvinas, after the French from St Malo who had established the first formal settlement, in 1764, and who had claimed them in the name of Louis XV). Of course I was in no position to judge the strength of the various claims: but I remember being impressed by the vigour and constancy with which Argentina asserted her title to the islands, and wondering if there was much more than obstinacy in the tone that successive British Governments had adopted towards the idea of any real negotiations over the islands' future. I was struck too by the suggestion that every Argentine schoolchild from the age of four knew in the minutest detail the history of the Malvinas, and had an unswerving belief in his country's entitlement to the islands; I cannot recall ever having heard anything about them at school at all, other than as a name in the stamp album. (The penny black-and-carmine issue of 1938, with the black-necked swan, and the halfpenny black-and-green with the picture of two sets of whale jaws, were my particular favourites; I promised myself I would look them out when I got back home in a week or two.) Like most Britons I neither knew much about the islands, nor cared greatly about their fate, nor who owned title to them.

Few of the early settlers seemed to have liked the islands. 'A countryside lifeless for want of inhabitants . . . everywhere a weird and melancholy uniformity' was the verdict of Antoine de Bougainville, the leader of the settler band from St Malo. Dr Johnson established the colony's reputation in 1771, noting that it had been 'thrown aside from human use, stormy in winter, barren in summer, an island which not even the southern savages had dignified with habitation'. 'I tarry in this miserable desert,' wrote the first priest of the Spanish community, Father Sebastian Villaneuva, 'suffering everything for the love of God.' And again, one of the first Britons to live on East Falkland Island, an army lieutenant, recalled some years later that the colony was 'the most detestable place I was ever at in all my life'. 'A remote settlement at the fag end of the world,' said one Governor in 1886; 'the hills are rounded, bleak, bare and brownish,' wrote Prince Albert Victor, who had sailed in aboard HMS *Bacchante*. The hills, he added, 'were like Newmarket Heath'.

Charles Darwin went to the Falklands aboard the *Beagle* in 1833, the same year that the Union flag was first raised by a visiting naval vessel. He knew that the existing Argentine garrison had been ordered to leave, and was scornfully dismissive of the Admiralty's action. He delivered a judgement as haunting as it was economical: 'Here we, dog in manger fashion, seize an island and leave to protect it a Union Jack.' Ten years later the islands were formally colonised – an Act of Parliament in London, twenty-eight-year-old Mr Richard Moody came south on the brig *Hebe* to be the first Governor, a Colonial Secretary and Colonial Treasurer were appointed and the dismal new possession was inserted into the Colonial Office List, sandwiched between British Honduras and Gambia (although by the beginning of this century Cyprus and Fiji had become its closest alphabetical neighbours). Port Stanley was chosen as the capital, thirty pensioners were sent down from Chelsea Barracks, and thirty-five Royal Marines and their families followed shortly afterwards. Governor Moody's first Imperial decision was to curb the colonials' keen liking for strong drink. Spirits, he declared, 'produce the most maddening effects and disorderly excesses', and he slapped a pound a gallon on liquor brought in to the islands from home.

I must have slept fitfully for a while, for it was morning when I next looked out of the windows, and we were coming in to land at Rio. The Brazilian newspapers were full of news about the Malvinas, and there were pictures on the front pages of the warships *Drummond* and *Granville*, the two Argentine destroyers (despite their names) that were even now cruising around the fjords of South Georgia. Both ships had been built in Barrow-in-Furness, and sold to the Argentine Navy – a measure, it was said, of the enduring amity between Britain and Argentina. Back in London politicians and diplomats set great store by this long-established friendship: here, to the extent I could translate the Portuguese headlines, it seemed to count for rather less. There was definitely the smell of trouble.

A day later and I was in deepest Patagonia. This was very different from the steamy warmth of the River Plate. Here it was very much a high latitude autumn. The wind howled down from the Andes, and whipped up the dust in cold, gritty flurries. I was in Comodoro Rivadavia, a town which I had long thought to be blessed with one of the prettiest names in the Americas. I had tried to get there two years before to write about a simmering dispute between Chile and Argentina over the ownership of a group of small islands off the coast of Tierra del Fuego;

but the Pope stepped in to moderate, and the dispute collapsed, and there was no reason to go. Now I was here, and the place was a terrible disappointment. It was littered with the accumulated debris of the oil drilling business – rusty iron girders, enormous pulley blocks, barrels, abandoned lorries, stores dumps behind barbed-wire fences. The buildings were modern, and ugly, and the people walked bent over into the cold gales that blew along the alleys. (It was the second time that I had come to expect too much from a lovely city name: years before I had spun wondrous fantasies about a place called Tucumcari in New Mexico; but when I got there it was just an oily little truckstop on Route Sixty-six, best avoided. I felt much the same way about Comodoro Rivadavia.)

Flying to the Falkland Islands has never been easy. In 1952 a seaplane made a remarkable journey all the way from Southampton to Port Stanley, by way of Madeira, the Cape Verde Islands, Recife and Montevideo. She took seven days, turned round a few days later and flew home. Then in 1971 a lighthouse keeper – the Cape Pembroke Light on East Falkland was one of the few remaining outposts of the Imperial Lighthouse Service – fell ill, an amphibious aircraft of the Argentine Navy flew in to evacuate him, and then agreed to fly to and from Port Stanley twice a month with passengers and mail. A year later the state-run Argentine civil airline took over the task, and ran a weekly service to the islands. It was an excellent arrangement for both sides: the Falkland Islanders had an air service, and the Argentines could keep an eye on the colony. Moreover, with a small office in Port Stanley, manned by a serving naval officer (to which the colonial authorities seemed to express no objection), the Argentine military had a foothold – one that was to prove useful just a few days after I arrived.

It was Tuesday, 30th March when I presented my ticket at Comodoro airport, and the political atmosphere had become electric. Two days before – the Sunday – the intelligence community had told the British Prime Minister that Argentina was probably going to take action against the Falkland Islands; three atomic-powered submarines had been ordered to proceed with all deliberate speed to the South Atlantic; one, HMS *Spartan*, was being loaded with live torpedoes in Gibraltar dockyard at the very moment I was walking up to the ticket counter.

I knew nothing about this, nor did I know that the Argentine authorities had decided to invade the islands – though the Comodoro aerodrome was filled with Hercules transport planes, and fighters were flying overhead for much of the day. My only inspiration had come the day before, via a chance remark from a Royal Navy officer I had met at the British Embassy in Buenos Aires. I had asked him if, in his view, it was worth my while trying to get to Port Stanley – the BBC had said that no journalists were going to be allowed to go, and I would have to use some degree of subterfuge to get aboard the plane. The Argentine authorities might be rather annoyed if they found out – so, was it worth the risk? 'Go,' was all he said. 'It should be worth it.' (Some months later he told me that, having a fair idea of what was going to happen over the coming days, he had wondered guiltily how I ever planned to get back.)

But no complicated subterfuge was necessary. The little plane took off on time, and all the passengers who had queued were aboard. No matter that task forces and battle fleets were even at that moment assembling at the two ends of the Atlantic Ocean, and satellites were being interrogated hourly for information on troop movements and diplomatic messages, no matter that the world's spying community was working overtime, and that presidents and prime ministers were engaging in urgent late-night telephone calls for advice and support – of all of these events that history now insists were taking place that day, the plane's passengers were quite insensible. I had lengthy conversations with three men aboard who had come to the Falkland Islands to buy land. One was a minor Spanish count; one was a High Tory gentleman farmer from Shropshire; the third was a Scotsman who lived in Egypt. Each one had the fullest confidence in the ability of the mother-country to prevent any unpleasantness: no one in the plane was thinking of war, except perhaps the uniformed men in the cockpit, who may well have known what we did not. Only London was expecting trouble, and Buenos Aires was less than sixty hours away from delivering it.

I felt a thrill of excitement as the plane bumped its way downwards an hour later, and the seat-belt signs snapped on. There was a thick and dirty layer of cloud, and it was several minutes before I could see anything below through the Lockheed's picture windows. But then, grey and heaving and white-veined in the gale, there was the sea. It had everything I expected of a Cape Horn sea. It was shallow – the South American continental shelf was only thirty fathoms down – and the waves were short, and steep. The sea here had a vast emptiness, and a subdued fury to it – not at all like the North Sea, for instance, across which ships of all kinds are for ever making way. This was a deserted quarter of the ocean, and the clouds were very low, and ragged wisps blew down to the crests of the swell, where big seabirds – albatross, I imagined, or the southern ocean mollymauks – whirled lazily on the storm.

We were coming in north of the islands, and making a tight turn into the wind, landing from the east. The charts ('Islands Surveyed by Captains R. Fitz Roy and B. J. Sulivan, RN, 1838–1945') were not entirely helpful. Macbride Head, for which I looked in vain, had a notation beside it. 'Reported to lie one mile further northward, 1953'. The cliffs around Cape Bougainville were said to be a mile and a half further south than depicted by the Victorian captains. And the interior of East Falkland, which they either never took time to see, or else found too intimidating to describe, was curtly dismissed as being crammed with 'Rugged mountain Ranges and impassable Valleys'. I trusted that the Air Force men up front were using more accurate maps.

And as we turned for the final approach, so I spotted my first glimpse of this uttermost outpost of the old Empire. A chain of black rocks, streaked with white foam, surrounded by a tangled web of weed, heaved up from the seabed. There was a tiny beach, and on it the lumbering forms of seals, frantically racing into the comfort of the surf to escape our noisy approach. There were said to be four types of pinnipeds on the Falklands – the southern elephant, the southern sea lion, the South American fur, and the leopard. True seals walk by flexing their stomach muscles (unlike sea lions, which use their flippers) and furs are the most common Falkland seals, and as these below seemed to be both numerous and heaving themselves about on their bellies, I assumed these to be furs. But before I could be sure two more islands, these covered with tall bushes of tussac grass, flashed by and we bumped down on the most southerly governed dominion of the United Kingdom.

The rain lashed cruelly out of the rugged ranges and impassable valleys to the west, though it was not cold. Two bedraggled and dejected baggage men waved us into the low block of the arrivals' hall, where there was the smell of cigarette smoke and damp corduroy, and where a rather dated picture of the Queen and Prince Philip hung, steamed up, on a whitewashed wall. A small and cheerful man in blue oilskins welcomed us, said his name was Les Halliday, customs and immigration officer and harbour master, and could he have our passports? Much inspection, and questioning followed – how long was I staying, did I have enough funds to support myself, where was my return ticket, what was my business – before Mr Halliday felt confident that I was not an Argentine zero pilot out on the islands for a recce, and he chalked my dripping bags and stamped my passport.

A small oblong stamp in blue-black ink: 'Immigration Department 30 March 1982 Falkland Islands'. Neither Les Halliday nor I knew that was to be the last mark he would put in a passport for a long while, and that the plane even then refuelling in the storm outside would be the last international civil flight into the Falklands for five years, at least. The next foreign aircraft to land at Stanley airfield would arrive in three days' time; it would fly the blue-and-white flag of Argentina, all of its guns would be loaded with shells, and Mr Halliday would be under strict curfew, ordered to stay indoors and pay the arrival no official heed at all.

A clutch of mud-spattered Land Rovers stood outside, and a pleasant-faced girl took my bags and led me to one of them. Her voice sounded vaguely Australian, though she was rather shy, and clearly rather uneasy with the strangers who piled into the cab. She unbuttoned her anorak once the heater got going, and she was wearing a tee-shirt with a Union Jack, and the slogan

'British and Proud of It' over an outline of the islands. We lurched forward with a belch of diesel smoke and crunch of wet gravel, and set off for the colony's capital.

A few weeks before I had been on the island of Lewis, in the Outer Hebrides, and the similarities were remarkable. No trees. Bare rocks, ever wet from the rain and salt spray. Endless stretches of green bogland, fading into the fog and the drifting squalls. Lines of black diggings, some with tiny figures in black plastic coats moving slowly among the pools of inky water, stacking fuel for the coming winter. Gulls mewed and squawked as they wheeled in the eddies. Discarded cars lay rusting beside the road, which was either deeply rutted, or covered with thick patches of beach sand scattered by the last storm waves. And through the holes torn in the Land Rover's canvas top, the sweet smell of peat smoke, and, as we rounded a bend and breasted a low rise, the sight of it blowing in blue streams from a hundred mean cottage rows in Port Stanley herself.

We passed a small forest of radio aerials: this was where the Marconi Wireless Telegraph Company had set up its first transmitter in 1912, and had sent a message in morse to King George. The Admiralty built a second set of mighty aerials just before the Great War, in the mountains to the west of the capital; the first time they were tested some hapless matelot turned on too much power and miles of wiring burned out in a flash and a drizzle of sparks. A submarine cable laid to Montevideo snapped, twice. Then a set of rhombus aerials was built for a space-research team that came to the Falklands in the mid-Sixties, and a private circuit was established between the unlikely twin towns of Stanley and Darmstadt, in West Germany. But after seven years it closed, too – leaving behind, as seems the custom here, a cluster of odd-shaped radio masts. There may be no native trees on the Falklands, but the twentieth century's sterling efforts to allow the colonists to talk to the outside world has left many rusting iron masts and rotting hawsers that, from a distance and in a mist, look much the same.

Up in the Caribbean, where the winds are from the east, colonial capitals were usually built on the western sides of the islands – protected by the lee of the land, accessible for sailing

ships that used to bring and take the Imperial trade. Down in
the Falklands, where the winds – and what winds! – are from
the west, precisely the opposite is true. The eastern shores are
those protected from the gales, and logic and prudence thus
dictates that the trading vessels call and anchor there. The first
township was at Port Louis, on the eastern side of East Falkland,
but the approaches were shallow, and troublesome for the bigger
ships of the day; and when the Royal Navy surveyed the nearby
waters and tested the anchorages and decided on another spot,
it too was on the eastern side of the archipelago. The place they
considered most fit was a tiny settlement named Port William
at the southern side of an inlet called Jackson's Harbour. To
honour the peer who was then Under-Secretary for the Colonies,
it was renamed Stanley, and formally designated capital 'with a
turf hut and a small wooden cottage in progress' in 1844.

Like Bird's custard and the shapeless cardigan, the design and
structure of a British working-class town is quite unmistakable,
utterly unexportable and – to the British, and only to the British
– charming in a ghastly sort of way. As we bumped down the
final hill into Stanley there could be no doubt that this was the
creation of Britons, seeking familiarity and reassurance so far
from home. It was a town that appeared to have paid no heed
to its position so close to the Patagonian coast. (It is notable,
though, that Stanley is at almost exactly the same latitude
south – fifty-two degrees forty minutes – as Great Yarmouth,
Stamford, Cannock, Oswestry and Barmouth are north, and it
is similar to the poorer parts of all of those towns and has, in
winter, a not dissimilar climate, too.) There is nothing like it
anywhere in South America, though there are villages in the
older parts of Australia and New Zealand that have the same
ramshackle aspect – a blend of mining-town and fishing-port,
Industrial Revolution and Prince Albert, memorial hall and cenotaph, red brick terrace and tiled roof, pebbledash and peeling
paint, potting shed and allotment, conservatory and geranium
and privet hedge. I was never to see another Imperial town
quite like Stanley. The Caribbean capitals have more grandeur
and permanence about them; the old garrison cities – Gibraltar,
Hong Kong – have been subsumed by modern development,

the mid-Atlantic colonies have in their capitals stone constructions that proclaim the might and main and dignity of Empire.
But not poor Stanley. This is a truly forlorn and gimcrack little
town, creaking and damp, and with the feel of impermanent
permanence about it, as though it had been put up by a Ministry
of Works to solve an immediate housing problem, and never
removed. There used to be rows of what were called prefabs
in some English towns, erected to ease the shortage of housing
after the Hitler war. They stayed for years – ugly, and yet not
hated. Stanley seemed to me rather similar – a town that has
suffered from too little money, too little confidence, too little
care taken in its design and its maintenance. It does have a
certain charm – but that tends to derive from its people, rather
than from its appearance. No historian, surveying the architec-
tures of Imperial power, would ever select the Falklands capital
as an exemplar of what the world's greatest Empire had done.
The Imperial ties that bound Chowringhee and Pedder Street
and Albert Road, Hong Kong, never extended as far south as
Ross Road, Stanley.

Stanley was built on the northern flanks of a steep hill, its
streets running down to the waters of Stanley Harbour. The
light, in consequence, is intense – the sun always hanging in the
northern skies and reflected back by the riffled and sparkling
sea. As we turned down the hill the town suddenly became
curiously luminous, everything bathed in the pastel brightness
of a low sun and the sea. From here the town looked like a
freshly painted water-colour of itself, shining with the damp.
The rain had stopped, the sun had broken through and the gale
had eased to a stiff breeze. There was washing flapping on
the lines, the peat smoke rose half-vertically from a hundred
chimneys, gulls were finding it possible to land on rooftops, and
children, in oiled pullovers and Wellingtons, spilled out on to the
streets, to play. This might have been a Scottish islands capital
– Stornoway, perhaps, or Tobermory, on a brisk morning after
a night of storms.

The Upland Goose Hotel, made famous by the events of that
autumn, was rather less of a hostelry than would be found in a
Scottish fishing town. It was more like a youth hostel – spartan,

old-fashioned, worn out. The name comes from the wild goose that island sheep farmers loathe, regarding it as an absolute pest. They call it 'Magellan's grass-eater', and claim that seven geese can wolf down as much grass each day as the average healthy sheep. There was a plan to slaughter 15,000 a year and offer a bounty of fifteen shillings for every hundred beaks, but the conservation lobby won the day, and the geese remain, to be shot for food, and served with redcurrant jelly and slices of orange.

I had a cup of instant coffee and sat in the conservatory, basked for a while in the afternoon sun and read old copies of *Weekend* and *Titbits*, and smelled the geraniums and the roses. Mutton, too: it was lamb for dinner at the Upland Goose, as it is so often that the islanders call the meat three-six-five (or so it is said; I never actually heard anyone call it anything but mutton).

There was a purr of heavy tyres on the road outside, and a new, bright green Land Rover shot past. Royal Marines, members of Naval Party 8901, the Falklands garrison. I might have supposed they were bent on some secret military expedition – setting up fortifications, perhaps; or making a last-minute reconnaissance. But as I strolled out into Ross Road to look, it turned out to be much more mundane. They had stopped at the grocer's, and were inside buying Mars bars. They were curious when I told them I had come all the way from London. Everything was pretty relaxed, they said. No crisis, except that a few lads had come across from Montevideo and were crowding out the barracks up at Moody Brook. Come over and have tea, they said. Or even a drink. The major's a pretty decent sort, be glad to see you.

And off they rumbled, westwards, towards their little headquarters camp at the head of the sea-loch. Up in London matters were fast moving to a head; down here, 8,000 miles away from the diplomatic argument, the marines whose task was, in theory, to defend the integrity of the Colonial Government, were blithely unconcerned, or at least appeared to be.

As the sun began to slip its way westwards, and ease itself down behind the Saddleback and Mount Longdon, I strolled through town. (The 800-foot peak directly south from Stanley is called Twelve O'Clock Mountain, and islanders set their watches by it, when it is not raining, and covered with cloud.)

Christ Church Cathedral – 'the most southerly Anglican cathedral in the world' – was the only structure of any real Imperial value, it seemed to me, even though its roof is made of red corrugated iron. The first Falklands church had been wrecked in 1886 when a river of liquid peat had roared down from the hills; Sir Arthur Blomfield designed its replacement, and it might have been particularly grand had the Austrian stonemasons he employed not walked out after a year, leaving the tower half-finished, and forcing the abandonment of plans for a thirty-foot steeple. But what resulted was pleasant enough: a chunky, well-buttressed tower, and an impressive expanse of red roof – proof, if any were needed, that the Imperial deity was of the Church of England, and could survive even among the winds and the waves of the far south Atlantic.

I liked the cosy Britishness of it all, too. The altar had been carved by masons in Yorkshire, the kneelers had been embroidered by the good ladies of the parish, and there was a tiny stained-glass window in the south corner, dedicated to the memory of the island nurse, Mary Watson, who pedalled the rough roads of Stanley on her ancient Raleigh bicycle, visiting the new mothers and the old men and the sickly children, and who was much loved by her people.

Yes, there were the grander memorials, too – a battle ensign from the *Achilles*, which had streamed behind her as she tackled the pocket battleship *Graf Spee* off Montevideo in 1939, and a plaque for the sailors who died at the battle of Coronel, in 1914. But it was the gentler, less strident memorials that seemed more suited to this most gentle of colonies – like that to the old Dean, Lowther Brandon, who had travelled by horse and by ship to every corner of the islands (a complete tour took three months) bringing the post, books, his own *Falklands Islands Magazines*, and his magic lantern, which sat on the saddle of his second horse and with which he would entertain the island children. 'In appreciation of many years of faithful service' reads the memorial. No hectoring monuments to conquering generals

here, and only one governor (the splendidly named Herbert
Henniker Heaton) gets a mention.

The lights were coming on all over Stanley as I strolled back
to the hotel, and out in the bay, too, there were the pinpricks
of lanterns on the few ships at anchor. Two fixed lights showed
the Narrows, the entrance to the wonderfully sheltered anchorage; and beyond it there was the bulk of a vessel that, according
to a passing policeman, was a Polish fish-factory ship. Polish and
East German fishing vessels crawled all over Falklands waters,
he said, 'stealing our hake'. But, he added, 'we steal the Poles',
so it all works out fair.' It turned out that whenever a Polish
vessel came into Falklands waters a number of seamen jumped
ship, and asked the colonial authorities for asylum. There were
six in the police station outhouse just now, he said, and they
were being taught English by one of the local wives.

There were as many Poles as policemen. The force in Stanley
is smaller than in any other colony – one chief, from the Colonial
Police Service, an inspector, a sergeant and four constables.
One member of the thin blue line for every 300 colonists, a
number that Falklanders like to think compares favourably with
an island like St Helena where there is one policeman for every
hundred Saints. There is almost no crime – a little drunkenness,
the odd bout of sparring between spouses, and assorted beastliness with sheep (of which there are three-quarters of a million
– 400 for every islander). The task of the police force, then, is
limited to handing out licences for islanders wishing to collect
penguin eggs, and making sure dogs are regularly inoculated
against a worrying local ailment called hydatidosis. 'A pleasant
sort of life,' said the constable. 'Boring, though.'

The dinnertime rituals at the Upland Goose would have been
familiar to a travelling brush salesman who had ever worked his
way through a wet Wednesday night on the Ayrshire coast.
The dining room was cold, the furniture cheap, the ugly floral
wallpaper was scuffed and the glasses on each table were made
by Duralex, in France. The passengers from the plane were
seated at separate tables, and were not encouraged to talk to
one another, but to munch solemnly at small clumps of congealed
mutton and instant mashed potatoes, boiled carrots, and Bisto.

The waitresses caught the glumness of the hour, and moved with a sullen weariness from kitchen to table, finding it difficult to smile, impossible to talk. An excited babble of Spanish came from an adjoining room – a dozen workers for the Argentine natural gas combine were staying, someone explained; they were building a gasworks down by the docks.

I had met, and had dinner with, one other Argentine who was staying locally. He was a photographer named Raphael Wollman, and he had been on the island for a week. Des King, the owner of the Upland Goose, was very suspicious of him. 'Big coincidence, I'd say,' he remarked. 'All this talk of trouble, and we have an Argentine photographer here. Funny business.' And he shook his thin head with distaste. He didn't care much for the Argentines, he said. Impossible to trust. Unpredictable. Very emotional.

The radio was on in the kitchen, and at eight – midnight in London – the familiar jauntiness of *Lilliburlero* cascaded through the static, and the BBC newsreader came on air. All conversation stopped, forks hovered in mid-route. The South Georgia saga was the first on the list, and hotting up: Lord Carrington, the British Foreign Secretary, had broken off a trip to Israel and had made a statement to Parliament. 'The question of security in the Falklands area is being reviewed . . .' It was almost the first time the name of the colony had been mentioned, other than as a mere adjunct to the trouble 800 miles to the east. I felt the adrenalin pump briefly into my system, and my hands shook slightly with excitement.

There was more. Some newspapers in London were reporting that submarines had been sent south. The Navy High Command in Buenos Aires had declared its force 'in a high state of readiness', and there were reports that the Argentine flagship, the aircraft carrier *Veinticinco de Mayo*, had put to sea. (It was forty years old, built for the Royal Navy as HMS *Venerable*. But elderly or not, it was still a carrier, and sending a carrier to deal with a gathering storm on South Georgia suggested that someone in Buenos Aires had decided it was time to stop playing games.) There was said to be a row brewing between Britain and the United States over which side the Americans were on.

And to complicate matters still further, riots were breaking out all over the Argentine capital. The rioters were angry with the military government. Raphael Wollman, listening solemnly to all this, shook his head sadly. 'Madness,' he said. 'This will all come to no good.'

Everyone on the islands would have heard the news from London. Every house – and not merely those in Stanley, but in all the outlying settlements dotted across in the vast expanse of countryside they called 'the Camp' – was equipped with a brown walnut box, a gold-coloured grille on the front, and a single black bakelite knob below. This was 'the Box', the radio-rediffusion system that had been introduced to the islands in the Thirties, and which conveyed, by land-line and telephone circuit, every piece of news and gossip a remote colonial community was ever likely to need.

It was customary to keep it switched on all the time – the Box in the Upland Goose was always burbling away in the background, a combination of Muzak and a pictureless telescreen that I half-suspected would bring me news of increased chocolate rations and successes against Oceania. The feeling was enhanced by the acronym used by the Falkland Islands Broadcasting Service, FIBS. 'All they tell,' Des King laughed. The usual fare was music, very much from the Fifties, with interleaved snippets of news read by a man named Patrick Watts, and announcements – who would be on the next morning's float-plane departure to Fox Bay and Port San Carlos, who had flown in on the afternoon flight from Comodoro, what His Excellency the Governor was doing for the remainder of the week. 'And now – Edmundo Ros . . .' The BBC broadcasts were relayed, and were much listened to – particularly a brief fifteen-minute programme each Friday, 'Calling the Falklands', which generally consisted of birthday greetings of the 'to little Janice at Walker Creek from her Auntie Jill and Uncle Bert in Southampton' variety, and usually ended with sad promises that they would try to get down to see everyone 'before you're too much older', and which everyone seemed to know would never be fulfilled.

These days, of course, it was the news that stopped most islanders in their tracks. The names of the BBC readers – Roger

Collinge, Michael Birley, Barry Moss – were as familiar in this bleak corner of the ocean as were the Cronkites or the Days of the outside world. 'Always worry when Mr Collinge is reading the news,' said one man in the hotel bar afterwards. 'Reminds me of Frank Phillips in the last war. He always seemed to be given the bad news to deliver. Collinge seems the same. If it's grim stuff, give it to old Collinge.' Mr C – I had seen a picture of him once; he looked very gentle, and wore dark glasses – did seem to be on a lot these days.

The radio service, antique though it may have been, was the very soul of modernity when compared to the Falklands telephone system. I had decided to call the Governor. The telephone was enormous, made of bakelite, weighed twenty pounds and had a hand crank on the side. Not for the first time I felt that I had whirled backwards in time, and that I was playing a bit-part in a Rattigan play, all seedy gentility, brilliantine, ration cards and Utility furniture. But I followed the instructions on the card – picked up the 'instrument', twirled the handle – it rasped alarmingly – and was connected to a cheery lady whose name, I had read, was Edith. 'Thirty-eight two rings,' I said somewhat diffidently offering the number of Government House. 'His Excellency's having dinner,' said Edith, without a moment's pause. 'Can you try in ten minutes? Give him time to have his coffee.'

Rex Masterman Hunt, Governor and Commander-in-Chief of the Falkland Islands, Governor of the Falkland Islands dependencies and High Commissioner of British Antarctic Territory, presided over what is by far the biggest remaining land acreage of British Empire. The Falklands, which cover just under 5,000 square miles, are but a morsel. The dependencies of South Georgia and the South Sandwich Islands (which Governor Arthur, in the Fifties, represented by a stuffed king penguin at one end of his office, and which he kicked every so often to remind himself how irritating the dependency problems could be) add another few thousands of square miles; and the Antarctic Territory – the South Orkneys, South Shetlands and a massive wedge of Antarctica claimed by Britain – represent 100,000 more.

Despite the rigours of having to rule such a mighty Imperial domain, Mr Hunt said he would be delighted to have company, would I please come over right away, coffee was being brewed, and Mavis keen to hear all the gossip. Did I need a lift?

He had a red London taxi, just like the Governor on Grand Turk Island. Taxis were considered eminently suitable for gubernatorial transport because, the Foreign Office had said, they were unmistakably British, impressive-looking, and tall enough inside to allow governors to keep their plumed hats on their heads while on ceremonial drives. The Falklands taxi, I was glad to learn, did not suffer the depredations of its Caribbean colleague, which was always being gnawed to bits by inquisitive wild horses. Here the only snag was that the car got a little rusty.

Government House, Stanley, was a pleasant and unpretentious Victorian villa, looking rather like a cross between a manse and one of the smaller railway hotels found by the junction stations of the Scottish highlands. It had brick chimneys and a tiled roof, and conservatories and offices had been tacked on later, as business flourished. It was next door to the Cable and Wireless office, and there were a couple of wooden houses nearby where junior officials from the Foreign Office lived. A flagpole stood on the lawn and a copse of Douglas firs, some of the very few trees on the islands, and planted as a windbreak, so that His Excellency could read old copies of *The Times* in the garden, and not risk having the court and social news blown out to Cape Pembroke. The house was wholly unprotected – there was no guardian fence, just a tall pine hedge, and pipework cattle grids, to keep the sheep off the lawns. No duty soldier was in evidence, either – odd, considering the fuss in London and Buenos Aires; even odder, when you think that even on an island as tranquil as Montserrat a white-uniformed soldier stands constantly in a sentry-box beside Government House, Plymouth; and that in Hong Kong armed police patrol the grounds, on eternal watch for possible assailants.

Here there was no one. I strolled up the path, rattled the door, and the Governor and Commander-in-Chief opened it himself, as though we were neighbours calling in for a cup of

Nescafé. He was wearing, as I recall, a cardigan; Mavis was sitting by the peat fire, drinking brandy and soda from a tumbler and reading a copy of the previous week's *Times*. A Beethoven sonata was on the tape player, the velvet curtains were drawn, and on the spare armchair was a pile of mail from England, and a great number of recent London newspapers, all of which had come in with the diplomatic bag from Comodoro.

'Governors,' *The Times* wrote in the mid-Sixties, after the anonymous Latin American correspondent paid a visit, 'are fleeting birds of passage in this out-of-the-way colony.' Many would never have chosen to come to 'these islands of peat moorland, where people are few and sheep are many'. The place had many shortcomings – the water 'which the stranger finds has a peculiar taste and effect, looks like whisky'; the winds blow hard, trees are a rarity. Small wonder so many of Her Majesty's men – none of whom had ever been high fliers in the Colonial Service, and were always paid indifferently – were so hostile. Governor Arthur kicked his stuffed penguin; Governor Moore forced his staff to go to church, banned drink, and could be kind about nothing Falkland except his garden, in which he once grew a thirteen-pound cabbage; Governor Robinson let it be known he loathed this tiny settlement 'at the fag end of the world'. But Governor Hunt, who had paid his dues in the service of Empire – he had been a District Commissioner in Uganda, and had worked in Jesselton, Brunei and Kuala Lumpur, as well as flying Spitfires against Hitler's air force – seemed to like the place. Mavis Hunt, a stalwart of a colonial wife who preferred warm places, was not so sure about the weather; and Tony Hunt, the tearaway teenager who rode his motorcycle furiously around the rutted Stanley streets, was not keen at all. But they all liked the scenery, and the people; and they had no doubt that they were loyal British subjects, and intended to remain so.

The house was certainly very comfortable, with a kitchen big enough for a mansion, a billiards room, eight bedrooms, studies, drawing rooms, gun rooms and diplomatic offices. A small lair at the end of a corridor housed the communications centre, where there was a cipher machine and a telex for sending and receiving coded telegrams, and where Rex Hunt kept his one-time pads, the code books for those rare occasions when it was necessary to send messages in ultra-secret. The Government House secretary turned out to be a woman I had known some years before in Islamabad, in Pakistan.

In the kitchens I met the Governor's chauffeur, an islander named Don Bonner. He had been asked to stand by until I was ready to leave, and was nursing a cup of cocoa with one of the kitchen maids. He was a dignified man, grey haired and weather-beaten, with the manner and the accent of a countryman; he had been in the employ of the past three governors, both as driver and preserver of His Excellency's dignity. 'I make sure the flag's the right way up – that sort of thing.' He drove me back to the Upland Goose, in the little taxi with a crown in place of a number plate.

He admitted to being bewildered, and not a little alarmed, by all that seemed to be going on. 'We've had all sorts of troubles with the Argentines over the years, you know,' he said. 'They landed a plane on the racecourse once. They built a base on Thule Island, and no one in London seemed to mind. No one even knew about it for the best part of a year! And now all this. Landing planes at our airfield again – they did that last week – and all this nonsense at Leith. We've seen it all before, I suppose. But it doesn't sound good.'

Don set me down, and waved me goodbye. 'Cheers *che*!' he cried. There are a number of such residual Spanish words and phrases in use on the islands. Every part of the colony outside Stanley is known as the Camp – from *campo*, the Spanish word for 'countryside'. The islanders take a coffee-break each morning, only they call it 'smoko time'; the sheepskin fleece on the farm horses is known by its gaucho word, the *cojinillo*, and the noseband is the *recado*, the halter is the *cabezada*, the harness is the *apero*. And farms, too – Rincon Grande, Salvador, and San Carlos. (But Lafonia, the huge southern part of East Falkland Island, did not get its name from the Spanish: Samuel Fisher Lafone was a merchant settler who bought vast tracts of land in the 1840s, and later sold out to the magnificently named Royal Falkland Land, Cattle, Seal and Whale Fishery Company

– later to become the Falkland Islands Company, a subsidiary of an English firm of coal dealers. The firm's greatest land asset is the soggy waste of Lafonia.)

Next day dawned bright and clear, though the wind still stung, and as I walked by the sea after breakfast – Rice Crispies, bacon and eggs, damp toast and Chivers marmalade – droplets of salt spray whistled through the air like fine rain. Outside the hotel, mounted on a plinth on a patch of grass that ran down to the harbour, was the mizzenmast of the SS *Great Britain*, one of the many wrecks that litter the island. The *Great Britain* herself, built by Brunel in 1838 and one of the world's first iron ships, was dismasted off the Horn, and ran to Stanley for shelter, where she lay for more than a century. Eventually enthusiasts had her brought back to Bristol, leaving only the mast behind.

But there are other ships that remain intact: the huge ironclad *Lady Elizabeth*, with her three masts, lies on a sandbank near the airport; the *Snow Squall*, the *Vicar of Bray*, the *Charles Cooper* – and my own favourite, an East Indiaman known as the *Jhelum*, which was built in 1839 and now lies where she came to grief, in front of Government House. (I felt a certain affinity for this creaking old beauty, condemned and dangerous though she might be. I had been in Jhelum, in the Pakistan Punjab, only a week before leaving for Port Stanley: the symmetry seemed remarkable, to say the least.)

Close to the hulk of the *Jhelum* was the colony's most famous memorial – that commemorating the triumphal naval engagement of 8th December, 1914, and which has ever since (despite later happenings) been known as the battle of the Falkland Islands. Admiral Sturdee and the battle cruisers *Invincible* and *Inflexible* were on duty, defending the Horn from the German grand fleet, under the command of Admiral Graf von Spee, in his battleship the *Scharnhorst*. The Falklands Volunteers, islanders mounted on ponies and armed with two machine-guns, were sent out on watch; and at seven thirty on the morning of 8th December saw the smoke of the approaching Germans. (A Mrs Melton, who worked on the farm at Fitzroy Settlement, managed to get a message to Stanley that three German warships were lying off Port Pleasant.) Admiral Sturdee, accompanied by a mighty squadron of British Imperial naval power, put to sea, and sank the marauding Germans, sending von Spee to the bottom. The islanders have always been proud of having helped trounce the Kaiser's attempted domination of the South Atlantic, and celebrate the day each December – one of the few occasions when the Governor turns out in full Imperial rig, and the garrison steps out in style.

I called on the garrison at their tiny base at Moody Brook, a couple of miles along the sea-loch, to the west of Stanley. On the Wednesday the marines were said to be on yellow alert, but their officers seemed relaxed enough, and gave me tea and sandwiches from a silver mess teapot. There had been a small celebration, since one of their number – only forty in usual times, though more had come over from Montevideo since the South Georgia affair started – had married a local girl named Alana Cusworth. He was reckoned lucky by his chums, who saw their eighteen-month tour of the islands as 500 days and nights of excruciating sexual frustration. 'We give them lots of training exercises, and they run around, and sail a good deal,' their commander, Major Gary Noott, remarked over a piece of toast. 'But it is still tricky for them.' He took me to one of the marines' rooms: an entire wall was covered with pin-ups from floor to ceiling – there must have been a thousand nipples on display, and still the man wasn't happy.

Major Noott seemed unbothered by the gathering storm. He had his orders, he knew what to do in case of a 'threat', but as he had almost no weapons ('just enough to support a troop, spread among sixty of us') he considered his presence more symbolic than useful. 'If they were foolish enough to invade us,' a brother officer remarked, 'we have to remember that there are nearly 80,000 of them, and sixty of us, with just a few rifles and a machine-gun. I'd say our chances of success were – well, limited.' Everyone in the mess laughed, but sardonically.

It was a curious time. Diplomacy, away in London and New York and Buenos Aires, appeared to be staggering towards disaster. Ships were involved in complicated manoeuvres in the South Georgian waters: I managed to send a telex to HMS *Endurance*, asking the skipper, Captain Nicholas Barker, for some news on just what was happening, and he promised to reply on Friday morning. But here in the eye of the storm, all was uncannily calm. The *Penguin News* carried stories about the Horticultural Show (Harry Ford won a bag of fertiliser for displaying the 'most outstanding potatoes'); Stanley beat the marines in the annual soccer match; Timmy Bonner from Port Howard won seven races at Port Stephen, on horses named Happy, Parker, Trigger, Matcho and Ulster. Someone had written from New Zealand to say that diddle dee berries, which grow in great abundance on the Falklands, could make excellent aftershave if mixed with alcohol. And one of Stanley's little shops, the Kelper Store, was up for sale; its owner kept it open for only nine hours a week, and consequently found it woefully unprofitable.

The store's plight echoed one of the main troubles of the Falklands. There seemed a pathological lack of initiative and drive among the islanders. The shops were dreary, made no effort to compete with one another, never made a bid for excellence. There were no local industries – no whisky was produced, despite the ideal conditions for growing all the ingredients. No one tried to sell fresh vegetables to the marines, who had to buy their supplies from England. There were 600,000 sheep on the islands – yet no one tried to sell a single skin, or make a single coat, or spin a single ball of wool. There was but one restaurant in Stanley. (Its owners later upped and left.) There was no fishing industry – indeed, I found it hard to buy fish in any shop, or order it in any hotel. Nor was there a butcher's shop: the meat supplies were brought in the back of a Land Rover, which called at houses only if a sign was displayed – 'Meat today please'.

The marines had noticed it. The Governor had noticed it. A few of the islanders, and the more recent immigrants had noticed it. The place was dying on its feet. Islanders were leaving – a score or so each year, the population sagging now well below 2,000, the ratio of young women to young men declining rapidly, the social ills of a small, introverted group – alcoholism, divorce, depression – increasing fast.

I liked the colony very much; but I had no illusions about it.

This was no elysium, a remote and peaceful corner of the world in which the forgotten idylls of mankind were still performed. It was a place of change and decay, of decline and pointlessness – gentle, yes; harmless, yes; but a sorry kind of wasteland, the abode of the spiritually dying, and of the intellectually dead. It was, I realised after my first few days, a place that made me angry – that so much beauty and serenity had to be wasted on so many who were so unwilling or unable to reap the most from its natural goodness and potential.

There were, of course, places and people I came to like. I loved Cape Pembroke Lighthouse, with its brass gleaming and its lenses sparkling, and its keeper (who had worked for twenty years on an Imperial light on South Georgia) proudly showing me the log book, and telling me of the various vessels he had watched over the years as, despite the warnings of his ten-mile beam, they hurled themselves on to the rocks below. I loved the penguins – the rockhoppers and the gentoos, the kings, the magellans, and the improbably named macaronis. I found much pleasure in the names of the animals and birds and plants these strange sub-Antarctic islands provided homes for. There were Cuvier's beaked whales, Falkland foxes, South American sea lions. You could see steamers and loggerhead ducks, Johnny rooks and mollymauks, Pampa teal and Chiloe widgeon. You might walk across meadows of swamp rush and pigvine, the Cape Horn boxwood and the Christmas bush, the vanilla daisy and scurvy grass. And all under a wind so cool and fresh and clean that a quick turn of an evening left you feeling scrubbed down to bright metal, with the appetite of an ox and the fitness of an athlete. The Falklands felt a place that should have been good for the body and the soul, and it puzzles me still that so much was so evidently missing.

Some newcomers were not as disappointed as I, and did indeed find the islands a source of perfect peace and spiritual inspiration. A small community of Ba'hai had been started there in the mid-Seventies; I became friendly with one young Californian family, the Sheridans, Jeannie and Duffy. Duffy Sheridan worked by day writing road signs for the Government, and at night turned his talents to oil painting. He was good enough to be given an exhibition in London, devoted to portraits of the island people, and he made a considerable amount of money.

It was mid-afternoon on Thursday, All Fools' Day, when things started to go visibly wrong. The news from London was bad that morning, and when we stood in the kitchen, wreathed in porridge steam, and listened to the World Service, the girls clenched their fists until their knuckles turned white. Mrs King was from the Pitaluga family, well known in Gibraltar, and she knew a thing or two about the travails of Empire. She looked up from her cooking and scowled at the radio. 'Something's happening,' she said. 'Something's going wrong.'

That afternoon I made a brief attempt to get a ride to South Georgia, so that I could see exactly what was going on between the Royal Marines and the sailors on board *Drummond* and the *Granville*. There was history of a sort being written out there, and I felt I wanted to take a squint into the epicentre of the moment. A steel sloop had slipped into harbour overnight, sailed by a young Czech who was on a single-handed circumnavigation. He had left the Baltic a year ago, and had wandered down the Atlantic to Montevideo, and was now crossing to Cape Town in the roaring forties, and had stopped in the Falklands for shelter from the storm, like thousands of sailors before him.

He said he would take me to Grytviken. It was on his way, and he was bored with his own company. So we sailed out into the harbour, and swung the compass for an hour or so, tacking back and forth along the length of the loch. Two others came for the ride – Raphael, the Argentine photographer, and a stray Polish seaman who had jumped ship a few days before, and wanted to give his fellow crewmen a wave as we cruised cheekily close to the factory vessel. I rather fancied that the Czech planned to go back home when his journey was over, and might not look too kindly at his Polish friend thumbing his nose at fellow Pact-members, but he was a relaxed sort of fellow, as most lone yachtsmen have to be, and seemed not to worry.

It was about five, and we were sailing close to the Narrows

when, with a roar of exhaust and a plume of spray, three uniformed Royal Marines shot by in a rubber boat. I had seen them the night before, and I waved. They did not wave back, but sped ahead with a look of rather grim purpose. They landed at the westerly entrance, just by the tiny green navigation light, and began unloading weapons – a light machine-gun, and a pair of mortars. One marine remained behind, his colleagues sprang away again and unloaded more weapons at the other side of the entrance. Something, I said to myself, was definitely up.

When we got back to the tiny dock by the Upland Goose there was a telegram waiting for me. My masters in London had decided that, in view of the deteriorating situation, I should remain in the Falklands, and I was asked not to sail on to see the scrap men 800 miles to the east. Then I spied Dick Baker, the Colonial Secretary, striding purposefully to his car, which took off in a screech of rubber towards Government House. A friend who had had an appointment with him followed: it had been cancelled, he said. There was something urgent afoot.

At five minutes to eight, while I was struggling through another of Mrs King's ten thousand ways with mutton (though there was the promise of red mullet on the morrow) the Governor telephoned. He was calm, but in deep earnest.

He had requisitioned five minutes of radio time at eight fifteen, he said. Would I come round immediately afterwards, please? It was a matter of great urgency. He would not say what the matter was, other than there was trouble in the offing.

I put down the telephone. All of the King family stood around in silence, waiting for a word. They looked shrunken, and frightened. I told them all I knew, and went back to the dinner table, where one of the girls served me my ginger sponge, her hand shaking as she did so. 'Balloon going up, I expect,' bellowed the Shropshire farmer from across the room. 'Nasty business. Had to come one day, I suppose.'

I felt, quite suddenly, gripped by a terrible sadness for these people. I could imagine a little of how they felt. Here I was, on the verge of becoming witness to a classic episode of Imperial history, excited, absorbed, all the instinctual routines of journalism swinging into their familiar actions; and here were the Kings, and their neighbours and their friends, who had come here to this bleak and windswept rock because they thought it would be safe, and peaceful, and because they loved the land and the wind and the kindred spirits, and because they wanted somewhere that was securely British, with all the essential decencies and protocols of an England that was herself slipping away from the things they had come to love.

I once bought a house in an Oxfordshire village from a pair of elderly ladies who had decided to emigrate to New Zealand, because, they explained, 'it is like England was in the Fifties, and that's the time we liked so much. We don't like England today. We want to find a place that's like it used to be.' And as with New Zealand, so with the Falkland Islands. What these people had wanted, when they or their fathers set out on the ship so long ago, was just what my old ladies wanted: a country with no crime, no television, no permissiveness, no coloured people, no disco music, no drugs . . . These were a people for whom Carnaby Street meant the beginning of the end, and for whom progress was a dirty word. And the land they had found, and for all its faults the world to which they clung so eagerly, was about to be desecrated. I remember thinking, as I spooned up the last morsels of sponge and custard and poured a cup of watery coffee from the cheap steel pot, that this would be the last night ever during which all those things for which these people had become colonists would survive. I was not quite sure exactly what was about to happen, but I knew, and I could see these people knew, that from this moment on, in just a matter of hours, or minutes from now, nothing on the Falkland Islands would ever be the same again. It made the fact of this particular reliquary of Empire, with all its reasons and its history, seem suddenly to have been a pathetic waste of time.

Events then moved swiftly, in a blur. The announcer at the radio station had not quite grasped the urgency of the moment, and tried for a ribald tone. 'Lay your ears back, folks, for His

Excellency the Governor!' And Rex Masterman Hunt, the man
who had taken down the flag on the British Embassy in Saigon
and who thus knew some of the rules of diplomacy *in extremis*,
was on the air, with every house in Stanley and every settlement
in the Camp hanging on his every word. Not a sheep was shorn,
not a word was said, until the news was delivered.

The islands were going to be invaded. (Dick Baker was to
say later that up until Thursday afternoon London insisted they
would not be.) A battle group of Argentine warships – led by
that former British carrier, the *Venerable* – was on its way.
There were frantic discussions in the world's interested capitals,
but no one held out much hope. The first units of the force
could probably be seen by the keeper at Cape Pembroke in two
hours' time. The first men might be ashore by dawn. The local
Defence Force was being called up. There was no need for
alarm.

Nor was there any. Stanley was stunned into silence. A curfew
had been declared, and only soldiers were abroad. I walked the
deserted streets, which were like any working-class English
town during the screening of *Match of the Day* – every single
person was inside. Everyone was awake. The Governor was
back on the radio at four, declaring – as colonial governors have
the perfect right to do – a state of emergency. All the Argentines
staying at the Upland Goose were arrested and led away by
marines, lest they try to give some help to their arriving colleagues.

But the colleagues had already arrived. The first party was
ashore by four; the first shots were heard at eight minutes past
six. By this time I was in the small frame building beside Government House, under a bed upstairs. Don Bonner's
foot was in my ear, and a tabby cat, terrified by the
rattle and pounding of the guns, was huddled under a mess of
candlewick bedspread. A small island nation was busily changing hands.

The surrender came three hours later; the Union flag came
down, the blue-and-white banner of the Republic of Argentina
went up in its place. The Falkland Islands were instantly transmuted into Las Islas Malvinas, Port Stanley became Puerto

Argentina, the British colony, together with her dependencies and the Antarctic Territory were, in the minds of millions of jubilant Argentinians, part of the device that had for years been printed on all Spanish-language charts of the area: 'Territorio Nacional de la Tierra del Fuego Antartida e Islas del Atlantico Sur'. After a century and a half of argument, this windy quarter of the southern seas was now a province of Argentina.

The British Colonial Government was kicked out; Rex Hunt and his colleagues were on an Air Force plane to Montevideo by sunset. As a final humiliation he had been ordered to take off his white Imperial uniform and dress instead in sober style. He had to change behind a curtain in the Stanley airport, while impatient and unamused soldiers fingered their trigger-guards, and muttered Spanish imprecations under their breath.

Next morning the islanders awoke to find new road signs being painted: from now on they would drive their Land Rovers on the right, said the commanders. They were, after all, a part of Argentina, and it did not behove them to be different, in any way. And Spanish lessons would be started in all the schools, with immediate effect.

I stayed around for two more days, until the Argentine officials on the island expressed their irritation and deported us, back to Comodoro Rivadavia on the mainland. The following day I was in Buenos Aires, one of the hundreds of reporters assigned to cover the story from the perspective of the jubilant Argentine capital, wondering, like half the world, how it would all turn out. And to judge from the sounds of outrage howling down from London, the Empire, after years when it had seemed well on the way to becoming a wholly moribund and insignificant institution, was coming very much to life once again.

This is not the place in which to recount the events of the early northern summer of 1982 – the Falklands 'war' or 'operation' or 'recovery' has been well chronicled elsewhere, and for reasons I will explain in a few moments, I was not in the best position to report them. It will be sufficient to say that the Government in London responded with deliberate and brilliantly schemed ferocity, just as it might in times of earlier and more classically Imperial crises.

A massive battle fleet put out from Portsmouth, scores of civilian ships – liners, container vessels, tugboats, tankers – were requisitioned, soldiers, sailors, marines and airmen were brought from every corner of the world, arms and diplomatic assistance were sought and won from the Allies. And all with one single, uncomplicated end – to regain what had been so brusquely snatched from British hands. 'The Empire', *Newsweek* magazine perhaps inevitably wrote on its cover, 'Strikes Back!'

The British troops, replaying the grand manoeuvres of Normandy and Sicily and the Italian beaches, landed on East Falkland Island in mid-May. The next day one Falkland farm was liberated, and the Union flag flew on British soil once again. Some three weeks after that all of the island group was wholly dominated by the British forces.

The Argentine dream had lasted just seventy-four days and a little over sixteen hours. On 14th June, at 9 p.m., local time, the warring generals put their signatures to an Instrument of Surrender. Twelve minutes later a message was received in Whitehall, from Major-General Jeremy Moore. 'In Port Stanley at 9 o'clock p.m. Falkland Islands time tonight 14 June 1982 Gen. Menendez surrendered to me all the Argentine armed forces in East and West Falklands together with their impedimenta. The Falkland Islands are once more under the government desired by their inhabitants.' It had taken thirteen hundred deaths to accomplish the ending of this Argentine dream and this Falklands nightmare.

But I was not to see any of that. A week after I had returned to Buenos Aires – long before the British forces had landed at the Falkland settlement of San Carlos – I travelled down to Tierra del Fuego, in company with two friends, both from a rival newspaper. We were arrested in southern Patagonia, charged with spying, and spent the better part of three months locked up in a tiny cell in gaol in the small town of Ushuaia, the most southerly town in the world.

But once the British victory was announced, and once enough bail money had been collected to satisfy the pride of the local magistracy, we were released and flown back to London. The war had happened without us. I had been there at the beginning, but had never been allowed to witness the end. I felt slightly cheated, as if a mission had been left incomplete, and the journey had no symmetry to it. The paper sensed this, and suggested I go back down to the islands as soon as possible, to see what the war had done to the place I had thought so very peaceful and so serene.

And it changed everything, of course, and for always. It was a month later when I returned, in a Hercules transport plane. The airport at Stanley had been shattered by bombing and shellfire. There was torn metal and oil and devastation on every side, and a crush of soldiery with their tents and their radios and their portable latrines and all the other toys of military occupation. Stanley's roads were pitted, fences had been knocked down, tank-tracks and minefields and depot flags spoiled every view, and the air was constantly filled with the whirring and chugging and buzzing of helicopters as they carried the new residents back and forth over the once-peaceful little town.

I flew out to the Camp. The helicopter pilot and the army public relations men and the foreign office news managers pointed out the famous battlesites, as though they were Blenheims and Trafalgars and the salient at Ypres. There was Mount Tumbledown, and there Wireless Ridge; that's where Colonel 'H' Jones fell; that hut at Goose Green was where the bastards locked up the entire settlement; and that's where they kept the napalm, evil sods!

We stopped at the settlement at San Carlos, and had a cup of Typhoo and a bacon sandwich in the farmhouse kitchen. Woollen socks were drying over the Raeburn, and a small child came in with peat for the fire. The family sheepdog lay curled up on the floor. There were copies of the *Daily Express* on the table, and a bag of Tate and Lyle sugar, and a box of Capstan cigarettes. The islanders who stood beside the range said they were thankful for what had been done, and would now like

to be left in peace again. It had been a trying time, and still
was.

I walked outside, into the sunshine and the wind. The field,
beyond the gorse bush, was rutted with tyre marks, and the
helicopter sat to one side, its rotors bouncing in the breeze. Up
the hill a Nigerian gunnery sergeant was shouting abuse at a
squaddie: there was a Rapier missile battery near the summit,
and something had gone wrong with the tracking computer. The
squaddie set off on a khaki-painted motorbike, to seek out a
spare part.

To the west, shining gold in the afternoon sun, lay San Carlos
Water, and Falkland Sound. Three months ago there would have
been nothing there but the water and the birds – perhaps the
little island packet, or a yacht, or a child in a rowing boat off for
a day's fishing. This afternoon six warships steamed at anchor,
their guns ranged high, their radars swinging round and round
on perpetual watch. But no Admiral Sturdee here, with battleships and cruisers bent on some mighty task; these were mere
sentry ships, stationed to ensure that for the time being there
was some truth in the old Imperial axiom about Holding what
we Have.

'Come on – no time for gazing!' shouted the man from the
Ministry of Defence. The helicopter rotors were up and running,
and it was time to whirl away and leave the islanders to their
own devices. Their lives had been shattered, and changed for
ever – and all for the preservation of a sad corner of Empire
which, by rights and logic and all the arguments of history should,
by some device or other, be permitted and encouraged to fade
away. Arguments were later to be advanced about the need
for keeping the Cape Horn passage in safe hands, for the day
when Panama fell to the other side. But most of the world,
perhaps less sophisticated and more cynical than it should be,
saw this as quite simply the pointless preservation of Imperial
pride. And yet the preservation could only last a few more
years, or a few more decades; when finally it was allowed to
die, how senseless this tragedy would all appear, how wasted
all the lives.

And then I was aboard the plane again, and the islands were

falling away below, and had become a small green patch in the great grey ocean, with a British flag still flying, the guardian of the useless.

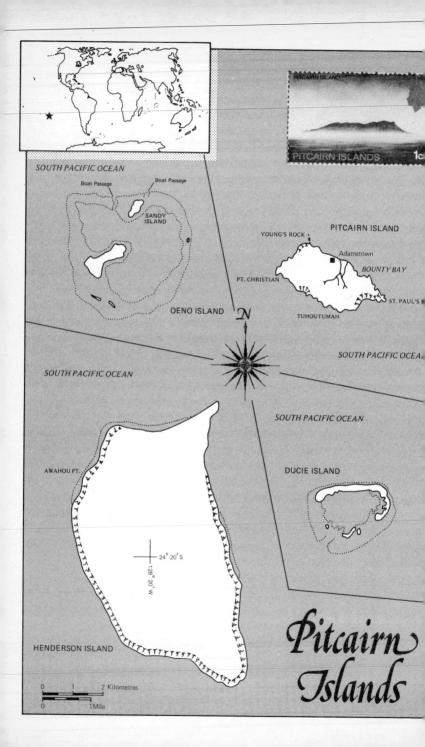

ELEVEN

PITCAIRN AND OTHER TERRITORIES

After three long years, and tens of thousands of miles, the Progress was almost over.

At the very start, when I first hauled out all the almanacs and atlases and diplomatic lists and gazetteers I counted rather more than 200 islands of any significant size that still belonged to the Crown – and thousands more, if you bothered to count every last skerry and reef where England's writ still ran and England's sovereign ruled. But I had done what I had wanted to do: I had managed to get myself to every colony that still had a British Imperial representative, and still had a population – everywhere, in other words, that was likely still to have the feel of Empire to it.

But I had had to make some hard decisions. One of the most difficult concerned whether or not I should go to Britain's sole remaining possession in the Pacific Ocean, the group of four tiny and barely inhabited rocks made notorious two centuries ago as the refuge of the *Bounty* mutineers – the Pitcairn Islands.

Three of the four islands of the colony have no population at all; the fourth, Pitcairn itself, has but forty-four islanders, and the number is declining slowly but steadily. There is no resident representative of the British Crown. (The Governor is also the British High Commissioner in Wellington, and he tries to make a brief visit every two years. The Island Administrator doesn't live on Pitcairn either, but in Auckland, 3,000 miles west.)

There is precious little communication between the Pitcairners and the motherland. Adamstown, the tiny capital named after one of the mutineers (and peopled by more than a dozen islanders whose surname is Christian, and can trace their roots back to Fletcher, the architect of the whole affair), does not rank high on Whitehall's diplomatic priorities. Hardly any British money is spent on the place: if the Pitcairners need anything urgently they have to talk to Auckland by morse code, though they have been helped in recent years by a market gardener near London, who listens out for the islanders on his ham radio set. If they want anything particular he will buy it out of his own pocket and see that it is loaded on to the twice yearly supply ships. There is no island doctor; when Betty Christian fell victim to a particularly pressing gynaecological problem the island pastor (a Seventh Day Adventist, to which church all the islanders belong) had to operate. He had never carried out surgery in his life before, and the instrument needed for the operation was not in stock among the rusty scalpels and plasters in the Adamstown dispensary. So they hand-forged the necessary item, and the pastor was led through the operation, step by step, by a surgeon speaking by radio from California, 8,000 miles away. At moments like this Pitcairners have good reason to think they and their tiny island are being shunned by the policy-makers and the bureaucrats in London.

The two supply ships usually call at Pitcairn while on their way somewhere else. Most of their skippers are reluctant to stop at all, and when they heave to off the lonely cliffs to take off stores they are invariably impatient to get under way again. A visitor who chooses this means of arriving is lucky if he gets ten hours on the island unless, by accident or design, he misses the boat, in which case he stays for the next six months. When I came to plan the journey the ten-hour option seemed worthless, the six months excessive. I decided, with some sadness, that I would not go at all.

I went instead to the village of Frog Level, Virginia. The connection between the tiny Pacific Crown colony and a rundown community in the Appalachian Mountains – not one that is immediately obvious, it has to be admitted – was provided by one of the local residents. He was named Smiley Ratliffe, and he lived in an extraordinarily vulgar mansion with fences, guntowers and a collection of five Rolls-Royces, each equipped with spittoons to accommodate his soggy plugs of Work Horse tobacco.

Mr Ratliffe, who knew nothing of the mutiny story and confessed to not having read a book since he was a GI in 1945, was a lonely and unhappy millionaire. He had made his fortune from running coal mines in the hills of Virginia and Tennessee and Kentucky, and he had developed a profound, almost pathological loathing for the insidious evils of Communism, Freudian analysis, big government, narcotics and Elvis Presley. For most of the 1970s he had spent his days flying and cruising around the world in search of a deserted and idyllic island where he could be guaranteed total freedom from all taint of the Red Menace, and all the other evils that disturbed his tranquil routines. In 1981, towards the end of another long and fruitless quest, when he was heading sadly homewards from Tahiti, he stopped by to see the good folks of Adamstown, liked them mightily and proceeded, as he tells the tale, to one of the three other islands that make up the Pitcairn group.

It was called Henderson Island, was four miles long, two miles wide, was surrounded by vertical cliffs forty feet high and was almost perfectly flat. Most mariners would not give the place a second thought. Pitcairners occasionally stopped by to pick up wood to carve, but thought little of their neighbour. Like Ducie and Oeno, the others of the forgotten Imperial quartet, Henderson was just another coral island, with nothing to commend it, and no particular quality aside from its isolation. A man had been put ashore there with a chimpanzee some years before, but had gone mad inside three weeks, and had to be taken off by a passing ship.

But Smiley Ratliffe very much liked what he saw. He had no doubts from the moment he first spotted her, that this was to be his island home. He had a sudden dream, a veritable vision. He saw his now-beloved Henderson Island nurtured and brought to civilisation by the best efforts of the fine folk of Frog Level. He saw an airstrip, a mansion, lovely ladies dancing under the Pacific stars, endless supplies of Work Horse tobacco, no taxes, no psychologists and, best of all, no Communists. And so, fired with evangelic fervour as befits a man who has discovered paradise, Smiley Ratliffe returned home to America, and with all the uncomplicated enthusiasm that is peculiar to the rural American millionaire sat down and wrote a letter: he wanted to buy Henderson Island, price (more or less) no object.

The Foreign Office gave a polite cough, and said that, no, actually, Crown colonies were not actually for sale, and certainly not to aliens. But Smiley was not that easily put off. He had heard the Pitcairn Islanders grumble about how London spent so very little on them – so he played a shrewd hand. He told the Foreign Office he would give the Pitcairners a million dollars if he could just lease Henderson – 999 years should do the trick, he said – and, moreover, he would throw in a ferry boat and would build an airstrip on Henderson so that the group of islands could have certain access to the world outside.

And this time – for such are the ways of today's Imperialist mind – the Foreign Office stopped short, and began to think very seriously about Mr Ratliffe and his money. Every Empire builder, it seems, has his price.

For a while – and particularly during those rainy summer days when I would go and see him at his desk in Frog Level – old Smiley was able to dream. He drew up the most elaborate plans – men would be shipped into Henderson by landing craft, and would have the airfield built in six months; then there would be dairy herds and a piggery and Smiley's gun collection and his thousands of cowboy videotapes, and his new mansion built and his girlfriends brought over . . . two years, maybe, and paradise would be ready for him. Lord Belstead, the Foreign Office man who was considering the case, had told Parliament itself, no less, that the Government was seriously considering the matter. Optimism reigned at Frog Level, and Smiley would drive his Silver Wraiths down the country lanes at a furious pace, scattering the chickens, singing southern songs and giving a war-whoop of victory as he sensed the imminent realisation of his life-long ambition.

But it was not to be. The World Wildlife Fund reminded the world that Henderson Island was a repository for great natural treasure. It wrote a report for the Foreign Office. 'The Island remains largely in its virginal state. It supports ten endemic taxa of flowering plants, four endemic land-birds (including the Henderson Rail, known to ornithologists as the Black Guardian of the Island), various endemic invertebrates, a colony of fifteen species of breeding seabirds and extensive and virtually unexplored fringing coral reefs.' There was a special breed of snail, a fruit-eating pigeon and a parrot that sipped nectar. Mr Ratliffe chewed tobacco, and could not under any circumstances be allowed to settle on Henderson, the Fund declared. Moreover, the island should be protected from settlement by any member of the human species, and left entirely for the world of animals and birds. Her Majesty's Government, the Fund concluded, 'has a profound moral obligation to take immediate steps to protect Henderson Island . . .'

Mr Ratliffe received his letter a few days later. So sorry to have indicated there might be cause for optimism, really cannot permit settlement, unique natural heritage, taxa here, taxa there, nice of you to offer such generous terms, great pain to have to decline kindness, no need to enter into correspondence on the matter, infinite regret, yours respectfully. And down in Frog Level that night there was much chewing and hawking, and sounds of disgust rattled around the Appalachian hills as Smiley Ratliffe unburdened himself of yet more invective, and prepared to begin his search once again, for a place where there were no drugs, no psychiatrists, no rock stars, no Commies and, particularly, no officials of the British Foreign Office. They, in Mr Ratliffe's view, were the worst of the lot of them. 'Hell, they were gonna sell me the goddam lease. They didn't give one tuppenny damn for the place. They jes' saw it as a way of making a million bucks – until them critturs weighed in on the side of some pesky little ol' snail, and some dingbat of a parrot, and the British realised they wouldn't look so good to a bunch of parrot-lovers. Damn hypocrites, you British! Just damn hypocrites.' And I left Frog Level forthwith, and have not spoken to Mr Ratliffe since.

On Pitcairn Island the news was received with sullen dismay. The islanders wanted the money, and the ferry, and thought an airfield on Henderson would be a good idea. Mrs Christian could have had a doctor flown in from Tahiti, they said. When we have a problem here someone could fly in, they said. Who cares about fruit-eating pigeons, and birds called Rails, they said.

The Foreign Office said it was moderately sympathetic. Glynn Christian, a young man related to most of the island families, and who now lives in London demonstrating cooking for early morning BBC television viewers, planned to lead an expedition to go to Pitcairn in 1989 and study the animals and birds. It would leave behind its boats and its buildings for the bicentenary the following year of Fletcher Christian's arrival; a royal visit would take place then as well, he hoped. Pitcairn would be put back on the map.

His idea was, essentially, to rescue the colony from extinction. He, and those few friends of Pitcairn to be found in Britain, are convinced the Foreign Office wishes the island to be depopulated totally – the last few islanders should go to New Zealand, or to Norfolk Island, and live a better life. If the trend of the last two decades continues, no one will be left on Pitcairn by the end of this century, and the rocky islands of this tiny and remote group will be left to the wind and the waves, the pigeons, the parrots and the snails.

But lately one additional argument is finding official favour: it concerns the strategic importance of the Pacific Ocean. The argument is simple. The sovereign sea area that surrounds the four islands of Pitcairn is vast. There are said to be dark forces – the very forces Mr Ratliffe so despises – who would dearly like to fill any Imperial vacuum that might be created in what President Reagan called 'the Ocean of the twenty-first century'. The depopulation of Pitcairn might create such a vacuum: the argument for trying to retain at least token inhabitation, a small band of colonists set down in the silver sea, is more powerful than can be influenced by mere considerations about ecology, or sentiment, or the bicentenary of an event that official Britain would prefer, in any case, to forget.

The decision not to visit Pitcairn was difficult. I felt no particular regret, however, at keeping away from both South Georgia and the British Antarctic Territory: neither has a population, neither has a resident administrator (though the chief official of the Antarctic Survey acts as magistrate and British Government representative should any problems arise – such as the illegal landing of the Argentine scrap men at Leith harbour in March 1982). The scenery, of course, appears to be stunning; but such architecture as the Empire has left is the gimcrack wreckage of scientific stations and whaling factories, and only the memorial cross to Shackleton on a snowy hillside above Grytviken appears to have a trace of the Imperial feel about it.

When I began the journey, and mentioned to friends that I was wandering around the world looking at the remaining British colonies, most would look puzzled. 'Do we have any left, then?' they would ask. Not a few, though, would assume a more sophisticated attitude. 'Places like the Isle of Man, the Channel Islands, that sort of thing?' And in the early days I grimaced inwardly, and gritted my teeth, and said that no, these were not colonies, not part of the Empire, not abroad, you see . . .

Technically, though, they were right to suggest these most British of Isles for inclusion. (And it is perfectly correct to call the Channel Islands British Isles. The word 'Britain' refers to two places – that wedge-shaped island comprising England, Wales and Scotland on the one hand; that duck's-bill of a peninsula known as Brittany on the other. The latter was always known as 'Little' Britain, the former 'Great' Britain. The Channel Islands, belonging to both, may have the sound of Gaul about them, but are British through and through.)

Both they, and the Isle of Man, are true dependencies of the Crown. They are not a part of the United Kingdom. They have their own laws, parliaments, taxes and customs. They have a British governor, the representative of the sovereign to whom they owe their allegiance and their loyalty. They are willing colonies, their citizenry colonials, in every sense the same as those in Bermuda, on Grand Turk, or up on the Peak in old Hong Kong.

But I did not go there. I decided not to for the most prosaic of reasons, though one tinged with a kind of logic. They are not, in the accepted sense, abroad. You don't have to have a passport to go there. They are not within the remit of the Foreign Office. They have not been within the remit of the Colonial Office. They do not appear in the histories of Empire, nor in the directories of dependent territories. Their governors were not chosen from the select lists of the Colonial Service, but from the same loyal rolls as came the lords lieutenants of the counties.

Their association with England, whatever the technicalities of their status, was far more intimate than the relation between, say, the United States and Guam, or between France and Martinique. In those latter cases the word 'colony' can, with some degree of literal truth, still be fairly applied; in the case of Man, in the cases of the Bailiwicks of Jersey and Guernsey, and of Alderney, Great Sark, Little Sark, Brechou, Lihou, Jethou and Herm, not even the most fervent apologist would suggest that an Imperial foot was placed against a colonial neck, and that any subjugation or inequality still obtained. These may not be part of the Kingdom; but nor are they part of the Empire, nor have they been for many centuries past.

And then, finally, I cast logic and good reason to the winds, and went back to Ireland.

The British had held Ireland for longer than any other people on the face of the earth. The First Empire – that of France, and of America, had come and gone; the great Imperial adventure, of which these three years of wandering may be a final journey, grew, reached its zenith, and began its decline. And yet still there was Ireland; the flag flew over Dublin Castle, the soldiers drilled in the parks and the squares, the police were still royal, the Viceroy still ruled a sullen and unforgiving people. For the Irish hated it, they resented it, and they were the first to throw the British out.

Conventionally the British think that the first colonies they lost were those in America; but that irruption of nationalism and violence did not spell the end of an Imperial attitude, merely the closing of one Imperial phase, and the dawning of another. When the Irish rose, with all that wonderfully misguided valour at the

General Post Office, the writing was truly on the wall for the Empire of the English. I have taken the common view that, in strict colonial terms, it was Weihaiwei in China that was the first real loss to the Empire; but the first wound was struck in 1916, the first grave and fatal blow was struck with Home Rule, the institution began to crumble from within – if not yet without – from the moment the Pale, eight long centuries old, ceased to exist in the Ireland of modern times.

True, there was the Act of Union: Ireland was not a colony, in the same strict technical sense that decided me to leave out journeying to Douglas or St Peter Port. But it felt like one. It felt like one to the Irish. And the English behaved as though it were one. There was a distinction drawn, and the Gael was on the distaff side of it, always.

And, what's more, so was the Planter, too. The English cared as little for the Protestants of Ulster as they had for the Catholics of Leinster, Munster and Connaught. The colonial mind ruled in the northern six counties too, even when the Free State had been born, and the North had been legally subsumed into the United Kingdom, and made to feel, constitutionally, part and parcel of and wholly equal to the motherland across St George's Channel. The republicans and the nationalists in the mean streets of Belfast and Derry belted it out as a slogan – 'Ulster – England's last colony!' and they were right, in a strange, indefinable sort of way, righter than they knew.

So I spent the last hours of the journey in the town of Hillsborough, in County Down, at the great stone mansion they called Government House, and where the symbol of Ireland as part of Empire had come to rest after being chased out of Dublin by the heroes of the rising and the architects of Home Rule. It had been called Hillsborough House back then – the family house of the man who had been England's first Colonial Secretary, and a man who believed passionately in Union with Ireland, and the denial of independence to the Americas.

In 1921 the family gave the house to the Crown – with provision that they might have it back should the Crown ever decide it had no need for it. The first of the five Governors moved in – to sign bills, to affix the great seal of Ulster to legislation, to hold investitures in the throne room, to hold garden parties on the lawn, to open fêtes, present awards, dress in full Imperial raiment on the sovereign's birthday, on Armistice Day, on the State Opening of Parliament at Stormont, and the delivery of the speech from the throne.

They were said to stand for no side, these men; and yet all were Protestant, all were loyal to the Crown, all stood for the very antithesis of what fully one-third of the people they ruled were said to want. In this way more than any other the Governors of Northern Ireland seem now to have been truly colonial – for like the viceroys of Ireland in Dublin Castle, they stood, to some extent, for subjugation and rule, rather than as a pleasant symbol of a universally accepted association.

There was the Duke of Abercorn, who had a decorative embellishment of soldiery at Government House, changing the guard each noon and night, to remind the passing people that the Crown ruled this corner of the island. Next the Fourth Earl Glanville, gruff, intemperate, unloved – but married to the sister of the Bowes-Lyon Queen, and thus beloved by association, if loathed by virtue of his person. Lord Wakehurst of Ardingley, come to Ireland from Governor-Generalling in New South Wales, a man so given to nocturnal excursions that his official portrait was painted with an open fly, and the newer paint ordered to conceal the white silks below is still visible to even the casual eye.

And then Lord Erskine of Rerrick, who was chased away by the beginnings of the Troubles, a man said by his biographer to have been tortured by his bewilderment of Ireland – not the first, and assuredly not the last to be so.

Finally, Lord Grey of Naunton, who arrived to govern at Hillsborough after governing both British Guiana and the Bahama Islands. I remember him – a jaunty man with a white moustache and a twinkle in his eye, one of the few dashes of style and colour in a country that, during the five years he held office, was collapsing in a miasma of blood and dirt and misery.

The British told Lord Grey to go in 1973. His butler, Albert Harper, who had buttled for all five Excellencies and their ladies, remains puzzled at the way they made him go. They tried, he told me one afternoon as we walked down the endless carpet of the throne room, they tried to make him take the ferry home, and said there was no Queen's Flight for him; they tried to stop a soldier's guard of honour for him; and they made him go in his civilian clothes, without his swan's-feather plumes, or his great sword, or his fine blue uniform.

But in the end Ralph Grey of Naunton left in style. There was a detachment of Scots Guards in the Square; there was a Heron of the Queen's Flight; there was a final salute. But he did go in his black suit, and the final wave, as he stepped from the North of Ireland and into his English plane, was not with a plumed hat, but with a black bowler.

There was a dinner at Hillsborough the night I last saw Albert Harper. The menu read 'Hillsborough Castle' – the name 'Government House' had long since gone. The silver knives were each an exact one inch from the table edge; the freesias were fresh from the garden; the servants were briefed, the fires were lit, the whisky glasses had been polished, the kitchen staff was at the ready.

But it was all a sad pretence. Where the Governor once sat, there was now but a Secretary of State, a mere politician, and usually one of little note, and with little reason to be noted. The footmen had long gone. The portraits of former Governors and Irish Viceroys triggered no memories, no conversations. The great seal of Ulster had been officially defaced with two great scratches of a knife, and the man who sat at this table's middle signed no bills, affixed no sign manual, had no role that was not dictated by a political superior in London.

The argument by which we called Ireland part of the Empire must apply, right or wrong, to the remanent six counties of today. This is, in a way, a colony still. But since Lord Grey waved that bowler hat down from the Heron that June afternoon in 1973, Ulster has just not had, for me, the feel of Empire any more. Nor for Butler Harper. He sat down at the long table, and gazed down over the lawns, to where a policeman stood with a machine-gun crooked under his arm. 'It was grand here in those days, right enough. But now – the Empire, if that is what we were part of, has vanished. Into thin air.'

And he stood up wearily and stretched his back. He opened the great door of Government House, and let me out into the afternoon sun and the fresh shower of rain. And as I walked away I heard him turn the great key in the lock, shutting himself in with a fine Imperial memory, while all outside the Empire had, as he realised, just vanished clear away.

TWELVE

SOME REFLECTIONS AND CONCLUSIONS

And what an Empire it had been! These little sun-bleached bones, scattered around the world in silent memorial to it all, stir some sadness and a lot of pride. It is a Saturday morning in St Helena – I came back for a second visit, early one recent southern autumn – and this could be an England of 6,000 miles away and a hundred years ago.

Before me, through the uneven glass windows of this East India Company mansion, a long garden slopes down towards the sea. There is a border of roses and marigolds; a row of fig trees, cow parsley hedges, a small jungle of banana palms, jacaranda trees and a magnificent magnolia. The sea sparkles in the warm morning, touched by a faint grey haze. There are a score of boats at anchor, including the Royal Mail boat the RMS *St Helena* from Bristol which came in last night, bringing me back to this speck of Imperial memories.

It is very quiet. If I stand still I can just hear the bells of St Paul's Cathedral ringing in muffled celebration: the servant girl says there is a wedding this morning, a friend of her sister's marrying a boy from Sandy Bay. Yes, there is a child already – a 'spare', she calls it, laughing – born a year ago. No one exactly certain who the father was. The girl, whose name is Annie, wants to go to England to be 'in service'; the Government will not allow any girl to leave the island until she is twenty-three, so she has another four years to wait until she sees her first bus, or train, aeroplane, television programme or daily newspaper. Until then she is happy to clear away the Weetabix and Hoover the bedrooms and earn a few pounds to put away in the savings bank. She yearns to know what the outside world is like. She met a girl from Tristan once, who came to St Helena and left in great confusion, unable to cope with the frantic pace of life in Jamestown – she was frightened by what she called the rush hour in the island capital, when perhaps ten cars leave for the hillside, and ten shops all shut at the same hour. 'They tell me that England's pretty busy when compared with us,' observed Annie, gravely. 'I often wonder what happened to little Jessica when she got up to London. I wonder what I will think, too. It's so quiet here – so very peaceful.'

The ship's arrival had, as always, caused great excitement. We carried tourists, wealthy Americans who were passing through to the Cape, and who fell upon the old streets of Jamestown with locust-like zeal. But we carried some Saints, too, and as they stepped from the dinghy through the great swirls of the rollers, there were tears and hugs and hoarse greetings, people who hadn't seen each other for months, even years, in touch and view again.

There was a Saint Helenian soldier, a man who had joined the Royal Engineers twenty-three years before and who had never been home. He had a young wife now, a frightened little girl from Liverpool, who, for days before our arrival, would scan the horizon ahead for the first glimpse of her new home. Her husband had promised to return, and she had agreed to come with him, to give up the rainy streets of Toxteth and the grey waters of the Mersey for a tiny island 700 miles from the nearest land. But on the morning we made our landfall and she had seen the low and ragged outline beneath the clouds, she retreated to the poop deck and silently smoked a cigarette while gazing at our wake, and back towards her old abandoned home. From time to time her husband, his eyes shining with his own excitement, would walk back through the ship to find her. But each time, seeing her staring into the distance, he would back away and leave her, understanding, no doubt, how she must have been feeling. I met him in the street next morning, his hand being pumped by an assortment of grizzled passers-by. His wife had been spirited away within minutes of the boat docking: her new in-laws had taken her home for tea, and by the time he caught up with her 'it was as though she had been living here all of her life'. He knew it would be all right, he said. The Saints 'are an awful nice bunch of people'.

The Empire had, on its better days, been both run by and peopled by 'a nice bunch of people' such as these. These places I had journeyed to and through were, by and large, *good* places – organised kindly, directed along traditional and well-meaning ways, peopled by men and women whose days moved to the comfortable English routines – from Weetabix to Ovaltine, from Sunday communion to the Friday knees-up, from Christmas and Boxing Day to the Queen's birthday and hot cross buns. They took their 'O' levels and their Royal School of Music examinations, listened to the BBC relay broadcasts, sent their telegrams from Cable and Wireless, dispatched their letters by the Royal Mail and learned to call the man in the big house on the hill 'Your Excellency'. They committed few crimes, stirred up little trouble, kept the Queen's peace and collected coloured pictures of Prince Charles and Princess Di. And they were, on a small scale, reflections of the larger, grander Empire – that vast assemblage of nations upon which the sun never set (though the original remark – 'the sun never sets on my dominions' was written in German by Schiller for Phillip II of Spain, and had nothing to do with Britain at all).

And so here I sit, in an East India Company room, looking down across a Royal Naval fortress, at a Victorian harbour and a Regency town. It is easy to slip into a fine Imperial reverie, and remember how we came to possess only morsels like these as the parting gift from our days of world dominion. Consider how once, from Aden to Zanzibar, from the ice-bound rocks of Arctic Canada to the bone-dry ovens of the Kalahari, from groves of Malayan durian trees to the apple orchards of Tasmania, from the 'friable and spongy rocks' of Malta to the granite peaks of Mount Kenya, and, most gloriously of all, from Kashmir to Kannayakumari, northern bastion to southern tip of India, Great Britain was, as the *New York Times* happily conceded on the Diamond Jubilee of Queen Victoria, 'so plainly destined to dominate this planet'. Endless tracts of land, a quarter of the world's peoples, every race and creed, from Ashantis and Assamese, Zeptiahs and Zulus, from Buddhists to Zoroastrians, fell under the seemingly eternal paramountcy of London.

True, some of the possessions were not possessed at all, as such: the self-governing colonies, Newfoundland, Cape Colony, Natal, New Zealand, Canada and the six Australian colonies made their own rules and deferred to London only rarely; India, a splendid law unto herself, above and beyond what she and her servants would have regarded as the undignified rabble of mere colonies; and the protectorates – Somaliland, Nyasaland, the Solomons and that part of Aden between Muscat and Yemen – which were, strictly, foreign countries, whose citizens may have been subject to but not necessarily of the British Crown, and were thus not entitled to the kind of amiable treatment supposedly handed down in the colonies themselves. There were other genera in the Colonial Office menagerie – protected states, trust territories, and a bastard tribe that included such forgotten ends of the earth as Starbuck Island and Vostok Island, and which were lumped together under the heading 'Miscellaneous islands and rocks'.

The Crown colonies, as varied in governmental form as they were in governed peoples, were at the centre of it all. Some had parliaments, some had appointed assemblies, some gave the vote to all, some to a few (to one-eighteenth of the population of Malta, for example), some had no laws at all. Some, gigantic and complicated, had all the trappings of independent states – the Gold Coast enjoyed the attentions of an administration that included a cinema technician, a tug master and a grade one foreman platelayer (in 1950 Mr Blackwood, Mr Stewart and Mr Reynolds, all shipped out from Britain); others had only the rudiments – Tonga, for instance, had just one British Minister (of Finance) and was otherwise run by colonial servants a thousand miles away in Fiji.

This immense and majestic collection of peoples and places was administered by the men of the Colonial Office. They were unhurried folk, bureaucrats of splendid aloofness and determined superiority who were encouraged to pursue any private field of endeavour or research for which they cared, rather as though the office was an out-station of All Souls. One note records that a Mr Darnley of the West Indian Department had a keen interest in whales, and spent much of his time before the fire contemplating, instead of the possibilities of a putsch in Jamaica, the complexities of ambergris and the relative blubber thickness of Fin and Sei.

The clubbability of the place led, perhaps inevitably, to a certain smugness. In 1956 Sir Charles Jeffries, Deputy Under-Secretary for the Colonies (and a contributor to *Punch* and the *Listener*), was content to declare that, 'The Colonial Office will still have immense continuing responsibilities for as long as any planner can usefully look ahead.'

It might have been useful had he looked ahead just ten short years; or he might perhaps have been a little suspicious that he and his colleagues had laboured for so long in temporary quarters of Sanctuary Buildings, Great Smith Street, and that the marvellous structure they had been promised just after the war had taken so long to materialise. That structure was never built; by 1966 the Colonial Office suffered the indignity of merger, subsumed into the Commonwealth Relations Office; a mere six months later, on 7th January 1967, it disappeared altogether. The existence of a Colonial Office meant the perpetuation of the colonial mind in an age that, quite suddenly, had developed a loathing for such things. And, in any case, most British colonies had disappeared: Aden had, and Zanzibar; not one of the protectorates was still protected, nor any trust territory, nor any protected state. India had gone, and Australia, Canada and her dominion colleagues were standing proud and alone. Yes, most of the colonies had gone. Most, but not quite all.

Historians of Empire will still argue over the reasons for Britain's Imperial decline. Was it deliberate, or did it happen by accident? Was the gathering of Empire deliberate, indeed? Did this greatest accretion of power and influence the world has ever known come about as a consequence of a sustained fit of absentmindedness? Theses for Doctorates of Philosophy and Bachelors of Letters – and books, of course – will continue to stutter from the typewriters and the word-processors for years to come. This book will certainly not attempt to answer the question. Before we take our final look at the stranded hulks of the Imperial adventure, though, it might be useful if, briefly, we pass by the way-stations of the great decline, if only because so many of the stations themselves bear a remarkable similarity to the fragments that remain.

Where did it all begin? The loss of the American colonies, of course, brought to an end one phase of the adventure; but the Treaties of Utrecht and of Paris had by then been signed, and the growing dominance of Great Britain within Europe was about to ensure that a new British Empire was about to rise from the wreckage of the old. It was the scuttling of that second Empire that was the long and painful affair which only today seems to be coming to an end.

The Indian Mutiny – or the First War of Indian Independence, as it is known today by every schoolchild from Amritsar to Assam – sent the first whisper of concern around the London clubs. The mutineers had been subdued, naturally, but not at all easily, and that came as a shock. Compared with the succession of easy victories that had secured most Imperial territories, India was proving, as they might have said in the gymkhana clubs over a not-so-chota peg or two, 'deucedly tricky'.

Then there was the Boer War, so hard fought and so hard won, often so humiliating in its losses and eventually so Pyrrhic in its triumph, a massive force of Britain's mighty army ranged against, and often punished by, a ragged mass of distempered Boer farmers. If the mutiny had checked the hubris, the events at Magersfontein and Spion Kop interrupted, then slowed, and finally stopped the progress. Sure, the aggressive temper could still be called up – Younghusband's invasion of Tibet, with its accompanying massacres that were, in truth, rarely committed by British empire-builders, took place in 1903, after the events in South Africa; but then there was the Great War, the Dardanelles and Gallipoli, and it could safely be said the Empire had reached and passed its apogee, and never would be quite the same, nor as powerful, nor its masters as confident again.

The first piece of property that was actually let go – if we forget Heligoland (which Lord Salisbury swapped for Zanzibar) and the Balearic Islands of Minorca and Majorca, which were ceded to Spain under the Treaty of Amiens in 1802 – was a tiny corner of China known as Weihaiwei. It was a port, on the southern side of the Gulf of Po Hai, and had long been regarded as strategically important, as well as having – a rare thing, in China – an extremely pleasant climate. The Chinese were accustomed to having it snatched away from them (the Japanese had occupied it in 1895, and destroyed the Chinese Imperial North Ocean Fleet at anchor, much as they were to do with the Americans in Hawaii – another station that was briefly in British hands – forty-six years later) and when the British demanded it, acquiesced, in 1898. The British wanted the port as a summer station for the Royal Navy China Squadron, and to provide some Imperial balance to the Russian occupation of the port on the northern side of the Gulf. (And the knowledge that the Germans also wanted Weihaiwei provided a final argument for Lord Salisbury to raise the Union Jack there.) The Russian acquisition was called Port Arthur; Britain renamed Weihaiwei Port Edward, and as such it remained for thirty-two pleasant years, most of them under the benign governorship of 'the charming, plump and unctuous' James Stewart Lockhart, who was said to have been a 'scholar-administrator in the Confucian sense'.

But American influence in the world had begun to grow; new arguments were interfering with the geopolitical assumptions that had emanated from Downing Street during the heyday of Empire; and when, at a conference in Washington in 1921 it was suggested that Britain might give up Port Edward, voluntarily, and leave China to run her own port at her own whim and leisure, Britain's Ministers agreed. Not without a grumble – Winston Churchill made a forceful argument that to abandon Weihaiwei would mean a massive loss of prestige for Britain in the Far East, and newspapers in London complained that the Government was knuckling in to pressure from an upstart rival to world dominion. But the nerve had gone, the purpose had faltered, the need for territory seemed to be on the wane. Britain gave up Port Edward, the famous sanatorium where unnumbered matelots had recovered from malaria and gazed out at the sea and the mountains of Shantung was handed over to the Chinese Navy, and the fleet sailed away, for ever. (Eight years after the British left the Japanese moved in again, and the place did not become properly Chinese until 1945. Since then it has been one of the very few Chinese cities where the population has actually fallen: Port Edward had 100,000 inhabitants, today there are only a tenth as many.)

The 'rendition', as Balfour called it, of Port Edward, may have been the first deliberate act in the rundown of the Empire; the fall of Singapore, that most terrible of wartime blows, showed beyond all doubt that Britain had lost both the Imperial touch and, more important, the Imperial ability. By 1942 – the date of the surrender, February 15th, was noted by some latter-day Imperialists as being particularly inauspicious: on the same day twenty-nine years later the Kingdom's shillings and pence gave way to the beastliness of the decimal currency – Britain was militarily incapable of keeping her Empire going. Singapore's fall was the beginning of the end.

It had been the axis of the eastern possessions. India, Australia, Borneo, Burma – all the colonial governments and governors had rested their confidence in the knowledge that the fleet was ready, that *Illustrious*, or *Revenge*, or *Indomitable* would sail at a moment's notice from a dockside only a few days' steaming away from whatever problem had arisen. Sixty million pounds had been spent after the Great War to turn Singapore into the Portsmouth of the East – the colonies to derive most security from its presence, the Malay States, the Straits Settlements and Hong Kong, all contributed towards the cost of pouring concrete and bending iron into the greasy swamp at the eastern end of the great peninsula.

But only two battleships ever stayed in the dockyard, and then for a week before sailing off. The fortress had guns with which to defend itself – but they were firmly bedded in concrete, faced the southern sea, and could not be turned around. So when the Japanese forces entered Thailand, and then overran Malaya, and found the colonial citadel without its Navy and without any effective firepower pointing towards them, they pushed on to victory without a second thought.

The colony's rulers still could not imagine that the Japanese would succeed; when a worried Churchill cabled that, 'The City of Singapore must be converted into a citadel and defended to the death', the Governor, Sir Shenton Thomas, laconically remarked that he trusted the British Army 'would see the little men off'. They couldn't, and they didn't. The Imperial Japanese met the Imperial British across the Johore Strait on 8th February; one week later General Percival sued for peace, and the surrender was signed in the old Ford motor car factory out on the Johore road. Singapore was renamed Syonan, and all the rubber and tin went off to Tokyo.

Never again would the Asians – from the Punjabis to the Cantonese – have full and complete faith in the word, the might or the ability of the British. The mirror cracked, the glass dimmed and the muscle became flaccid; no matter that the war was later won; no matter that Singapore came back into the royal fold in 1945 (after the period when it was officially recorded as being 'temporarily in hostile Japanese occupation'); no matter that the gin slings were slung at the Raffles Hotel and returned nabobs strutted and swaggered just as they had before and just as Sir Stamford would have wished – that February day was the moment when the Imperial will was challenged, and was found wanting.

Eight months later, and the British Government was to be found officially toying with the idea of running down the Empire. The Atlantic Charter, issued in 1941, had talked of 'the rights of all people to choose the form of government under which they live' – but when an apoplectic Governor of Burma wired to know if that meant that the Burmese were going to have such a right, he was told that no, of course the Charter did not apply to peoples under the benevolent charge of the British, but to hapless indigents like the Abyssinians who had been jackbooted into submission by less civilised powers, in this case, the Wop. No, no worries, old man – The Atlantic Charter not to be interpreted as end of Empire or any such damn fool idea.

But the next winter, after Singapore had fallen and India looked even more restless than usual and the Burmese Government was itself in exile (up in Simla – very cold in winter, the

Burmese aides complained), a new kind of policy began to be conceived. And these words were at its nub:

'It is therefore the duty of "Parent" or "Trustee States" to guide and develop the social, economic and political institutions of the Colonial peoples until they are able without danger to themselves and others to discharge the responsibilities of Government.'

And how they agonised over it! Mr Attlee and Mr Eden, Lord Halifax and Viscount Cranborne and Lord Stanley argued and dithered, sent copies to the nervous dominions, decided to act out the policy of the entire Declaration (which was a great deal longer), then decided not to, then decided to abandon the whole document and make it secret and pretend it had never happened. But it had: planted in the minds of two men who were later to become Prime Minister, and two others who were to have a long and continuing influence on British foreign and colonial policy, were the seeds of a new scheme of things: after the war India was going to be handed over to the Indians, and then, in an unending cascade, all those other dominions and protectorates and trustee states and protected states and mandated territories and Crown colonies were going to be helped, slowly and surely, to stand on their own two feet, with England looking on, less a weary Titan, more a proud parent.

But the war, and its ultimate result, briefly clouded this new appearance of policy. In victory, Britain seemed to regain her Imperial energies. She had doughtily recaptured all the lost particles of Empire – the West Kents fighting hand-to-hand with the Japanese on the tennis court at Kohima, to win back Burma, and no less a grandee of Empire than King George's cousin, Lord Louis Mountbatten, accepting the enemy surrender at Singapore. And the British sphere of influence in Europe and North Africa – particularly on the littoral of what was now truly, it seemed, the British lake of the Mediterranean – had actually increased, tremendously. But it was all an illusion: almost as swiftly as the dreariness of post-war Britain became apparent to her subjects – the rationing, the bitter weather, the bombed buildings, the shoddiness and weariness of it all – so, to the world, did her new and diminished role. She was on the second tier of a new grand alliance of nations that were richer, more powerful, more expansive and more confident than herself; and, fatally for the Empire, she had no stomach for foreign possession, no enthusiasm for hanging on to much more than the mere trappings by which her glories had been proclaimed, only three decades before, to a humble and obedient world.

If India went, the axioms had it, the end was inevitable. Curzon had foretold of that: 'If we lose it, we shall step straight away to a third-rate power . . . your ports and your coaling stations, your fortresses and your dockyards, your Crown colonies and your protectorates will go too. For either they will be unnecessary, or the tollgates and barbicans of an Empire that has vanished.' But India did go, swiftly and explosively, divided and perhaps cruelly misdirected by those Britons who were determined to get away. And once India had gone, and King George stopped signing his letters with the letter 'I' to denote him as Imperator, and once the Union flag that had flown night and day over the Lucknow Residency had been returned to Windsor Castle, so, gradually, and with some pain and not a little sadness, the remaining shards of Empire fell away – they were, it was felt, too costly, too inconvenient, too restive and anyway, in many cases ready (if not always quite able) to stand alone.

Burma and Ceylon were the first to peel away, and then, with consequences still so unhappily evident today, the mandated territory of Palestine. Newfoundland, Britain's oldest colony (Sir Humphrey Gilbert had taken possession of it in 1583), a place of codfish and pinewoods and where they used dogs for pulling carts, had gone bankrupt before the war; once the fight was over the Bank of England had a look at the Newfies' account book, pronounced all now well and – such was the fading Imperial spirit – organised a referendum so the loggers and the fishermen could decide what to do next. The first time round half opted to stay colonials, to considerable irritation and embarrassment; they had a second go, and voted to confederate with Canada, and nestle up alongside Nova Scotia, New Brunswick and Prince Edward Island. By January 1949 Newfoundland was out; one more colony down, seventy-odd to go.

There was a last rush of blood to the head in 1953; wet and miserable though that June day dawned, the coronation of Queen Elizabeth (the first monarch in nearly a hundred years not to be described as 'Imp.Ind.', but instead merely as 'of the United Kingdom of Great Britain and Northern Ireland and of her other Realms and Territories Queen, Head of the Commonwealth, Defender of the Faith') provided an opportunity for the final grand march-past of Empire. Suitably *The Times* announced a final Imperial triumph: Mount Everest had been climbed by a British party (though it was a New Zealander and a Nepali who actually made it to the top); the massed bands and regiments that thumped and clattered through the rain marched with even a little more spring and verve as a result.

There, behind Lieutenant-Colonel G. N. Ross of the Gordon Highlanders ('attached Royal West African Frontier Force'), were the massed thousands of the colonial contingents – armed police detachments from North Borneo and Trinidad, Air Force detachments from the Aden Protectorate Levies; the Barbados Regiment, the Leeward Islands Defence Force, the Kings Own Malta Regiment, the Malaya Federation Armoured Car Squadron, the Fiji Military Forces, the Somaliland Scouts, 154 HAA Battery, East Africa, the Northern Rhodesia Regiment and a dozen more besides. And there were the colonial rulers – the Sultan of Zanzibar sharing a carriage with the Sultan of Perak, the Sultan of Kelantan with the beaming and drenched (for she declined to carry an umbrella) Queen of Tonga. The entire procession, miles long and impeccably drilled, from Colonel Burrows, OBE, TD, of the War Office Staff who led, to the final man of the Fourth Division, the Sovereign's Escort, who brought up the rear, was a last celebration of Empire – a muted and diminished version of the great jubilee of Queen Victoria, on a warmer and sunnier June morning fifty-six years before.

One by one the colonies departed. Comets and VC–10s and destroyers and frigates brought ever more junior members of the royal family to the rituals of Independence – the lowering of the Union flag, the lament of a piper or the solitary bugle call, the celebration ball and the hopeful speeches, the luncheon at the Government House and the unnoticed departure for London on the morning after. Usually the pomp was perfect, sometimes not – at the Bahamas ceremonies an awning fell on poor Prince Charles's head, and the frigate dispatched to help St Lucia on her road to freedom collided with the mole, and all the sailors standing at attention along its decks fell over in a grand confusion.

But via evenings of grand ceremony or amusing bathos, and in the wake of ugly fighting or quiet agreement over lunch at Lancaster House, they went. The Sudan and the Gold Coast, Malaya and Somaliland, Nigeria and Sierra Leone, Tanganyika and Western Samoa, Uganda and North Borneo, Malta, Basutoland, Aden Colony, Mauritius and Swaziland, Grenada, the Gilberts, the Ellices, St Kitts, St Vincent, Antigua, British Guiana, British Honduras – even the Condominium of the New Hebrides which was jointly run by the British and the French and was so consequently ungovernable that, it was joked, cars would drive on the right on Mondays and on the left on Tuesdays. By the 1980s, when television viewers in England had seen what they assumed had been the last of the flag-lowering and heard the last echoing of the bugles, once Churchill was buried and Suez was relegated to history and no longer embarrassed anyone – by that time the colonial Empire was, it was safely imagined, dead, buried and if not forgotten at least consigned to the past and no longer wished for, if little regretted either. All was gone.

But stay! In truth it was not quite gone. Almost, but not quite. A few colonies did remain, unwilling to let go, or unable to stand alone. A few governors still were appointed each year or so, a few geese still had to be plucked to provide plumes for a few Imperial helmets, a few grand houses still had to be maintained and lawns mowed and servants paid to keep a relic Imperial enginework chugging along. And in the Foreign and Commonwealth Office in London, up a stairway so long and twisting, so dark and unmemorable that newcomers would take a week or so to learn just where they worked and all other workers in more glamorous departments professed ignorance of its whereabouts, even its existence – up in the eaves and among the gurgling radiators and the dusty collections of the registry and the accountants, was an office that ran it all.

I tried to get there once to see the place from where the Empire was directed. But the Foreign Office is a place without a soul these days, no longer peopled by the clever and the romantic; and I had a dry note from a head of department saying that no, a visit would not be possible, but that perhaps a few questions, if suitably and solemnly written, might be answered in due course. There seemed no point in an arid correspondence, so I gave up this small aspect of the quest – far easier to fly to Cockburn Town, or to sail to Edinburgh-of-the-Seven-Seas than to inspect the heart of Imperial power in London!

In a sense, though, it was a pity. The very reason for my journeying, after all, had been to make a last inspection of the Empire's remains, to try to see how we were managing these final responsibilities of ours. It might have been instructive to talk to the civil servants whose parishes were the faraway outposts I had seen. I would have liked to ask the lady on the St Helena desk why she took a full month to answer a simple query from the Castle, or to ask the gentleman whose allotted tasks included the daily management of Pitcairn Island just why it was that Mrs Christian's queries from Adamstown had to proceed across the sea by morse code, and that supplies for the colony were sent by courtesy of a market gardener in south London, who listened out for the plaintive cries from the island on his ham radio set.

I wanted to ask, I think, why it was we seemed to have given up on our last few charges – why, simply because they were so few, so far between, so unpeopled and so wanting in importance, they were of less intrinsic interest than when there had been many, and the Empire had been grand, and full of moment. The ethos of Empire had never been – or never during its accretion, anyway – an ethos that had much to do with global dominion, or the fierce assertion of naked power. We had power, of course, and once possessed power is a difficult thing to relinquish. But our success in making an Empire, in running it, in handing back and in winning the respect and, yes, the love even of those whom we had ruled – our success in all this grand endeavour came in no small part because we *cared*. We felt we had a mission, a divine right. We attended to the details of the thing. We managed the Empire with men and women of compassion and skill, energy and intellect, and something of a romantic dream about them. Whether they directed, from the Office, or whether they ruled, as members of the Service, the colonial mandarins seemed to be a breed who *cared*. They had no need to do so, these District Commissioners and these Colonial Secretaries and these Governors and Commanders-in-Chief. But they seemed by and large to have done – ambitions and territorial jealousies seemed to run second to fascinations and enthusiasms, as though the colonial officers were pursuing their private and amateur interests, and had come out here, or gone over there, in pursuit of obsessions and hobbies, rather than aggrandisement or Machiavellian intent.

I have beside me, on this fine old East India Company desk, a copy of *The Colonial Office List* for 1950. The Empire was just then beginning to wane; the thick pink book was a little less thick than the year before, and the editorials and the essays showed signs – easier to read now, in retrospect, than at the time – that the purpose was indeed faltering, that the steel was showing its fatigue. But there are, at the back of the book, 200 pages that display the human reason for the Empire having been, on so many levels, a force for general good. The pages contain the complete lists of all those men and women in the Colonial Service – all those currently stationed overseas, involved in the daily devotionals of Empire. I take a page at random, and the full complexity of the thing becomes immediately apparent:

William Henry DeLisle, organiser of the anti anthrax campaign on the island of Nevis; Cicely Denly, hospital matron, Mauritius; Arthur Dennier, engineer on the Ugandan telephone service; Thomas Dennison, district magistrate, Kenya; John Denny, superintendent of Police in Singapore; Ronald Derrick, author of *The History of Fiji, The Geography of Fiji, The Fiji Islands*; Lawrence Des Iles, Chief Inspector for Poor Relief, Trinidad; Frederick Deighton, OBE, mycologist, Saint Lucia; Frank Dixey, author of *A Practical Handbook of Water Supply*, now with the Geological Survey of Nigeria; Henry

Dobbs, Assistant Secretary to the Western Pacific High Commission and author of *Some Difficulties in Dirac's Representation Theory*.

They were, in truth, a remarkable body of men and women – Haileybury and Harrow schooled them, Balliol and Caius polished them, the finer ethos of Imperialism motivated them. A disproportionately large number of them came from the manse and the cathedral close – of 200 governors who served during the first sixty years of this century, thirty-five were the sons of clergymen: men of intellect and good sense, Church of England and high traditions, Barsetshire principles sent out to minister to the brown and yellow in the world outside.

Some are still in the traces. The sixteen last relic islands attract the final survivors of the Colonial Service, and they shuttle slowly around the globe, a treasurer here, a secretary there, and finally governor, or administrator, or commissioner at last. They all know each other – Dick Baker in St Helena sends his Christmas card to David Dale in Montserrat, Rex Hunt in Port Stanley writes the occasional letter to Eddie Brooks in the Turks and Caicos Islands; the Tristan Administrator takes up a new job in Hong Kong, the Treasurer in Jamestown takes a ship for Gibraltar and a post at the Convent, and nurtures the fond hope that he'll be made Governor in Anguilla before the place goes independent.

It would be pleasant to suppose that old colonial hands are still around to manage old colonies. Unhappily, though, there are now more surviving responsibilities than there are old hands to be responsible for them. The *corps d'élite* is winnowed to a very few, all about to retire from the service for all time; the surviving islands are having to be governed, run and – more unfortunately – directed from London – by the lesser men and women in a diplomatic service that has no time for and no interest in what Empire stood for, or what it stands for now. A colony may be lucky – it may still win the attentions of men who feel affection for the idea and the ideal; more usually these days it is unlucky, and its affairs are directed and its people ruled by civil servants who are either young, ambitious, and on their way to better and more exciting things, or by the old, the unsuitable, the drunk and the incompetent who are not able or willing to play in the greater games of major league diplomacy.

A fellow works in some minor capacity in our Embassy, in some remote country, pushing paper in disconsolate fashion, upsetting no one, inspiring even fewer. His fifty-fifth birthday comes up, and the Personnel Department in London decides he must be given his head-of-mission job before he leaves the service. He can't go to Khartoum – too tricky, too potentially important; he can't go to Lima, or Ulan Bator, or even to Fernando Po. But how about, let's see – Ascension Island, or the British Virgins? No trouble there – parish pump stuff, really, a few cocktail parties in the evening sun. Very pleasant. Fellow ought to be rather glad.

And so off goes the Third Secretary (Commercial) to take up the post of Colonial Administrator; he lives in his lovely old bungalow up in the hills, drives his Ford with the Union flag flying from the bonnet, he invites the island grandees to drinks and 'At homes' and – if the entertainment allowance provides – to dinners as well – and keeps his territory out of the public eye for the three years of his posting, and then he leaves. If he ever realised that his job was unimportant, the pleasantness of its routines softened the realisation; he could have made something of it – could have nagged and irritated and cajoled and tried to leave the island in better shape than when he found it. But as like as not he wouldn't have bothered: too much trouble, London didn't care for the place, and so, keen for an easy last few years in Diplomatic life, why should he care either?

And in that lies the problem. The islands that remain are not, by and large, places for which London has any time to spare. No one – either those who labour in the bureaucratic labyrinths in Whitehall or, more sad to say, those who find themselves in the Government Houses and colonial bungalows out in the far-flung fragments – has time, or energy, or the inclination to spare to deal with problems that, when set beside the graver matters of the world, must appear so monumentally insignificant. The matter of where to place the petrol storage tanks in St Helena or how to find a ship to take toilet rolls to Pitcairn or

what to do when there is a massive rainstorm over Ascension
that washes out the road to Two Boats village – all these are,
quite reasonably, of almost no significance at all.

But an ailment untreated has a habit of becoming an affliction
untreatable. To ignore the needs – small, insignificant needs
maybe, but needs nonetheless – of our remote dominions is to
court disaster. The Falkland Islands proved that to all the world
– for though there can be no argument that the events of April
1982 sprang as a direct consequence of Argentina's invasion of
the islands, it was Britain's inability and unwillingness to deal
with a nagging colonial problem that led to the frustration that
prompted Argentina to make her foolish and fatal move. I hold
no brief for the Argentine Government in this matter; nor is this
account concerned with the merits of the various claims to those
windy islands – that 'bunch of rocks down there' as President
Reagan liked to call them. But some aspects of the early chapters
of the tale are incontrovertible: Argentina had a passion to win
the islands back for her own; the British refused to countenance
the claim, kept Argentina talking about the claim – and sundry
other less momentous matters, too – for nearly two decades,
coquettishly hinting at a willingness to discuss the claim, but
never doing so. Signals were sent out suggesting that a deal
might be possible – the Royal Naval vessel that guarded the
islands was to be withdrawn, private exasperation was
expressed about the islanders' intransigence, diplomats talked
of the need to consolidate the long-standing friendship between
the two great sovereign states on either side of the Atlantic.
And yet the years went by, and precisely nothing of any substance happened. The problem was not considered a great
one; the men and women who were deployed to manage it,
to contain it, were not of sufficient calibre or commitment
to realise its potential, nor to devise a means of reaching a
solution.

And so a small problem became a large tragedy. Thirteen
hundred men died, hundreds more were maimed, thousands of
millions of pounds were expended in an unnecessary war over
a piece of territory whose only function was as a symbol of
power and strength, and had no intrinsic use at all. 'Like two

bald men fighting over a comb,' Jorge Luis Borges remarked sardonically when it was all over. 'When will our country realise,' said Robin Renwick, the then Counsellor at our Embassy in Washington, 'that we have a duty to solve our old Imperial problems before tackling those in which we have no direct role? There are more problems than the Falklands out there – and yet we see ourselves as primarily concerned with mediating between Moscow and Washington, or dealing with the Lebanese situation. More attention to the problems that beset us directly might head off such things as the Falklands war.'

In almost every territory I visited there was some stark indication that the mother-country had neither the time nor the energy to waste on correcting an irritation, righting a wrong, recognising an ominous trend, bowing to a subtle need. The Cayman Islands, for instance, was gaining a fearful reputation as a place for 'laundering' money from highly questionable sources – did the country that gave us the Bank of England and the highest standards of fiscal propriety care if one of her distant Caribbean colonies became a loose cannon on the decks of the world money markets? It did not – it neither cared, nor cared to interfere. The Turks and Caicos Islands now have a reputation as one of the region's major centres for drug smuggling – the Chief Minister no less was arrested by the American narcotics authorities a few days after I took tea with him – and yet Britain, a country of supposedly Himalayan moral standards, does no more than emit a benign harrumph! and lets the islands go on their sorry way. In Bermuda there is anxiety as more and more American – and, specifically, American military – influence is brought to bear, and secret plans are announced to station American nuclear weapons on the island in the event of an emergency. The Bermudian people grumble, and make their anxiety known to London – and London does nothing to alleviate their anger or to calm their fears.

We ignore the St Helenians – though we grudgingly pour money into the island economy, priding ourselves on our largesse, while failing to understand that by maintaining the island solely by public handouts we condemn the islanders, who deserve better, to a life stripped of self-respect. We ignore the

Pitcairn Islanders, and they drift away on each passing cargo boat, until by the end of the century there are expected to be no Pitcairners left at all, and the colony will, as the Foreign Office would anyway prefer, fade from existence altogether. And we deal – or rather we dealt – with horrifying callousness with the people of the Indian Ocean, when we evicted them from their homes, transported them to a foreign country against their will, and lied and evaded our responsibilities for years before a writer discovered the scandal, and told it to the world. Of all the events of post-Imperial British history, those of the late 1960s that occurred in the archipelago we customarily call Diego Garcia remain the most shabby and the most mean. No excuses can be made, by politicians of any persuasion: Diego Garcia is a monstrous blot on British honour, and shames us all, for ever.

To illustrate the evident lack of caring, or prescience, or sympathetic understanding that too often seems to characterise Britain's dealings with her final Imperial fragments, consider those few hundred square miles at the northern end of the Leeward Island chain – square miles in which four foreign powers still maintain dependent territories.

There is the island of Ste Martin – Dutch run in the south, under the Netherland Antillean name of Sint Maarten, French run in the north; there are the United States Virgin Islands; and there are the British Virgin Islands. From Washington, Paris, the Hague and from London, four foreign nations try to direct the affairs of the descendants of their former slaves, and with varying degrees of success.

Ste Martin is an overseas department of the French Republic: she is administered by a prefect, she sends deputies to the National Assembly. The laws of France are the laws of Ste Martin. A *citoyen* of Ste Martin is a citizen of France, able to come and go as he pleases, providing, of course, he can afford the fare. But Air France flights between Paris and the Caribbean departments are well subsidised, and holidays are cheap.

Sint Maarten enjoys much the same privileges as does its neighbour. The laws of Holland apply; the Netherlands Antilles are represented at the Hague; citizenship is mutually exchangeable, regardless of the colour or the background of the particular Dutchman involved.

The United States Virgin Islands are run by a locally elected assembly, with a governor who is elected by the islanders themselves. The territory sends a representative to Congress, though he has no vote. Citizens of the US Virgins are citizens of the USA, and all American federal laws apply in the islands. To all practical intents and purposes, the Virgin Islands are another American state.

But the British Virgin Islands, once a small department of the great colony of the Leeward Islands, seem isolated by more than geography from its mother-country. True, there is a functioning democracy there, and the island runs itself efficiently enough, and without trouble. The Governor – always white, since he is the representative of the Crown – is appointed by London, with no reference made to the islanders' wishes. There is no Virgin Islands representation in London, save for one small lobbying organisation that carries out public relations and trade relations on behalf of a number of small West Indian states.

The laws of England apply on the Virgin Islands – but not all of them. Capital punishment is still in use, and there is a law permitting public flogging (it is administered by the Chief of Police, usually to youthful miscreants).

Citizens of the Virgin Islands do not enjoy full citizenship of the United Kingdom – they are entitled to some of the consular protection of the Crown, but they may not settle in Britain, and are treated by the immigration authorities with as much, or as little consideration as if they were Iranians, Venezuelans, or citizens of Turkey.

This, above all, seems the greatest insult. There are five and a quarter million people in all the Empire that remains – five million of them in Hong Kong. They have been, and in the main still are, fiercely loyal to England and all for which she stands. They have fought and in many cases have been wounded or have died for her. They fly the Union flag, they worship at the Church of England, they believe themselves immensely fortunate when, on Christmas Day each year, they hear Her Majesty address them all from Buckingham Palace and remind them they are citizens of that splendidly worthy agglomeration of peoples once, or still, ruled by Britain, the Commonwealth. But let them try to come to London to find work, or fly to Manchester to spend time with their relations, or take a holiday in Scotland. Then all the loyalty and the feeling of privilege and good fortune counts for nothing. The law – the British Nationality Act – marks them out as suspect visitors; for the inspectors know full well that the only reason a Montserratian or a Pitcairner or an Anguillian comes to Britain is to settle, and thus become a charge upon the parish; and so the inspector harasses and interrogates and demands this and that, certificates and bank statements and return tickets and marriage licences, far more evidence of some legal reason for the visit than would be asked, one suspects, of an American or a man from Dresden or Valparaiso.

The law applies to all colonial citizens, apart from those in two colonies – Gibraltar and the Falkland Islands. Parliament, which wrote the laws, specifically excluded both groups – 25,000 people, all told – and permitted them full right of access to Britain as and when they might want. No logical reason was ever given – indeed, the Falkland Islanders were only given the status after their war – but the inference is obvious. They were given free access because they were white; every other colonial citizen is coloured either black or brown, or yellow.

The stated reason for the Act's introduction was to prevent the possible tidal wave of five million Hong Kong Chinese into Britain once the agreement with China is finally implemented in 1997. The implied secondary reason is to ease the immigration burden posed by tens of thousands of other non-white colonials who might think of arriving in a country already displaying the effects of widespread immigration from the Indies, East and West, in the post-war years. And yet, ironically, it seems very much as though few would-be immigrants actually want to come to Britain to take up their prize. Few Gibraltarians have come, and even fewer from the Falklands. And surveys claim to show that even the St Helenians – most loyal and devoted of all – would come with great reluctance. Of the 6,000 islanders, perhaps 800 would come if the law were changed tomorrow.

But the principle seems an insulting and unkind device, whatever its actual practical results might or might not be. It seems a modest and appropriate reward to all those remaining citizens of Empire, that should they feel they want to come home, they should be permitted so to do. It is the feeling of rejection that is so hurtful to them – and it is a feeling that could be reversed with a change in the law that would have almost no effect, no detrimental effect, at least, upon the welfare of the Britons themselves. The Foreign Office says it will not change the law: Anguillians and Pitcairners and the people of Grand Turk remain foreigners, aliens, for the time being. Only when Hong Kong is safely back in Chinese hands will any minister look at the law again – and it is doubted in Whitehall that it will, in fact, ever be changed. The few thousand remaining colonials are condemned to live for ever denied the small honour of being full citizens of the country that took so much from, and made such use of, the colonies from which they come.

This law aside, there have been some few successes. The Hong Kong agreement was a piece of skilful diplomacy; there seems likely to be some amicable arrangements between Britain and Spain over the future of Gibraltar. For one thing the gates are now open. And it can fairly be said, in the particular case of St Helena, that since 1984, when the Overseas Development Administration took over the day-to-day running of their colony from the Foreign Office, island morale has perked up, there is more optimism than before. Some cynics might suggest this is because ODA is a money-spending arm of the British Government, while the Foreign Office is not; others might suggest that the calibre of people working within the ODA is more suited to the particular needs of small and helpless states, and that there is no attempt by the mandarins at ODA to do more than assist in development – which is all that most colonies want – and no attempt to formulate policy of which, it must be said, there is none currently that relates to the colonies.

But generally, I must conclude that the state of the Empire – that state I thought I might try to divine when first I planned the journeys – is less than ideal. How is the Empire? Were the King to ask, one might fairly reply: 'Lamentable, Your Majesty,' and be fairly right. There are exceptions – Hong Kong is one, the Falklands another, Tristan da Cunha, for very peculiar reasons, a third. In the main, though, the tail-end of Empire is an unhappy collection of peoples and places, wanting in imagination, in policy, in a future, in money, in sympathetic administration or talented leaders. Some islands may seek, and win, their independence; others, I fear, will become relentlessly poorer and more morose, trapped by their history, condemned to an eternity of begrudged expenditure, parsimonious direction, second-rate thought and government, to listlessness and ill-fortune. For those, the former glories of that grand assemblage of the British Empire must have a bitter aftertaste today, must trigger the sardonic laugh in the bar, a smirk, and some grim remark about the England of far away and long ago.

There is, I feel, one way out. The idea is not new, and others – notably the French – have tried it with some degree of success.

All the colonies that wish to remain linked to and ruled by the British Crown should continue to be so, as full and integral parts of the United Kingdom, or associated with it in some intimate and constitutionally attractive way. The six West Indian colonies, for example – Bermuda, Anguilla, Montserrat, the Turks and Caicos Islands, the Caymans and the Virgins – could be made into the External British County of the West Atlantic, with their own Member of Parliament (who could sit in the Lords if needs be). The new 'constituency' would have a population of some 45,000 people – about the right size for representation at Westminster. The same arrangement could be made for the South Atlantic possessions of Ascension, St Helena, Tristan, the Falklands, the Falklands Dependencies and the British Antarctic. The population would be considerably lower – no more than nine thousand; but the six territories are of a kind, their needs and peoples more similar than separate. (I have long found it odd, for instance, that the BBC has for many years broadcast a regular brief weekend programme to the people of the Falklands – 1,800 of them – but has never thought it worthwhile to broadcast to its equally loyal colleagues in St Helena and Tristan, where there are nearly four times as many British subjects. 'Calling the South Atlantic' might be a programme well worth considering – the 'Saints', certainly, would feel a little less neglected by London were they to hear direct from Bush House every week or so, in the way the Falklanders do now.)

Gibraltar could quite easily be made an External County of the Kingdom, having the population, the proximity and the desire. As for the remainder – sadly it has to be admitted that Pitcairn is too small, British Indian Ocean Territory has no resident population, and Hong Kong is leaving for fresh pastures shortly before the end of the century. For the two first of these, perhaps some Protectorate status – and would it really harm the interests of the British people if all forty-four members of Pitcairn were offered free and permanent access to the United Kingdom, if such they wanted? I rather think not.

Once thus assimilated into the mainland system, the people of the External Counties would be at one with the people of home – the same laws, the same taxes, the same grants, the same rights of access to each other's territories. A man from Plymouth in Montserrat would enjoy precisely the same rights and freedoms as the man from Plymouth in Devon. A child in Edinburgh-of-the-Seven-Seas would have the same future as the child from Edinburgh on the Forth. And the Common Market could take upon itself the burden of financing some of the less well developed parts of the newly expanded but now truly United Kingdom – a grant for an emergency air strip on St Helena, technical help for the new hospital in Road Town, or a broadcasting station on Anguilla. The arrangement would be tidy, it would be kind, and it would recognise the debt an Imperial power owes to those of its Empire who are, for whatever reason, unable to stand upon their own feet and march into the world alone. For those who want us to stand by, we should do so with enthusiasm, with efficiency and with grace: such a scheme as the French – and, to a lesser extent the Americans – have found ideal might well work for ourselves. I fervently hope some minister, some day, might champion the cause, rather than leave the old Empire to fade and decay in a way unworthy of our greater traditions.

Since I began these final pages I have left the fine old East India Company desk, and the colony of St Helena, too. I am in a cabin down by the waterline of the little cargo ship that brought me here. I have said my farewells to the island that, of all in the remaining Empire, I feel I have come to know most intimately, the one for which I feel most sympathy, the one I suppose I would say I like above all others.

It is a bright autumn morning, a few minutes before noon. Out at sea there are white horses racing across the wave tops, and in the anchorage a dozen yachts are rolling gaily in the swell. On board our ship there is a silence, pregnant with anticipation.

At noon a bell is struck at the forepeak, and the rumble of the engines shakes the entire vessel. White foam races from the stern, and as the anchors are winched from the seabed, so the ship begins to move forward and into a tight turn to port, out of the anchorage and into open water. The loudspeakers begin to blare their traditionally Imperial farewells: 'Anchors Aweigh', 'Hearts of Oak', 'A Life on the Ocean Wave' and, last of all, 'Rule Britannia'. Down here the Empire is still alive and well, the memory is the reality, and glorious history is the stuff of the present.

The ship's siren sounds – three immensely loud blasts which boom and reverberate around the cliffsides. Some of the nearer yachts begin to bounce and rear in our wash. We are turned now, on a heading away from the island, and the engines growl up to their cruising speed. The cliffs move away. The church tower slips behind the jacaranda trees. The great ladder moves out of sight. The Union flags at the summit of Ladder Hill and down beside the Governor's Castle stream in the trade winds.

The ship begins to roll in the ocean swell, and then to heave as she comes out of the island's lee and the winds begin to make their own impression on her superstructure. We have the Governor aboard, and his personal standard flies from the stern mast, cracking in the wind. People are waving. A few are in tears. It will be a long time before the next boat to St Helena, and some in the crowds will not see their friends and children and loved ones for many months, or years, or perhaps ever again. Such is the isolation of this most perfectly preserved Imperial relic.

But soon the watchers turn away. There is no point in prolonging the sadness. The ship is moving fast now, and nothing can stop it. The island is fading into the clouds on the far horizon, her cliffs becoming a little hazy as they plunge into the limitless sea. Soon the island vanishes, to be replaced by a patch of settled grey cloud, and even that fades before long, and the horizon becomes an unbroken line of steel. Before another hour has gone it becomes simple to muse that if there ever were an outpost of the Empire back there, or anywhere, it lingers on only in the memory, and on the maps that no one these days seems to have time to read.

ACKNOWLEDGMENTS

'Not another tropical island!' they would groan at the *Sunday Times*, each time I returned, tanned and fit, from one more expedition to an outpost of Empire. In vain would I protest that on this occasion I had been to somewhere cold and windy or on that had suffered from terrible seasickness. To them all – the *Sunday Times* editor, Andrew Neil, the foreign editor, Stephen Milligan, his deputy, Cal McCrystal and to Peter Jackson, the editor of the *Sunday Times Magazine* – I must have seemed to have been on a perpetual holiday, endlessly away from base, writing far less than is customary for a *Sunday Times* correspondent. I gladly take this opportunity to give them my thanks for their tolerance, forbearance and suppression of envy during my absences and on my returns. And for letting me hang on to my job, through it all.

Out there, the following were among many who gave their help and advice, and in many cases hospitality, for which I am most grateful. In Bermuda, Lord Dunrossil, Sir Edwin Leather, Helen Rowe, Jack Arnell, Gillian and Dai Lewis; in Anguilla, Alastair Baillie, Alan Hoole, Ronald Webster; in the British Virgin Islands, David and Margaret Barwick, Arden Shaw, Jefferson and Jinx Morgan; in Montserrat, Elizabeth McEwan, John Cashin, Reginald Lucie-Smith; in the Cayman Islands, Peter Lloyd, the Tradewinds calypso group; in the Turks and Caicos Islands, Christopher Turner, Edward Brooks, Norman Saunders; on Ascension Island, Ian Thow, Steven Devitt; on St Helena, the Hon. John Massingham, the Hon. Dick Baker, Philip Dale, Ethel Yon, Maureen Jonas, Richard Saltwell, Frederick Ward, Clive Warren; on Tristan da Cunha, Roger Perry, Richard and Margaret Grundy; en route to and in British Indian Ocean

Territory, the crew of the tugboat *Robert W.*, the staff of Cable
and Wireless on Male and Diego Garcia, John Beasant, John
Topp; in Hong Kong, David Akers-Jones, Clare Hollingworth,
Cecilia Wong, Donald Wise, Teresa Ma; in the Falkland Islands,
Sir Rex Hunt, Patrick Watts, Graham Bound, Les Halliday; in
Gibraltar, Admiral Sir David Williams.

In addition I am grateful to Andrew Bell and Simon Sugrue of
Curnow Shipping Ltd., for their help in arranging voyages to the
South Atlantic, and to Captain Bob Wyatt and Chief Officer
David Roberts for taking me there. The Foreign and Commonwealth Office was less eager to offer its assistance after I had
made my unwelcome voyage to Diego Garcia than when I began
the project; but Walter Wallace of the Dependent Territories
Section of the West Indian and Atlantic Department was helpful
throughout, and read and criticised several of the typescript
chapters. Wing Commander Ian McCoubrey made helpful com-
ments after reading the Hong Kong chapter, and General Sir
William Jackson gave me many useful pointers during my study
of the history of Gibraltar.

I am grateful to Mia Stewart-Wilson for her invaluable help
with picture research, and to Tracey Skelton for digging
out much useful material on the islands in the Caribbean and
Atlantic.

Donald Simpson, that most kindly and helpful librarian, who
has presided for many years over the finest and most congenially
atmospheric of all colonial collections – that at the Royal Commonwealth Society in London – has my keenest gratitude, as
do his immensely knowledgeable staff; and I made much use of,
and was greatly helped by the librarians and their colleagues at
both Queen Elizabeth House and Rhodes House in Oxford.

Any errors that survived the attentions of the scrutineers
are, of course, my own.

The Press Facilities Office of the Royal Air Force made
possible flights to and from Ascension Island, and to them and
the crews of Strike Command based there and at Brize Norton
I owe a great deal.

The idea for the book was suggested by the literary agent,
Anthony Sheil; his colleague, Gill Coleridge, kept my enthusiasm

alive on those occasions when it seemed likely that the project would never be completed. To them and to my ever-tolerant family and friends, who put up with a lot, my deepest gratitude.

SBAW
Iffley,
Oxford

August, 1986

FURTHER READING

For anyone fortunate enough to be able to contemplate a journey to these last specks of the British Empire there are, sad to say, rather few relevant books that are worth taking. I have ploughed through scores of works that linger over the stately decline of the Empire and any number of papers that suggest fates for those islands that, for one reason or another, escaped the great retreat. But most are a little dull; I would be loath to advise any friend bound for Montserrat or Tristan, for instance, to lug along *The Cambridge History of the British Empire*, or Mr D. J. Morgan's *Guidance Towards Self-Government in British Colonies* 1941–1971, invaluable though they were for me. So I have omitted that kind of book, meaning no disrespect to the authors. Those few I have mentioned below are books that in my view are best suited for the traveller, in that they combine accuracy and interest with a sense of the atmosphere of the places they seek to describe. They are books both to be of use as sources of information and, in all cases, to enjoy. But I was only too well aware, after reading through all the others available – and there are many – that had these islands been more important places, a greater range of authors might have tried their hands, and this list of suggestions would have been rather easier to compile.

DIEGO GARCIA

Robert Scott, *Limuria*, Oxford University Press, 1961
John Madeley, *Diego Garcia*, Minority Rights Group, London, 1985

TRISTAN DA CUNHA

Derrick Booy, *Rock of Exile*, Dent, 1957
Peter Munch, *Crisis in Utopia*, Longman, 1971

GIBRALTAR

John D. Stewart, *Gibraltar the Keystone*, John Murray, 1967
George Hills, *Rock of Contention*, Hale, 1974

ASCENSION ISLAND

John Packer, *The Ascension Handbook*
Lawrence G. Green, *South African Beachcomber*, Timmins,
Cape Town, 1958

ST HELENA

E. L. Jackson, *St Helena the Historic Island*, Ward Lock, 1903
Tony Cross, *St Helena*, David and Charles, 1980
Lawrence G. Green, *There's A Secret Hid Away*, Timmins, Cape
Town, 1956

HONG KONG

Richard Hughes, *Hong Kong – Borrowed Place, Borrowed Time*,
Deutsch, 1968
David Bonavia, *Hong Kong 1997*, Columbus Books, 1983
Maggie Keswick, *The Thistle and the Jade*, Mandarin Publishers,
1982

BERMUDA

Henry Wilkinson, *Bermuda in the Old Empire*, Oxford University Press, 1950

THE BRITISH WEST INDIES

There are many brief accounts of the five island groups that still belong to Britain, though most appear to have been written more for academic interest than literary pleasure. I would refer the reader to just two volumes. The first does not specifically cover any of the five colonial possessions, but wanders gently across islands and seas belonging to a variety of foreign owners; the second is, I think, the very best guidebook available about anywhere in the world, and it deals at very respectable length with all of Britain's West Indian territories.

Patrick Leigh Fermor, *The Traveller's Tree*, John Murray, 1950
John Brooks, *The South American Handbook*, Trade and Travel Publications, updated annually

THE FALKLAND ISLANDS

Michael Mainwaring, *From the Falklands to Patagonia*, Allison and Busby, 1983
Ian Strange, *The Falkland Islands*, David and Charles, 1972
Natalie Goodall, *Tierra del Fuego*, Ushuaia, 1979
John Brooks, *The South American Handbook*, Trade and Travel Publications, updated annually

THE FALKLAND ISLANDS DEPENDENCIES
AND
BRITISH ANTARCTIC TERRITORY

Robert Fox, *Antarctica and the South Atlantic*, BBC, 1985

THE PITCAIRN ISLANDS

Robert Nicolson, *The Pitcairners*, Angus and Robertson, 1966

AND IN GENERAL

George Woodcock, *Who Killed the British Empire*? Jonathan
   Cape, 1974
Colin Cross, *The Fall of the British Empire*, Hodder and Stough-
   ton, 1968
James Morris, *Farewell the Trumpets*, Faber, 1978

If there is room for just a single volume, pack the last.

MELVYN BRAGG

THE CUMBRIAN TRILOGY

'It is an extraordinary blend of delicacy and harsh simplicity which makes Melvyn Bragg a remarkable novelist'
The Times

Melvyn Bragg's celebrated trilogy – THE HIRED MAN, A PLACE IN ENGLAND and KINGDOM COME – traces four generations of Tallentire history: from John in the rural Cumbria of 1898 to Douglas in the competitive and backbiting metropolis of the Seventies. From 'hired man' to media man worlds have been bridged, but the old ideals of success, freedom and happiness seem ever elusive as each Tallentire must come to terms with private uncertainty and pain.

'An uncommonly high talent. The people are "real" enough to leave footprints right across the page'
The Guardian

'A novelist of power and imagination. It is one of Bragg's gifts to create his own atmosphere and so heighten feeling'
New Society

'Quite masterly'
The Daily Telegraph

sceptre

MELVYN BRAGG

SPEAK FOR ENGLAND

Melvyn Bragg returned to his home town, Wigton, Cumberland, to interview over sixty locals from all walks of life. The result is a memorable testimony to the first three-quarters of this century. The people speak for themselves, for their inheritance, their culture, and for their country.

'These vivid recollections, scrupulously edited, make a book which lays plausible claim to being representative of England's history as lived and felt by her people in the twentieth century . . . The considerable pleasures and insights to be gained from the book are to be found in real memories, the measure of a life'
Dennis Potter, in The Guardian

'What leaps from these pages is the authentic voice of direct experience'
The Listener

'Full of humour, hope, common sense, stoicism, courage, decency . . . The voices speaking for England here are not just a collection of characters – odd, outspoken, eccentric – but give a real insight into England, past and present . . . They are intelligent and individual, all sorts, all classes and conditions'
Los Angeles Times

'A very decent and straight book . . . I believe he's right in saying "Speak for England" '
Richard Hoggart,
author of THE USES OF LITERACY

LYALL WATSON

DREAMS OF DRAGONS

Ideas On The Edge Of Natural History

'Each of these essays takes an odd idea, something from the soft edges of science, and tries to nourish it with natural history – to work it, somehow, into the fabric of Earth . . .'

Lyall Watson first challenged many scientific 'sacred cows' in SUPERNATURE. Following in that tradition, this cycle of twelve essays probes the frontiers of the unknown, covering topics as diverse as crowd behaviour, cannibalism, plant sensitivity, salamanders and dragons. The result is a sequence of perspectives of the natural world as intellectually challenging as they are eminently readable. This is a book that cannot fail to make you think again about the enigmatic kaleidoscope of life on earth . . .

Current and forthcoming titles from Sceptre

MELVYN BRAGG

THE CUMBRIAN TRILOGY
SPEAK FOR ENGLAND

LYALL WATSON

DREAMS OF DRAGONS

CHRISTOPHER ANDREW

SECRET SERVICE

MARK CHILDRESS

A WORLD MADE OF FIRE

W. H. DAVIES

YOUNG EMMA

IRMGARD KEUN

AFTER MIDNIGHT

BOOKS OF DISTINCTION

MARK CHILDRESS

A WORLD MADE OF FIRE

In early-century backwoods Alabama, Jacko, crippled and strange-eyed, is brought up by his twelve-year-old sister Stella. Sudden fire has destroyed their house, killed their mother. In the heat-hazed Southern air, reality distorts into mystery. At night the Klan rides, white-hooded, while black voodoo flourishes in the deep woods. Then, as an epidemic sweeps the county, rumour and superstition wreathe and mingle to produce the terrible demand for a scapegoat . . .

'A writer of almost uncanny stylistic ability and clear vision. His eye for detail is extraordinary'

Stephen King

'Terrific. What is so good about it, I suppose, is that it's like nothing else'

Fay Weldon

'A memorable story out of the land and people of the Deep South'

Erskine Caldwell

CHRISTOPHER ANDREW

SECRET SERVICE

'The first serious and reliable history of Britain's Intelligence Service, most carefully researched and also very funny indeed. Dr Andrew succeeds admirably in demythologizing the history of Intelligence. Splendid and astonishingly good value'
Keith Jeffrey in History Today

'Dr Andrew's determined research and admirable prose, besides giving working historians much that is new, provide the amateur *aficionado* of history with an irresistible brew: a record of exciting successes laced with ludicrous ineptitude . . . As well timed as it is well executed'
Peter Calvocoressi in The Sunday Times

'A history of the Secret Service as exciting as any spy novel, and which also makes the most powerful case I have seen for greater public accountability'
David Cannadine in The New York Review of Books

'Excellently informed, well researched, compulsive reading . . . A fascinating story of triumph and failure'
D. Cameron Watt in the Daily Telegraph

'A great deal of military and diplomatic history will have to be rewritten in the light of some of these revelations . . . remarkable'
Robert Blake in The Illustrated London News

'Scholarly, balanced and highly entertaining'
Hugh Trevor Roper

W. H. DAVIES

YOUNG EMMA

'This new life . . . seems to be much greater than the longer
life that is past, because of its greater intensity. Let us judge it
then, not by its number of breaths, but by the number of times
that breath is held or lost, either under a deep emotion caused
by love, or when we stand before an object of beauty'

W. H. Davies

This object of beauty is young Emma whom W. H. Davies
meets at a bus stop on the Edgware Road. She is twenty-
three, poverty-stricken and pregnant. He is fifty, and a celebrated poet. YOUNG EMMA is the moving, personal account
of their love affair and marriage which survived against all the
odds. Written in 1924, the history of its publication is as
remarkable as the love affair itself.

'YOUNG EMMA is a masterpiece, and stranger than any
fiction'

Sunday Telegraph

'Classic . . . remarkable . . . an extraordinary manuscript'

The Observer

'An amazing document'

George Bernard Shaw

sceptre